Chinese Cash

Identification and Price Guide

David Jen

DEDICATED

TO

MY MOTHER

AND

THE AMERICAN PEOPLE

D.J.

Published by

krause publications

700 E. State Street • Iola, WI 54990-0001
Telephone: 715/445-2214
Web: www.krause.com

Please call or write for our free catalog.

Our toll-free number to place an order or obtain a free catalog is 800-258-0929 or please use our regular business telephone 715-445-2214 for editorial comment and further information.

Library of Congress Catalog Number: 99-67648
ISBN: 0-87341-859-X
Printed in the United States of America

CONTENTS

INTRODUCTION

Chinese cash coins are fascinating to study and collect. They were made from at least as early as 700 BC to 1911 AD. They were copied in many parts of East Asia. They were issued by every major ruler of China and many pretenders and rebels. Their study opens up a fascinating book of colorful history to which few Westerners are exposed in school. They are also interesting as objects. The earlier types, unlike Western coins, were made in a fascinating variety of shapes and sizes. The later ones, while almost all round with square holes, come in a variety of sizes and metals. And the calligraphy — the shapes and forms of the characters — can become interesting and beautiful after a little exposure, even to people who do not read Chinese. (It is easy to read the legends on the coins: only a hundred or so characters were used, which can be listed in a single-page table.) The precision of the casting, the patina and the state of preservation are also esthetic values.

Fortunately for the collector, the more common types of Chinese cash coins were made in immense quantities — millions per year, even 2,000 years ago. In ancient times coins were often included in tombs, too. As a result many survive and most interesting types can be obtained at affordable prices. It is a pleasure to inform a person who has a cash coin in a piece of jewelry or a family collection that the coin is indeed genuine and centuries old. Unfortunately, however, it is then usually necessary to inform the person that the coin is common and worth no more than one dollar!

Until recently the English language literature on Chinese coins was very limited. There were a few specialized books on specific categories of coins, usually difficult to obtain and not all reliable. There was only one comprehensive catalog, Chinese Currency by F. Schjoth. With few exceptions it provides only a one-line identification for each coin, with no historical or comparative discussion. A better catalog appeared about ten years ago, Fisher's Ding, Ding Fubao's catalog in Chinese, translated and annotated by George A. Fisher, Jr., is more comprehensive than Schjoth, contains some useful reference tables, and provides a value for each coin. Unfortunately the values are now obsolete, and (like Schjoth) there are practically little discussion of the individual coins. In 1994 A Monetary History of China, by Peng Xinwei and translated by Edward H. Kaplan, was published by the University of Western Washington. This monumental work presents all Chinese money in the context of the history and economy of the time, with extensive reference to original sources. Although indispensable to the student it is not a good catalog: the references to individual coin issues are scattered through the text and no effort is made to comprehensively list individual coins.

As a result, there is a clear need for this book. It accompanies groups of coins with capsule presentations of the history of the period they represent, including entertaining anecdotes and fantastic-but-true stories: no other book has so effectively combined the functions of history and catalog. This book also separates "Mainstream Dynastic coinage" from "Varieties and Variants", which is very helpful to the less-than-expert reader. There are so many varieties of some issues that the reader trying to identify a common type in a comprehensive list can get lost. Values are given for all the coins, not as absolutes but on a relative scale tied to absolute prices existing in 1998. This sensible approach permits the reader to adjust the values easily to match changes in the market. The book is also unique in its emphasis on the rare and interesting "seed coins", and appends several interesting discussions of more detailed topics. Even if irrelevant to a particular reader's needs, these illustrate the kind of information that thorough scholarship can elicit. Finally, the book confronts squarely the issue of identifying reproductions and fakes. These unfortunately exist, but most books do not help the reader identify them. Because of these virtues, this book is essential for every collector and scholar.

The author writes English very well, but main reasons for the book's success are his knowledge and integrity. He knows so much more than I do about Chinese history and numismatics that I cannot evaluate his knowledge — does anyone know more? And his integrity as a judge of quality and authenticity cannot be praised too highly. It is evident in his comments on the esthetic qualities of the fascinating coins he presents. This book cannot fail to be both useful and entertaining.

FREDERIC G. WITHINGTON

FOREWORD

People often meet me at coin shows and ask for Chinese coin catalogs to supplement the Schojth and Fisher's-Ding references they are now using. Over half a century had passed since their publication, and though many new ones have come out, they are all in Chinese, simply inaccessible to the western reader. Since I can read and write in both Chinese and English, why not compile a catalog with notes in English and make available the material from Chinese sources to readers in the western world?

Preparing such a book has its difficulties and rewards. I am happy that I have an opportunity to introduce Chinese cash coin culture to the western public, a culture spiced with exotic patterns and vivid tales, leaving with us a record of three thousand years of evolution, a lost horizon awaiting the adventurer to enter.

I have spread the material into four parts to avoid presenting too much at one time, thus making it easier for the reader to stay in focus. I am trying not to encumber this book with material that can be found in other catalogs prepared carefully by western writers providing hints on how to cross the language barrier. The modern Pin Yin given under the illustrations should be a reliable guide serving the same end.

In Section I are the mainstream dynastic issues. On the pages facing the illustrations are some brief notes for each coin. In the next section appear some other species not included in the first section to avoid a cluttering of material; and also some that vary a little from the mainstream issues. Although no notes are given in this section, it would suffice to refer to those provided in the previous one. In the third section are the seed coins and patterns. They are placed apart from the others to alert the reader not to mistake one for the other, which would prove very unfortunate for the dealer who might sell a seed coin at the price of a most common counterpart, or the buyer who took a regular issue for a seed or pattern. In the last section are some hints to the collector having interest in the sport of identifying and sorting variations of a certain specie. And lastly, a word on detecting forgeries. No one likes experiencing a rip-off. The Six-word Key to detecting fakes is from a Chinese source, with some additional observations drawn from my personal field experience.

Providing a price-list poses quite a problem. Fifty years ago in Ding Fu-bao's time a Chinese silver dollar could purchase a hundred eggs. Market conditions have since changed, and many new species have emerged, their value and price unresolved during this time. In recent years, several new Chinese catalogs have reached the store shelves. The quoted prices may provide the reader with a general idea of the comparative value of marketed cash coins, which is quite helpful; but actual transactions are quite another matter. In this catalog, I gave a price for each coin, ranging from very good to very fine, the pricing based on the current Chinese market conditions. Of course, one must not suppose that a coin available for 10 Chinese yuan in China could still be purchased in the United States for 10 Chinese yuan. The standards of living and income in the two countries are quite different. In Chinatown I buy a dish just for one US dollar, which is available in China for one Chinese yuan; the difference is 1:8, surely a handsome profit. Now, would an American collector be willing to pay 8,000 dollars for a coin marked 8,000 Chinese yuan? In this case, a price nearer to the conversion rate 1:8 would be more acceptable, that is, 1 to 3 thousand dollars, whichever is acceptable to both parties; with profit and other expense taken into account.

In the first two sections a price-listing system is used; while in the next two sections a grading system preferred by some Chinese numismatists is chosen simply for the reason that seeds and variants are graded on a more stable basis than that of the regular dynastic issues. The grading system is as follows:

Grades	**US Dollars**
ER (Extremetly rare)	Unpriced
VR (Very rare)	10,000.00
R (Rare)	5,000.00
S (Scarce)	2,000.00
1	1,000.00
2	700.00
3	400.00
4	250.00
5	150.00
6	100.00
7	70.00
8	50.00
9	25.00
10	10.00
11	5.00
12	1.00

MODERN PIN YIN & WADE-GILES SYSTEM

A Cross Reference Table *

Pin Yin	Wade-Giles	Remarks
a	a	father, pronounced as the underlined part.
ai	ei	ei pronounced as aisle
bie	pieh	p pronounced as be.
Bo	po	bought
ca	ts'a	lots
ce	ts'é	e as away
cheng	ch'éng	ch pronounced with lips rounded.
chong	ch'ung	ung as in the German "yungfrau".
chun	ch'un	un as in wendy
ci	ts'i	ts• voiced.
di	ti	detail
dian	tien	ien as in Yana River.
dui	tuei	uei as way.
e	ê	e as in away.
ge	kê	k as ge
gong	kung	k as ge
ji	chi	ch as jack
jian	chien	janitor
jie	chieh	Jerry
jin	chin	ginger
jing	ching	jingle
jiong	chung	Joan + ng = joang.
ju	chü	jura
jue	chüeh	ch pronounced as jet with lips rounded.
kui	k'uei	quake
liu	liu	lieu
lu	lu	loop
lu	lü	lu pronounced with tongue forming a groove.
lun	lun	lwen
mian	mien	e as a
miu	miu	mew
nu	nu	canoe
nu	nü	said with sides of tongue raised into a groove.
nüe	nüeh	manure
pian	p'ien	piano
pie	p'ieh	pianissimo
qi	ch'i	cheeta
qie	ch'ieh	chess
qin	ch'in	chin
qing	ch'ing	matching
quan	ch'uan	ch pronounced with lips rounded.
qun	ch'ün	chin with lips rounded.
ran	jan	Zanzibar, z pronounced with lips rounded.
rong	jong	j pronounced as z with lips rounded.
rui	juei	radar, r as z with lips rounded.
run	jen	rent, r as z with lips rounded.
sha	sha	sh said with mouth rounded and tongue grooved.
shui	shuei	
tie	t'ieh	
tun	t'uen	
weng	wêng	we as woe.
xi	his	she
xie	hsieh	
xun	hsün	
yan	yen	Yana River
yi	i	eat
yuan	yüan	
yue	yüeh	
za	tsa	ts as adze
ze	tsê	
zha	cha	adze said with lips rounded.
zhi	chi	
zi	tsi	
zong	tsong	
zui	tsuei	

* Self-explanatory material is not included.

QUALITY GRADING

A word needs to be said about the grading of Chinese cash coins. For western coins a 14 grade system is usually used, but for Chinese cash a 5 grade system would be sufficient; since the most recently minted cash coins are almost 90 years old and copper corrodes more easily than gold or silver; hence it would be quite unrealistic to assume that a coin 2,000 years old might now still be in mint or unculated condition. However, the seed coins of the Qing Dynasty may qualify as uncirculated pieces. Abbreviations for the grades are as follows:

Uncirculated	UNC
Extremely Fine	EF
Very Fine	VF
Fine	F
Good	G

According to the practice of dealers and buyers in the Chinese coin market, the quality of the cash coins is governed by four factors: the clearness of the legend, the degree of wear, the intactness of the coin, and the condition of the patina, the beauty of which may influence the buyer's decision whether to acquire it as a collectible.

1. Uncirculated – Seed coins of the Qing Dynasty that have not gone underground, golden-yellow in color, bright and shiny, with no signs of wear or damage.
2. Extremely Fine – The legend sharp and clear, no signs of wear or damage, very beautifully patinated.
3. Very Fine – Very little sign of wear or corrosion, all brushstrokes of the characters sharp and clear, nicely colored patina.
4. Fine – Showing rather serious signs of corrosion or wear, yet all brushstrokes still discernible, patina not attractive.
5. Good – The coin quite worn or badly damaged, some of the brushstrokes rubbed out, the patina spoiled, marring the profile. Coins in such condition not usually imported to the United States, unless specified by the buyer.

ACKNOWLEDGEMENTS

This work is a compedium of the information gathered from various sources and contributed by many groups and individuals. I owe special gratitude to the American Numismatic Society for granting me access to the Society's great collection of Chinese cash coins and numismatic works, making available to me much invaluable reference material. Dr. Michael Bates, ANS Curator of the Islamic and East Asian Department, imparted to me professional expertise on diverse numismatic subjects, for which I am especially grateful. I am much indebted to Mr. Zhao-qing Jiang, renown Chinese numismatist and a man of integrity, for helping me in the pricing of the coins, drawing from field experience accumulated through 20 years of active participation in the Chinese coin market. I cannot thank Mr. Frederick Withington enough for the very nice introduction he wrote for this catalog; I could not have hoped for a better one; and besides, he made many suggestions and helped in the editing of the text. Through the kindness of the Shanghai Numismatic Society, China, and the Shizuoka Numismatic Society of Japan, I obtained the needed information to present the section on Tang and Song cash varieties. A special thanks to Mr. Wei-dong Zhang for helping out in typing the Chinese characters imprinted on the reverse of the Song Dynasty iron coins and those used in several other places.

The encouragement from numismatic friends and support from my loving wife all deserve special acknowledgement, for without them this work would still be a piece of unwritten fantasy.

SECTION I

Coinage of the Dynasties (Major Issues)

THE DAWN OF CHINESE MONEY

The dating of the Chinese monetizing process relies mainly on excavation finds and what fragments of written history that have survived the passage of time. From the little that we know, the Chinese started using cowrie shells for money towards the end of the Xia Dynasty (c. 2200 B.C., according to Chinese historians), the first of China's feudal dynasties. The shells came a long way from the South China Seas and were often in short supply; and to meet the market demand, imitation shells were carved from bone, stone, jade, or made from other materials (Nos. 1-4).

Towards the end of the Shang Dynasty (c. 1766-1154 B.C.), the second feudal dynasty, bronze shells appeared on the scene (No. 5), heralding the era of metal coinage in human history, antedating the coinage of the Lydians, which were first struck around 630 B.C.

1

Later on, any bronze artifact could become acceptable for payment, the value determined by its weight. The fish shown here (No. 6) is an interesting sample. It has raised controversy among Chinese numismatists as to whether it is an ornament or a piece of money. Surely no one would refuse to accept it for payment so long as it is not valued way over its own weight.

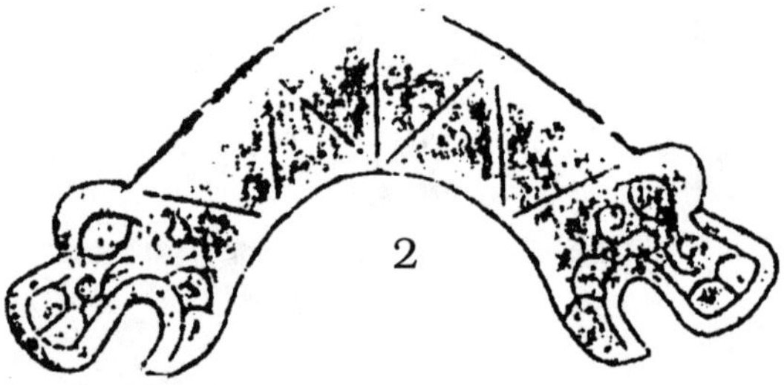

2

5

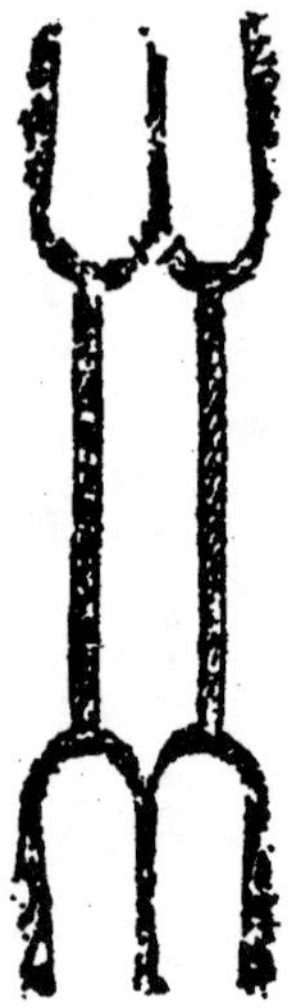

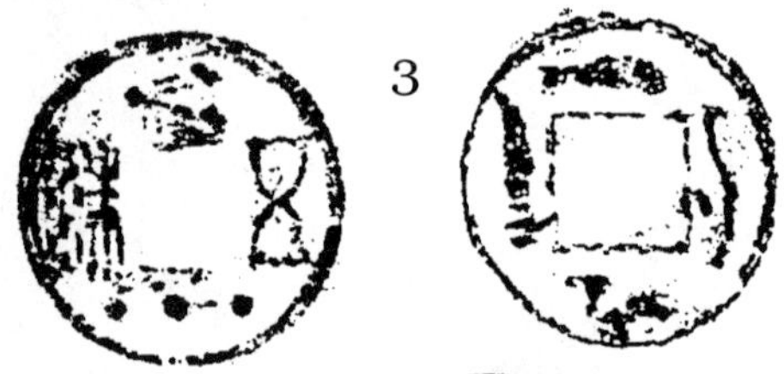

3

4

The bridge coins (Fig. 1) and brambles (Fig. 5), among others, may have the dual function of ornament and money. As far as kinship is concerned, they might not come near to money as the fish, which is a homonym of the word "prosperity". It is quite probable, therefore, that the fish were actually circulating currency; as were the dolphins of Olbia, one of the Greek Black Sea colonies. Fish patterns appeared on pottery as early as the Neolithic Age, and on Wu Zhu coins (Fig. 3) and other coins beginning from the Han Dynasty 206 B.C.-220 A.D. The Huo Quan coin (Fig. 4) was minted by Wang Mang the Usurper (9-23 A.D.). The dragonhead coin (Fig. 2) is a variant of the bridge coin. As for the brambles, people only know that they were made of bronze, hence eligible for circulation.

I. XIA AND SHANG DYNASTIES

2nd Millennium-1st Millennium B.C.

1

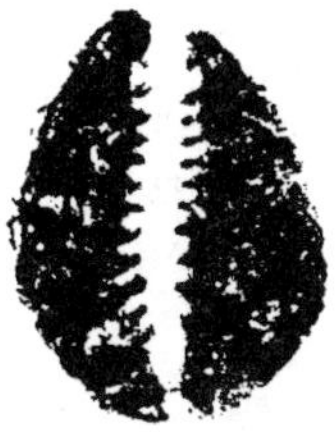

2

3

4

5

6

	VG	VF
1. Shell Cowrie FD-1	5.00	15.00
2. Bone Cowrie FD-2	20.00	40.00
3. Stone Cowrie	20.00	40.00
4. Jade Cowrie	150.00	250.00
5. Bronze Cowrie FD-3	70.00	120.00
6. Bronze Fish	80.00	150.00

THE SPRING AND AUTUMN PERIOD

After founding the Zhou Dynasty, the king bestowed fiefs on his sons, brothers, other lines of the royal family, members of the Jiang family, and members of other families. As time went by, these fiefdoms grew into independent petty states, competing against each other, and plunging the entire kingdom into a boiling cauldron brimming over with military campaigns and political intrigues. In 770 B.C. the Zhou capital was moved east to Loyang. The era covering the events starting from this date to 475 B.C. is commonly called the Spring and Autumn Period, after the name of a chronicle compiled by the Chinese sage Confucius.

The first Chinese currency appeared in this period in the shape of spades and knives, which derived their shape from the common work implements of everyday use — the spades having a hollowed-out handle and the knives a cutting edge. Each state minted its own currency, despite the fact that the Zhou court was still existing and operating as the central government. The coins were made with the same material and technics as the actual work tools. But for its size and fragileness, the primitive spade coin (No. 7) could have passed as the real implement shown here. Some of the coins have characters on them, mostly depicting place names, numerals, or the characters of the Heavenly Stems and Earthly Branches. The characters Wu and San Chuan on the other two spades are place names.

II. ZHOU DYNASTY

Spring & Autumn Period
(770-476 B.C.)

7

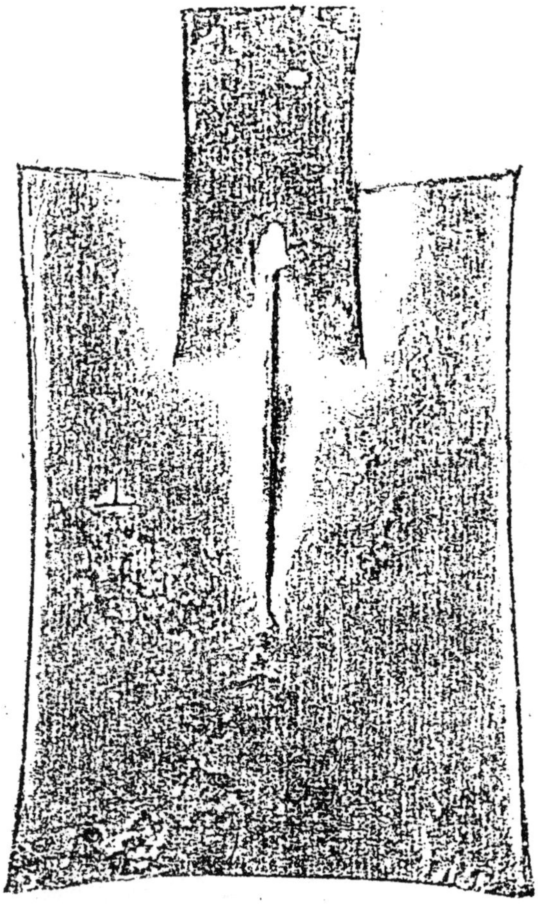

8

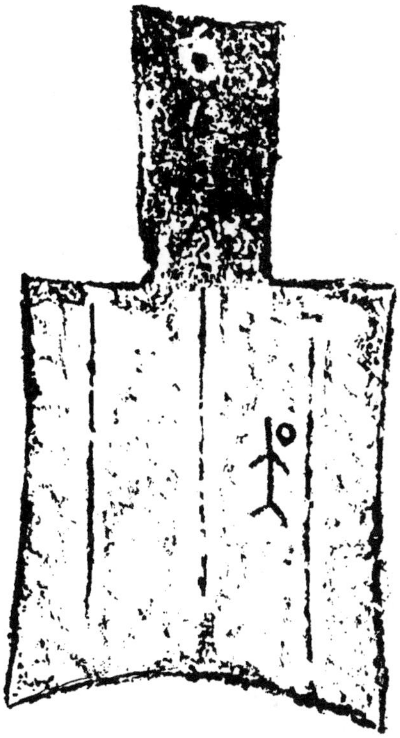

9

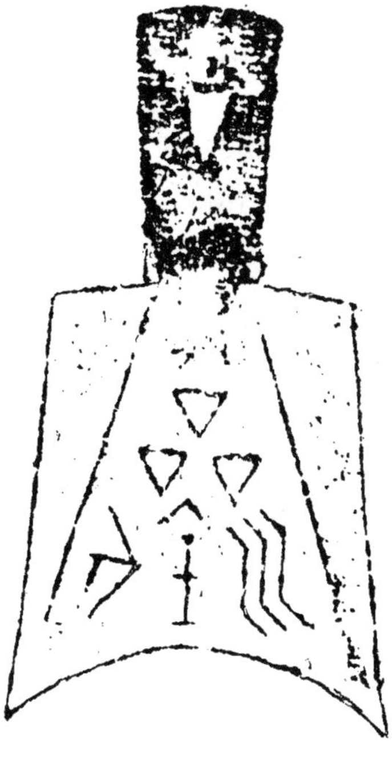

	VG	VF
7. Primitive Spade	1500.00	2500.00
8. Wu Spade FD-16	300.00	500.00
9. San Chuan Spade, S-42/FD-98	400.00	750.00

10. Slope-shouldered Hollow-handle Spade — This type of spade is smaller and lighter than the earlier level-shouldered variety. The character on it is Wu, a place name.

11. Dong Zhou Hollow-handle Spade — Minted by the Dong (Eastern) Zhou Dukedom, it is one of the most coveted of spade coins. In 367 BC, what remained of the Zhou empire split into two dukedoms. Dong Zhou and Xi (Western) Zhou. Aside from the spades, the Dong Zhou Dukedom also minted rounded coins and flat-handle spades; The Zi Zhou Dukedom minted only round coins. All coins of these two dukedoms are very rare.

12. Pointed-feet Hollow-handled Spades — Minted by the state of Jin. This spade emanated from the farming tool Lei.

13. Needle-tip Knife — This knife derived its shape from the knife tools used by the nomadic tribes in northern Chins, namely, the Huns; hence it is also called a Hun knife.

14. Sharp-tip Knife — Minted by the State of Yan. The cutting edge is at the back of the knife; when viewed from the top of the front part of the knife has no blade, but flattened out into the shape of the letter T.

HALBERD COINS

Recent finds have added a new relative to the spades and knives of this period

First discovered in 1986, this heretofore unknown coin type was found only at the location of the State of Yue, sited in present-day Shaoxing City and its suburbs, Zhejiang Province, China.

The said Kingdom existed in the Spring and Autum period. Since almost all major battles involving the kingdom were staged on the water, the Halberds were best suited for that type of warfare, and became the standard weaponry for the soldiers to be used on boats and ships. The coins are not yet listed, pending further information.

At about the time that the Chinese were using spades and knives, the Lydians were minting electrum and silver staters in Asia Minor, setting up a tradition that spread throughout the western world, enriching the coin culture of the human race.

10

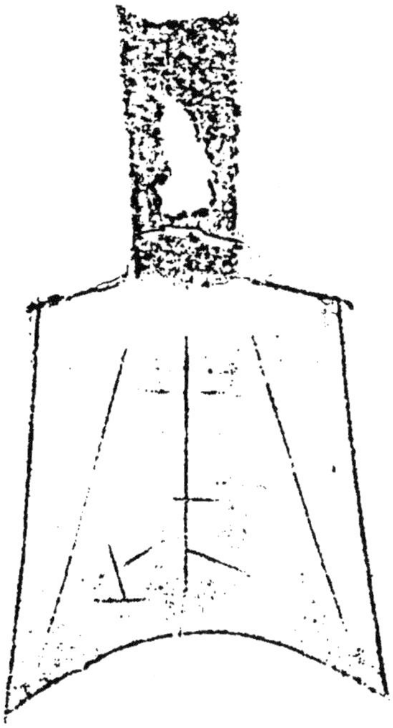

11

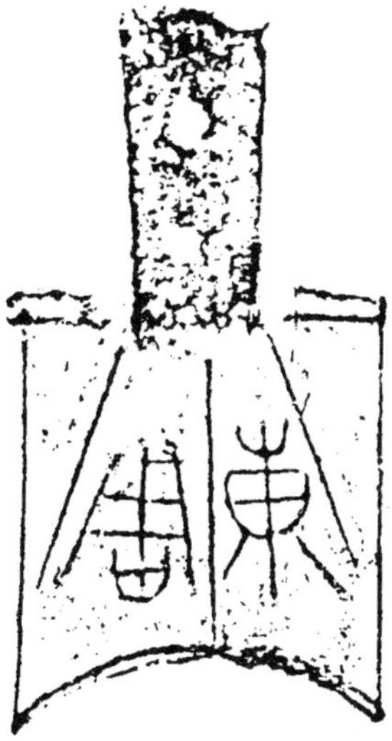

12

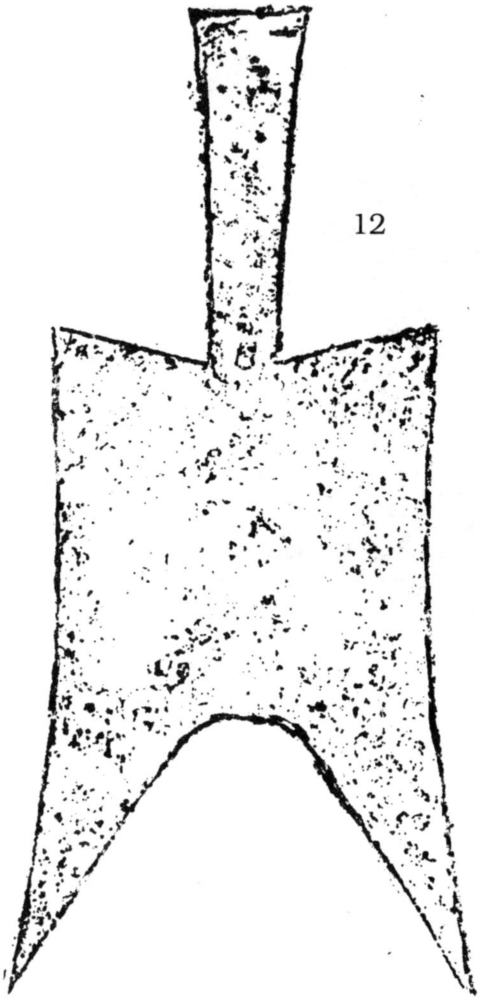

13

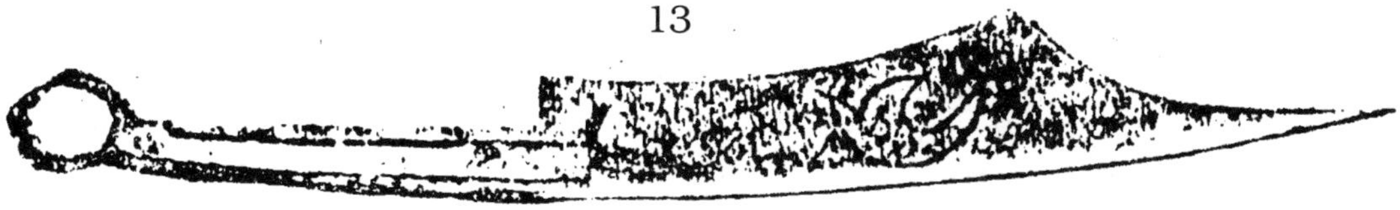

14

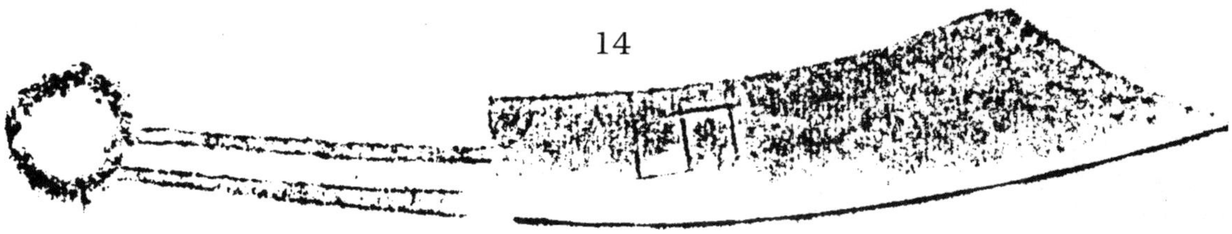

	VG	VF
10. Slope-shouldered Hollow-handle Spade FD-23	200.00	400.00
11. Dong Zhou Hollow-handle Spade FD-8	1500.00	3000.00
12. Pointed-feet Hollow-handle Spade S-43/FD-11	300.00	600.00
13. Needle-tip Knife	200.00	350.00
14. Sharp-tip Knife FD-338	80.00	150.00

THE WARRING STATES PERIOD

The 5th century B.C. ushered in the Warring States period, the era of contention among the seven great powers for hegemony. The following is a general sketch of their domains:

Qi – Shandong province.
Chu – Hubei province.
Yan – Hebei province.
Zhao – Henan province.
Han – Liaoning province.
Wei – Shanxi & part of Hebei.
Qin – Shaanxi province.

The spades of this period no longer had hollowed-out handles. Round coins eventually replaced the clumsy spades and knives. Units of weight appeared on the currency, the most commonly used being the Jin, Zhu, Lei, and Liang; the following figures are rough estimates:

釿 Jin = 14g. Yi Jin means one Jin, Er Jin is two Jin, and Ban Jin one half of a Jin.

寽 Lie = 1,400g.

銖 Zhu = 0.7g.

兩 Liang = 28g. Ban Liang means Half Liang (ounce). The Ban Liang of the Qin state are about the same in weight as the Wei spades.

The six spades listed below are all Wei spades:

15. Liang Yi Jin Spade — Commonly called an Arched-feet spade for the shape of the coin between the two legs. The legend is inverted. Some numismatists insist that the character on the left is unreadable.

16. An Yi Er Jin Spade — This is a 2 Jin spade; the legend is also inverted.

17. Liang 8-characters Spade — The legend reads: New 2 Jin Spade of Liang, fifty worth 1 Lie. The Roman X stands for 5, the cross 10, and the equal sign an iterative symbol for both the 2 and 50 numerals.

18. Yu Yi Jin Spade — Yu is a place name; legend inverted.

19. Shan Yang Spade — Place name; legend reads from left to right.

20. An Yang Spade — Place name; This is a half Jin square feet spade. These small spades bring the use of spades as currency to a close.

21

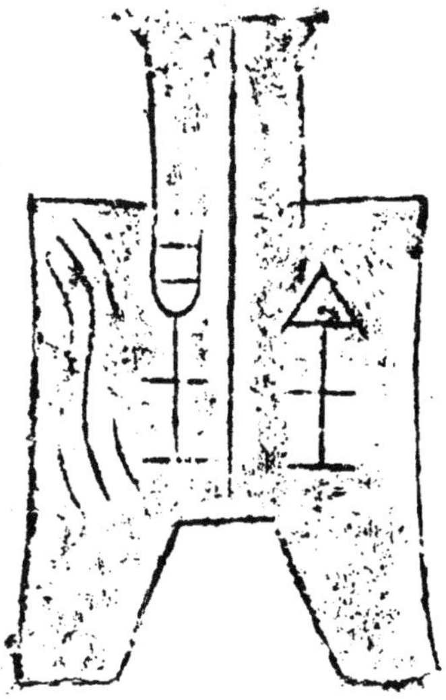

22

23

24

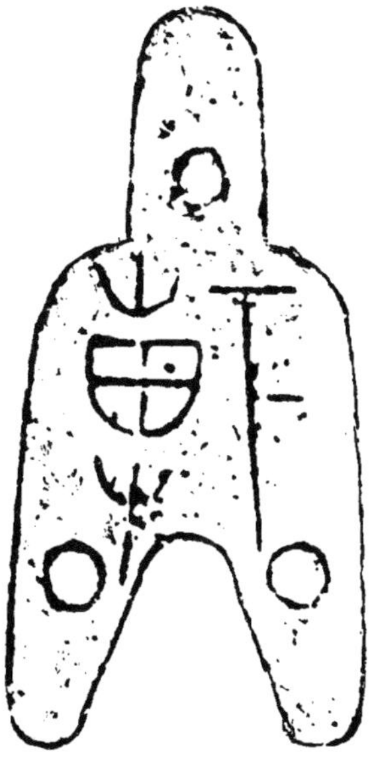

25

26

	VG	VF
21. Jin Bi (Nie Jin) Spade FD-284	350.00	550.00
22. Si Bu Dang Jin Spade FD-288	1000.00	1600.00
23. Li Shi Round-feet Spade FD-318	500.00	800.00
24. Xia Zhuan 3-hole Spade FD-326, VR	—	—
25. Ming (Yi) Knife S-51 FD-341	15.00	30.00
26. Qi Fa Hua 3-characters Knife S-46 FD-351	150.00	300.00

ROUND-HOLED COINS

Round-holed coins marked another step forward in the progress of currency. As these were convenient to carry, they eventually replaced the clumsy knives and spades.

- Coin No. 27, like the Dong Zhou spade, was also the currency of the Dong Zhou regime.

- Coins No. 28, 29, and 35 are Wei coins. The characters are place names.

- The legend on the coin No. 30 means 6 cach. This coin comes in three values: 1, 4 and 6. Yi is a place name.

- Coin No. 31 has the same legend as the Ming knife, its earlier counterpart.

  Coin No. 32 is a Qin coin. Liang means Two. Zi is equal to 6 Zhu. 2 Zi is 12 Zhu, the weight of a Qin Ban Liang coin.

- The legend on Coin No. 33 means 1 cash.

- Coin No. 34 is a Qin coin. Chinese numismatists are not quite agreed on the exact meaning of the legend.

27

28
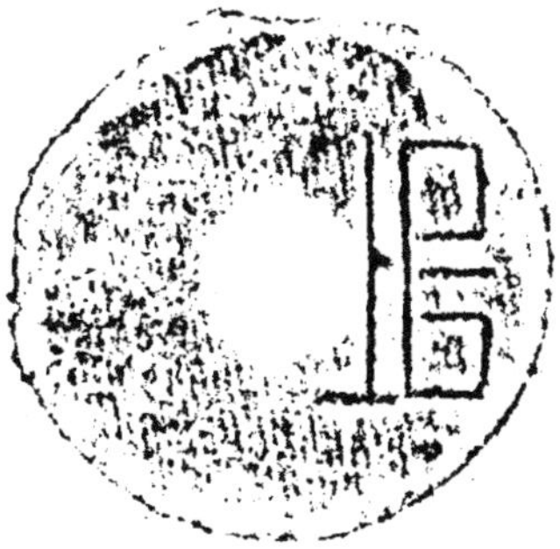

29

30
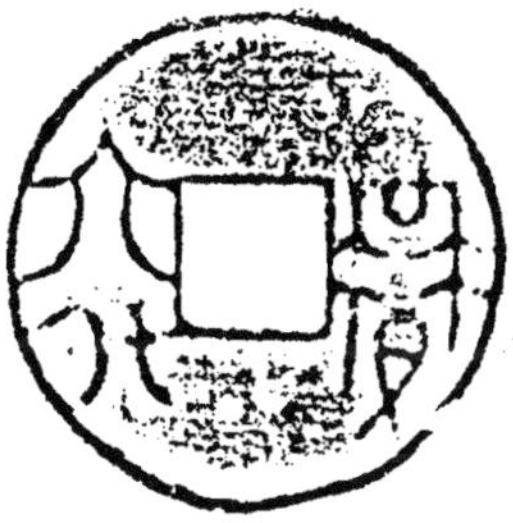

31

32

33
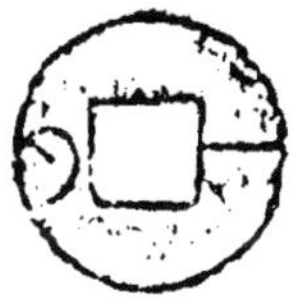

34

35

	VG	VF
27. Dong Zhou FD-9	3500.00	5000.00
28. Yuan coin S-73/FD-357	70.00	120.00
29. Gong coin S-75/FD-359	250.00	400.00
30. Yi Liu Hua S-71/FD-440	50.00	120.00
31. Yan Dao S-76/FD-379	40.00	80.00
32. Liang Zi FD-395	300.00	500.00
33. Yi Dao S-77/FD-382	15.00	25.00
34. Yi Zhu Zhong Yi Liang, Shi Si FD-391	2000.00	3000.00
35. Lin coin FD-369	4000.00	7000.00

THE BAN LIANG COIN

While the other six states were using spades, knives and round-holed coins, the State of Qin adopted the Ban Liang design for its currency. In the 2nd year of his reign (336 B.C.), King Hui Wen gave the order to mint large coins, generally presumed to be the Ban Liang coin, a presumption supported by the fact that coins minted 30 years later bearing the Ban Liang legend and more advanced in style and workmanship were discovered in a tomb marked with the exact date of the first year of King Zhao (336 B.C.).

The early Ban Liang coins were thick and heavy, the legend written in a casual hand, and the workmanship crude; the center holes were square in front but round at the back, being roughly chiseled out for lack of better skills.

The term Pre-Qin Ban Liang is generally used for those coins minted in the Warring States period, to differentiate them from those of the Qin Dynasty proper.

III. QIN DYNASTY

221-206 B.C.

36

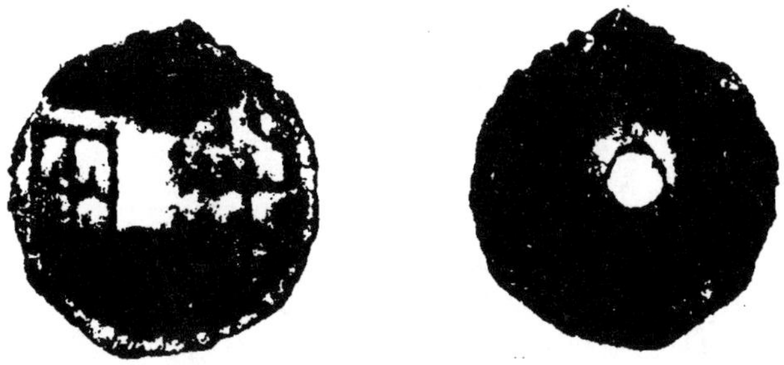

37

38

39

40

41

42

43

A. Ban Liang coins minted by the State of Qin, Warring States Period 475-221 B.C.

	VG	VF
36. Primitive Ban Liang, 33mm, 10.5g	40.00	70.00
37. Ditto, 42.5mm, 64g		
38. Ban Liang, Short Script 33mm, 10g S-82	40.00	70.00
39. Ban Liang, Early, 34mm, 12.6g	50.00	100.00
40. Ditto, Long Script	40.00	80.00
41. Small Ban Liang	10.00	20.00
42. Needle-stroke Ban Liang	15.00	30.00
43. Biscuit Ban Liang, Primitive	150.00	300.00

THE BAN LIANG COIN of the QIN DYNASTY

In the 26th year of his reign (221 B.C.), Shi Huang Di of the State of Qin eliminated the other six states, unified the whole country, and established the Qin Dynasty — the first of Chinese imperial dynasties. He proclaimed himself the first emperor of the Middle Kingdom, and decreed the Ban Liang coin to be the standard currency throughout the empire.

To tell which Ban Liang coin belonged to the Warring States and which to the Qin Dynasty is not an easy matter. Judging from excavation finds, it is generally agreed that the legend on the Qin coins were more neatly written; the two lower strokes of the character Ban on the right are about even in length, and the two upper strokes of the character Liang on the left also about the same in length; and the vertical stroke of the Ban a bit longer than the pre-Qin species. The Qin coins were larger but thinner, usually 33 to 36mm in diameter (Nos. 44-48).

It did not, however, take long for the Ban Liang to shrink to the size of Coin No. 48, a result of his indulgence in numerous projects of gigantic proportions, of which the Great Wall and the army of terra cotta soldiers guarding his tomb are still seen standing today.

The Qin Ban Liang is also called 12 Zhu Ban Liang. Ban Liang means one half of a Liang, equal to 24 Zhu, thus Ban Liang is equal to 12 Zhu, hence its name.

No. 49. Minted by Lu Bu-wei, Marquis of Wen Xin, the alleged father of Shi Huang Di.

No. 50. Allegedly minted by the emperor's brother, the Marquis of Chang An.

44

45

46

47

48

49

50

	VG	VF
44. Ban Liang, Large, Neat Script, 38mm	80.00	140.00
45. Ditto, Medium, Neat Script	20.00	40.00
B. Ban Liang coins of the Qin Dynasty 221-206 B.C.		
46. Ban Liang, Large, 36mm FD-386	70.00	120.00
47. Ditto, Medium, 32mm	25.50	50.00
48. Ditto, Small, 26mm	5.00	10.00
C. Other coins issued during the Qin Dynasty		
49. Wen Xin FD-3090	1500.00	2500.00
50. Chang An FD-3088	2000.00	3500.00

HAN DYNASTY COINAGE

No. 51. Emperor Gao Zhu considered the Qin Ban Liang too heavy for practical use, so he ordered the minting of the Elm Leaf Bar Liang, so dubbed for their small size and light weight (No. 51).

No. 52. Finding the Elm Leaf coins too light, Empress Gao Hou (Lu Hou) minted the 8 Zhu Ban Liang in 186 B.C. (About 5.3g). These coins were smaller and thinner than the Qin Ban Liang and the legend minted in low relief.

No. 53. Minted by Gao Hou in 182 B.C. 5-fraction means the fifth of a Qin Ban Liang (2.4 Zhu).

No. 54. Emperor Wen Di minted the 4 Zhu Ban Liang in the fifth year of his reign (175 B.C.).

No. 55. Minted by Emperor Wu Di in 140 B.C. and withdrawn five years later.

No. 56. Emperor Wu Di resumed minting the 4 Zhu Ban Liang, which had an outer rim, and so it was called the Rimmed Ban Liang.

No. 57. In the 5th year of Yuan Shou (118 B.C.), Emperor Wu Di ordered the withdrawal of the Ban Liang and the circulation of the Wu Zhu. From then on it became the standard form for almost all succeeding dynasties up to the Sui Dynasty until its withdrawal in the 4th year of the Tang Dynasty. It enjoyed a circulation of 739 years, the longest record in Chinese numismatic history.

IV. HAN DYNASTY
206 B.C.-220 A.D.

A. Western Han 206 B.C.-25 A.D.

52

53

51

54

55

56

57

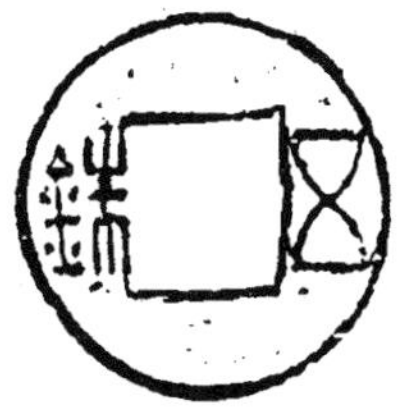

	VG	VF
51. Elm Leaf Ban Liang S-86/FD-411	0.50	1.00
52. 8 Zhu Ban Liang S-89/FD-415	2.00	4.00
53. 5-fraction Ban Liang	1.00	2.00
54. 4 Zhu Ban Liang S-93/FD-422	1.00	2.00
55. San Zhu S-103/FD-429	40.00	80.00
56. 3-fraction Ban Liang S-104/FD-432	2.00	5.00
57. Wu Zhu S-114/FD-441	2.00	5.00

MAJOR WU ZHU VARIETIES

1. Jun Guo Wu Zhu (Nos. 58-60) — The earliest Wu Zhu coins were minted by the central authorities as well as the prefectural nobility with permission by the emperor Wu Di of the Western Han Dynasty, hence the name Jun Guo, meaning Prefectures and principalities. The adoption of the Wu Zhu pattern started in the 5th year of Yuan Shou (118 B.C.) and stayed in use for 739 years, when it was discontinued in the Tang Dynasty. The first issues were large and heavy, the legend casually written, and with splashes of copper around the edges, which imperial decree forbade to file off. Due to the increasing number of pirate minters, the size and weight of the coins deteriorated rapidly, thus three years later, in the 2nd year of Yuan Ding (115 B.C.) the emperor retracted his decree and turned over all minting rights to the central authorities.

2. Chi Ze Wu Zhu (No. 61) — In the same year (115 B.C.), the Chi Ze Wu Zhu coins were released, each equal in value to 5 Jun Guo coins, with the imperial decree that all taxes be paid in this currency. To prevent the theft of copper, the sides were filed, showing a reddish color, hence its name — Chi in Chinese means red, and Ze the sides of the coins. No documentation is available to identify its features. Scholars presume that the ones in the inner burial chamber of Liu Sheng, Prince of Zhong Shan, to be Chi Ze coins. They average 25.4mm in diameter and 4.45g in weight, setting them apart from both the Jun Guo coins they were meant to replace, as they were heavier and larger, and the later San Guan coins that were smaller and lighter; the workmanship and writing were also different.

3. San Guan Wu Zhu — The Chi Ze species had hardly been in use for 2 years when it was denigrated by counterfeits and withdrawn from circulation. Its successor, the San Guan Wu Zhu, was released in B.C. 113, San Guan being the collective name of the three authorities responsible for minting operations. The new issues averaged 25mm in diameter and 3.5g in weight, with a bar over the center hole, which pattern all subsequent Western Han emperors adopted.

58

59

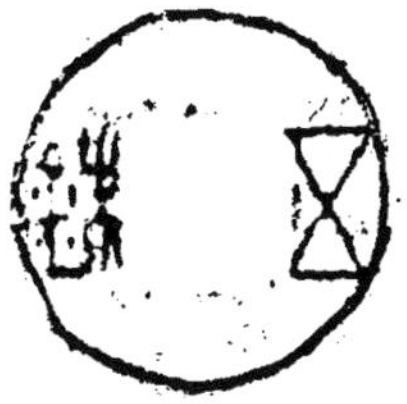

60

61

62

	VG	VF
58. Jun Guo Wu Zhu, 28.89mm, 6.53g	40.00	70.00
59. Ditto, 25mm, 3.55g	20.00	40.00
60. Ditto, 25mm, 5.36g	20.00	50.00
61. Chi Ze Wu Zhu, 27mm, 4.7g FD-442	5.00	15.00
62. Shang Lin San Guan, S-115	3.00	10.00

The Wu Zhu's long circulation history of over seven centuries and the adoption of its pattern by almost all successive regimes has made it quite impossible to identify each Wu Zhu specie discovered so far. The efforts of generations of scholars, both Chinese and foreign, have contributed to establishing the identity of the Wu Zhu varieties listed here, one or two of which are still open to discussion.

4. Zhao Di Wu Zhu — Excavated dies with specific dates on them have helped ~~contribute~~ this variety (No. 63) to the emperor Zhao Di (86-73). The Wu resembles a pair of glasses, there being a bridge in the middle, separating the Wu into two lens. The legend is longer than that of the San Guan coin (No. 62) and there is also a bar over the hole.

5. Xuan Di Wu Zhu — There exists 3 types of dies with Xuan Di's reign title. The 2nd one dated 64 A.D. is shown here, as it is easier to identify. This specie resembles 2 cannon shells joined tip to tip with the sides running in parallel directions (No. 64).

6. Wang Mang Wu Zhu — There is no documentation confirming Wang Mang having minted any Wu Zhu coins. However, one particular Wu Zhu (No. 65) has long attracted the attention of numismatists for its resemblance in style to the Da Quan Wu Shi (Large coin value 50) minted by Wang Mang. The said coin is large and thick, 27-28mm in diameter and over 2mm in thickness. The workmanship is excellent, the legend in low relief with the outer rim rising high, a feature characteristic of his coins; the inner and outer rims on the reverse are both thick and high rising, another characteristic of the Da Quan coin.

   In 1975, some Wu Zhu coins fitting the above description were found in a casting works along with Da Quan coins at Heichen in Ningxian County, Liaoning Province; no coins of other rulers mingling with this hoard. The Wu Zhus resembled the Da Quan coins in style, thick and solidly made, with a diameter of 27mm. This finding supports the presumption that No. 65 is the Wang Mang Wu Zhu in question. This coin certainly does not fit into any other Western Han category.

7. Geng Shi Wu Zhu — Geng Shi is the reign title of Liu Xuan, Prince of Huai Yang, a kin of the Han family. He joined the Green Forest rebels and was elected emperor after they overthrew Wang Mang the usurper. An existing Wu Zhu die dated the 2nd year of Geng Shi depicts the features of this coin (No. 66). The legend and rims are in low relief and the hole is larger than usual. The 2 characters are thin and long and the head of the Zhu round, setting the pattern for the Eastern Han coins. Liu Xuan betrayed the cause of the rebels a few months later and was defeated by the Red Eyebrow rebels who were in turn defeated by Liu Xiu, who founded the Eastern Han Dynasty.

63

64

65

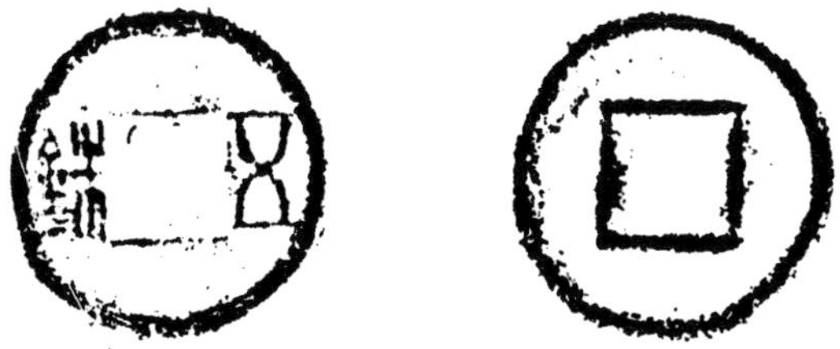

66

67

	VG	VF
63. Zhao Di Wu Zhu	5.00	15.00
64. Xuan Di Wu Zhu FD-443	5.00	15.00
65. Wang Mang Wu Zhu, 2.74mm, 3.68g	20.00	30.00
66. Geng Shi Wu Zhu, FD-507 (Ding Fu-bao had Nos. 507 & 501 switched)	10.00	35.00
67. Gong Sun Shu Wu Zhu (iron) FD-509	30.00	50.00

The Geng Shi Wu Zhu deserves a good rating for its historic significance, as it was the first coin ever minted by a peasant regime, predating the Ying Yun Yuan Bao coin (No. 307) minted by the insurgent Li Shun (995 A.D.) by 900 years.

WANG MANG'S COINAGE

This usurper set about reforming the currency even though he knew nothing about economy. However, he did know how to make money, the real incentive behind his actions. Four times did he reform the currency, setting up monetary systems too complex to be practical and doomed to failure from the start, but to his profit.

Wang Mang started his first reform in the 2nd year of his regency (7 A.D.). The knife coins Yi Dao value 5,000 (No. 69), Qi Dao Value 500 (No. 68) were circulated along with his Wu Zhu coins mentioned on page 22 (No. 65), and the Da Quan value 50 (No. 75).

His 2nd reform began in 9 A.D. when he usurped the throne and set up his Xin Dynasty, casting aside everything linked with the royal Liu family. As three of the four coins mentioned above contained parts of the character Liu, the surname of the Han family, he withdrew the two knife coins and the Wu Zhu, and issued the Xiao Quan Zhi Yi (No. 70) to be circulated along with the Da Quan Wu Shi, equal in value to 50 Xiao Quan coins.

Incidently, the character Liu is made up of three parts:

卯 mao

金 jin

刀 dao

The two knife coins contained the Dao part while the Wu Zhu the Jin, hence offending his sensitivity!

The 3rd reform began in 10 A.D., which resulted in the release of the renowned six Quan and ten Bu (Nos. 70-85), to be used along with gold, silver, and turtle and cowrie shells, the rates of exchange so complex no one could figure them out properly.

However, three failures were not sufficient to dishearten him, and after five years of silence (14 A.D.) he undertook his 4th reform, releasing the value 1 Huo Quan and the spade-shaped value 25 Huo Bu. In 20 A.D. the Da Quan value 50 was withdrawn from circulation, and two years later his regime collapsed.

B. Wang Mang the Usurper 9-22 A.D.

68

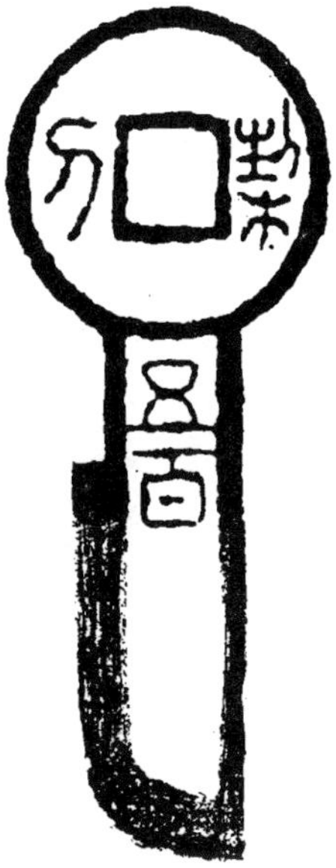

69*

70

71

72

73

74

75

* The characters Yi Dao, inlaid with gold, are level with the field, making it impossible to make impressions.

	VG	VF
68. Qi Dao Wu Bai S-116/FD-454	120.00	250.00
69. Yi Dao Ping Wu Qian S-119/FD-~~456~~ 457	700.00	1500.00
70. Xiao Quan Zhi Yi S-139/FD-459	10.00	25.00
71. Yao Quan Yi Shi S-141a/FD-462	700.00	1200.00
72. You Quan Er Shi S-142/FD-463	1000.00	1700.00
73. Zhong Quan San Shi S-142a/FD-464	2000.00	3000.00
74. Zhuang Quan Si Shi S-142b/FD-465, R	3000.00	—
75. Da Quan Wu Shi S-120/FD-446	10.00	30.00

76

77

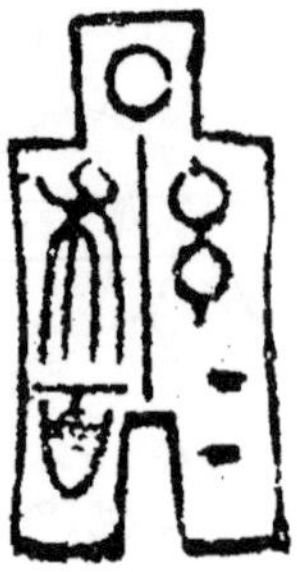

78

79

80

81

82

83

	VG	VF
76. Xiao Bu Yi Bai FD-~~466~~ 467	300.00	500.00
77. Yao Bu Er Bai FD-~~470~~ 468	300.00	500.00
78. You Bu San Bai FD-~~472~~ 470	300.00	500.00
79. Xu Su Si Bai FD-~~474~~ 472	300.00	500.00
80. Cha Bu Wu Bai FD-~~476~~ 475	300.00	500.00
81. Zhong Bu Liu Bai FD-~~478~~ 476	300.00	500.00
82. Zhuang Bu Qi Bai FD-~~480~~ 479	300.00	500.00
83. Di Bu Ba Bai FD-~~482~~ 481	300.00	500.00
84. Ci Bu Jiu Bai FD-~~484~~ 482	300.00	500.00
85. Da Bu Huang Qian S-1~~45~~, 146 FD-~~485~~ 486	300.00	500.00

84

85

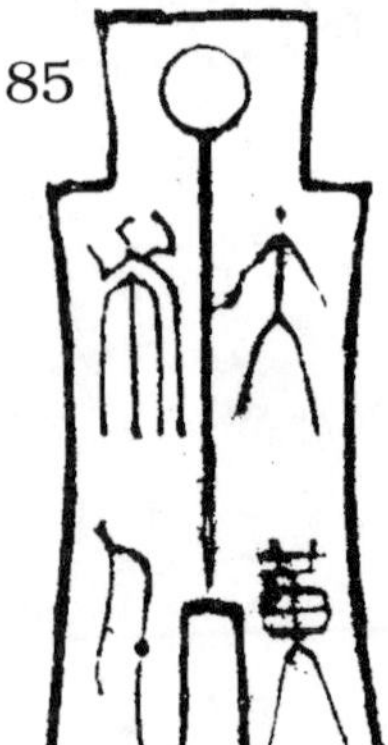

86

87

88

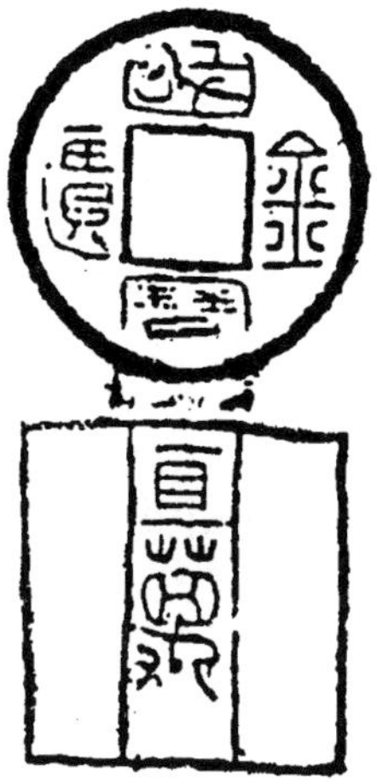

89

90

	VG	**VF**
86. Huo Quan S-149/FD-490	0.50	1.50
87. Biscuit Huo Quan FD-496	10.00	20.00
88. Guo Bao Jin Gui FD-3091, ER	—	—
89. Bu Quan S-175/FD-502	10.00	30.00
90. Huo Bu S-148/FD-486	15.00	30.00

Wang Mang, as a tyrant, ruined the economy with his monetary reforms, bringing chaos and misery to the masses. His coins, though, have become highly prized collectibles for their quaintness, beauty, and variety. His head, cut off by the rebels and preserved for censure through all eternity, was consumed by fire along with the shoes worn by the great sage Confucius when the royal treasury burned down near the end of the Western Jin Dynasty 300 years later: The wise and the ignorant going down together!

GONG SUN SHU WU ZHU

After Liu Xuan and his followers defeated Wang Mang, Gong Sun Shu seized Sichuan and proclaimed himself emperor of Shu in 25 AD. He used iron to mint his Wu Zhu coins (No. 67), making use of the original Western Han moulds. He died in 36 AD.

EASTERN HAN WU ZHU COINS

1. Jian Wu Wu Zhu — Sixteen years after setting up the Eastern Han Dynasty, the emperor Guang Wu Di (Liu Xiu) issued his first Wu Zhus (40 AD). Jian Wu being his reign title, they are popularly called Jian Wu Wu Zhu (No. 91). The legend and rims are in low relief, and thinner than their Western Han counterparts. The head of the Zhu radical is round  instead of square  as on the Western Han variety, it being one of the main features relied upon to discern the difference between the two species.

2. Ling Di Wu Zhu — This coin was minted in 186 AD, and there is an interesting story connected to it (No. 92). The emperor's avarice knew no bounds, and when his coins were released, the common folk whispered among themselves that his treasures would follow the four rays on the reverse of the coins and flow out of a ruined city and scattered to the four winds, which was what actually happened soon afterwards when upheavals left the capitol city in ruins.

3. Dong Zuo Wu Zhu — In 190 A.D. Dong Zuo usurped the throne. He melted the giant statues inherited from the Qin Dynasty and used the copper to mint small blank coins, passing from one extreme to the other – the largest statues ever cast turned into small goose-eyed coins (No. 93).

4. Yuan Shao Wu Zhu — Yuan Shao led an army against Dong Zuo, but victory went to the three leaders who eventually set up the Three Kingdoms. The legend on his coin is reversed and four rays are imprinted on the reverse of the coin (No. 94).

HAN DYNASTY – continued

C. Eastern Han 25-220 A.D.

91

92

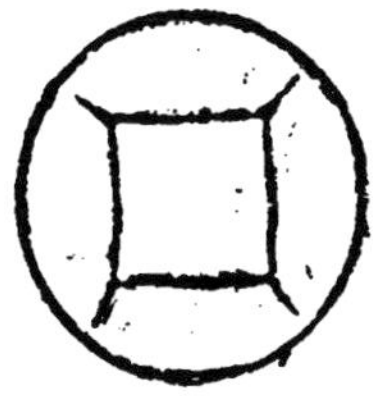

93

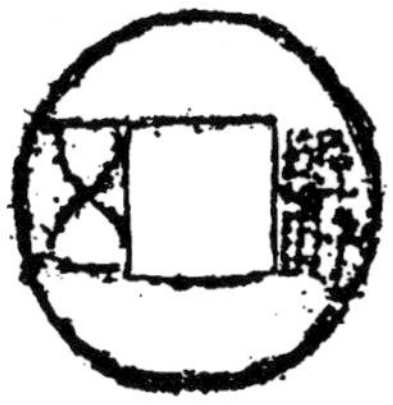

94

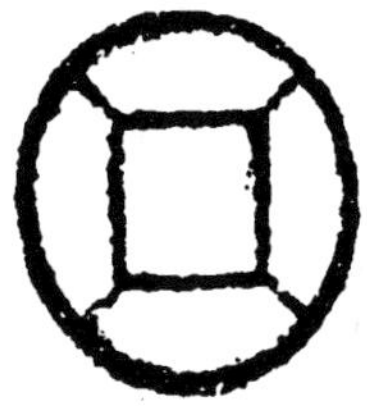

	VG	VF
91. Jian Wu Wu Zhu S-178/FD-510	1.00	5.00
92. Ling Di Wu Zhu S-179/FD-512	3.00	8.00
93. Dong Zuo Wu Zhu S-180/FD-514	0.50	1.00
94. Yuan Shao Wu Zhu FD-~~515~~ 513	25.00	40.00

THE THREE KINGDOMS

1. Shu Wu Zhu — Attributed to Liu Bei, King of Shu. As many such coins were unearthed in the Gansu Corridor, doubts have been raised about their origin. The Kingdom of Shu was by far the weakest of the three, but Liu Bei, helped by his legendary adviser Zhu Ge-Liang, kept his two adversaries at bay. His son, though an indulgent weakling, heeded obediently Zhu's last words and miraculously kept the kingdom afloat for forty years. The coin is No. 95.

2. Zhi Bai Wu Zhu — Meaning value 100 Wu Zhu (No. 96). Liu Bei faced empty coffers when he took over Sichuan and minted this coin as an emergency measure, which was Wang Mang's way of doing things; but his plans fared better. The Tai Ping 100 cash is also attributed to him (No. 97).

3. The Da Quan series — Sun Quan, King of Wu, went even further, and the outcome was the minting of the large coins Da Quan (Large coin) 500, 1,000, 2,000, & 5,000 (Nos. 98-101).

4. Wei Wu Zhu — Minted by Ming Di, King of Wei, in 227 AD. The kingdom had plentiful resources and a stable economy. The founder, Cao Cao, was a great leader, but no match for Zhu Ge Liang, who humiliated him time and again on the battlefield. Zhu's ingenious strategies are colorfully narrated in the "Romance of the Three Kingdoms". The coin No. 102 is traditionally regarded as Wei coinage; however, at a recent Chinese numismatic conference, a conclusion was reached that the one shown here is of Wei origin. No mention was made of the original coin No. 102.

V. THREE KINGDOMS
220-265 A.D.

95

96

97

A. Kingdom of Shu (221-263)

98

99

100

101

B. Kingdom of Wu (222-280)

102

C. Kingdom of Wei (220-265)

	VG	VF
95. Wu Zhu FD-525	10.00	25.00
96. Zhi Bai Wu Zhu S-181/FD-515	20.00	50.00
97. Tai Ping Bai Qian S-200/FD-545	25.00	40.00
98. Da Quan Wu Bai S-192/FD-530	40.00	70.00
99. Da Quan Dang Qian S-195/FD-536	50.00	80.00
100. Da Quan Er Qian FD-538	300.00	500.00
101. Da Quan Wu Qian FD-539	3000.00	5000.00
102. Wu Zhu FD-529	10.00	40.00

THE JIN DYNASTY

The Western Jin Dynasty started out with full depositories and solid national strength when it unified the whole country. However, the later years of this epoch turned out to be another story. Whether any currency of its own was minted was not mentioned in the historical records.

Not fifty years had passed before the rebellion of the eight princes dislocated the empire. The northern and western nationalities took advantage of the situation, crossed over into Jin territory and set up their own regimes – sixteen in all, four of which are known to have minted their own currencies (Nos. 104-108).

1. Shen Lang Wu Zhu – Shen Cong of the House of Wu minted this coin after Emperor Yuan Di was forced to cross the river and establish the Eastern Jin Dynasty. This coin is commonly called Shen Lang Wu Zhu (No. 103). Minted around 317 A.D., the left part of the Zhu is omitted intentionally, serving as its hallmark.

2. Han Xing – Li Shou, King of Chen Han, adopted the reign title Han Xing in 337 A.D. and minted this coin (No. 104, 105), the first cash to bear a reign title. The legend is either horizontal or vertical.

3. Feng Huo – Meaning "The cash of plenty", this coin was minted by Shi Le, King of Later Zhao in 319 A.D. (No. 106).

4. Liang Zhao Xin Quan – Minted by Zhang Gui (317-376), King of Anterior Liang (No. 107), the legend is interpreted as "New coinage of the State of Liang".

5. Da Xia Zhen Xing – Minted by He Lian Bo Bo, King of Xia, in 425 A.D. (No. 108), Da meaning great and Zhen Xing the reign title.

6. Dismembered Wu Zhus – Towards the end of the Eastern Han era, there arose the malpractice of chiselling one Wu Zhu into two, the outer part called "Yan Huan" (Thread ring, No. 109), and the inner part "Zao bian" (Chiselled-out, No. 110) Wu Zhu. This practice continued through the Jin Dynasty into the next epoch, when coins patterned after the chiselled-out specie were actually cast, the difference shown by the splashes of copper around the edges.

VI. JIN DYNASTY & 16 KINGDOMS
(265-420 A.D.)

103

104

105

106

107

108

109

110

	VG	VF
103. Shen Lang Wu Zhu S-227/FD-550	5.00	20.00
104. Han Xing S-213/FD-~~559~~ 560	40.00	70.00
105. Han Xing FD-~~560~~ 559	100.00	200.00
106. Feng Huo S-211	100.00	150.00
107. Liang Zhao Xin Quan FD-505	800.00	1500.00
108. Tai Xia Zhen Xing FD-561	2500.00	4000.00
109. Yan Huan Coin S-304/FD-583	5.00	10.00
110. Zhao Bian Wu Zhu S-306/FD-~~582~~ 581	0.50	1.00

THE SIX DYNASTIES

This epoch is commonly called the Six Dynasties for the six regimes that made Nanjing their capital — the Wu regime of the Three Kingdoms, Eastern Jin and the four successive southern dynasties. To be exact, the nomenclature should be the Northern and Southern Dynasties, five in the north — Northern Wei, Western and Eastern Wei, Northern Qi, Northern Zhou; and four in the south — Song, Qi, Liang, Chen.

1. Si Zhu — Si means four. This coin was minted by Emperor Wen Di of the Song Dynasty in 441 A.D. (No. 111).

2. Xiao Jian — A Song coin, minted in 454 A.D. (No. 112). It was first cast with Si Zhu on the other side. Later the Si Zhu was removed and only the Xiao Jian remained.

3. Yong Guang & Jing He — Both coins (Nos. 113, 114) were cast in the same year (465 A.D.) by the emperor Fei Di, an intemperate and ruthless tyrant. First came the Yong Guang, and after a few months it was replaced with the Jing He, which had not seen circulation for three months when the emperor was assassinated while playing hide and seek.

4. Gong Shi Nu Qian — Translated literally, it means "Female" cash for its lack of an outer rim (No. 115). It was minted by the Liang emperor Wu Di in 502 A.D.

5. Two Pillar Wu Zhu —So called for the two dots on the obverse (No. 116). It is a Liang coin, equal to 10 cash in value.

6. Four Pillar Wu Zhu —Two dots on either side of the coin. Also a Liang coin, it was cast in 557 A.D. (No. 117), value 20 cash.

7. Iron Wu Zhu — Also minted by the Liang emperor Wu Di in 523 A.D. (No. 118), with 4 rays on the reverse.

8. Chen Wu Zhu — Minted by Emperor Wen Di of the Chen Dynasty in 562 A.D. (No. 119). At first glance it resembles the Sui Dynasty Wu Zhu (No. ~~168~~ (138)) for its wide rim and small legend. However, it lacks the vertical bar to the left of the character Wu.

VII. SIX DYNASTIES
(420-581 A.D.)

A. Southern Dynasties

111 112 113 114

115 116 117 118

119 120

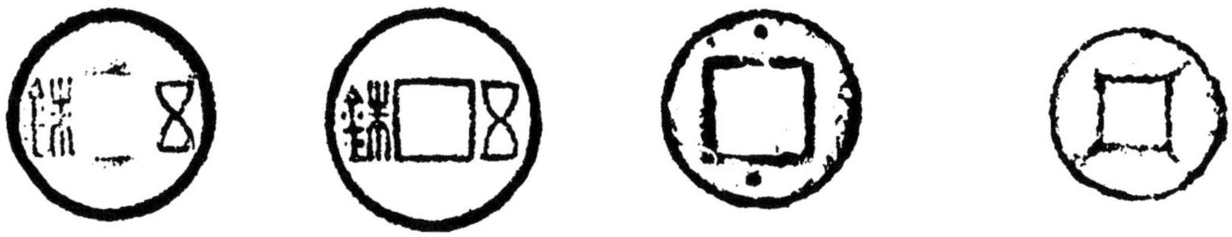

121

	VG	VF
111. Si Zhu S-215/FD-562	40.00	70.00
112. Xiao Jian S-221/FD-567	40.00	70.00
113. Yong Guang FD-584	2000.00	3500.00
114. Jing He S-222/FD-585	2000.00	3500.00
115. Gong Shi Nu Qian S-225/FD-589	0.50	1.00
116. Liang Zhao Wu Zhu FD-595	20.00	30.00
117. Si Zhu Wu Zhu FD-596	30.00	60.00
118. Liang Wu Zhu (Iron) S-232, FD-591	2.00	15.00
119. Tian Jia Wu Zhu S-223/FD-598	5.00	11.00
120. Chen Wu Zhu FD-587	10.00	20.00
121. Tai Huo Liu Zhu S-243/FD-599	40.00	70.00

9. Wu Zhu with inner rim — The identity of this coin is still an open question (No. 120). It resembles the following coin (No. 121) in style, giving rise to the conjecture that it is a Chen coin, while some contend it to be of Liang origin. In recent years many of them were unearthed in Shaanxi Province, former site of the Northern Zhou Dynasty, a reason for its being taken for a Zhou coin by some people.

10. Tai Huo Liu Zhu — Liu means six, a Chen coin minted in 579 A.D. (No. 121), value 10 cash. The coin soon depreciated, and in the course of exchange the people sustained great losses, there circulating the saying that the character on the right resembles a person crying before the emperor with arms akimbo. This and the following Number 136 are among the most beautiful of Chinese cash coins for the subtle balance and flowing style of the brush strokes.

11. Tai He Wu Zhu — Minted by Emperor Xiao Wen Di of Northern Wei in 495 A.D. (Nos. 122-124). These coins come in varying sizes, good and bad intermingled, as coins from private mints were tolerated.

12. Yong An Wu Zhu — This coin comes in three versions — plain reverse minted in 529 A.D. (No. 125) by Emperor Xiao Zhuang Di of the Northern Wei Dynasty; with the character Tu on the reverse (No. 126), the Tu and the hole combining to form the character Ji, meaning "Lucky"; and with four rays on the reverse (No. 127), minted by Gao Chen, the son of Emperor Xiao Jin Di of Eastern Wei in 542 A.D.

13. Yong Ping Wu Zhu — Minted by the Northern Wei regime in the 3rd year of Yong Ping (No. 128). The legend of this coin is longer and narrower than the Han Dynasty varieties.

14. Da Tong Wu Zhu — Minted in 535 A.D. by Emperor Wen Di of the Western Wei Dynasty (No. 129), the rim of this coin is wide and the Wu is written with straight crossing strokes. Number 130 is from the same regime. Coin No. 129 was usually listed as a Sui Dynasty specie for its resemblance to No. 137. No supporting evidence, however, could be offered so far, as no such coins were ever found in tombs dating from the Sui Dynasty.

B. Northern Dynasties

122

123

124

125

126

127

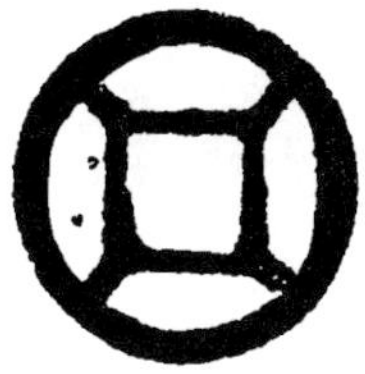

128

129

130

	VG	VF
122. Tai He Wu Zhu S-237/FD-601	60.00	100.00
123. Ditto, Large FD-600	90.00	150.00
124. Ditto, Top character with 2 dots FD-603	150.00	250.00
125. Yong An Wu Zhu S-239/FD-608	20.00	35.00
126. Ditto, Character Tu on reverse S-241, FD-610	80.00	120.00
127. Ditto, 4 rays on reverse FD-611	25.00	50.00
128. Yong Ping Wu Zhu FD-607	10.00	20.00
129. Da Tong Wu Zhu	30.00	50.00
130. Xi Wei Wu Zhu FD-612	15.00	30.00

15. Chang Ping Wu Zhu — Minted by the Northern Qi emperor Wen Xuan Di in 553 A.D. (No. 131). The legend means Constant Equity.

16. Goose-Eye coins — When and where these coins were minted is unknown (Nos. 132 & 133). No stable monetary system could withstand the tumultuous social situation during the epoch of the six dynasties without giving way to anarchism in the exchange market. It is quite understandable that many numismatists have the tendency to attribute all kinds of base coins to this epoch.

17. Bu Quan — This and the following two coins comprise a set, minted by Emperor Wu Di of Northern Zhou (Nos. 134-136). The Bu Quan came first (56 A.D.), equal in value to five Yong An Wu Zhu.

18. Wu Xing Da Bu — Minted in 574 A.D., the legend meaning Large Coin of the 5 Elements, a value 10 coin.

19. Yong Tong Wan Guo — Also a value 10 coin cast in 579 A.D., the legend meaning The Everlasting Currency of the Empire. It would be probable that the Bu Quan and Wu Xing species both depreciated to the status of one cash soon after their release, a fate that the Yong Tong coin was also likely to share.

This coin deserves special mention for its aesthetic value. The sinewy and supple quality of the lines lend a jadelike grace and charm to the characters, a writing style appropriately termed "Jade Tendon". Together with the "Hanging Needle" style seen on Wang Mang's Huo Bu and Bu Quan coins, and the "Iron Thread, Silver Hook" style of the Song Dynasty Hui Zong used on his Da Guan and Chong Ning coins, the three styles stand out in ageless radiance, exotic gems of the Chinese coin culture.

20. Sui Wu Zhu — This coin brought the seven-century long Wu Zhu tradition to a close. Minted in A.D. 581, it has very distinct features (No. 137) — the rim is wide and the Wu written with straight crossing lines, instead of the usual curves; and there is a bar to its left, forming a rim on the right side of the hole, leaving the remaining three sides open. There is another variety with the Wu written in the usual curved lines and alloyed with tin or lead, giving it a light, brassy color, thus earning the name "White cash".

131

132

133

134

135

136

VIII. SUI DYNASTY
(581-618 A.D.)

137

138

	VG	VF
131. Chang Ping Wu Zhu S-242/FD-613	20.00	35.00
132. San Zhu FD-614	50.00	80.00
133. Si Zhu FD-616	30.00	60.00
134. Bu Quan S-245/FD-639	25.00	40.00
135. Wu Xing Da Bu S-246/FD-640	30.00	50.00
136. Yong Tong Wan Guo S-251/FD-644	70.00	120.00
137. Sui Wu Zhu S-253	1.00	5.00
138. Wu Zhu Bai Qian FD-650	5.00	20.00

TANG DYNASTY COINAGE

In the 4th year of his reign (621 A.D.), Emperor Gao Zhu of the Tang Dynasty abolished the Wu Zhu then in use and released the Kai Yuan Tong Bao coin, ten equal in weight to one Liang. The dignified yet graceful legend was written by the renowned calligraphist Ou Yang Xiu and could be read either from top to bottom or clockwise — Kai Yuan Tong Bao or Kai Tong Yuan Bao. As its size and weight was just right for use in the market, the coin became a model for almost all later regimes, with the legend stating the reign or year title plus Tong Bao or Yuan Bao, both meaning "Currency".

The Kai Yuan coin was minted all through the Tang Dynasty, its standard currency for 300 years. The legend stayed the same, but the quality did not. The coins cast during the early and prosperous Tang period were the finest, mirroring the economic situation of that era. For 120 years the economy had advanced in a steady upsurge and during the reign of Emperor Xuan Zong culminated in the mightiest and most glorious of Chinese feudal empires. The coinage of the emperors of this period grew in size and weight, each larger and heavier than the one before it, a phenomenon unparalleled in Chinese history.

No. 139 — Wu De Kai Yuan. The early issues generally go under this name, Wu De being the reign title of the first emperor Gao Zhu. The copper is of a whitish color and the workmanship excellent.

No. 140 — Emperor Xuan Zong (713-756 A.D.) preferred the legend on his coins written in this style. To fight illicit casting, he ordered the size and weight of his coins to be raised, and he had the means to do so — for under his reign the Tang empire reached its zenith. The copper coins are as large as the silver one shown here: 26mm.

No. 142 — A value 10 coin minted by Emperor Gao Zong in 666 A.D. to cope with the rising court extravaganzas and military expenses. To avoid incurring exchange losses, merchants suspended business and the public hid their money, which sent prices skyrocketing. The coin was withdrawn the following year.

IX. TANG DYNASTY
618-907 A.D.

139

140

141

142

143

144

145

	VG	VF
139. Kai Yuan Tong Bao S-132/FD-672	0.50	4.00
140. Ditto, Silver	200.00	450.00
141. Ditto, Gold, VR	—	—
142. Qian Feng Quan Bao S-350/FD-685	50.00	80.00
143. Qian Yuan Zhong Bao, Cloud on reverse FD-688	70.00	120.00
144. Ditto, Large S-355/FD-694	30.00	60.00
145. Kai Yuan Tong Bao, Large S-365/FD-707	300.00	500.00

No. 144 — A 10 cash coin minted by the emperor Su Zong in 758 A.D. to revive the economy shattered by An Lu Shan's revolt and to raise military funds. This measure did somewhat ease the situation, but prices got out of control — a decalitre of rice soon rose from 10 cash to 7,000. A 50 cash coin was released the following year; however, after 3 years the public accepted it only as a 1 cash coin, and small Qian Yuan were then released. In 763 A.D. the Kai Yuan coin was again recognized at its original value and the exchange rate to the Qian Yuan coins set at 1 to 1.

Some Qian Yuan coins have a cloud or bird pattern on the reverse (No. 143), meant to be signs of good luck. Such coins were mainly found in Sichuan Province, probably minted there to commemorate the emperor Xuan Zong's having taken refuge there during the An Lu Shan revolt.

No. 145 — Large Kai Yuan coins were of a commemorative nature, not meant to go into circulation. Those most resembling the small coins in style and workmanship are of Tang make.

Nos. 146-149 — In the 5th year of Hui Chang (845 A.D.), Emperor Wu Zong, a believer in Taoism, ordered the demolition of all but a few of the Buddhist monasteries and melted the copper Buddhas and sacrificial artifacts to mint new coins. Yang Sheng, the Revenue Commissioner of Yangzhou cast Kai Yuan coins with the character "Chang" on the reverse to represent the emperor's reign title, whereupon the emperor gave orders for the other mints to follow suit and print their mint names on the reverse of their coins. Hence the name of this series of coins is Hui Chang Kai Yuan – twenty-three in all, "Yong" being the rarest. The quality of these coins was a far cry from that of their early counterparts. They marked the beginning of the Late Tang Period, the twilight of the empire. The complete set is shown in the next section.

No. 150 — Orders came for its withdrawal just as it was coming out, hence its rarity.

Nos. 151, 152 — Minted by Shi Si Ming, An Lu Shan's partner during their revolt. The De Yi coin was withdrawn after a few months as the legend sounded an ominous tone, something like "Having only one year".

146

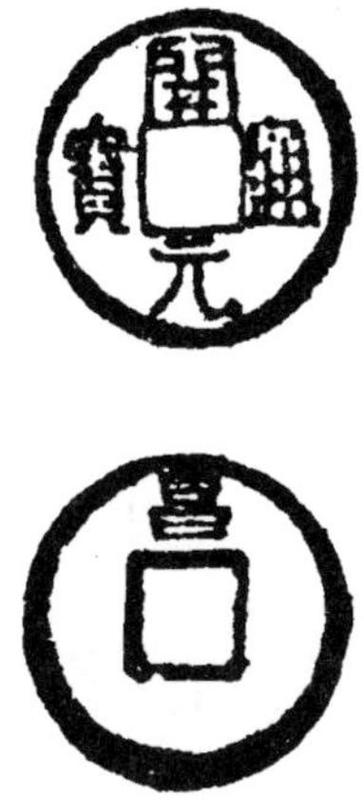

147

148

149

151

152

150

153

154

155

	VG	VF
146. Kai Yuan Tong Bao, Chang on reverse, S-366-FD-709	5.00	10.00
147. Ditto, Fu on reverse FD-738	40.70	70.00
148. Ditto, Dan on reverse S-405/FD-740	40.00	70.00
149. Ditto, Yong on reverse FD-735	1000.00	2000.00
150. Xian Tong Xuan Bao FD-746, R	3500.00	6000.00
151. De Yi Yuan Bao S-407/FD-747	70.00	150.00
152. Shun Tian Yuan Bao S-409/FD-751	40.00	70.00
153. Da Li Yuan Bao FD-702, *		
154. Jian Zhong Yuan Bao FD-704, *		
155. Gao Chang Ji Li FD-1819, *		

* See Xinjiang Section.

THE FIVE DYNASTIES

This was one of the most tumultuous and short-lived of dynastic eras, lasting only 53 years. Many regimes were wiped out before they had a chance to mint their own coins, and those who did produced some of the rarest specimens, some of which are known to have existed only from early rubbings (Nos. 166, 184).

1. Posterior Liang — Set up by the ruthless villain Zhu Wen after he toppled the Tang regime. He minted No. 156 and another Tong Bao specie; only one of each exist, their authenticity still unestablished.

2. Posterior Tang * — No. 157 was cast during A.D. 926-930. The price of copper rising, the melting of cash for making utensils became a profitable business for the public and the casting of currency a losing one for the government, which explains the rarity of this coin.

3. Posterior Jin * — To meet the money shortage, the regime legalized private minting in A.D. 938, and when inferior coins flooded the market, countermanded the order and took back all minting rights the following year. Coins smaller than No. 158 and inferior in workmanship must be from private mints.

4. Posterior Han * — Left resourceless by the invasion of northern tribes, the regime had to extort copper throughout the country to cast currency (No. 159), which started in A.D. 948. Kai Yuan moulds from the Tang Dynasty were used, changing only the top character.

5. Posterior Zhou — To collect copper, the government closed down 3336 monasteries and allowed the public to retain only copper mirrors, paying a reimbursement of 100-150 cash per jin (1/2 kg). In 955 A.D. the emperor ordered dozens of furnaces set up inside the palace and personally watched the minting process. His coins are of very fine make (No. 160), and as they were cast with copper from melted Buddha statues, people believed they could heal certain diseases and give relief to difficult delivery, thus many imitations appeared over the years with various patterns on the reverse.

* The founders of these regimes were descendents of the Western Turks, called "Sha Tuo" in Chinese.

X. FIVE DYNASTIES & TEN KINGDOMS
907-960 A.D.

A. Five Dynasties

156

157

158

159

160

B. Ten Kingdoms

161

162

163

164

165

	VG	VF
156. Kai Ping Yuan Bao FD-753, ER	—	—
157. Tian Cheng Yuan Bao FD-757, R	2500.00	—
158. Tian Fu Yuan Bao FD-759	100.00	500.00
159. Han Yuan Tong Bao S-411/FD-761	30.00	80.00
160. Zhou Yuan Tong Bao S-414/FD-764	5.00	30.00
161. Yong Ping Yuan Bao FD-770	2500.00	5000.00
162. Tong Zheng Yuan Bao FD-772	30.00	100.00
163. Tian Han Yuan Bao S-430/FD-773	15.00	30.00
164. Guang Tian Yuan Bao S-431/F-774	15.00	30.00
165. Qian De Yuan Bao S-433/FD-775	15.00	30.00
166. Qian De Yuan Bao, Large, ER	—	—
167. Xian Kang Yuan Bao S-434/FD-776	10.00	20.00

166

167

168

169

170

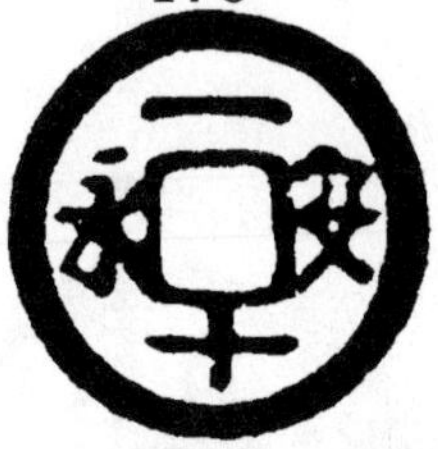

171

172

173

174

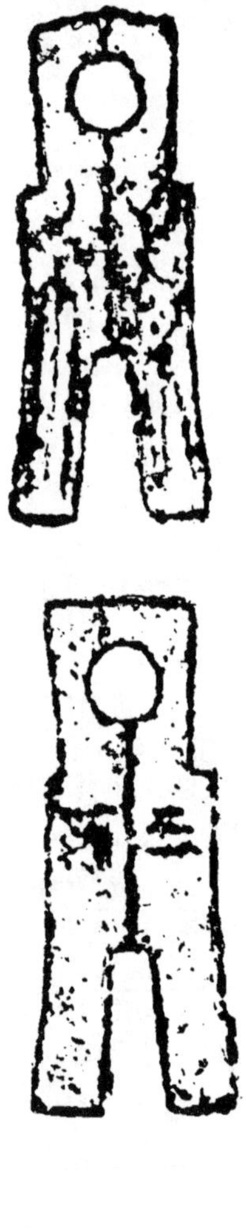

	VG	VF
168. Qian Heng Tong Bao FD-829	1200.00	2500.00
169. Qian Heng Zhong Bao FD-824	100.00	200.00
Lead S-436/FD-825	5.00	25.00
170. Yong An Yi Shi FD-832, VR	—	—
Iron FD-833	800.00	1500.00
171. Yong An Yi Bai FD-834	800.00	1500.00
Iron FD-835	70.00	120.00
172. Yong An Wu Bai FD-836, VR	—	—
Iron FD-837	2000.00	3000.00
173. Yong An Yi Qian FD-838	3000.00	5000.00
Iron FD-839	100.00	300.00
174. Huo Bu, Iron FD-842	150.00	300.00

175

176

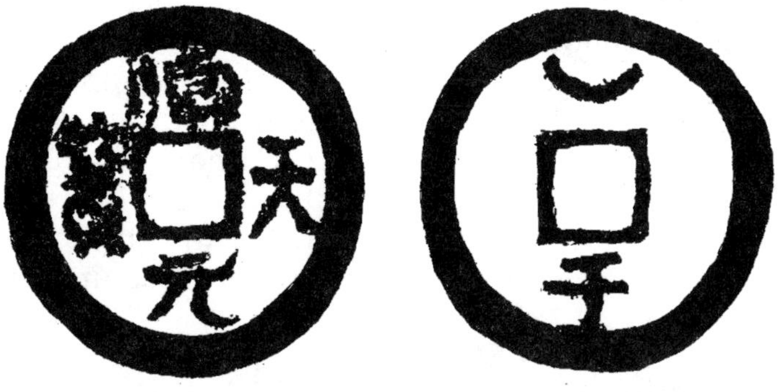

177

178

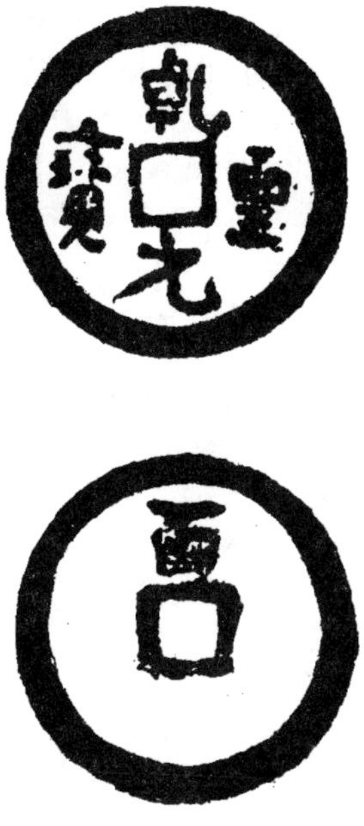

179

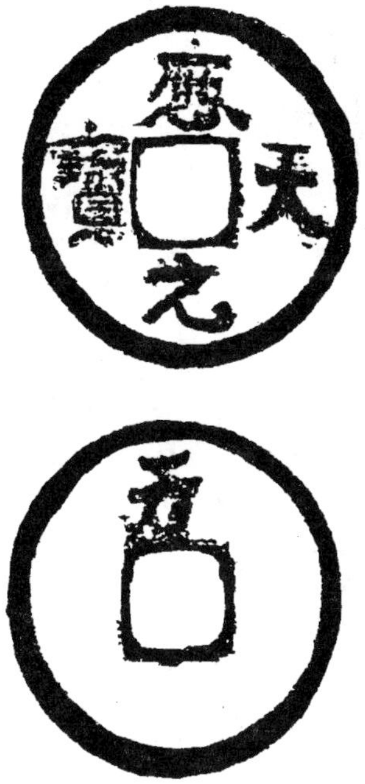

	VG	VF
175. Shun Tian Yuan Bao, Iron FD-843	400.00	700.00
176. Shun Tian Yuan Bao, Yi Qian on rev. FD-845	2000.00	4000.00
177. Ying Sheng Yuan Bao, Shi on rev. FD-846, ER	—	—
178. Qian Sheng Yuan Bao, Bai on rev. FD-847, ER	—	—
179. Ying Tian Yuan Bao, Wan on rev. FD-848, ER	—	—

1. - 8. missing

9. Min — As his regime was located in Fujian Province, Wang Shen Zhi cast 1 cash lead Kai Yuan coins in 916 A.D. with Fu or Min on the reverse, both words meaning Fujian. Large Kai Yuan coins followed in 922 A.D. with a large star or Min with half moon on the reverse (Nos. 180, 181), copper coins being very rare. In 939 Wang Yan Xi became the ruler and issued Yong Long lead and iron coins (No. 182). No copper coins have been discovered so far. The Tian De coin (No. 183) was cast by another ruler Wang Yan Zheng in 944 A.D. with Yin on the reverse, his state title. Both copper and iron varieties are very rare.

10. Chu — Ma Yin the carpenter rose swiftly through the ranks through his ability and bravery from rank and file to Governor General of Tian Che Fu in Hunan Province. He issued iron and lead coins (No. 184) to be circulated within the city, and copper species to be used only in the suburbs, quite similar to that of Southern Han, but in this case by his orders. These coins were cast in 911 A.D. after he became King of Chu to commemorate the occasion, thus they are also commemoratives and highly valued by numismatists at home and abroad. Later he followed his minister Gao Yu's advice and cast iron Qian Feng coins in several sizes with a variety of characters on the reverse.

Few circulators of iron coins achieved the success that he did with his. He adopted a protective policy toward traders and allowed the use of vouchers in transactions, thus relieving them of the cumbersome iron coins; and moreover, commercial tax was exempted. Merchants far and near flocked to Hunan with their wares, and as the easily acquired iron coins were unusable outside the province, they readily bought local products, speeding up the exchange of commodities, gaining large profits for the government silk and tea businesses. Of this coin (No. 185) copper ones also exist, very rare specimens. Coin No. 186 is attributed to him.

180 181 182 183

184

185

	VG	VF
180. Kai Yuan Tong Bao, Bronze FD-778, VR	—	—
Iron, FD-779	250.00	400.00
181. Ditto, Min on rev., Iron FD-781	300.00	500.00
Lead, FD-779	80.00	150.00
182. Yong Long Tong Bao, Bronze FD-782, ER	—	—
(All three have Min & crescent) Iron FD-783	700.00	1200.00
Lead	1500.00	3000.00
183. Tian De Zhong Bao, Yin on rev. Bronze FD-785, VR	—	—
Iron FD-786	2000.00	4000.00
Tong Bao, Bronze FD-784, ER	—	—
184. Tian Ce Fu Bao, Bronze, FD-787, VR	—	—
Iron FD-788	700.00	1200.00
185. Qian Feng Quan Bao, Tian Fu on reverse, VR	—	—
FD-792 Iron FD-798	100.00	500.00

11. Posterior Shu — After the fall of Anterior Shu, Meng Zhi Xiang entered Sichuan and set up this regime. The coins existing today with his Meng De reign title are Annam coins, not his. In 934 A.D. Meng Zhi Xiang proclaimed himself Emperor of Da Shu (Great Shu). Opinions differ on who cast the Da Shu coins (No. 188), father or son, as he died a few months later, the time not sufficient to cast coins. His son Meng Xu, however, continued to use the same reign title for four years, so we cannot rule out the possibility of his having cast the coins. In 938 A.D. he adopted the reign title Guang Zheng and minted coin No. 187. Eighteen years later he minted iron Guang Zheng coins to meet military expenses. These coins were so excellently made that they passed off as copper coins to many people. Both copper and iron coins are scarce. The Da Shu species are great rarities.

12. Southern Tang — In 937 A.D. Xu Wen's adopted son Xu Zhi Hao succeeded to the throne and adopted the state title of Da Qi, but soon took up his original family name of Li and changed the state title to Great Tang – Southern Tang. The Da Qi coin (No. 189) is accredited to him. This coin ranks among the rarest of cash coins. Only two have been discovered, one with a part of it missing and the other with four holes on it. The first one faded into oblivion when its owner committed suicide and the second one also disappeared after its owner brought it over to the United States half a century ago.

After the throne passed to Li Jing, coins No. 190-196 were minted. The Tang Guo coins are quite good looking and some of them are very hard to find. Some of them came in pairs, both the same size but written in different scripts. The Kai Yuan coins differ from their Tang Dynasty predecessors by their wide rims and also come in pairs, one in seal script and the other in Li script. The last emperor Li Hou Zhu was one of the most tragic of emperors. He was an incompetent ruler, but as a poet he ranks among the greatest. His poems are chanted in schoolrooms all over the Middle Kingdom to the present day.

How many woes do you have, O Sire?
As a River of Spring Water eastward flowing.

He died as a hostage in captivity.

186

187

188

189

190

191

192

193

194

195

196

	VG	VF
186. Qian Yuan Zhong Bao FD-800, VR	—	—
187. Guang Zheng Tong Bao FD-801	2000.00	4000.00
Iron FD-804	400.00	700.00
188. Da Shu Tong Bao S-435/FD-806, VR	—	—
189. Da Qi Tong Bao FD-822, ER	—	—
190. Bao Da Yuan Bao FD-811, VR	—	—
Iron	800.00	2000.00
191. Yong Tong Quan Huo S-439/FD-810	1500.00	3500.00
↳ 33mm Iron	800.00	1500.00
192. Tang Guo Tong Bao S-444/FD-815	15.00	30.00
193. Ditto, Large FD-818	700.00	1200.00
194. Da Tang Tong Bao S-440/FD-819	70.00	120.00
195. Kai Yuan Tong Bao, Seal script S-446/FD-821	2.00	5.00
196. Ditto, Li script	1.00	5.00

THE SONG DYNASTY

In terms of prolificness, no dynasty can stand a chance against the Song Dynasty with its 15 emperors and 48 reign titles, not to mention the coin pairs and triplets, mother coins and test pieces, and a variety of species with dozens of variations each; and to top it all, from there come the iron coins with their countless mint marks. Tackling such a state of affairs poses a challenge indeed.

Four forms of script are used in writing the coin legends:

1. Regular script — The kind of script used in China today;
2. Seal script — This is the form of script standardized in the Qin Dynasty and often used on seals. The brush strokes coil back and forth tastefully;
3. Running script — This is a form of rapid writing, the brush strokes running into each other;
4. Scribbling script — To the layperson the characters are simplified beyond recognition, somewhat resembling cipher; it is also called running script. Schjoth terms it "Grass character".

The emperors are listed here in chronological order. Actually there were 18 emperors, but the last three issued no coinage of their own, as they were being chased from place to place by Yuan troops.

1. Tai Zhu (960-976) — He adopted three reign titles but on his coins he used instead the year title Song Yuan (No. 197). The legend is in Li script, modelled after the Kai Yuan coins.
2. Tai Zong (976-998) — Coins No. 198-206. He was a good calligraphist and the legends are in his own hand. The difference between three scripts are shown on these coins (Nos. 201-206); regular script varieties also exist. Iron coins were cast in Sichuan after its occupation as the copper was looted and taken back to the capital. One cash iron coins are plentiful but the large ones are scarce.

XI. SONG DYNASTY
960-1279 A.D.

A. Northern Song 960-1127 A.D.

197

198

199

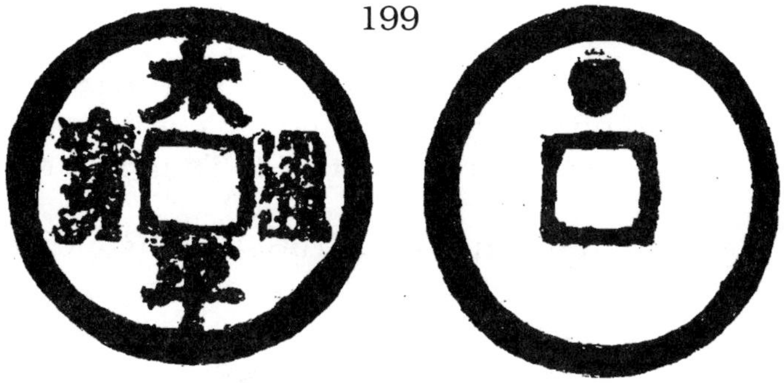

200

201

202

203

204

205

206

	VG	VF
197. Song Yuan Tong Bao S-451/FD-849	0.50	2.00
198. Tai Ping Tong Bao S-460/FD-860	0.50	2.00
199. Ditto, Large FD-865, VR	—	—
Iron	100.00	300.00
200. Chun Hua Yuan Bao, Iron FD-871	70.00	120.00
201. Ditto, Li script S-463/FD-867	0.50	1.00
202. Ditto, Running script S-464/FD-868	0.50	1.00
203. Ditto, Scribbling script FD-869	0.50	1.00
204. Zhi Dao Yuan Bao, Running script S-467/FD-873	0.50	1.00
205. Ditto, Li script S-466/FD-872	0.50	1.00
206. Ditto, Scribbling script S-468/FD-874	0.50	1.00

3. Zheng Zong (988-1023) — Four of his five reign titles appeared on his coins. The Qian Xing title was not used, and so was Da Zhong, which was represented by Xiang Fu. Some Xian Ping and Xiang Fu varieties are large and thick and with very wide rims, coming in various sizes. Their denominations and function are unknown. At the time Sichuan was still being fleeced by the central government and iron coins were circulated for currency. As a result, iron coins depreciated and the buying power of copper coins skyrocketed. The value of these large coins must have been determined by the market conditions of the day. The one cash Xiang Fu coins with stars or half moons on the reverse are rather scarce. The Tong Bao specie is his handwriting.

4. Ren Zong (1023-1064) — His 4th reign title was changed to Huang Song, since two Baos appearing on the same coin was considered bad form — the title would have read Bao Yuan Yuan Bao or Bao Yuan Tong Bao. The Kang Ding title appeared only on iron coins ordered cast in Shaanxi Province for frontier needs. For some reason his Huang You title was not used. The chronicles mentioned over one million strings of cash were minted during the middle of that period, but no Huang You coins have ever surfaced except forgeries, therefore the coins cast must have been the Huang Song species.

a. Tian Sheng — Two pairs were issued, one large and one small. Iron coins were also issued.
b. Ming Dao — Also in pairs. There is a larger coin in regular script.

208

207

209

210

211

212

213

214

215

216

217

218

219

	VG	VF
207. Xian Ping Yuan Bao S-469/FD-876	0.50	1.00
208. Xian Ping Yuan Bao, Large FD-880, VR	—	—
209. Jing De Yuan Bao, Iron S-472/FD-882	70.00	120.00
210. Jing De Yuan Bao, One Cash S-471/FD-881	0.50	1.00
211. Xiang Fu Yuan Bao S-474/FD-883	0.50	1.00
212. Xiang Fu Tong Bao S-476/FD-891	0.50	1.00
213. Tian Xi Tong Bao S-480/FD-894	0.50	1.00
214. Tian Xi Tong Bao, Iron S-493	40.00	70.00
215. Tian Sheng Yuan Bao S-486/FD-895	0.50	1.00
216. Ditto, Seal script S-484/FD-896	0.50	1.00
217. Ditto, Iron S-487	12.00	25.00
218. Ming Dao Yuan Bao S-490/FD-899	12.00	25.00
219. Ditto, Seal script S-489/FD-900	12.00	25.00

c. Jing You — Coins No. 220 & 221 comprise a pair, though the rims are not the same in width. Copper coins of the size of No. 222 are mother coins used for casting iron ones and fetch a high price in the market.

d. Huang Song — Also in pairs. These come in many sorts and sizes as their minting covered a period of 20 years, with over a million strings issued annually.

The nine-folds variety (No. 225) has a very artistic design and is much coveted by collectors. The legend is the same as Nos. 223-224, the difference showing in the brush strokes that fold back and forth — a kind of script in vogue on official seals in the Song era.

e. Qing Li — The legend was printed in two ways. On No. 227 the legend reads from top to bottom and then from right to left; on No. 228 it reads clockwise. The small Qing Li (No. 226) might be a depreciated 10 cash specie, as Zhong Bao is usually used for coins of large denomination.

f. Kang Ding — Only 1 cash iron coins exist. Ten cash or copper coins are forgeries. The Xi Xia minorities to the west were then constantly harassing the border regions and this coin was cast in Shaanxi Province to cover military expenditures. Huang Song coins continued to be minted in the other provinces.

220

221

222

223

224

225

226

227

228

229

	VG	VF
220. Jing You Yuan Bao S-494/FD-901	0.50	1.00
221. Ditto, Seal script S-492	0.50	1.00
222. Ditto, Iron S-495/FD-903	60.00	90.00
223. Huang Song Tong Bao S-499/FD-904	60.00	90.00
224. Ditto, Seal script S-497/FD-905	60.00	90.00
225. Ditto, Nine-folding Seal script FD-906	2500.00	4500.00
226. Kang Ding Yuan Bao, Iron FD-911	70.00	200.00
227. Qing Li Zhong Bao, Read from top to bottom S-504/FD-914	4.00	8.00
228. Ditto, Read clockwise S-505/FD-913	5.00	10.00
229. Ditto, Small S-506/FD-916	25.00	40.00

g. Zhi He — Coins No. 230 & 231 make a pair and so do coins No. 233 & 234; the beautifully written No. 232 has no partner. Copper Zhi He Zhong Bao coins are mostly mother coins used for casting No. 235 and others; the ones with a character on the reverse are rare.

h. Jia You — Also issued in two pairs, one Yuan Bao and one Tong Bao. Only 1 cash coins were minted.

5. Ying Zong (1064-1068) — Zhi Ping is the only reign title appearing on his coins (Nos. 240-244). The Yuan Bao variety (Nos. 241-242) is a triplet, written in regular, seal and Li scripts; and the Tong Bao pair in regular and Li scripts.

The Song Dynasty stands out among other dynasties for turning out great quantities of cash coins, reaching 3 million strings of cash (1 string = 1,000 cash) per year during this emperor's reign. No wonder tons of Northern Song coins have been unearthed over the years, most of them of no value whatsoever. In his time, however, some coins of great merit or value were produced: the Nine-Folds Huang Song, the 2 cash wide rimmed coin with the same legend, and the Zhi He mother coins. As they are not easily available, the nice Zhi He coin written in Li script (No. 232) and the Kang Ding specie (No. 229) are attractive collectibles for representing this emperor.

	230		231		232	

230

231

232

233

234

235

236

237

238

239

240

241

242

243

244

	VG	VF
230. Zhi He Yuan Bao S-511/FD-919	0.50	1.00
231. Ditto, Seal script S-510/FD-920	0.50	1.00
232. Ditto, Li script FD-918	50.00	80.00
233. Zhi He Tong Bao S-513/FD-922	0.50	1.00
234. Ditto, Seal script S-512 FD-923	0.50	1.00
235. Zhi He Zhong Bao FD-924	150.00	300.00
236. Jia You Yuan Bao S-515	0.50	1.00
237. Ditto, Seal script S-514/FD-933	0.50	1.00
238. Ditto, Li script FD-934	0.50	1.00
239. Jia You Tong Bao S-517/FD-936	0.50	1.00
240. Zhi Ping Yuan Bao S-523	0.50	1.00
241. Ditto, Seal script S-521/FD-937	0.50	1.00
242. Ditto, Li script S-522/FD-939	0.50	1.00
243. Zhi Ping Tong Bao S-526/FD-942	0.50	1.00
244. Ditto, Seal script S-525/FD-940	0.50	1.00

6. Shen Zong (1068-1086) — Two reign titles appear on his coins, Xi Ning and Yuan Feng (Nos. 245-254). The amount of coins minted annually reached a record high of 5 million strings of cash, so it is not surprising that numerous variations and sizes of each reign title exist.

a. Xi Ning — The three coins make a triplet (Nos. 245, 246, 247), rendered in regular, seal and Li scripts. One cash coins with the character Heng on the reverse are quite scarce. The 2 cash coins also comprise a pair (Nos. 249, 249), the 1st in regular and the 2nd in Li script; and they come in various sizes. Large iron Tong Bao coins were also cast, and fortunate is the collector who finds a copper one, which without exception is a rare mother coin. The iron coins were cast in two denominations, 1 cash and 3 cash. Almost from its founding, the Song Dynasty was in constant trouble with its two bellicose neighbors, the Liao regime to the north and Xi Xia to the west; and later the Jin regime, which first overthrew the Liao regime and then the Northern Song Dynasty — which accounts for the fact that all the emperors of that period resorted to casting iron coins to settle their financial problems.

b. Yuan Feng — These coins were issued in three values; one, two and three cash, all in pairs. (Nos. 250-254). Deserving special mention is coin No. 252. The legend, written in Li script, was said to be the work of the noted poet and calligraphist Shu Dong Bo. Some said this could not be, as he had fallen from favor with the emperor and was demoted to places far from the capital. He was rehabilitated by the next emperor Zhe Zong, and it might be possible that some of the legends on this ruler's coinage were in his handwriting. There is another version of the Li script in smaller characters which is quite common. The 1 cash specie with a crescent moon on the reverse is quite scarce. The copper 3 cash mother coins are most beautifully written.

245

246

247

248

249

250

251

252

253

254

	VG	VF
245. Xi Ning Yuan Bao S-533/FD-952	0.50	1.00
246. Ditto, Seal script S-529/FD-945	0.50	1.00
247. Ditto, Li script S-532/FD-951	0.50	1.00
248. Xi Ning Zhong Bao S-542/FD-956	1.00	2.00
249. Ditto, Seal script, S-538/FD-955	1.00	2.00
250. Yuan Feng Tong Bao, Running script FD-963	0.50	1.00
251. Ditto, Seal script S-545/FD-964	0.50	1.00
252. Ditto, Li script FD-969	200.00	400.00
253. Ditto, Large S-556/FD-971	1.00	2.00
254. Ditto, Seal script S-553/FD-972	1.00	2.00

7. Zhe Zong (1086-1101) — Three varieties bear his reign title (Nos. 255-267), each denomination appearing in pairs, and the large 3 cash copper species being mother coins.

a. Yuan You — Of the many 1 cash varieties, the one with the character Shaan on the reverse is rare. It comes in pairs. Coins No. 257 & 258 appear to be mother coins in points of calligraphy, but they are too thin and too coarse in quality to be passed as such, and should be regarded as just regular issues.

b. Shao Sheng — Coins No. 259 & 260 are a pair. The Tong Bao variety (No. 261) was written in regular script. Of this variety both copper and iron coins were cast, the copper ones being slightly higher in value – let the buyer beware. They must not be mistaken for mother coins or test pieces.

c. Yuan Fu — Like the two preceding varieties, the legend on this coin also used the seal and running script. It is interesting to note that one of each pair in all three varieties and denominations carried the running script, a form of writing much appreciated for its elegance and flowing rhythm, and greatly favored by calligraphists as a form offering great freedom of artistic expression. In the later years of this emperor's reign, larger quantities of iron coins were minted than those of any other Northern Song emperor.

255

256

257

258

259

260

261

262

263

264

265

266

267

	VG	VF
255. Yuan You Tong Bao, Seal script S-565/FD-979	0.50	1.00
256. Ditto, Running script S-567/FD-980	0.50	1.00
257. Ditto, Large, Seal script S-575/FD-983	1.00	2.00
258. Ditto, Large, Running script, S-576/FD-984	1.00	2.00
259. Shao Sheng Yuan Bao, Seal script S-582/FD-990	0.50	1.00
260. Ditto, Running script S-586/FD-991	0.50	1.00
261. Shao Sheng Tong Bao S-592/FD-1002	10.00	20.00
262. Shao Sheng Yuan Bao, Large, Seal script, S-593/FD-995	1.00	2.00
263. Ditto, Running script S-595/FD-996	1.00	2.00
264. Yuan Fu Tong Bao, Seal script S-599/FD-1005	0.50	1.00
265. Ditto, Running script S-603/FD-1004	0.50	1.00
266. Ditto, Large, Running script S-605/FD-1009	1.00	2.00
267. Ditto, Large, Seal script S-604/FD-1010	1.00	2.00

8. Hui Zong (1101-1126) — His coins are remarkable for their excellent make and superbly written legends, many done in the emperor's own hand, whose forceful and elegant calligraphic style has been figuratively described as strokes of steel and hooks of silver, of which coin No. 275 is a representative specimen; reminding one of supermodels, skinny yet vigorous and graceful.

Hui Zong was another tragic emperor whose life, like the emperor Li Yu of the Southern Tang Dynasty, ended in captivity. As a calligraphist and painter he ranks among China's best; but as an administrator, he was self-indulgent and let his power slip into the hands of his villainous minister Tsai Jing.

a. Sheng Song — The legends on this coin were written in running, seal and Li scripts (Nos. 268-277). These are only a few out of many varieties; others are shown in the 2nd part of this book. The Tong Bao coin (No. 271) is very rare, only one known existing specimen.

b. Chong Ning — The 1 cash coins (No. 274) are fewer than the large ones (No. 275) of which large quantities were minted. This beautiful coin is a typical sample of his unique "Slender Gold" penmanship style. It is fortunate that they exist in large numbers, making it easy on the collector's pocketbook. The Chong Ning Zhong Bao (No. 276) in Li script also exists in large numbers; the Yuan Bao coin, whether the copper mother coin or its iron offspring, are quite rare. Sometimes one comes upon a white copper Chong Ning coin, the ones of excellent workmanship usually regarded as patterns.

268

269

270

271

272

273

274

275

276

277

	VG	VF
268. Sheng Song Yuan Bao, Running script, S-609/FD-1018	1.00	5.00
269. Ditto, Seal script S-607/FD-1017	1.00	5.00
270. Ditto, Li script FD-1021	1800.00	3000.00
271. Sheng Song Tong Bao FD-1033	3500.00	5000.00
272. Sheng Song Yuan Bao, 2 Cash, Running script S-614/FD-1026	2.00	5.00
273. Ditto, Seal script S-613/FD-1025	2.00	5.00
274. Chong Ning Tong Bao, Slender Gold Style, S-619/FD-1038	40.00	80.00
275. Ditto, 5 Cash S-621/FD-1040	5.00	20.00
276. Chong Ning Zhong Bao, 5 Cash, Li script, S-623/FD-1049	2.00	10.00
277. Chong Ning Yuan Bao, Iron S-626/FD-1054	100.00	200.00

c. Da Guan — This series (Nos. 288-292) excels as miniature masterpieces of design, balancing the top character composed of three strokes against the multi-stroked character below it. The 1 cash coin (No. 288) expanded into dozens of variations, among which this variety is considered the original version rendered in the emperor's own hand. Some of the variations are quite rare, especially the mother coin done in running script. One cash coins over 26mm are scarce.

d. Zheng He — This variety also claims many variations, the grading of which range from scarce to the bottom line. Many of them come in pairs. The pair shown here (Nos. 283, 284) is quite beautiful. As the writing style has some resemblance to the Zhong He pair below (Nos. 288, 289), they are commonly called Zhong He style Zheng He coins. In fact, the Zhong He pair came afterwards and to be exact, it was the Zhong He that imitated the Zheng He style. Two cash (Nos. 286, 287) and three cash were minted in large quantities. Some 3 cash varieties are much sought after by collectors for their beauty. Zheng He Zhong Bao coins are listed as rarities even though they were made of iron, not to mention the copper mother coins.

e. Zhong He — Collectors of Northern Song coins find this pair (Nos. 288, 289) quite difficult to acquire, and many of them have left their collections of this epoch in an uncompleted state. This reign title was in use for only one year, which accounts for its scarcity. The Legend is also pronounced Chong He.

278

279

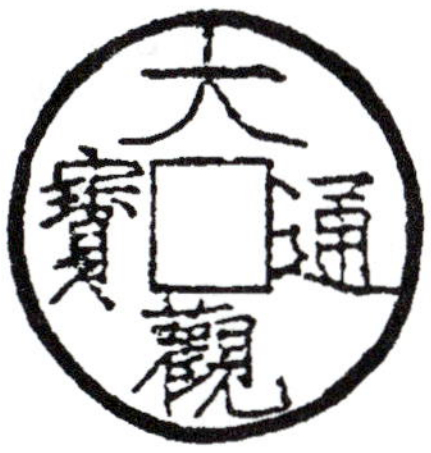

280

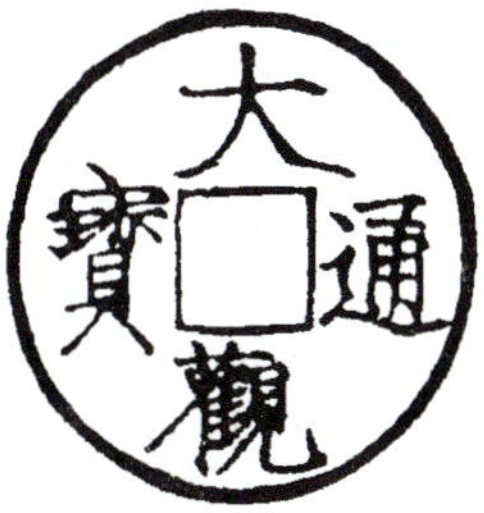

281

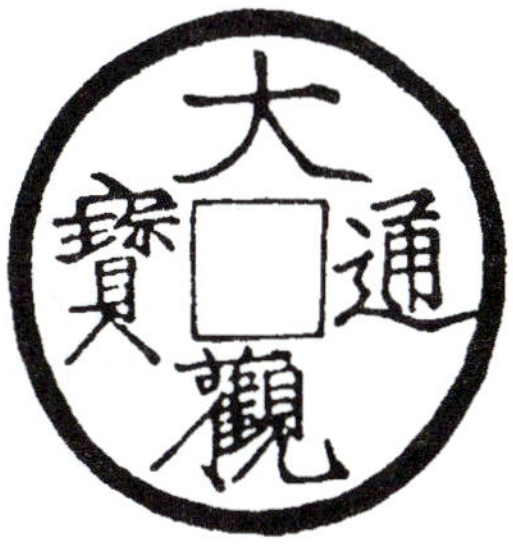

282

283

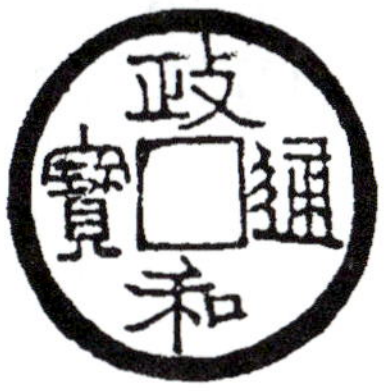

284

285

286

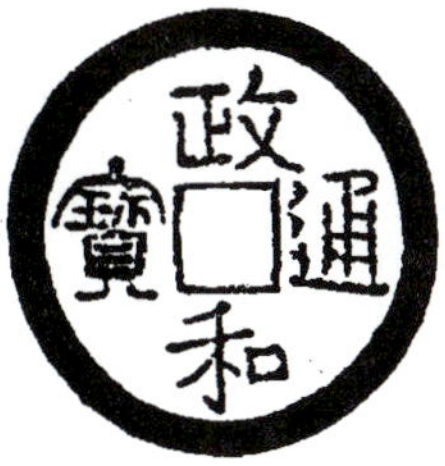

287

288

289

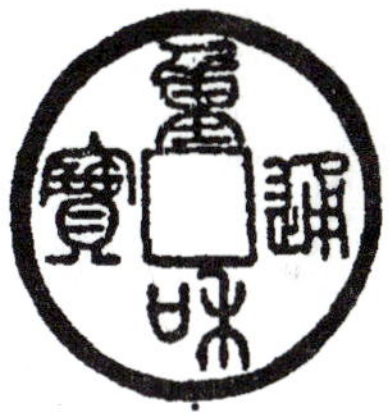

	VG	VF
278. Da Guan Tong Bao S-629/FD-1055	0.50	1.00
279. Ditto, Two Cash	25.00	40.00
280. Ditto, Three Cash S-632/FD-1059	30.00	50.00
281. Ditto, Five Cash FD-1961	150.00	250.00
282. Ditto, Ten Cash S-630/FD-1062	20.00	40.00
283. Zheng He Tong Bao S-635/FD-1074	0.50	1.00
284. Ditto, Seal script S-633/FD-1076	15.00	30.00
285. Ditto, Regular script S-640/FD-1073	20.00	50.00
286. Ditto, 2 Cash S-639/FD-1078	1.00	5.00
287. Ditto, Seal script S-638/FD-1077	1.00	5.00
288. Zhong He Tong Bao, Li script S-647, FD-1096	200.00	400.00
289. Ditto, Seal script FD-1095	250.00	500.00

f. Xuan He — This variety embraces the greatest number of variations among Song coins; the major types will appear in the second section of this book. First to be minted were the Yuan Bao varieties (Nos. 290, 291) displaying magnificently written legends, supposedly done by the emperor himself. Most of the Yuan Bao varieties came out in pairs, and so it was with the Tong Bao coins (Nos. 292, 293). The legend on coin No. 294 was written in the emperor's "Slender Gold" style; the character Shaan on the reverse stands for Shaanxi Province. Both copper and iron coins were issued, the copper ones much fewer than their iron counterparts; they are in fact regular issues and should not be regarded as mother coins or test pieces.

As the 2 cash & 3 cash species do not possess much artistic merit or market value, numismatists just concentrate their attention on the 1 cash species and let the large ones go by. However, one must be on the alert for 3 cash mother coins. These are recognized as such if an iron coin is found that matches them in appearance. The serious collector of mother coins needs to have a comprehensive catalog on hand and be well informed of excavation findings, as many iron coins are not published in catalogs for the reason that they take up too much space.

290

291

292

293

294

295

296

297

298

	VG	VF
290. Xuan He Yuan Bao, Seal script FD-1099	250.00	500.00
291. Ditto, Li script FD-1101 / S-652	250.00	500.00
292. Xuan He Tong Bao, Seal script S-649, FD-~~1102~~ 1103	5.00	50.00
293. Ditto, Li script S-653/FD-~~1103~~ 1102	5.00	50.00
294. Ditto, Slender Gold Style, Shaan on reverse, Iron S-666/FD-1119	5.00	10.00
295. Ditto, 2 Cash, Seal script S-656/FD-1112	2.00	5.00
296. Ditto, Regular script S-657/FD-1115	1.00	3.00
297. Ditto, 3 Cash, Seal script S-659/FD-1111	2.00	5.00
298. Ditto, 3 Cash, Li script ~~S-660~~/FD-1116 S 661	2.00	5.00

9. Qin Zong (1226-1227) — With this shamed reign title the Northern Song Dynasty came to a close. For all its humiliations, this title that lasted only one year produced quite a few rarities. In the face of the troops of the Jin regime advancing on the capital, the terror-stricken emperor Hui Zong abdicated the throne and passed it on to his son, who assumed the reign title of Jin Kang. Surrounded by capitulators, the father and son retreated time and again without putting up a fight. Even though there were patriotic and capable generals who tried their best to save the kingdom, they were shoved aside; making it easy work for the Jin troops to capture the two useless emperors along with thousands of family members and concubines. The father and son were dispatched to the far north where they died in galling humiliation.

a. Jin Kang Yuan Bao — The 1 cash (Nos. 299, 300) is very rare; the 2 cash variety (Nos. 301, 302) is more often available. Both denominations come in pairs.

b. Jin Kang Tong Bao — Though rare, the Tong Bao varieties (Nos. 303-306) come in many different versions, some in pairs. Despite the many variations of the Tong Bao and Yuan Bao coins, the legends seem to have come from the same hand – Emperor Qin Zong's. He must have followed in his father's footsteps and wrote the legends himself; like father, like son.

10. Rebel coins — Coins No. 307 & 308 were minted by the rebel leader Li Shun in A.D. 995. He and his partner Wang Xiao Bo rose up against the Song regime in A.D. 993. After his partner's death, Li Shun proclaimed himself King of Da Shu with the reign title Ying Yun, and later Ying Gan. He was killed in the same year (995 A.D.).

299

300

301

302

303

304

305

306

307

308

	VG	VF
299. Jing Kang Yuan Bao, Seal script FD-1122, R	3500.00	—
300. Ditto, Li script FD-1121, VR	—	—
301. Ditto, 2 Cash, Seal script FD-1125	150.00	300.00
302. Ditto, Li script FD-1126	150.00	300.00
303. Jing Kang Tong Bao, Seal script FD-1130	2500.00	4000.00
304. Ditto, Li script FD-1129	2500.00	4000.00
305. Ditto, 2 Cash, Regular script FD-1135	900.00	2000.00
306. Ditto, Seal script FD-1134	900.00	2000.00
307. Ying Yun Yuan Bao FD-1612, VR	—	—
308. Ying Gan Tong Bao FD-3099	3000.00	5000.00

THE SONG DYNASTY (SOUTHERN SONG)

When the Jin troops took the capital, one powerful member of the royal family escaped the fate that befell the others — Zhao Gou, Prince of Kang. He and his troops were stationed in Shandong Province at the time. His assistant commander Zong Zhe had been tailing the Jin troops while they were heading for the capital and beat them 13 times. Now, as the enemy troops were heading homeward with their booties, he attempted to cut off the enemy's retreat and rescue the two emperors. He called upon the Song troops in all parts of the country to join forces, but on the appointed day no one showed up; so he hailed the Prince as emperor and rebuilt the imperial court — the Southern Song Dynasty, the reign title as of Jian Yan.

Southern Song coins, on the whole, are far fewer than those of Northern Song. Paper currency had come into use — the first in the world, so the minting of coins was hard affected, especially 1 cash coins. Another reason for the shortage of coins was that the Jin Dynasty used mainly Song currency, so large quantities of Song coins flowed northward; furthermore, overseas trade was developing, increasing the outflow of hard cash.

1. Gao Zong (1127-1163) — He gave orders to cast coins in the first year of his reign. One chronicle recorded the date as November, the legend being Jian Yan Tong Bao, while another record showed the date to be September without mention whether the legend was Tong Bao or Yuan Bao. The two dates gave rise to the speculation that before the minting of Tong Bao coins started in November, the minting of Yuan Bao coins had already begun in September and came to a halt upon arrival of the new imperial edict. This supposition is supported by the fact that very few Yuan Bao coins are known to exist. Among the Tong Bao varieties the ones with a dot on the upper left corner of the topmost character (Nos. 315, 316) are much sought after by collectors.

B. Southern Song 1127-1279 A.D.

309

310

311

312

313

314

315

316

317

318

319

	VG	VF
309. Jian Yan Tong Bao S-671/FD-1140	30.00	50.00
310. Ditto, Seal script S-673/FD-1141	30.00	50.00
311. Ditto, 2 Cash S-676/FD-1148	1.00	5.00
312. Ditto, 2 Cash, Seal script S-675/FD-1147	1.00	5.00
313. Ditto, 3 Cash S-674/FD-1153	2.00	5.00
314. Ditto, 3 Cash, Seal script FD-1154	2.00	5.00
315. Ditto, with Dot on upper left of top character FD-1142	200.00	400.00
316. Ditto, 3 Cash, with Dot on upper left top ~~corner~~ FD-1152	300.00	500.00
317. Jian Yan Yuan Bao FD-1156	800.00	1500.00
318. Ditto, Seal script FD-1155	800.00	1500.00
319. Jian Yan Zhong Bao FD-1157	350.00	500.00

Four years later the emperor changed his reign title to Shao Xing. Both Tong Bao and Yuan Bao coins were minted. As mentioned before, the 1 cash coins issued during Southern Song were far fewer than those of larger denominations, which is especially true with the Shao Xing 1 cash species, scarcest among the coins of this value. But for the neat and beautifully written legends, the larger coins, with the exception of the 5 cash No. 330, are practically worthless. The script on the 1 cash coin No. 320 is in the same style as that on the 2 cash specie. The legends in seal script were also nicely done (Nos. 321, 325 & 327).

The writing style of the regular script used on coin No. 324 set the pattern for the legends on all later Southern Song coins. Bookprinters in the Song Dynasty preferred this style for their typeface for its neat and clear lettering. Today this kind of script is named Song Script, and it has been developed by decorative artists into a form widely used on ads, documents, newspapers and other printing matter.

320

321

322

323

324

325

326

327

328

329

330

	VG	VF
320. Shao Xing Yuan Bao S-679/FD-1159	400.00	600.00
321. Ditto, Seal script FD-1158	400.00	600.00
322. Ditto, Private mint	5.00	10.00
323. Shao Xing Tong Bao, Bronze FD-1165	50.00	80.00
324. Shao Xing Yuan Bao 2 Cash S-685/FD-1161	1.00	10.00
325. Ditto, 2 Cash, Seal script ~~S-689~~/FD-1160	1.00	10.00
326. Ditto, 3 Cash FD-1163	1.00	10.00
327. Ditto, Seal script FD-1162	1.00	10.00
328. Shao Xing Tong Bao, 2 Cash S-690/FD-1166	1.00	10.00
329. Ditto, 3 Cash S-691/FD-1168	5.00	15.00
330. Ditto, 5 Cash FD-1169, VR	—	—

2. Xiao Zong (1168-1190) — This emperor changed his reign title three times. Disliking the first one for its resemblance to the one his opponent the king of Jin was using, he used it for two years and then changed it to Qian Dao. Nine years later he decided it was time to change again, as Nine was the highest of odd numbers, and anything related to Nine symbolized Heaven and therefore, the Emperor. Since this number must not be overpassed, he adopted the title Chun Xi, meaning radiance throughout the kingdom with the coming of victory. For fear of irritating the Jin rulers, this title was again discarded. The title had already been proclaimed throughout the empire, and so it was allowed to exist for a few days. That coins bearing this reign title (No. 335) could have come out of the mint in such a short time is quite surprising. Coin No. 335 was recovered from an ancient submerged pier in 1985.

a. Long Xing — As the minting of coins had come to be an unprofitable business, no 1 cash coins were cast. The 2 cash coins were issued in pairs, one in Song script and the other in seal script. Song script is a variant of the regular script. Coins No. 331, 333, 339 and 340 are good samples of this form. Iron coins were issued in 1 cash and 2 cash denominations.

b. Qian Dao — During this time no 1 cash coins were cast either. The minting of iron coins had increased considerably. Seven mints were set operating, as contrasted to one mint during the time of Xiao Zong's predecessor, Gao Zong. The iron coins bore the names of their respective mints on the reverse.

c. Chun Xi — Starting from the 7th year of this title, the year of mintage was cast on the reverse of the coins, a practice that all succeeding emperors followed, down to the last years of this dynasty; it was a way of dealing with illegal minters who lacked the skills to place the reverse moulds properly, thus making forgeries easily recognizable.

3. Guang Zong (1190-1195) — During his reign, only the Shao Xi species were issued, beautiful samples of the Song script writing style. Iron coins were cast with various mint marks.

331 332 333 334

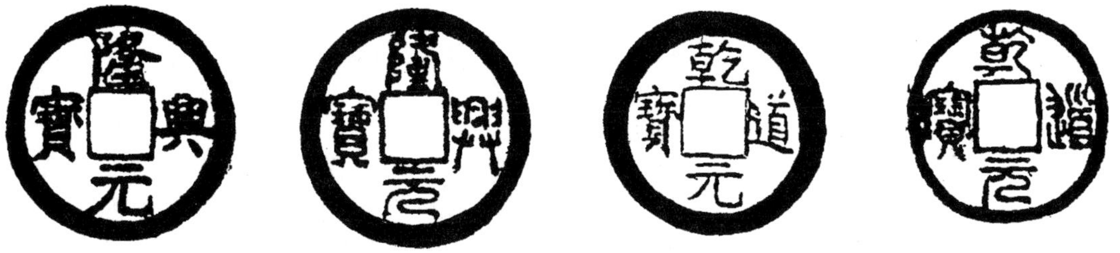

335 336 337 338

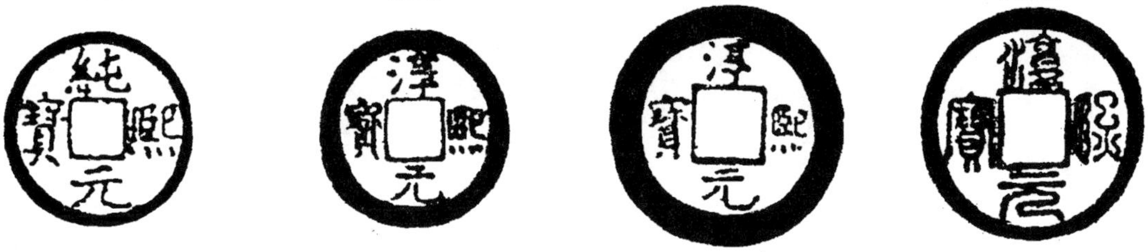

339 340 341 342 343

	VG	VF
331. Long Xing Yuan Bao S-699/FD-1174	10.00	20.00
332. Ditto, Seal script S-698/FD-1175	10.00	20.00
333. Qian Dao Yuan Bao S-706/FD-1182	5.00	10.00
334. Ditto, Seal script S-702/FD-1183	5.00	10.00
335. Chun Xi Yuan Bao	800.00	1500.00
336. Chun Xi Yuan Bao S-714/FD-1198	1.00	3.00
337. Ditto, 2 Cash S-730/FD-1201	1.00	5.00
338. Ditto, Seal script S-727/FD-1203	1.00	5.00
339. Shao Xi Yuan Bao S-758/FD-1223	5.00	10.00
340. Ditto, 2 Cash S-764/FD-1225	2.00	10.00
341. Qing Yuan Tong Bao S-788/FD-1243	2.00	3.00
342. Ditto, 2 Cash S-794/FD-1245	1.00	5.00
343. Ditto, 3 Cash FD-1247	10.00	20.00

4. Ning Zong (1195-1225) — Four reign titles appear on his coins: Jia Tai, Qing Yuan, Kai Xi and Jia Ding (Nos. 341-343 and 346-353); also issued was the iron Sheng Song Zhong Bao (No. 354) with a borrowed reign title. Unity of design and script form had become the order of the times, colorful diversity now a thing of the past.

a. Jia Tai — Issued in 3 denominations (Nos. 341-343). The legend on the 3 cash specie is read clockwise. Large amounts of iron coins with a variety of mint marks were issued.

b. Qing Yuan — Also cast in three denominations (Nos. 344-46). A large coin exists with the character Yong on the reverse, cast by the Yong Ping mint in Jiangxi Province. The legend is written in the emperor Hui Zong's Slender Gold style. The coin is seen in the 2nd part of this book.

c. Kai Xi — One of the few coins with this title worth mentioning is a large coin with the character Li on the reverse, a product of Li Zhou mint in Sichuan Province. Only 2 specimens are known to exist. Kai Xi mother coins are also rare. These are used to make moulds for casting iron cash. These are recognizable in that they are made of copper instead of iron and that there is invariably a mint mark on the reverse.

d. Jia Ding — The iron coins under this reign title were cast with numerous variations both in the legend and the mint marks. Eighteen different words were used for one of the two characters indicating "Currency". As for the number of different mint marks, few people would bother to count them.

e. Sheng Song — Minted by the Li Zhou mint in Sichuan Province in the 1st year of Jia Ding, probably by the frontier authorities at their discretion to cover pressing military expenses. The Sheng Song legend was originally a reign title of the Northern Song emperor Hui Zong, but here it does not serve in this capacity, since the coin was not a product of the central mint. Only 2 cash coins were minted (No. 352).

344

345

346

347

348

349

350

351

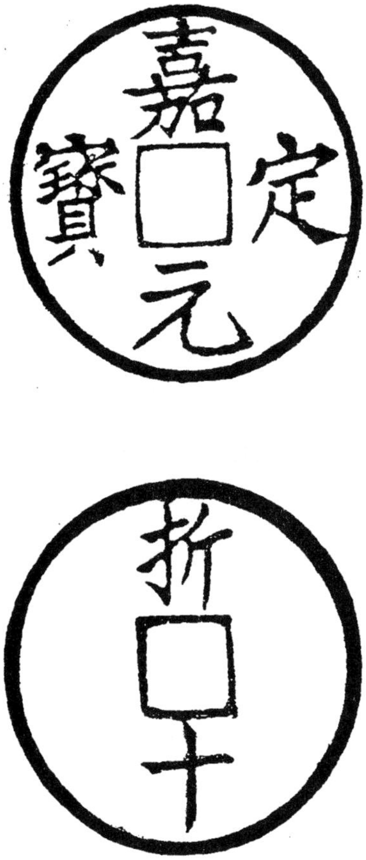

352

353

354

	VG	VF
344. Jia Ding Tong Bao S-835, FD-1301	1.00	3.00
345. Ditto, 2 Cash S-839/FD-1305	1.00	5.00
346. Ditto, 3 Cash S-843/FD-1309	20.00	40.00
347. Kai Xi Tong Bao S-857, FD-1329	1.00	3.00
348. Ditto, 2 Cash S-860/FD-1332	1.00	5.00
349. Jia Ding Tong Bao, S-877/FD-1348	1.00	1.00
350. Ditto, 2 Cash. S-890/FD-1362	1.00	1.00
351. Jia Ding Yuan Bao, 10 Cash S-95/FD-1417	250.00	500.00
352. Sheng Song Zhong Bao, Iron, FD-1450	20.00	40.00
353. Bao Qing Yuan Bao, Iron, FD-1451	30.00	60.00
354. Ditto, 2 Cash FD-1452	40.00	100.00

5. Li Zhong (1225-1265) — He enjoyed a long reign, as seen from his many reign titles, eight of them. Once again there is a profusion of varieties, whetting the collector's interest.

a. Bao Qing — Only iron coins were minted (Nos. 353, 354). No copper coins were officially cast by the central mint. Instead, an imperial edict was given to mint currency with the year title of Da Song, which is not a reign title, in the 7th month of Bao Qing. As in the case of the Bao You title of Northern Song, which was to be later replaced by Huang Song, the use of Bao Qing would result in two Baos appearing in the legend, not considered proper form. Therefore the court showed hesitancy and did not issue currency before the Da Song title was decided upon. Meanwhile the situation on the Sichuan Front was pressing, so the frontier authorities couldn't wait and cast the Bao Qing coins.

b. Da Song — Coins with this title were the first to be officially minted by this emperor, while the Bao Qing coins were only cast in a state of emergency. The 1 cash & 2 cash coins use Yuan Bao in the legend and the 10 cash Tong Bao. Superbly made, the 10 cash variety (No. 357) is appreciable for its rareness and beauty; the words in regular script are well balanced and written in a flowing style.

c. Shao Ding — Except for the 3 cash iron coins, most other varieties are quite common.

d. Duan Ping — The 1 cash bare-back specimen is worthy of the collector's interest. As said before, starting from the Chun Xi period, few coins do not have the year of mintage on the reverse, and this specie is one of them. The 10 cash coins, though common, are quite nice (No. 361). Delicately featured, the 10 cash Zhong Bao variety is quite hard to come by in the market (No. 362). One must be on the alert for mother coins that sometimes escape the dealer's notice.

e. Jia Xi — The Zhong Bao specimen is quite nice despite its low grading; 1 cash coins do not have good grades either.

355

356

358

359

357

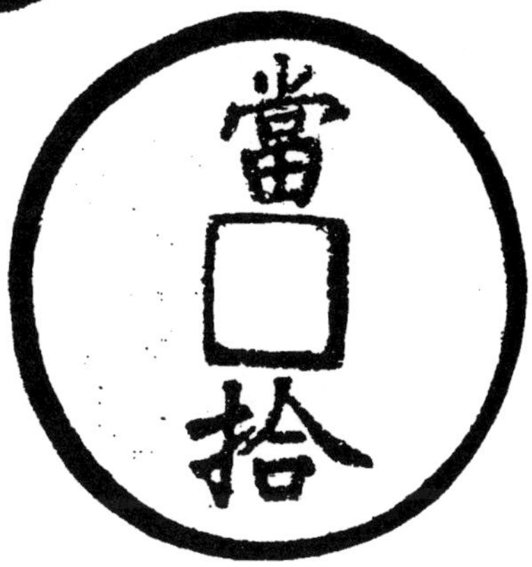

360

361

362

363

	VG	VF
355. Da Song Yuan Bao S-959, FD-1455	10.00	20.00
356. Ditto, 2 Cash S-961/FD-1459	5.00	10.00
357. Ditto, Value 10 FD-1467, R	4000.00	—
358. Shao Ding Tong Bao S-967, FD-1470	1.00	5.00
359. Ditto, 2 Cash S-973/FD-1476	1.00	5.00
360. Duan Ping Yuan Bao S-981, FD-1487	15.00	35.00
361. Duan Ping Tong Bao S-983, FD-1498	25.00	50.00
362. Duan Ping Zhong Bao FD-1504	700.00	1500.00
363. Jia Xi Tong Bao S-991, FD-1505	1.00	3.00
364. Ditto, 2 Cash S-994/FD-1509	1.00	5.00
365. Jia Xi Zhong Bao S-999, FD-1517	15.00	30.00

364

365

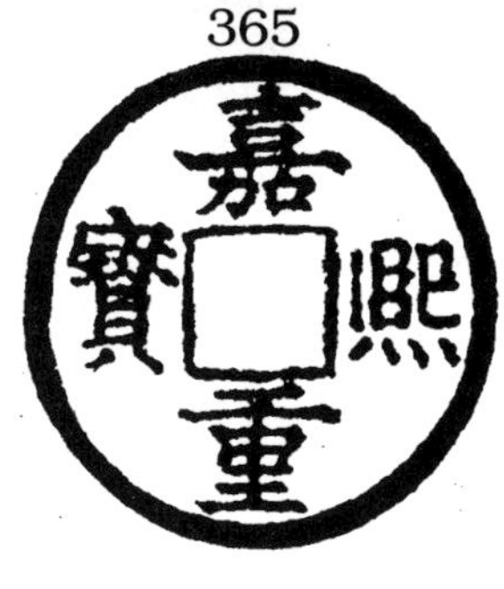

f. Chun You — Both Yuan Bao and Tong Bao were used in the legend: 1 & 2 cash for the Yuan Bao (Nos. 366, 367); and 1, 2 & 3 cash for the Tong Bao (Nos. 369-371). The Tong Bao species do not have mint marks on the reverse and all three are quite scarce. The 100 cash coins come in two sizes (Nos. 371, 372), the smaller one about the same in size as the 3 cash. The minting of small denomination iron coins had come to a halt. Some iron coins of large denominations do exist, such as the value 20 cash and value 100 cash (Not shown here); since very few have been found, it is presumed that the quantity minted was quite small.

The emperor was now in a desperate position. The Mongol troops had overrun the Jin Dynasty and were charging into his territory like they did in Asia Minor and Eastern Europe. With the coffers empty Li Zong resorted to printing paper money to sustain his crumbling empire. Copper cash was still coming out of the mints, but in largely reduced quantities. From then on the varieties minted with each reign title did not go beyond 1 & 2 cash species – the end was not far off.

366

367

368

369

370

371

372

	VG	VF
366. Chun You Yuan Bao S-1001/FD-1519	1.00	2.00
367. Ditto, 2 Cash S-1011/FD-1531	1.00	2.00
368. Chun You Tong Bao 1543	1000.00	2000.00
369. Ditto, 2 Cash FD-1544	2500.00	4000.00
370. Ditto, 3 Cash FD-1545	2500.00	4000.00
371. Ditto, Value: 100 S-1022/FD-1552	80.00	150.00
372. Ditto, Value: 100, Large S-1023/FD-1548	100.00	250.00

g. Huang Song — The reign title for this period was Bao You, which again presented the same problem as Bao Qing and Bao Yuan. The Huang Song title was then borrowed and the Tong Bao in the legend was changed to Yuan Bao to differentiate it from its Northern Song Counterpart — Huang Song Tong Bao. Only 1 & 2 cash denominations were minted (Nos. 373, 374).

h. Kai Qing — This reign title was used for only one year (Nos. 376, 377).

i. Jing Ding — Only cast in 1 & 2 cash denominations (Nos. 375, 376).

6. Du Zong — He stayed on the throne from 1265 to 1275, and his Xian Chun cash (Nos. 379, 380) were the last of the Southern Song coinage. Although four other emperors succeeded to the throne after him, the court had by now become a government in exile, chased by the Mongol troops from place to place, left with no time whatever to set up any mints.

For each reign title the year of mintage cast on the reverse of the coins are listed below, starting from Chun Xi:

1) Chun Xi: Years 7-16
2) Shao Xi: Years 1-5
3) Qing Yuan: Years 1-7
   Year 7 minted in 6th yr
4) Jia Tai: Years 1-4
5) Kai Xi: Years 1-3
6) Jia Ding: Years 1-14
7) Da Song: Years 1-3
8) Shao Ding: Years 1-6
9) Duan Ping: Years 1-3
10) Jia Xi: Years 1-4
11) Chun You: Years 1-12
12) Huang Song: Years 1-6
13) Kai Qing: Year 1
14) Jing Ding: Years 1-5
15) Xian Chun: Years 1-8

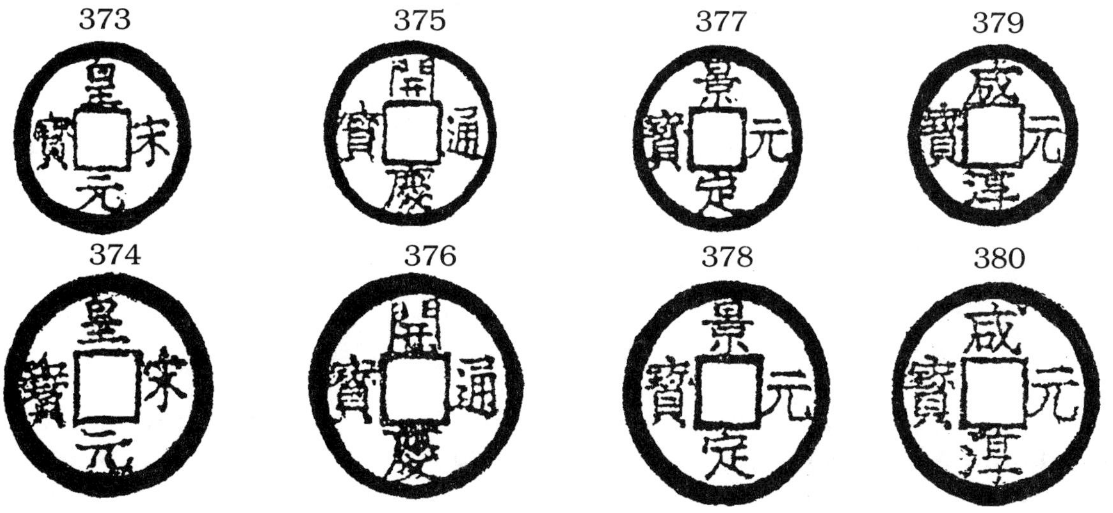

	F	VF
373. Huang Song Yuan Bao S-1024/FD-1560	5.00	10.00
374. Ditto, 2 Cash S-1030/FD-1565	3.00	8.00
375. Kai Qing Tong Bao S-1036/FD-1571	10.00	30.00
376. Ditto, 2 Cash S-1037/FD-1572	10.00	30.00
377. Jing Ding Yuan Bao S-1038/FD-1073	5.00	10.00
378. Ditto, 2 Cash S-1042/FD-1078	10.00	20.00
379. Xian Chun Yuan Bao S-1049/FD-1583	10.00	20.00
380. Ditto, 2 Cash S-1055/FD-1591	10.00	20.00

N.B. The Chinese numerals from 1 through 12 are given below. The character on the reverse of the first coin is read "Yuan", meaning the first in order.

TWO INTERESTING SPECIMENS
Of the Southern Song Dynasty

1. Bronze Tallies — These were cast around the time of Li Zong's Jing Ding period (1260-1265). A contemporary wrote in his book: "Since the money system had broken down, tallies were minted and circulated in the city of Hang Zhou (Lin-an Fu – the capital). His successor Du Zong tried to restore the money system and prohibited their use. The tallies were already very hard to come by in the Ming and Qing dynasties, not to mention the present day.

The legend on the obverse means: For use in Lin An Fu. The first word on the reverse means "value" and the last word implies "seventy-seven cash to be equal to one hundred"; the words in between gives the denominations: 200, 300 and 500. Lead tallies were also issued in smaller denominations.

2. Pass coins — The coin Zhao Na Xing Bao (No. 384) was intended for use by soldiers of the Jin army who wanted to desert and join the Song ranks. In 1231 A.D. the Jin troops again advanced against the Southern Song Dynasty. The two armies were stationed facing each other across the river. The Song commander Liu Guang Shi got word that many of the Jin soldiers were of Han nationality and were longing for home, so he had these coins minted and gave them to captive Jin soldiers after setting them free with the word to give them to those who wanted to come over and join his ranks; the coins would serve as passes and anyone bearing them would receive a warm welcome. It was not long before tens of thousands deserted the Jin army, forcing the Jin commander to withdraw his troops and return home. The top character on the reverse means envoy and the bottom one a signature.

381

382

383

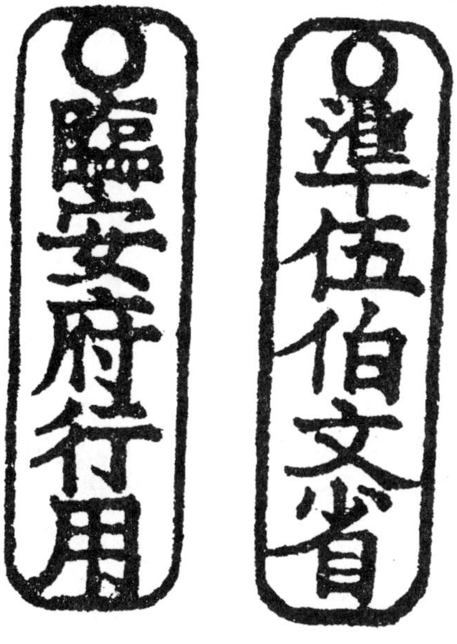

384

	VG	VF
381. Lin An Fu Xin Yong, Value 200, S-1064a/FD-1600	2500.00	5000.00
382. Ditto, Value 300 FD-1602	—	—
383. Ditto, Value 500 S-1064/FD-1606	—	—
384. Zhao Na Xin Bao FD-1609	1500.00	3000.00

LIAO DYNASTY COINAGE

This dynasty was founded by the Qidan Tartars of Northeastern China. As a dynasty, it was a small one, never having extended its influence far south of the Great Wall; yet its coinage occupy a niche of no small importance in Chinese numismatic culture, without which no collection of cash coins would be considered complete. Due to a shortage of copper and severe currency control, the regime minted its coinage in rather small amounts, about 500 strings annually as compared with the 6 million strings in the time of the Song emperor Shen Zong. The copper alloy is of a reddish color and the workmanship inferior to that of the Song coins. No wonder Liao coins are hard to come by and lucky is the person who can see one of the early issues, let alone acquiring one specimen.

1. Tai Zhu (907-925) — Coin No. 385 is accredited to him, of which only one or two have been found so far.

2. Tai Zong (925-947) — No mention has been made of his having issued any money in either the annals or numismatic works. Not long ago a coin bearing the legend Hui Tong Tong Bao was recovered from a salvage station in northeast China, the locality of the Liao Dynasty. Hui Tong is the second of this emperor's reign titles. This discovery made certain that he did issue coins (Not yet cataloged).

3. Shi Zong (947-951) — Of this specie that he minted, not more than 20 are known to exist (No. 386).

4. Mu Zong (951-968) — Of his Ying Li coins, around 5 have been found (No. 387).

5. Jing Zong (968-985) — This emperor minted Bao Ning Tong Bao (No. 388) which, like the above varieties, is also quite rare.

XI. LIAO DYNASTY

916-1125 A.D.

385

386

387

388

389

390

391

392

393

394

395

396

	VG	VF
385. Tian Zan Tong Bao FD-1613, ER	—	—
386. Tian Lu Tong Bao, VR	—	—
387. Ying Li Tong Bao FD-1614	—	—
388. Bao Ning Tong Bao FD-1616	—	—
389. Tong He Yuan Bao FD-1618	1200.00	2500.00
390. Zhong Xi Tong Bao S-1065/FD-1619	70.00	150.00
391. Qing Ning Tong Bao S-1066/FD-1622	60.00	90.00
392. Xian Yong Tong Bao S-1067/FD-1623	50.00	80.00
393. Da Kang Yuan Bao S-1068/FD-1624	35.00	70.00
394. Da Kang Tong Bao S-1069/FD-1625	35.00	70.00
395. Da An Yuan Bao S-1070/FD-1626	35.00	70.00
396. Ditto, Character An very long FD-1627	80.00	150.00

6. Sheng Zong (983-1031 A.D.) — The Tong He Tong Bao coin of his time (No. 390), though not so rare as the others, is not available either.

7. Xing Zong (1031-1055 A.D.) — From this emperor on, coins were minted in much larger quantities, as one can see from the not so attractive grading of the following varieties. The Zhong Xi Tong Bao coin (No. 391) appears in several versions, the legend on each one a little bit different from the others; the larger the characters, the higher the grading.

8. Dao Zong (1055-1101) — Five reign titles were used on his coins (Nos. 392-397), and what's more, the legends offer a lot of brushwriting variety, which is always welcome to the collector. The long An version of Da An Yuan Bao (No. 386) is an attractive collectible.

9. Tian Zuo Di (1101-1125) — The legends on his coins were better written than most Liao coins (Nos. 398-400). This ruler caused much trouble for the Northern Song troops, for he was an aggressive strategician in the field, forcing the Song regime to sign a peace treaty which was observed until the Liaos were terminated by the Jurchens in A.D. 1125.

Unlike Song currency, red copper was used for minting Liao coins, instead of the customary bronze material of the regimes south of the Great Wall. Some large coins exist of which nothing is known about the role they played in their day (Nos. 399-491).

The three coins shown here are alleged to be of Liao origin:

1) Tong Xing Quan Huo — The legend means circulating currency. The writing style of the legend comes close to the traditional Liao style. One such coin was unearthed in Inner Mongolia in 1981, a habitat of the Liaos. All such coins discovered up to now were found buried alongside other Liao coins.

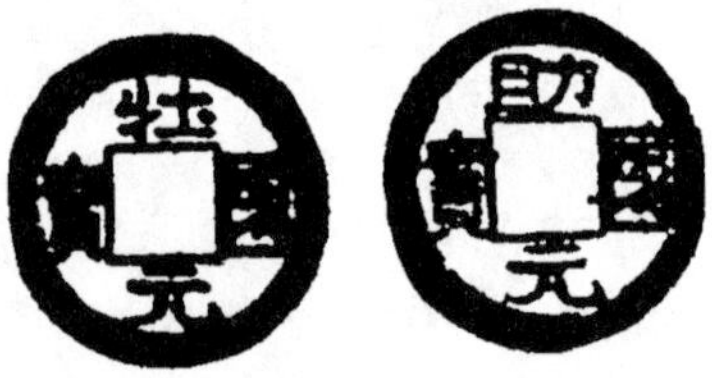

2) The two coins Zhuang Quo Yuan Bao and Zhu Guo Yuan Bao were originally considered to be of Annam origin; as with the above Tong Xing Quan Huo, they also showed up in recent years in Northeast China, the domain of the Liao people, therefore it would not be without reason to identify them as Liao coins.

397

398

399

400

401

	VG	VF
397. Shou Chang Yuan Bao S-1072/FD-1628	30.00	60.00
398. Qian Tong Yuan Bao S-1073/FD-1629	25.00	50.00
399. Ditto, Large FD-1630, VR	—	—
400. Tian Qing Yuan Bao S-1074/FD-1632	30.00	60.00
401. Tian Chao Wan Shun, in Qidan Tartar script, R	3500.00	—

JIN DYNASTY COINAGE

After terminating the Liao Dynasty, the Jin emperor Tai Zong turned his attention southward and advanced against the Song empire, the northern half of which fell into his hands together with the capital Kaifeng and the two emperors Hui Zong and Qing Zong as hostages. His victorious armies crossed the Yangtze River with the intention of conquering the remaining half of the Song empire, but the unruly Han people in the occupied Song territory and defeat at the hands of the Song generals Yue Fei and Han Shizhong prompted him to withdraw back across the river after signing an armistice, with the Songs as subjects and paying yearly tribute to the Jins.

His successor Hai Ling Wang took up where he had left off and again crossed the river. However, his first encounter with the Song troops wound up in a crushing defeat for him, and his subjects seized the opportunity and set up Shi Zong as emperor in his stead. The policy of conciliation with the Southern Song Dynasty and its other southern neighbor, the Xi Xia regime, was continued, gaining a peaceful respite of 70 years; during which time the Jin Dynasty issued a series of coins comparable in quality to the Chong Ning Tong Bao coins of his hostage, the emperor Hui Zong of the Northern Song Dynasty.

1. Xi Zong (1135-49 A.D.) — Only one specimen of his coins exist (No. 402). It was not until his two successors that the Jins started minting currency in large quantities.

2. Hai Ling Wang (1149-61 A.D.) — His coins were excellently made and exist in large numbers (No. 403).

3. Shi Zong (1161-70 A.D.) — The casting of the superb Da Ding Tong Bao coins (No. 405) became a possibility, as he had now in his hands the highly skilled captive Song regime mint workers.

4. Zhang Zong (1190-1209) — His Tai He Tong Bao coins in regular script (Nos. 405-408) are beautifully written and enjoy a high repute among numismatists. They are quite rare, unlike their large cousin in seal script, which fortunately, are quite plentiful today. Their large numbers, however, do not detract from their value as collectibles for the beauty of the legend written in the Jade Tendon Seal Script style, so called for the suppleness and

XII. JIN DYNASTY
1115-1234 A.D.

402

403

404

405

406

407

408

409

410

	VG	VF
402. Huang Tong Yuan Bao, ER	—	—
—403. Zheng Long Yuan Bao S-1083/FD-1637	1.00	10.00
404. Da Ding Tong Bao S-1085/FD-1640	1.00	10.00
405. Tai He Tong Bao FD-1652	800.00	1500.00
406. Ditto, 2 Cash FD-1654	400.00	800.00
407. Ditto, 3 Cash FD-1655	400.00	800.00
408. Ditto, 5 Cash FD-1657	1200.00	2500.00
409. Tai He Zhong Bao S-1093/FD-1661	70.00	150.00
410. Ditto, Legend in another style, FD-1660	600.00	1200.00

hidden strength of the brush strokes. This style, first appearing on the Yong Tong Wan Guo specimen (FD-644), together with Wang Mang's Hanging Needle Seal Script on his Huo Bu coins (FD-486) and Emperor Hui Zong's Slender Gold Regular Script on his Chong Ning Tong Bao coins (FD-1040) are the ultimate expression of Chinese brush artistry on cash coins.

5. Wei Shao Wang (1209-1213) — During his reign the Jin empire was weakened still further from internal problems. The Southern Songs took advantage of the situation and began their counteroffensive in the south, and Genghis Khan attacked from the north. The coins that he issued are all very rare (Nos. 411-13); only one or two of each are known to exist, perhaps survivors from the fire and looting brought about by Genghis Khan's troops as they laid level the Jin capital of Zhong Du in 1215. A recent discovery of two Zhi Ning Yuan Bao 1 cash coins were reported by Mr. Op den Velde in his article published in the Journal of East Asian Numismatics, No. 12, 1997.

Coinage of the Puppet Da Qi Kingdom (1130-1136 A.D.)

To govern the unruly Han people in the vast expanse of occupied Song territory north of the Yangtze River, the Jins resorted to the ancient strategy of playing one foreign power against the other and set up the puppet Da Qi Kingdom with the collaborator Liu Yu as emperor. Six years later, the Jins abolished the puppet regime and demoted him to the rank of Prince of Shu. The coins he minted are as good as his name is bad, a meeting of opposites (Nos. 415-20).

The three denominations shown here come in pairs, one in regular script and the other in seal script. The legends are beautifully written and the workmanship superb, on a par with the coinage of his Jin masters. It is probable that these coins were cast by the same captive Song craftsmen then serving under the Jin yoke.

411

412

413

414

415

416

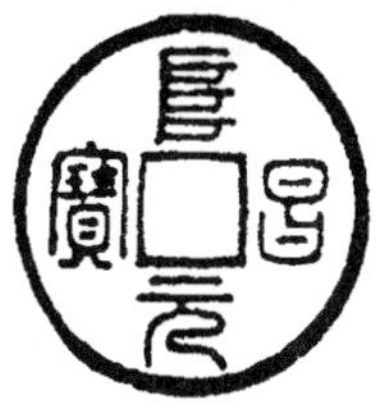

417

418

419

420

	VG	VF
411. Chong Qing Tong Bao FD-1665, VR	—	—
412. Ditto, Seal script FD-1663, VR	—	—
413. Zhi Ning Yuan Bao FD-1667, ER	—	—
414. Zhen You Tong Bao FD-1669, ER	—	—
415. Fu Chang Yuan Bao S-1075/FD-1672	300.00	600.00
416. Ditto, Seal script S-1076/FD-1673	400.00	700.00
417. Fu Chang Tong Bao, 2 Cash FD-1674	300.00	600.00
418. Ditto, Seal script FD-1675	300.00	600.00
419. Fu Chang Zhong Bao FD-1676	400.00	700.00
420. Ditto, Seal script, FD-1677	400.00	700.00

COINAGE OF THE XI XIA EMPIRE

Strategically situated in the remote northwest, the Xi Xia empire existed for 200 years, about parallel with its two neighbors, the Song and Jin Dynasties. Like the Liao and Jin regimes of the north, this power did not abstain from harassing the Songs, but as a military power, it was weaker than the other two and posed no serious threat other than looting raids along the border region. The Xi Xia people had their own language, and some of their early coins had the legends written in their own script. In A.D. 1227, Genghis Khan's horsemen trampled the Xi Xia empire and its culture into oblivion.

1. Fu Sheng Bao Qian (No. 421) — Cast by Emperor Xi Zong (1040-1069 A.D.) around A.D. 1055-57. The legend is written in the Tangut script.

2. Da An Tong Bao (No. 422) — Minter and minting date unknown. This specimen was discovered in Xi Cheng Yao County, Inner Mongolia. The Liao version (No. 395) is Yuan Bao, not Tong Bao.
3. Yuan De Tong Bao (No. 423) – Cast by Emperor Chong Zong (1087-1139 A.D.) around A.D. 1120-27. The Zhong Bao variety (No. 424) must be a 2 cash coin, judging by its size. All the above varieties are quite rare.

4. Tian Sheng Yuan Bao (No. 425) — Cast by Emperor Ren Zong (1149-71 A.D.) These were cast in large quantities, both in copper and iron, the iron coins being scarcer than the copper ones.

5. Qian You Yuan Bao (No. 426) — Cast by the same emperor around A.D. 1171-94. Copper coins are much scarcer than the iron ones.

6. Tian Qing Yuan Bao (No. 427) — Cast by Emperor Huan Zong (1194-1206 A.D.). He adopted only one reign title.

7. Huang Jian Yuan Bao (No. 428) — Cast by Emperor Xiang Zong around A.D. 1210-11.

8. Guang Ding Yuan Bao (No. 429) — Cast by Emperor Shen Zong around A.D. 1211-23, the years of his Guang Ding reign title, this being his only title. A recent discovery of a Guang Ding Yuan Bao written in seal script (No. 430) made known that this coin was cast in pairs, one in regular and one in seal script.

XIV. XI XIA DYNASTY

1002-1227 A.D.

421

422

423

424

425

426

427

428

429

430

	VG	VF
421. Fu Sheng Bao Qian FD-1678	500.00	1000.00
422. Da An Tong Bao	2500.00	5000.00
423. Yuan De Tong Bao FD-1682	3500.00	—
424. Yuan De Zhong Bao FD-1681, VR	—	—
425. Tian Sheng Yuan Bao S-1078/FD-1683	10.00	30.00
426. Qian You Yuan Bao S-1079/FD-1686	200.00	400.00
427. Tian Qing Yuan Bao FD-1691	200.00	400.00
428. Huang Jian Yuan Bao S-1081/FD-1693	40.00	70.00
429. Guang Ding Yuan Bao 1082/FD-1094	40.00	70.00
430. Ditto, Seal script, R	3500.00	—

YUAN DYNASTY COINAGE

Little is known about the monetary system of the Mongol empire except that some coins were issued for use within the occupied Jin territories. When Kublai Khan set up his Yuan Dynasty, he patterned his monetary system after the Song and Jin systems, which circulated both cash coins and paper bills. He showed preference for paper money and stopped issuing his Zhong Tong and Zhi Yuan coins shortly after their circulation. Of the ten emperors after him, only three issued coins, which accounts for the scarcity of coin varieties of that era.

1. Da Chao Tong Bao (No. 431) — Presumably cast by Genghis Khan when he raised his capital Karakorum. The cities and empires that he raided: Xi Xia, Samarkand, Bukhara and others, all had been using currencies of their own. To say that he followed suit and cast some Da Chao coins as commemoratives or tokens of sovereignty would sound reasonable. The few Da Chao coins discovered so far all came from the northwest regions of Gansu and Ningxia, outside the bounds of the Jin empire. After its downfall seven years after his death, silver conversion coins were cast for use in that area (Nos. 432, 433) in keeping with the silver currency and paper money then in use. From that time on, for 70 years Jin and Song cash circulated alongside the new currency into the early years of the Yuan Dynasty. The phrase Da Chao, meaning "Grand court", was already in use in Genghis' time. As early as 1208 A.D,, the Jins referred to the Mongols as Da Chao. The Song chronicles recorded that the Song regime and the "Grand Court" reached an agreement to attack the Jins from the north and south at the same time, resulting in the Jin emperor's suicide and the fall of his empire.

2. Zhi Chao Ban Fen (No. 432) — Zhi Chao means convertible to paper money, and Ban Fen half candareen. This coin was probably meant for circulation in the occupied Jin territories, as the Jins were using both silver and paper money.

3. Da Guan Tong Bao (No. 433) — Also probably cast for use in the occupied Jin region along with coin No. 432. The Ban Qian on the reverse means half mace.

4. Zhong Tong Yuan Bao (Nos. 434 & 435) — Minted by Kublai Khan around 1260-64 AD. He issued coins and bills bearing this reign title, both of which are very rare.

5. Zhi Yuan Tong Bao (Nos. 436-9) — Cast by Kublai Khan in 1285 A.D. Two species were issued, one in Han and one in Mongol script. It was not until 1280 A.D. that he was actually seated as emperor of the Yuan Dynasty, after the last boy emperor of the Southern Song Dynasty plunged into the sea in the embrace of his loyal minister Lu Xiu-fu.

XV. YUAN DYNASTY

1279-1368 A.D.

431

432

433

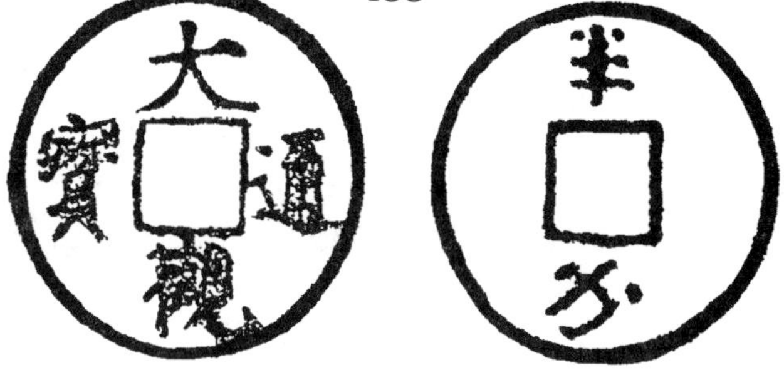

434

435

436

437

438

439

	VG	VF
431. Da Chao Tong Bao, Silver FD-1695	300.00	600.00
432. Zhi Cao Ban Fen FD-1818	2500.00	5000.00
433. Da Guan Tong Bao, Ban Qian on reverse, FD-1064	2500.00	5000.00
434. Zhong Tong Yuan Bao FD-1699, R	3500.00	—
435. Ditto, Seal script FD-1701, R	3500.00	—
436. Zhi Yuan Tong Bao FD-1702	400.00	700.00
437. Ditto, 2 Cash FD-1704	1000.00	2000.00
438. Ditto, 3 Cash FD-1705	1500.00	3000.00
439. Ditto, Legend in Mongol script FD-1707	300.00	600.00

7. Yuan Zhen Tong Bao (Nos. 440-1) — Cast by the emperor Cheng Zong (1285-1308) in A.D. 1295. The legends also come in two kinds of scripts.

8. Da De Tong Bao (Nos. 442-3) — Also cast by Chong Zong in two scripts. The emperor Chong Zong of Xi Xia also cast Da De coins, the legend written in a more graceful style as contrasted with its Yuan Dynasty counterpart, brimming with the rugged spirit of the grasslands. During its early years, the Yuan regime's standard currency was paper money, time and again prohibiting the use of cash coins, which accounts for the scarcity of the above species.

9. Zhi Da Tong Bao (Nos. 446-7) — Cast by the emperor Wu Zong (1308-12 A.D.) in the second year of his reign. Although he was on the throne for only four years, the 1 cash coins were cast in rather large amounts.

10. Da Yuan Tong Bao (Nos. 446-7) — Also cast by Wu Zong in the same year as the Zhi Da specie. The large 10 cash coin in Mongol script is nicely made. Among Yuan Dynasty coins, this and the Zhi Da 1 cash coin are affordable for the starter's collection.

11. Da Yuan Guo Bao (No. 448) — Minted in the Zhi Da era, this coin did not go into circulation. The dragon design on the reverse suggests that it must have been a commemorative. The legend is in seal script.

440

441

442

443

444

445

446

447

448

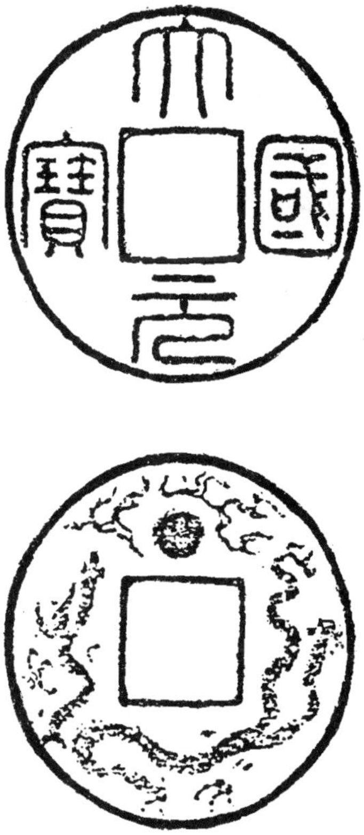

449

	VG	VF
440. Yuan Zhen Tong Bao FD-1712	1500.00	2000.00
441. Ditto, Mongol script FD-1713	1000.00	2000.00
442. Da De Tong Bao S-1097, FD-1718	1000.00	2000.00
443. Ditto, Mongol script FD-1720	1000.00	2000.00
444. Zhi Da Tong Bao S-1098, FD-1723	10.00	20.00
445. Ditto, 2 Cash FD-1724	1000.00	2000.00
446. Da Yuan Tong Bao FD-1730, R	3500.00	—
447. Ditto, Mongol script S-1099, FD-1733	30.00	60.00
448. Da Yuan Guo Bao, Dragons & Fireball on rev., R	3500.00	—
449. Zhi Yuan Tong Bao FD-1778	2500.00	5000.00

12. Zhi Yuan Tong Bao (No. 409) — Probably cast during the Zhi Zhi era of the emperor Ying Zong (1321-24 A.D.). As to the four characters on the reverse, there are different interpretations. One source claims that the top character is in Mongol script, the bottom one Jurchen, the left one Tangut, and the right Uighur; another saying has it that both the top and bottom characters are in Mongol script, the left one Tangut, and the right one Chagatai. No agreement on the interpretation of either the script or the meaning has yet been reached. This kind of arrangement must have been for the solidarity and good will between the various ethnic groups concerned, the backbone of such a vast empire, the largest land empire the world has ever seen.

13. Zhi Zheng Tong Bao (Nos. 450-69) — Minted by the last emperor of the Yuan Dynasty, Shun Di (1333-68 A.D.), the reign title Zhi Zheng being also his last one (1341-68 A.D.).

The emperor Shun Di first issued a set of coins coming in three denominations: one, two, and three cash; the characters on the reverse representing some of the twelve Earthly Branches used by the Chinese in combination with the Heavenly Stems to designate years, months, days, and hours. Five of the twelve Branches were used on the coins: Yin, Mao, Chen, Zi, and Wu, starting from the year 1350 A.D. (10th year of Zhi Zheng, one for each year). Only three are shown here: Yin, Mao, and Wu. Since the Chen and Zi coins are graded the same as Mao, they were omitted to conserve space.

450 451 452

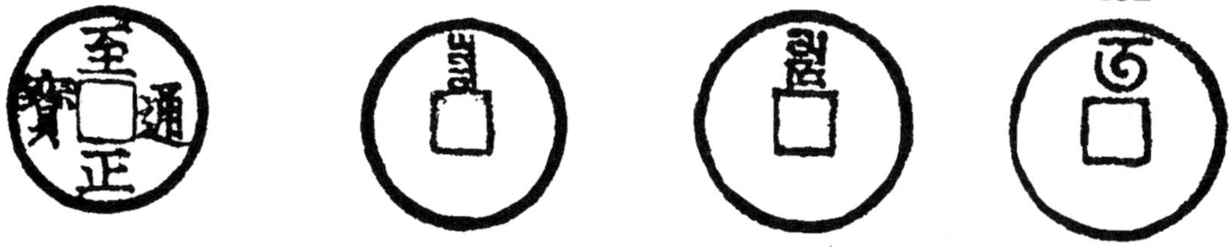

453 454 455

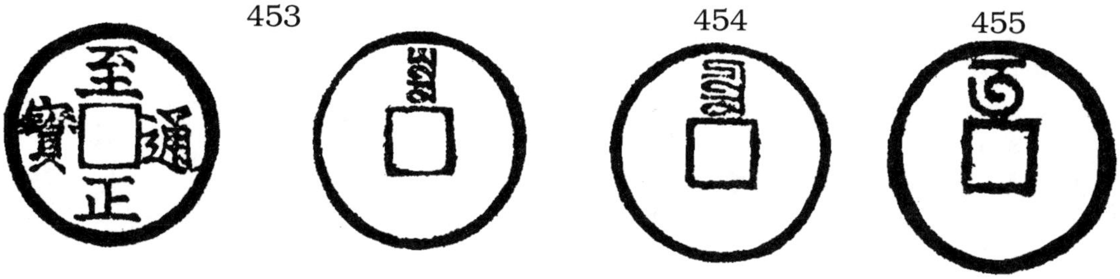

456 457 458

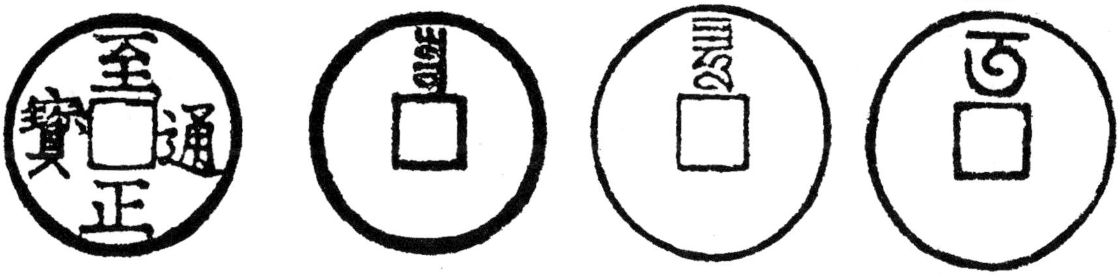

	VG	**VF**
450. Zhi Zheng Tong Bao, Yin on rev. FD-1785	200.00	400.00
451. Ditto, Mao on rev. S-1003/FD-1786	20.00	40.00
452. Ditto, Wu on rev. FD-1789	100.00	200.00
453. Ditto, 2 Cash, Yin on rev. S-1105/FD-1790	150.00	300.00
454. Ditto, Chen on rev. FD-1793	30.00	50.00
455. Ditto, Wu on rev. FD-1794	100.00	200.00
456. Ditto, 3 Cash, Yin on rev. FD-1795	200.00	400.00
457. Ditto, Zi on rev. S-1108/FD-1797	40.00	80.00
458. Ditto, Wu on reverse	100.00	200.00

The coins listed on the following pages reflect a diversity of denomination denotations on the reverse sides of the coins, reflecting confusion within the Yuan monetary system; some have the denominations rendered in both the Mongol and orthodox Han script (Nos. 459, 461, 462, 464, 465, 467, 468, and 469), while others only in Mongol script (Nos. 460, 463, and 466). By that time thirteen mints were in operation, and central control being weak, a diversity of style would only be natural. The coin No. 469 can be used as a 10 cash and also convertible into paper money.

Notwithstanding their complexity, these coins may be sorted into three groups. First come the coins with Earthly Branches denoting the year of mintage in Mongol script (Nos. 450-58); next come the ones with denominations in Mongol script (Nos. 460, 463 & 466); then come those with denominations in both Mongol and Han scripts (Nos. 459, 461, 462, 464, 465, 467 & 468); and lastly the one with both denomination in Mongol script and unit of weight in Han script, convertible into banknotes, not silver (No. 469), as were those issued in the occupied Jin territories.

Due to the reckless issuing of banknotes, prices skyrocketed; and coins of small denominations, not capable of adapting to the dire inflation quandary, became practically worthless. By the 14th year of Zhi Zheng (1350 A.D.), all mints were closed down and the random issuing of paper money continued as usual.

459

460

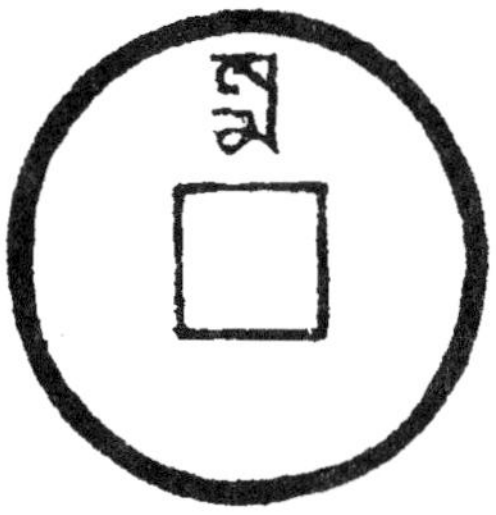

461

462

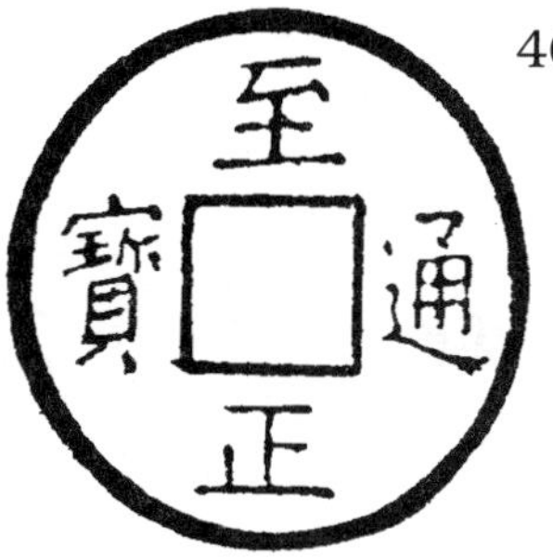

463

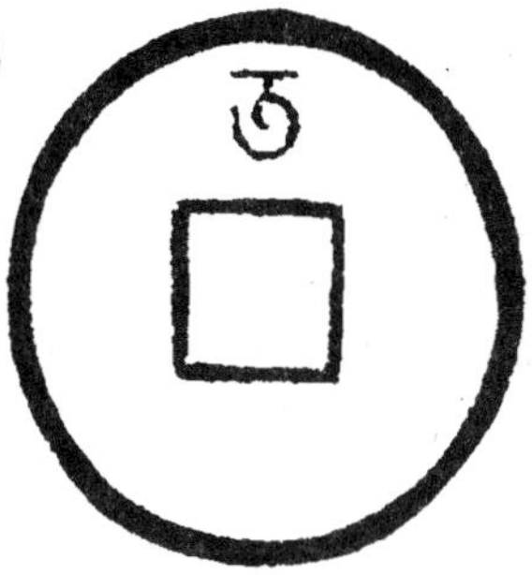

464

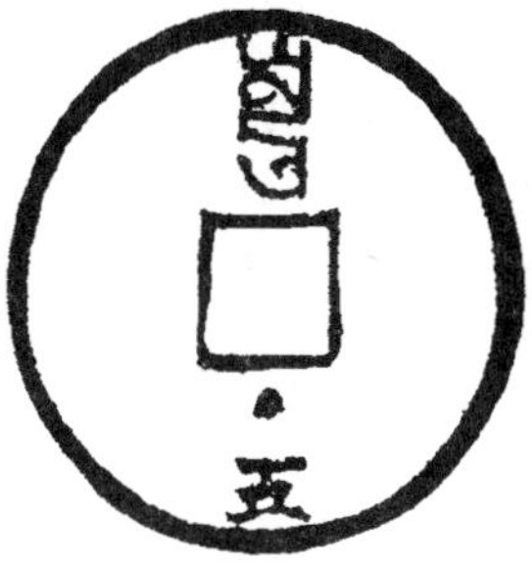

465

466

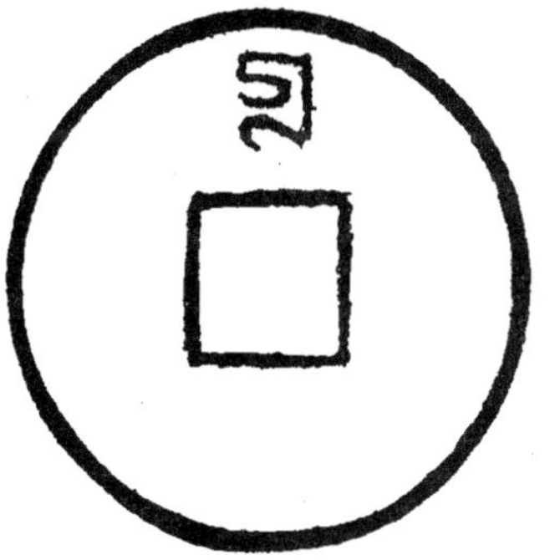

467

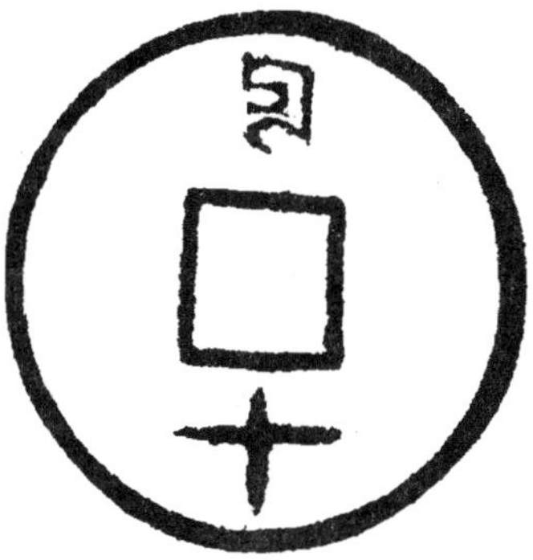

468

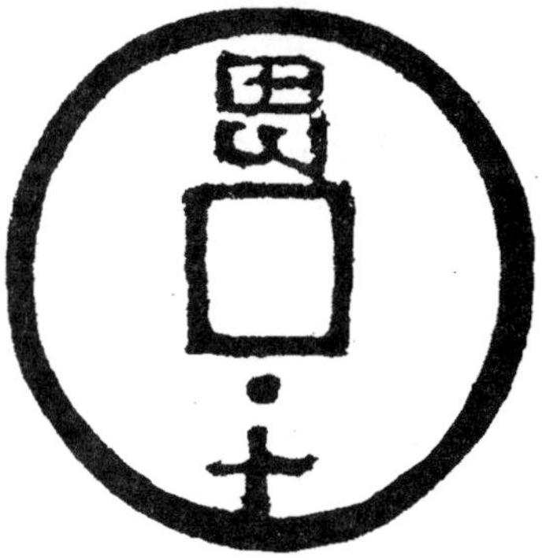

469

	VG	VF
459. Zhi Zheng Tong Bao, Numeral 2 in Mongol & Chinese script on Rev. S-1109/FD-1800	20.00	40.00
460. Ditto, Numeral 3 FD-1802	150.00	300.00
461. Ditto, Numeral 3, Wide rim, FD-1803	30.00	50.00
462. Ditto, Narrow rim FD-1805	100.00	200.00
463. Ditto, 5 Cash, Wu on rev. FD-1804	300.00	500.00
464. Ditto, Wu & 3 on rev. FD-1806	400.00	800.00
465. Ditto, Hai & 5 on reverse	400.00	800.00
466. Ditto, 10 in Mongol script, FD-1808	40.00	80.00
467. Ditto, 10 in both scripts, FD-1810	1500.00	3000.00
468. Ditto, Hai & 10 on reverse	400.00	800.00
469. Ditto, 10 & Weght 1 Tael, FD-1812	300.00	600.00

14. Zhi Zheng Zhi Bao (Nos. 470-74) — This group is the last of the Zhi Zheng series, minted probably after A.D. 1352. The flames of rebellion were spreading and inflation crippling the economy. To cope with the crisis, the government started issuing these coins of large denomination. The top character Ji symbolizes good luck or a place name; the two characters on the right, Quan Chao, show that they were meant to be complementary currency of equal value and circulating along with the banknotes; the two on the left denote the value. It was decreed that the bills were to be principal currency and the coins as subsidiary. This relation between the two was referred to as mother and son, with the bills as the mother. The public, however, reversed the relationship and rejected the bills; since there were not enough large coins to go around, the monetary system floundered. The measure was intended to resurrect the credit of the banknotes, but actually, it only served to accelerate the downfall of the Yuan empire. For all its explosive debut and the 70 years gone into its making, this empire lasted only 88 years, one of the shortest of Chinese dynasties.

Coin No. 470, though not the rarest in the group, makes a handful to the collector for its size and weight; and it is also the largest among Chinese cash minted for circulation. The 5 candareen coin No. 471 is the rarest of the five. There is mention of a small-sized 1 mace coin in the Monetary Museum of the Bank of Japan. The character Chen appears on the reverse, indicating that it was minted in the 12th year of Zhi Zheng (1352 A.D.). It is not listed in Chinese works, perhaps for the simple reason that no such coin has ever made its appearance before the Chinese public.

Little was said about the currency of the Yuan Dynasty in the Yuan chronicles. The first emperor of the Ming Dynasty, Zhu Yuan Zhang, summoned a group of 30 scholars to write the chronicles, who completed the work in 300 days. Omissions and errors are to be expected from such a hastily compiled work, and which could not but present a hazy sketch of that era.

470

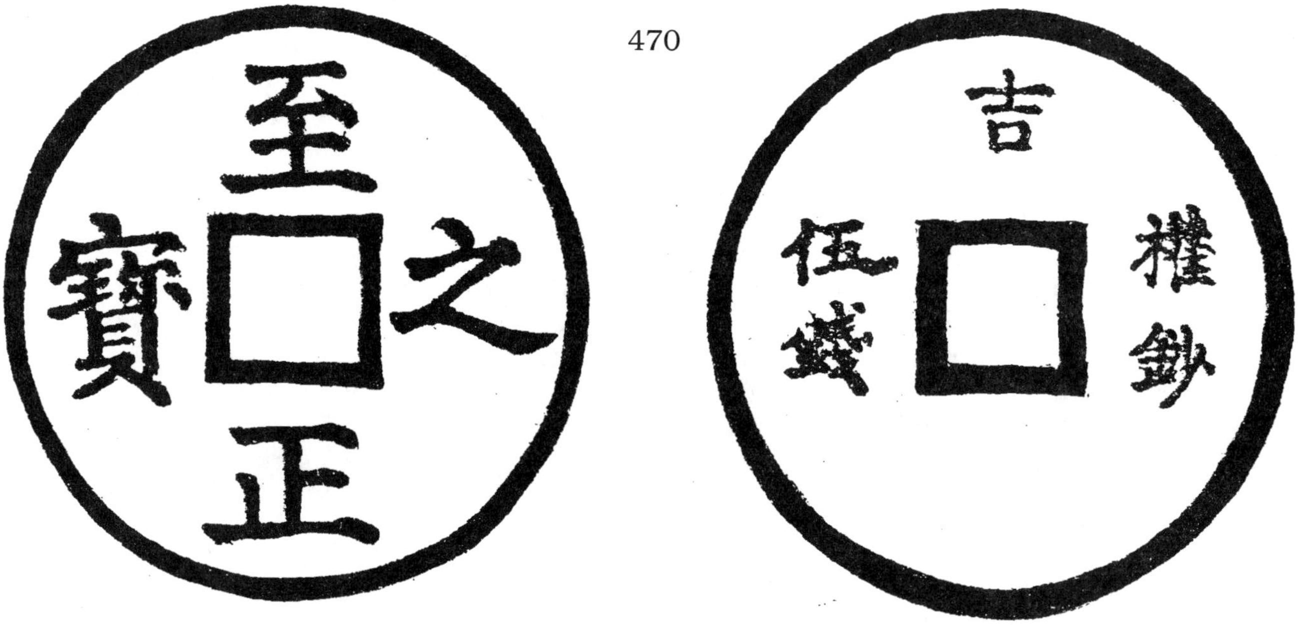

471

472

473

474

	VG	VF
470. Zhi Zheng Zhi Bao, Ji & 5 Mace on rev. S-1114/FD-1817	1200.00	2400.00
471. Ditto, 5 Candareens, S-1113/FD-1814	2000.00	4000.00
472. Ditto, 1 Mace FD-1815	1200.00	2400.00
473. Ditto, 1 Mace & 5 Candareens FD-1813	1200.00	2400.00
474. Ditto, 2 Mace & 5 Candareens FD-1816	1200.00	2400.00

TEMPLE MONEY

The coins in this category stand unique in the currency of the Yuan Dynasty. The imperial family were advocators of Buddhism, and large sums of money were appropriated for the building of temples and monasteries, the larger ones of which cast coins of their own for offerings to Buddha. As the abbots and high priests were themselves mostly high-ranking government officials, the temple mints were, in a sense, official mints, and the coins cast held the status of legal tender. Paper money being the standard currency at the time, seven of the Yuan emperors issued only banknotes; their reign titles appearing, nevertheless, on some of the temple coins. Such cash were crude in make, the legends poorly written, and most of them smaller in size than government issues; still they were hard cash and readily accepted by the public in lieu of the discredited banknotes.

No. 478 — Yan You Yuan Bao, cast around A.D. 1314-21, the Yan You period of the emperor Ren Zong (1312-21 A.D.)

No. 479 — Da Yuan Zhi Zhi, bearing the year title Da Yuan and the reign title Zhi Zhi; cast around A.D. 1321-24, during the reign of the emperor Yin Zong (1321-24 A.D.).

No. 481 — Tai Ding Tong Bao, cast during the reign of the emperor Tai Ding (1324-8 A.D.).

No. 482 — Zhi Shun Tong Bao, cast during the reign of the emperor Wen Di (1330-3 A.D.).

No. 483 — Yuan Tong Tong Bao, cast around A.D. 1333-5, the Yuan Tong period of the emperor Shun Di's reign.

No. 484 — Zhi Yuan Qi Nian, meaning the seventh year of Zhi Yuan. The characters Xiang Dian on the reverse is probably the name of a temple.

No. 485 — The characters Mu Qing must be a temple's name.

No. 486 — The characters on the reverse are in Hindu script, the meaning unclear.

475

476

477

478

479

480

481

482

486

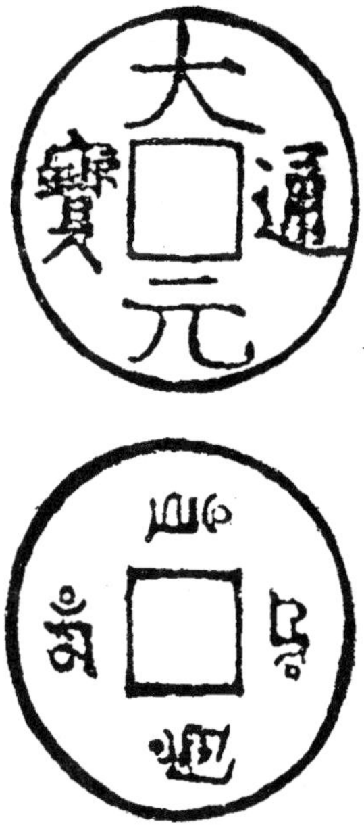

485

484

483

	VG	VF
475. Zhi Yuan Tong Bao, Mongol script FD-1706	400.00	700.00
476. Zhi Da Yuan Bao FD-1725	80.00	150.00
477. Da Yuan Zhi Bao	80.00	150.00
478. Yan You Yuan Bao FD-1741	300.00	500.00
479. Da Yuan Zhi Zhi FD-1737	300.00	500.00
480. Zhi Zhi Tong Bao FD-1751	150.00	250.00
481. Tai Ding Tong Bao FD-1757	300.00	500.00
482. Zhi Shun Tong Bao FD-1764	400.00	800.00
483. Yuan Tong Tong Bao FD-1772	350.00	500.00
484. Zhi Yuan Qi Nian, Xiang Dian on reverse FD-1781	200.00	400.00
485. Zhi Zheng, Mu Qing Tong Bao on reverse FD-1784	350.00	500.00
486. Da Yuan Tong Bao, Sanskrit on reverse FD-1732	2000.00	4000.00

REBEL COINAGE

All through the Yuan Dynasty, the Han people that made up the majority of the population were rebelling against their alien masters. Reduced to the status of second class citizens, they were at the mercy of any Mongol individual that came their way, knowing all too well that fair hearings were not to be expected from the officials, nor was there solace to be found in the temples, which harbored priests who all too willingly came to visit them in their homes and deprive them of any little property they had.

The discredited banknotes had shattered the economy, destroying the livelihood of the city folk, while exorbitant taxes and levies drove the peasants from their land. Chaos was widespread, sowing the seeds of revolt; and that was just what happened in the 1300's of that century. Peasants rallied around several insurgent leaders, who set up their own regimes and monetary systems. They issued hard cash to restore the economy within their territories, winning the support of the masses, who flocked to their standards in the tens of thousands. A cordon was forming in the south and the toppling of the Yuan empire seemed imminent. The rebels, however, did not combine their forces and take advantage of the situation, but instead, they fought against each other for supremacy and to reap the rewards of victory alone. It was for Zhu Yuan Zhang to emerge the victor, terminate the Yuan empire, and found the Ming dynasty.

Rebel coins occupy an important seat in Chinese numismatic history. They were symbols of the oppressed fighting against tyranny for justice and survival, striking a common chord with all freedom-loving peoples. Circulated in small areas and in small amounts, they exist in very limited numbers, hence their popularity with collectors.

REBEL COINS

487

488

489

490

491

492

493

494

495

496

497

	VG	VF
487. Long Feng Tong Bao S-1115/FD 1822	300.00	600.00
488. Ditto, 2 Cash FD-1823	700.00	1500.00
489. Ditto 3 Cash FD-1824	300.00	600.00
490. Ditto, 5 Cash FD-1825	800.00	1500.00
491. Tian Ding Tong Bao S-1122/FD-1833	80.00	120.00
492. Ditto, 2 Cash S-1123/FD-1832	80.00	120.00
493. Ditto, 3 Cash S-1124/FD-1831	80.00	120.00
494. Tian Qi Tong Bao S-1117/FD-1826	1200.00	2000.00
495. Ditto, 2 Cash FD-1827	2000.00	4000.00
496. Ditto, 3 Cash S-1118/FD-1828	600.00	1000.00
497. Ditto, Seal script FD-1829, VR	—	—

1. Long Feng Tong Bao (Nos. 487-90) — Cast by Han Lin Er in 1355 A.D.. His father Han Shan Tong and Liu Fu Tong were planning an uprising when the news leaked out and Han was killed. In 1351 A.D. Liu Fu Tong organized the Red Turban Army and rose up in revolt. In 1355 he set up the Da Song Kingdom, declared Han Lin Er emperor (1355-66 AD), with himself as minister and commander-in-chief of the army. The Long Feng coin comes in three denominations: 1, 2 & 3 cash. Coin No. 488 is actually a 1 cash variant. The legend is most attractive – Long meaning Dragon and Feng Phoenix.

2. Tian Qi Tong Bao (Nos. 494-7) — Cast by Xu Shou Hui (1351-60). On learning of Liu's uprising in Anhui, Xu followed suit, and in 1351 A.D. set up his Tian Wan Kingdom in Hubei Province, with Qu Shui for capital; first using the reign title Zhi Ping and then Tai Ping. After moving the capital to Hanyang, Hubei, he moved it a third time to Jiangzhou, Hubei Province, and in 1358 started minting his Tian Qi coins. This series comes in three denominations: 1, 2, and 3 cash. The Tian Qi 3 cash coin in seal script is the rarest of his coins (No. 497).

3. Tian Ding Tong Bao (Nos. 491-3) — This coin was cast in 1359, one year after the Tian Qi variety. It also came in three values: 1, 2, and 3 cash.

4. Da Yi Tong Bao (Nos. 498-500) — In 1360 A.D., Xu Shou Hui was slain by his comrade-in-arms Chen You Liang, who changed the name of the kingdom to Han and the reign title to Da Yi. His Da Yi coins, cast in 1360, also came in denominations of 1, 2, and 3 cash. He was routed and captured by Zhu Yuan Zhang in 1364 A.D.

5. Tian You Tong Bao (Nos. 501-4) — Cast by Zhang Shi Cheng (1353-7) in his Tian You years. The Tian You coins come in four values: 1, 2, 3, and 5 cash, inscribed in seal script on the reverse.

Aside from the above rebel coins, there exist two Tian Tong Tong Bao 1 cash coins, said to be cast by the rebel Ming Yu Zhen, who set up the Kingdom of Da Xia in Sichuan Province, with the reign title of Tian Tong (1363-6 A.D.). For lack of supportive evidence, the coins are considered controversial.

498

499

500

501

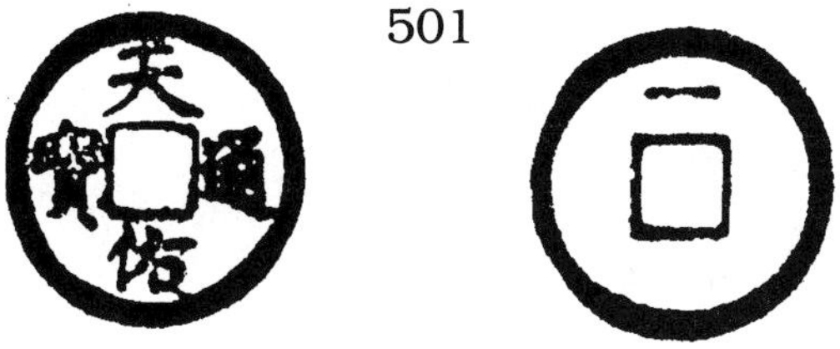

502

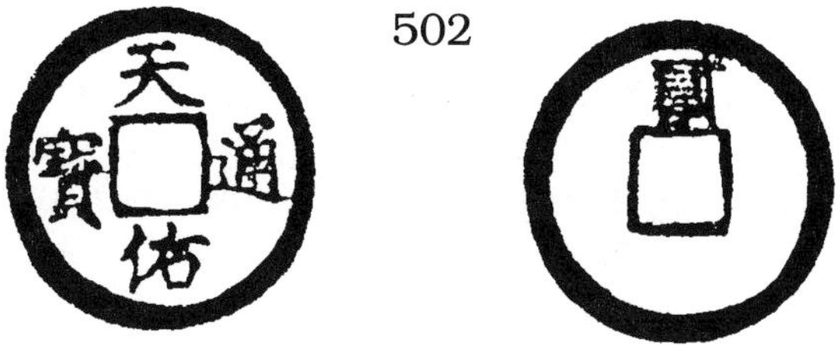

503

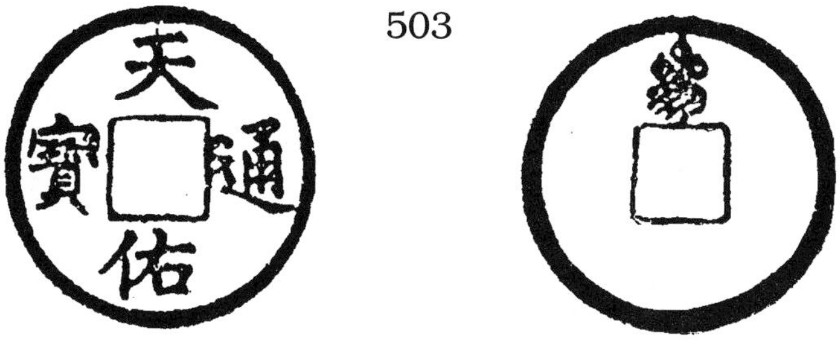

504

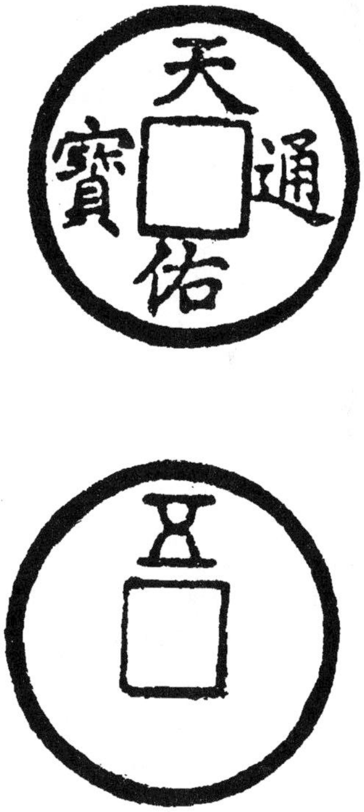

	VG	VF
498. Da Yi Tong Bao S-1119/FD-1834	80.00	120.00
499. Ditto, 2 Cash S-1120/FD-1835	80.00	120.00
500. Ditto, 3 Cash S-1121/FD-1836	80.00	120.00
501. Tian You Tong Bao 1 on rev. S-1125/FD-1840	400.00	800.00
502. Ditto, 2 on rev. FD-1839	200.00	400.00
503. Ditto, 3 on rev. FD-1841	200.00	400.00
504. Ditto, 5 on rev. S-1126/FD-1842	300.00	500.00

MING DYNASTY COINAGE

Among the rebels revolting against the Yuan regime was a young man who would one day rise to the very top — from beggar to emperor. His name was Zhu Yuan Zhang, son of a peasant family. A famine took away his parents and he entered the priesthood. Finding life unbearable, he went out to beg dressed in a monk's attire. In 1352 he joined the rebel army led by Guo Zi Xing, who was impressed by his appearance, the bone structure out of the ordinary. Zhu quickly proved his mettle and resourcefulness, unerring in his judgement in the field. After Guo's death he joined Han Lin Er's forces. His attention was now divided between the Mongols and the two rebels, Chen Yiu Liang and Zhang Shi Cheng, who invaded his Nanking home base. By A.D. 1367 they were both disposed of; and the following year the Yuan emperor fled the capital, abandoning it to Zhu's troops. Like Genghis Khan, he won the day with his superior generalship.

Zhu used two reign titles for his coins, first casting Da Zhong Tong Bao in A.D. 1361 when he was Prince of Wu, and Hong Wu Tong Bao after he became emperor. Set up with the central Bao Yuan mint were the following provincial mints:

Yu — Henan, Ji — Shandong, Jing — Nanjing (Nanking), Fu — Fujian, Beiping — Beijing (Peking), E — Hubei, Gui — Guangxi, Guang — Guangdong (Canton).

N.B. The variety with plain reverse must have come from the Jiangxi mint.

The Da Zhong coin comes in three varieties: plain reverse, value, both value and mint place on the reverse; the Hong Wu is more varied: plain reverse, value, value and mint place, and both value and weight on the reverse. Some Da Zhong coins were probably cast in the Hong Wu period to make up a series; Beijing did not fall until after the Ming Dynasty was founded and Hong Wu coins gone into circulation.

XVI. MING DYNASTY

1368-1644 A.D.

A. Pre-Ming

505

506

507

508

509

510

511

512

513

514
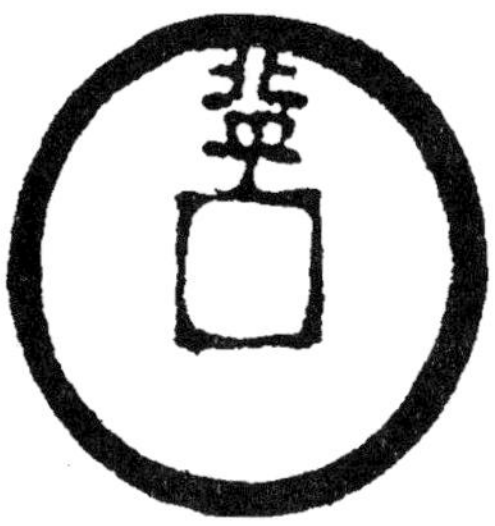

515

516

	VG	VF
505. Da Zhong Tong Bao S-1127/FD-1843	5.00	10.00
506. Ditto, Beiping on reverse S-1128/FD-1844	10.00	20.00
507. Ditto, Fu on reverse FD-1850	1000.00	3000.00
508. Ditto, Jing on reverse FD-1846	1000.00	3000.00
509. Ditto, 2 Cash S-1130/FD-1854	10.00	20.00
510. Ditto, Zhe on reverse FD-1858	5.00	10.00
511. Ditto, E on reverse FD-1856	1000.00	3000.00
512. Ditto, Gui & 2 on reverse FD-1860	1000.00	3000.00
513. Ditto, 3 Cash S-1131/FD-1864	10.00	20.00
514. Ditto, Beiping on reverse FD-1865	1000.00	3000.00
515. Ditto, Ji on reverse FD-1869, VR	—	—
516. Ditto, Gui & 3 on reverse FD-1870	1000.00	3000.00

517

518

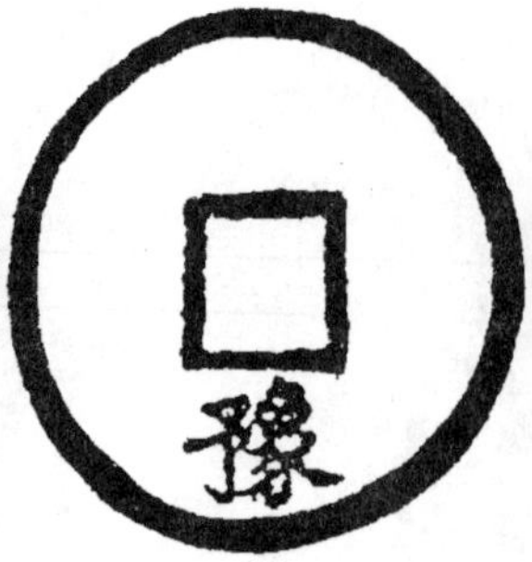

519

520

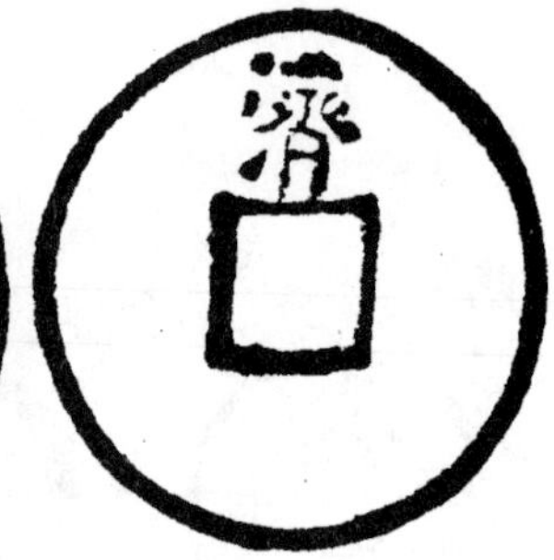

521

522

523

524

	VG	VF
517. Da Zhong Tong Bao, 5 Cash S-1132/FD-1874	20.00	40.00
518. Ditto, Yu on reverse S-1133/FD-1882	70.00	120.00
519. Ditto, E on reverse FD-1876	1000.00	2000.00
520. Ditto, Ji on reverse FD-1879, R	3000.00	—
521. Ditto, 10 on reverse S-1134/FD-1884	20.00	50.00
522. Ditto, Jing & 10 on reverse FD-1888	40.00	80.00
523. Ditto, 10 & Fu on reverse FD-1893	250.00	500.00
524. Ditto, 10 & Guang on reverse FD-1889	500.00	1000.00

B. Ming Proper

525

526

527

528

529

530

531

532

533

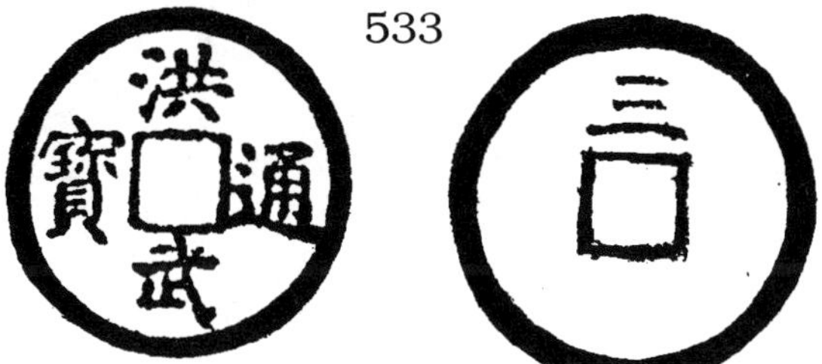

534

535

536

	VG	VF
525. Hong Wu Tong Bao S-1137/FD-1895	1.00	5.00
526. Ditto, Beiping on reverse, S-1143/FD-1897	2.00	10.00
527. Ditto, Guang on rev. FD-1907	200.00	400.00
528. Ditto, Jing on rev. FD-1899	1000.00	2000.00
529. Ditto, 2 Cash, Plain reverse, FD-1908	1000.00	2000.00
530. Ditto, Beiping on reverse, FD-1910	300.00	500.00
531. Ditto, E on reverse FD-1911	2000.00	4000.00
532. Ditto, 2 & Fu on reverse, FD-1916	120.00	200.00
533. Ditto, 3 Cash, 3 on reverse, FD-1920	700.00	1500.00
534. Ditto, 3 Mace on reverse, S-1155/FD-1922	15.00	30.00
535. Ditto, Ji on rev. FD-1927	1500.00	3000.00
536. Ditto, Gui & 3 on reverse, FD-1928	1700.00	3500.00

537

538

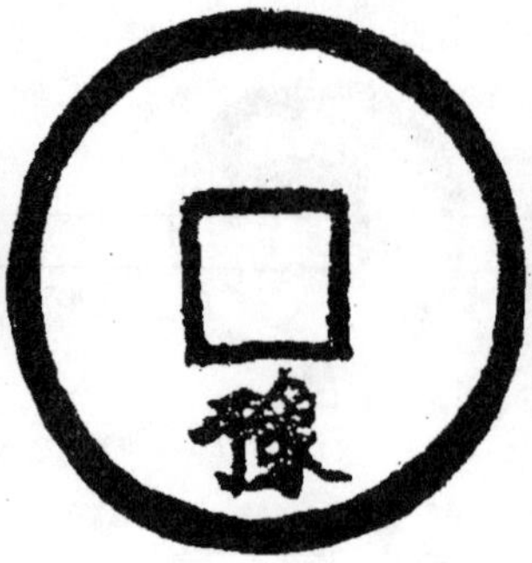

539

540

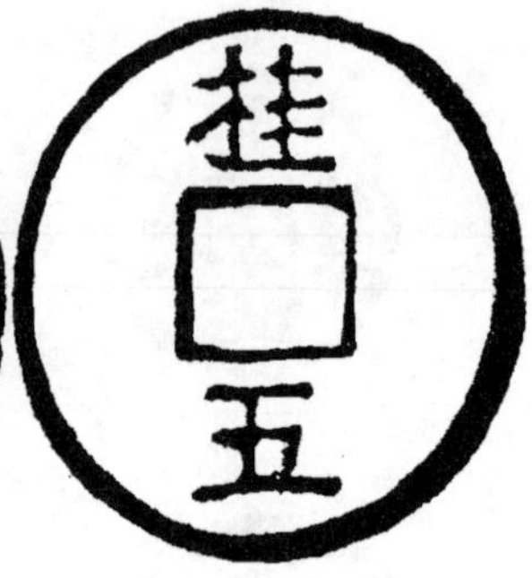

541

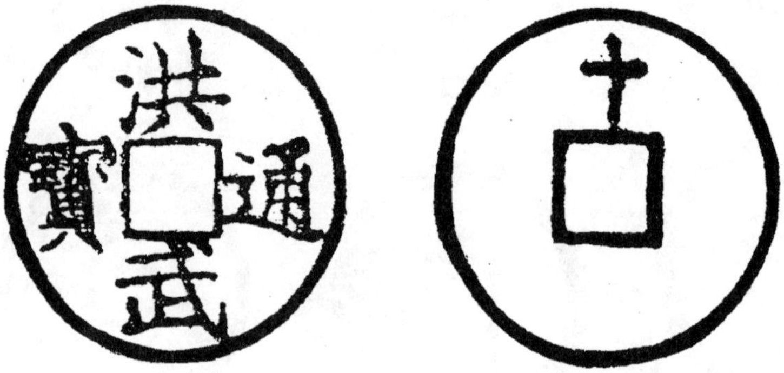

542

543

544

545

	VG	VF
537. Hong Wu Tong Bao, 5 Cash S-1139/FD-1932	400.00	600.00
538. Ditto, Yu on reverse 1943	1500.00	3000.00
539. Ditto, 5 & Fu on reverse, S-1156/FD-1942	80.00	120.00
540. Ditto, Gui & 5 on reverse, FD-1940	1500.00	3000.00
541. Ditto, 10 Cash, 10 on rev., FD-1945	80.00	120.00
542. Ditto, 10 & Guang on reverse, FD-1949	600.00	1200.00
543. Ditto, Jing & 10 on reverse, S-1159/FD-1948	30.00	60.00
544. Ditto, Gui & 10 on reverse, FD-1952	150.00	300.00
545. Ditto, 10 & 1 Tael on reverse, FD-1946	30.00	60.00

OX BACK HONG WU CHARM COIN

Hong Wu is the reign title of the emperor Zhu Yuan Zhang, founder of the Ming Dynasty. His is the success story of the man who rose from the gutters to the very top of the social ladder. Unlike many other successful people, however, he resents the mention of his early beginnings. Several persons used the phrase "Zuo Zhe" to eulogize the emperor. The phrase itself was beyond criticism, but the word Zhe was the homonym of thief, so the emperor thought they were lashing out at him and had them beheaded.

Among cash coins bearing his reign title, there is one with an ox pattern on the reverse and a cowherd sitting on it playing a flute. It is an interesting piece, but certainly not from the official mint, for no one at that time would have been foolhardy enough to make such a coin for the above reasons. It could only have come out in the Qing Dynasty, when such taboos had passed away together with the Ming Dynasty.

Several varieties of this coin exist. The alloys used are also varied — bronze, yellow copper, red copper and brass. The coins are commonly regarded as charms. Zhu Yuan Zhang's success has motivated people to think big and dare to do their best to realize their dreams and attain such heights of success as he did, at least to become a somebody in this world, hence the popularity of this coin.

In the time of Ming Tai Zhu (Zhu Yuan Zhang, a.k.a. Hong Wu), Da Ming banknotes were issued, circulating alongside the cash coins. In A.D. 1394 the use of cash was prohibited. Tai Zhu's successor, Hui Di (1399-1403), followed suit, and no coins bearing his reign title actually exist.

Yong Le Tong Bao (No. 546) — Cheng Zhu (1403-25 A.D.) cast these coins in the 6th year of his reign (1408 A.D.). The 1st series must have been patterned after the Hong Wu 5-grade system, but the plan was not approved. Only one 3 cash coin of this series exists. It could have been a trial piece.

Xuan De Tong Bao (No. 547) — Minted in the 8th year of the emperor Xuan Zong's reign. As he died two years later, the amount minted was far less than the Yong Le coins. He reigned from 1426-36 A.D.

Hong Zhi Tong Bao (No. 548) — Minted during Xiao Zong's reign (1488-1506 A.D.). His predecessors Ying Zong, Dai Zong, and Xian Zong minted no coins; those coins with the reign titles Jian Wen, Hong Xi, Zheng De, Zheng Tong, Jing Tai, Tian Shun and Cheng Hua are all forgeries. Two Hong Xi coins do exist; however, their authenticity is still an open question.

Jia Jing Tong Bao (Nos. 549-53) — Minted in the 23rd year (1544 A.D.) of Shi Zong's reign (1522-67 A.D.). Patterned after the Hong Wu series, all coins of this set are very rare, especially the 1 cash, of which only one specimen is known to exist. These coins were cast in low relief, the rims and legends easily worn away.

Long Qing Tong Bao (No. 554) — Minted by the emperor Mu Zong (1567-73) in the 4th year of his reign. The amount minted is quite small, creating a difficulty for the collector interested in Ming cash. Of the seventeen Ming emperors, only ten of them cast coins, the Long Qing being the fewest; hence ten reign titles comprise a set of Ming Dynasty coins.

Wan Li Tong Bao (No. 555) — Minted by Shen Zong (1573-1623 A.D.) in the 4th year of his reign (1576 A.D.). The official minting rights were transferred in part to the individual princes, who set up their own mints, resulting in a decline in coin quality and a profusion of varieties.

546

547

548

549

550

551

552

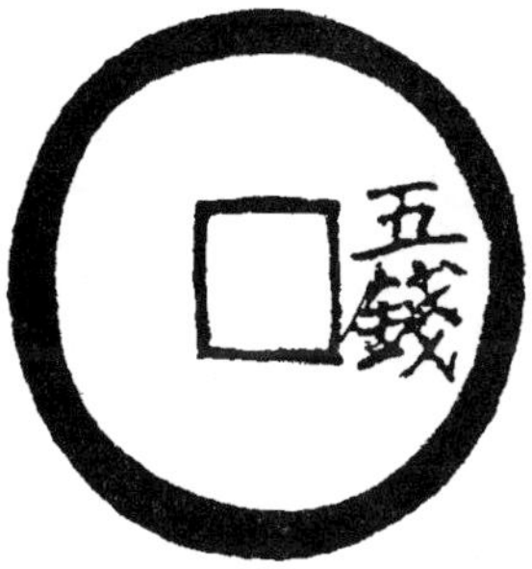

553

554

555

556

557

558

	VG	VF
546. Yong Le Tong Bao S-1166/FD-1958	5.00	15.00
547. Xuan De Tong Bao S-1170/FD-1959	10.00	20.00
548. Hong Zhi Tong Bao S-1176/FD-1960	10.00	20.00
549. Jia Jing Tong Bao S-1181, FD-1961	1.00	5.00
550. Ditto, 2 Candareens on reverse FD-1962	2000.00	4000.00
551. Ditto, 3 Candareens FD-1964	1200.00	2000.00
552. Ditto, 5 Candareens FD-1965	1200.00	2000.00
553. Ditto, 10 (?)/FD (?) 1 mace, loon top & left. Tael on the right FD-1967	(?)	(?)
554. Long Qing Tong Bao S-1183/FD-1969	25.00	50.00
555. Wan Li Tong Bao S-1185/FD-1970	1.00	5.00
556. Ditto, Large characters	20.00	50.00
557. Ditto, 2 Cash FD-1980	15.00	30.00
558. Tai Chang Tong Bao S-1199/FD-1984	5.00	15.00

Tai Chang Tong Bao (No. 558) — Issued posthumously for the emperor Guang Zong by his son Xi Zong (1621-28). Guang Zong was on the throne for only one month.

Tian Qi Tong Bao (Nos. 559-79) — Minted by Xi Zong (1621-28), who set up 156 mints; which explains the large quantity of coins issued and the diversity of the inscriptions on the reverse, coming in four groups:

- Marked with dots, crescents and strokes on the reverse.
- With weight values (Nos. 562-8).
- With mint names (Nos. 560-1, 569-70).
- Characters with special meaning (No. 571). The two characters Feng Zhi mean: On the Imperial Order. This coin might have been cast when orders were given to withdraw the coins of large denominations in A.D. 1626.

The mints denoted on the reverse are as follows:

Hu — Board of Revenue (No. 560).
Gong — Board of Works (No. 561).
Xin — New Minting Office of the Board of Revenue (No. 569).
Jing — Nanking (No. 570).
Zhe — Zhejiang Province.
Fu — Xuan Fu, Zhili (No. 577).
Zhen — Ji Zhen, Zhili (No. 578).
Mi — Mi Yun, Zhili (No. 579).
Yuan — Privy Council.

The standard weight for the 1 cash should be 1 mace & 2 candareens (No. 567); coins of such weight were the first issues, while those under 1 mace are substandard. The coins with 1 mace on the reverse (Nos. 562-566 & 568) are all good currency.

Xi Zong ascended the throne after Guang Zong's short-lived reign of one month in the 48th year of Wan Li (1620 A.D.). The reign title had just been changed to Tai Chang. To honor his father, Xi Zong decreed that the year remain Tai Chang until the next year A.D. 1621, when his reign title Tian Qi would then be formally adopted.

559

560

561

562

563

564

565

566

567

568

569

570

	VG	VF
559. Tian Qi Tong Bao S-1202, FD-1988	1.00	5.00
560. Ditto, Hu on reverse, S-1207/FD-1990	5.00	10.00
561. Ditto, Gong on reverse, S-1210/FD-1991	5.00	10.00
562. Ditto, 1 Mace (Yi Qian) FD-1992	300.00	500.00
563. Ditto, 1 Mace in orthodox script, FD-1993	300.00	500.00
564. Ditto, 1 Mace on the right side, FD-1998	200.00	400.00
565. Ditto, 1 on top & Mace below, S-1216/FD-1997	200.00	400.00
566. Ditto, 1 Mace & 1 Candareen, FD-1994	1000.00	1500.00
567. Ditto, 1 Mace & 2 Candareens, FD-1995	70.00	120.00
568. Ditto, Xin on top, 1 Mace on right & 1 Cand. on the left, S-1212/FD-1996	20.00	40.00
569. Ditto, Xin on rev., FD-1999	20.00	40.00
570. Ditto, Zhi on top & Feng on the right, FD-2005	400.00	800.00

571

572

573

574

575

576

577

578

579

	VG	VF
571. Tian Qi Tong Bao, 2 Cash, Dot on top, S-1218/FD-2009	30.00	60.00
572. Ditto, 2 on top & Dot below, FD-2008	1500.00	2500.00
573. Ditto, Hu on top	30.00	60.00
574. Ditto, 10 Cash S-1220/ FD-2016	30.00	60.00
575. Ditto, 10 on top & Dot below, S-1222/FD-2018	25.00	50.00
576. Ditto, 10 on top & 1 Tael on the right, S-1223/FD-2020	30.00	60.00
577. Ditto, Fu on top S-1224/FD-2023	80.00	150.00
578. Ditto, Zhen on top & 10 below S-1225, FD-2024	180.00	350.00
579. Ditto, 10 on top, 1 Tael on right & Mi on the left, FD-2020	500.00	1000.00

CHONG ZHEN COINS

The last Ming emperor, Chong Zhen, tried to improve the situation of the empire, but it had already rotted to the core. The markings on the reverse of his coins are even more complex than his predecessor's. They can be grouped into seven types:

1. Plain reverse (No. 581).

2. Dots & crescents, symbolizing the sun, moon & stars (581-2).

3. Celestial stems – Seven of the ten were used (Nos. 586-7), starting from Jia; some of the rest are shown in Part II of this catalog.

4. Weights (Nos. 584-5) – The first issues were made to weigh 1 mace, 4 coins convertible to 1 tael of silver; but some weighed only 4 candareens, though marked 8 candareens.

5. Mint & place names (Nos. 588-602):
   Hu – Board of Revenue.
   Gong – Board of Works.
   Xin – New minting office.
   Jiu – Old minting office.
   Bing – Board of War.
   Ju – Nanjing official mint.
   Jing – Nanjing mint.
   Jian – Control Yuan (Office).
   Yuan – Privy Council.
   Jiang – Chaojiang, Nanjing.
   Ning – Jiangning, Nanjing.
   Yu – Yuling, Shaanxi.
   Chong – Chongqing, Sichuan.
   Yin – Yintian, Nanjing.
   Qing – Qingyang, Nanjing.
   Gui – Guiyang, Guizhou.
   Guang – Guangdong.
   Taiping – Taiping Jian, Gansu.
   Fu – Xuanfu, Hebei.
   Gong – Gongqing, Hebei.
   E – Ezhou, Hubei.

6. Other:
   Zhi – Imperial Order. (No. 589).
   Zhi – Measure (No. 590).
   Zhi Feng – Measure, by Decree (No. 591).
   Chi – Imperial Decree (No. 586).
   Unidentified – Xing, Dao, He, Qi, Jing Zhong.

7. Galloping horse – This is the only regular issue with an animal pattern on the reverse. What it signifies is not known. The real coins are rather thin, while the thick ones are forgeries.

580

581

582

583

584

585

586

587

588

589

590

591

	VG	VF
580. Chong Zhen Tong Bao S-1229/FD-2025	0.50	2.00
581. Ditto, Dot on top S-1234/FD-2026	2.00	5.00
582. Ditto, Concentric circle S-1235/FD-2030	20.00	40.00
583. Ditto, Horse Pattern S-1278/FD-2079	30.00	60.00
584. Ditto, 1 Mace on right side S-1243/FD-2034	5.00	10.00
585. Ditto, 1 Mace on left side	80.00	120.00
586. Ditto, Yi on top S-1237/FD-2039	5.00	10.00
587. Ditto, Gen on top FD-2044	30.00	60.00
588. Ditto, Jia on top	350.00	700.00
589. Ditto, Zhi on top FD-2073	800.00	2000.00
590. Ditto, Zhi FD-2076	150.00	300.00
591. Ditto, Zhi on top & Feng on the right, FD-2077	20.00	40.00

592

593

594

595

596

597

598

599

600

601

602

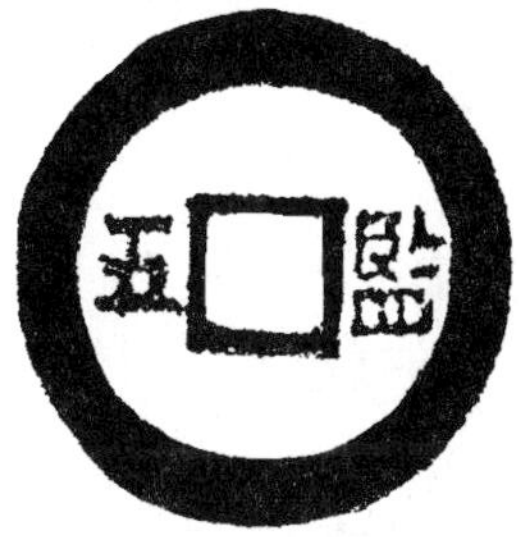

	VG	VF
592. Chong Zhen Tong Bao, 2 Cash FD-2083	40.00	70.00
593. Ditto, Hu & 2 from right to left S-1280/FD-2085	15.00	25.00
594. Ditto, Large version FD-2084	600.00	1000.00
595. Ditto, Hu on top & 2 below, S-1279	20.00	35.00
596. Ditto, Chi on top & 2 below	1000.00	1500.00
597. Ditto, Ji on right & 2 on the left	1000.00	1500.00
598. Ditto, Jiang on top & 2 on the right	300.00	500.00
599. Ditto, 4 on top & Shou on the left FD-2089	1500.00	2500.00
600. Ditto, 5 Cash, Hu on right & 5 on the left FD-2093	15.00	25.00
601. Ditto, Gong on right & 5 on the left FD-2094	70.00	120.00
602. Ditto, Jian on right & 5 on the left S-1284/FD-2095	15.00	25.00
603. Ditto, 10 Cash FD-2096	500.00	1000.00

603

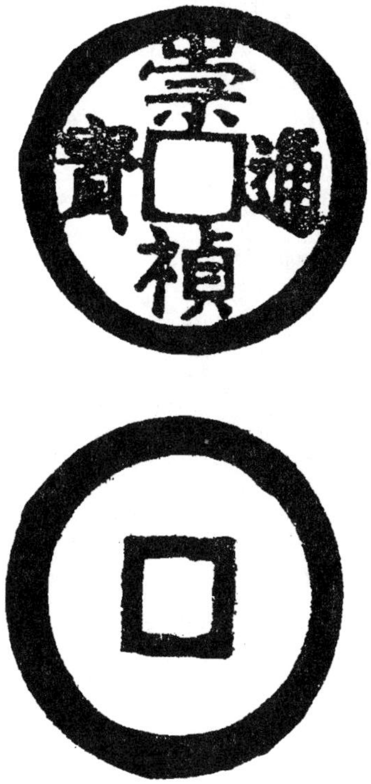

SOUTHERN MING COINAGE

After the fall of the Ming capital Peking, the royal family fled south. Prince Lu set up his regime in Zhejiang, Prince Fu in Nanking, Prince Tang in Fujian, and Prince Gui in Canton and Guangxi. These four issued their own currency.

• Da Ming Tong Bao (Nos. 604-7) — Minted by Prince Lu (1644-52 A.D.). The character Shuai stands for Commander-in-chief.

• Hong Guang Tong Bao (Nos. 608-10) — Minted by Prince Fu (1644-5). The character Feng on the reverse of No. 609 means phoenix, and the one on No. 610 is the numeral 2 in orthodox script; it is a two cash coin.

• Long Wu Tong Bao (Nos. 611-2) – Minted by Prince Tang (1645-6 A.D.). No. 612 is a 2 cash coin.

• Yong Li Tong Bao (Nos. 613-4) — Minted by Zheng Cheng Gong (1661-83 A.D.) in Taiwan. The 1st one is in running script and the 2nd one in seal script. They are 2 cash coins; interesting to say, they were minted in Nagasaki, Japan. Zheng Cheng Gong borrowed Prince Gui's reign title for his currency. He was not a member of the royal family, but he saw himself as part of the Han people's resistance to the Manchu aggression, who were considered foreigners at the time, thus the reason for his using the reign title. He holds a unique place in Chinese history as the liberator of Taiwan from western hands.

B. Southern Ming 1644-1662 A.D.

604

605

606

607

608

609

610

611

612

613

614

	VG	VF
604. Da Ming Tong Bao S-1285/FD-2099	40.00	80.00
605. Ditto, Hu on reverse S-1286/FD-2102	40.00	80.00
606. Ditto, Shuai on the right FD-2101	80.00	120.00
607. Ditto, Shuai on the top FD-2100	90.00	150.00
608. Ditto, Hong Guang Tong Bao S-1284/FD-2105	1.00	5.00
609. Ditto, Feng on the top S-1289/FD-2106	30.00	60.00
610. Ditto, Er on the right S-1290/FD-2107	90.00	150.00
611. Long Wu Tong Bao S-1291/FD-2108	1.00	5.00
612. Ditto, 2 Cash S-1295/FD-2111	5.00	10.00
613. Yong Li Tong Bao in Running Script, S-1316/FD-2128	20.00	40.00
614. Ditto, in Seal script S-1315/FD-2129	20.00	40.00

• Yong Li Tong Bao (Nos. 615-24) — Minted by Prince Gui (1646-62 A.D.). When the Qing (Manchu) troops reached Canton, he fled to Yunnan Province and then into Burma. In A.D. 1661, the Burmese surrendered him to the Qing troops, who had entered Burma; he was executed the following year. On leaving Canton, he issued an imperial decree to Li Ding Guo, his commander-in-chief to remain there and assist in affairs of State. A set of coins was issued with the 12 characters of the decree on the reverse, one on each coin as follows:

> YU (imperial), CHI (decree), DU (oversee), BU (Board of War), DAO (regional commanders), FU (prefectures), LIU (remain), YUE (Canton), FU (assist), MING (Ming Dynasty), (to) DING (first character of Li Ding Guo's first name), GUO (second character of his first name).

Five of them are listed here: Ming (No. 616), Dao (No. 617), Ding (No. 618), Guo (No. 619), and Chi (No. 620); the rest are given in Section II of this catalog.

The regular issues of Yong Li coins come in four denominations: 1, 2, 5 and 10 cash (1 candareen).

615

616

617

618

619

620

621

622

623

624

	VG	VF
615. Yong Li Tong Bao S-1296, FD-2113	5.00	10.00
616. Ditto, Ming on reverse, S-1308/FD-2122	10.00	20.00
617. Ditto, Dao on reverse, S-1304/FD-2110	200.00	400.00
618. Ditto, Ding on reverse, S-1309/FD-2126	20.00	40.00
619. Ditto, Guo on reverse, S-1310/FD-2124	20.00	40.00
620. Ditto, Chi on rev. S-1301	70.00	120.00
621. Ditto, 2 Cash S-1317	5.00	10.00
622. Ditto, 3 Cash S-1318/FD-2130	25.00	50.00
623. Ditto, 5 Cash S-1319/FD-2131	10.00	20.00
624. Ditto, 1 Candareen S-1322, FD-2133	15.00	30.00

REBEL COINAGE OF THE MING DYNASTY

Like all previous dynasties, the Ming empire had its share of peasant revolts, and eventually collapsed under the assault of Li Zi Cheng's peasant army. Li Zi Cheng (a.k.a. Chuang Wang A.D. 1644) had not occupied Peking for 100 days before he was driven away by Manchu troops that poured in through San Hai Guan, a strategic pass of the Great Wall. He set up his Da Shun Kingdom in Shaanxi in A.D. 1644, with the reign title Yong Chang. The coins he issued (Nos. 621-2) exist in quite large numbers.

Zhang Xian Zhong set up his Da Xi Kingdom in Chengdu, Sichuan, in the same year as Li Zi Cheng set up his, with the title Da Shun. His coins are thick and large, (Nos. 623-4), superior to those of the Ming Dynasty. His Xi Wang Shang Gong coin (No. 625) might have been made in A.D. 1623 when he took over the King of Chu's palace in Wu Chang, Hubei Province, and set up court there. He was slain by the Manchus in A.D. 1646.

After Zhang's death, his adopted son Sun Ke Wang entered Yunnan Province and proclaimed himself Prince of Ping Dong (1649-55 A.D.). The Xing Chao Tong Bao coins (Nos. 626-8) were minted in A.D. 1649.

Wu San Gui (1674-8 A.D.) was a double dealer, first betraying the Ming Dynasty and then the Qing Dynasty. The garrison commander of Shan Hai Guan, a strategic pass, he opened the gates and let the Manchus in; and then, as a vassal posted in Yunnan, he seized Hengzhou in Hunan Province and proclaimed himself emperor of Da Zhou Dynasty, with the reign title of Zhao Wu. He died a few months later. Of his coins, the one with the right-hand Yi in orthodox script (No. 636) is quite scarce, and the pair in seal script (Nos. 638-9) are nicely written.

Wu Shi Fan was Wu San Gui's grandson. He ruled in Yunnan from A.D. 1678 to 1681. He minted only 1 cash coins (No. 640).

Geng Jing Zhong (1674-76) occupied Fujian Province. In A.D. 1676 he surrendered to the Manchus, revolted, and was executed. No. 641 is the scarcest of his coins. The character Zhe on the right stands for Zhejiang Province, and the two on the right, one mace.

C. Rebel Coins

625

626

627

628

630

631

629

632

	VG	VF
625. Yong Chang Tong Bao S-1323, FD-2134	15.00	25.00
626. Ditto, 5 Cash S-1325, FD-2136	20.00	40.00
627. Da Shun Tong Bao S-1326/FD-2137	15.00	25.00
628. Ditto, Chuan on top & Hu below	1500.00	3000.00
629. Xi Wang Shang Gong, Gold, ER	—	—
Silver, ER	—	—
Bronze, VR	—	—
630. Xing Chao Tong Bao S-1329/FD-2139	2.00	5.00
631. Ditto, 5 Cash S-1332/FD-2142	10.00	20.00
632. Ditto, 1 Candareen S-1333/FD-2143	10.00	20.00

633

634

635

636

637

638

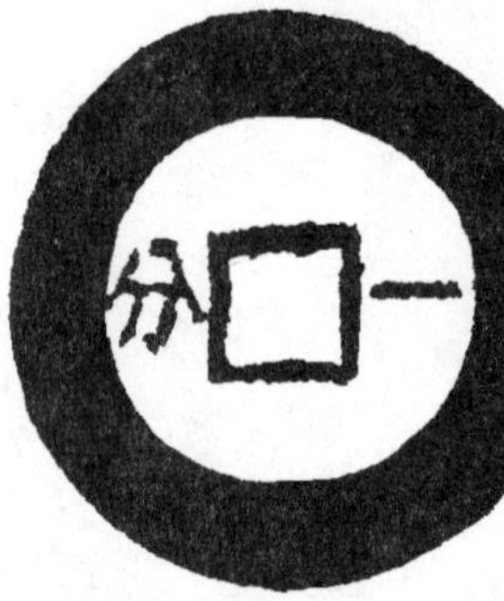

639

640

	VG	VF
633. Li Yong Tong Bao S-1335/FD-2144	1.00	3 .00
634. Ditto, 2 Cash on reverse S-1340, FD-2150	10.00	20.00
635. Ditto, 5 Cash S-1341/FD-2152	10.00	20.00
636. Ditto, 1 Candareen on reverse FD-2157	20.00	40.00
637. Ditto, 1 Candareen, smaller version, S-1343/FD-2153	15.00	25.00
638. Ditto, 1 on right & Candareen on the left S-1342/FD-2154	25.00	45.00
639. Ditto, Value in orthodox script on the reverse, 1 on top & Candareen at the bottom FD-2155	30.00	60.00
640. Ditto, 1 Candareen in orthodox script from right to left FD-2156	80.00	120.00

641

642

643

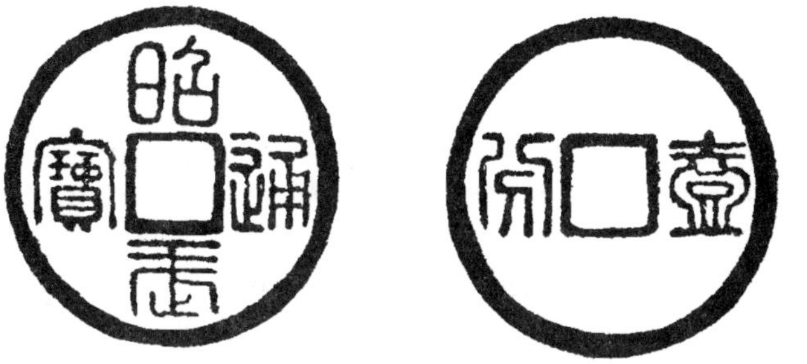

644

645

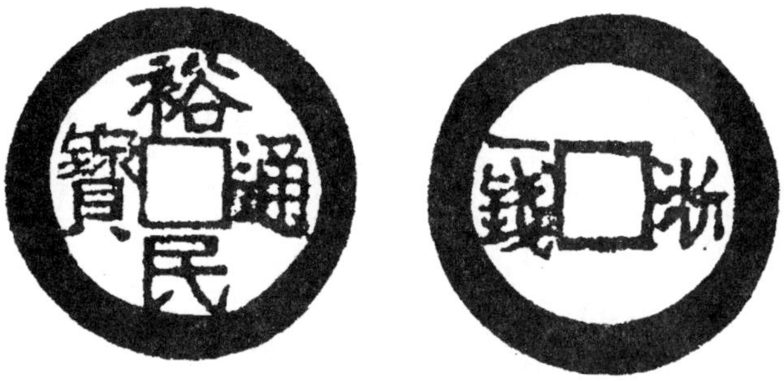

646

647

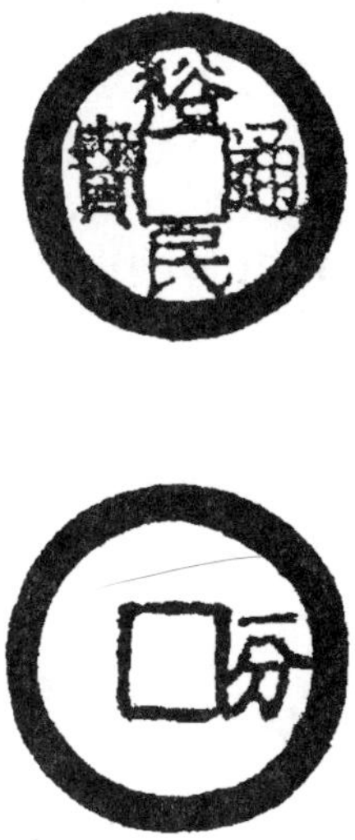

	VG	VF
641. Zhao Wu Tong Bao S-1345/FD-2158	5.00	10.00
642. Ditto, Seal script S-1344, FD-2160	25.00	50.00
643. Ditto, 1 Candareen on rev. S-1347/FD-2161	20.00	40.00
644. Hong Hua Tong Bao S-1348, FD-2162	2.00	5.00
645. Yu Ming Tong Bao, Zhe & 1 Mace on reverse, from right to left FD-2168	70.00	120.00
646. Ditto, 1 on right & Mace on the left S-1354/FD-2167	30.00	60.00
647. Ditto, 1 Candareen on rev. S-1353/FD-2166	10.00	20.00

QING DYNASTY COINAGE

After the Mongols terminated the Jin Dynasty in A.D. 1234, the Jurchens retreated to their home grounds in Northern China. In the 1600's, they adopted the name Manchus, banded together again under the leadership of Nurhachi, who founded the Posterior Jin regime. Three decades later, with the Ming Dynasty traitor Wu San Gui opening the Shan Hai Guan passe to let them through, they overran the entire Middle Kingdom and set up the Qing empire, the last of the Chinese dynasties.

The Tianming coins (Nos. 644-5) were cast by Nurhachi in A.D. 1616, and Tian Chong (No. 646) by Abatai, his successor in A.D. 1627. They both did not live to see their troops advance toward Beijing. Shun Zhi, their successor, was the one who accomplished the mission. His coins may fall into six groups:

1. Plain reverse — Coin No. 647.

2. With numerals 1 & 2 on reverse (648-9). The 2 cash may have been a trial piece.

3. With a single character in Han script denoting mint name on the reverse (Nos. 650-65).

4. With mint name in Han script on the right & value 1 cash on the left (Nos. 667-70). No. 667 has 1 at the top and cash below the center hole.

5. With mint name in both Han and Manchu script on the reverse (No. 671).

6. With mint name only in Manchu script (No. 672).

The large 10 cash was modeled after the Ming Dynasty system of 10 cash Tian Qi and Chong Zhen coins (No. 673), but it was not adopted for regular use: The large 2 cash piece also did not see circulation.

XVII. QING DYNASTY
1644-1911 A.D.

648 649 650

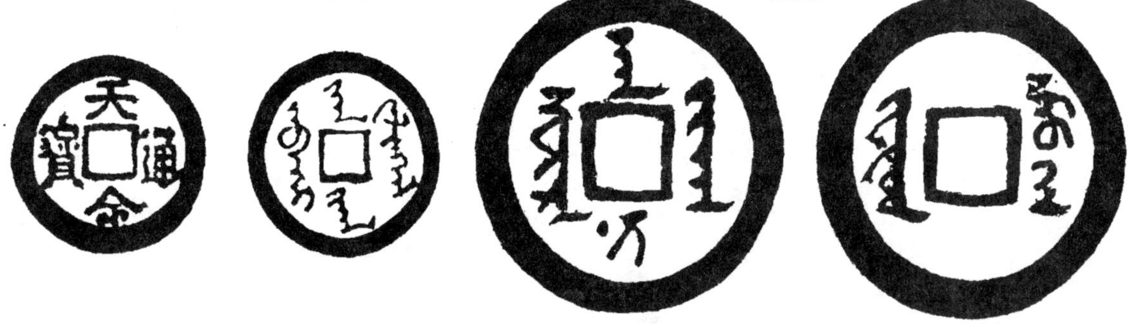

651 652 653

654 655 656 657

	VG	VF
648. Tian Ming Tong Bao S-1356/FD-2172	40.00	80.00
649. Ditto, in Manchu script S-1355/FD-2173	20.00	40.00
650. Tian Cong Tong Bao FD-2175	500.00	1000.00
651. Shun Zhi Tong Bao S-1359/FD-2176	1.00	5.00
652. Ditto, 1 on reverse FD-2178	15.00	30.00
653. Ditto, 2 on reverse	150.00	300.00
654. Ditto, Xiang on top S-1385/FD-2215	25.00	40.00
655. Ditto, Fu on top S-1382/FD-2210	15.00	25.00
656. Ditto, Tong on right S-1372/FD-2197	10.00	20.00
657. Ditto, Nan on top FD-2201	1500.00	3000.00

658

659

660

661

662

663

664

665

666

667

668

669

	VG	VF
658. Shun Zhi Tong Bao, Hu on top FD-2180	30.00	60.00
659. Ditto, Hu on right S-1362/FD-2179	5.00	10.00
660. Ditto, Gong on right S-1360/FD-2181	10.00	20.00
661. Ditto, Dong on right S-1380/FD-2211	10.00	20.00
662. Ditto, Ji on top FD-2191	80.00	150.00
663. Ditto, Ji on right S-1374/FD-2192	40.00	80.00
664. Ditto, Jing on top FD-2201	60.00	90.00
665. Ditto, Jing on right FD-2200	30.00	60.00
666. Ditto, Xuan on top S-1368/FD-2189	80.00	120.00
667. Ditto, Xuan on right S-1367/FD-2190	10.00	20.00
668. Ditto, Yan on top FD-2195	500.00	1000.00
669. Ditto, Yan on right FD-2194	120.00	200.00

670

671

672

673

674

675

676

677

	VG	VF
670. Shun Zhi Tong Bao, Dong on right, 1 on top & Cash below	400.00	800.00
671. Ditto, Dong on right & 1 Cash on the left FD-2221	10.00	20.00
672. Ditto, Jiang on right & 1 Cash on the left S-1392/FD-2217	15.00	25.00
673. Ditto, Tong on right & 1 Cash on the left FD-2231	150.00	300.00
674. Ditto, Bao Quan Mint in Manchu script S-1405/FD-2233	1.00	2.00
675. Ditto, Dong in Han script on right & Manchu script on the left S-1409/FD-2238	1.00	2.00
676. Ditto, Bao Quan Mint, 2 Cash	1500.00	2500.00
677. Ditto, 10 on top & 1 Tael on the right FD-2249	1000.00	2000.00

Kang Xi Coins
1662-1723 A.D.

The emperor Kang Xi was an accomplished man-of-letters despite his Manchu origin, and a wise administrator as well. The Middle Kingdom flourished under his 61-year reign. The quantity of currency minted in his time was much larger than his predecessor's, but the varieties were fewer, only two major series:

1. Kang Xi Tong Bao on obverse and mint name in Manchu script on reverse.

2. The mint names in both Han and Manchu script on reverse. This series is also known as the Kang Xi Verse Coins*. As there were 21 mints, there were 21 Han characters on the reverse sides, and 20 of the Han characters were arranged into a poem rhyming AABA. To be exact, it was a poem only in sound, with no meaning. The coin from the Bao Gong (Gansu) was not included, since it was very rare. The coin from the Taiwan mint was smaller than the rest, so to satisfy collectors' demands, some large ones to match the rest were cast during the reign of his grandson, Qian Long. Many forgeries have since entered the market. Let the buyer beware!

Aside from these, an interesting set of coins were issued by the Fujian mint to commemorate the emperor Kang Xi's 60th birthday in March, 1713. The mint meant to issue this series over a period of 12 years. Each year in March a new one was to be issued. The characters at the top on the reverse are the earthly stems, twelve in all, which are used to designate the years, so twelve would be minted. No. 676 is Zi, denoting the year 1713, No. 677 for 1714, and No. 678 for 1715. Kang Xi died in 1723; therefore the minting of this set was discontinued, thus ten were actually made. They are very rare.

Nos. 679, 680 may also be commemoratives. The legend on the reverse of No. 679 means: The Great Qing (Dynasty). No. 681 is a 10 cash commemorative.

678

679

680

681

682

684

683

	VG	VF
678. Kang Xi Tong Bao S-1419/FD-2250	1.00	3.00
679. Ditto, Zhi on top, Fu on right in Han script & Manchu script on the left FD-2273	700.00	1200.00
680. Ditto, Chou on top & Fu on the two sides FD-2274	700.00	1200.00
681. Ditto, Yin on top & Fu on the two sides FD-2275	700.00	1200.00
682. Ditto, Da Qing on the reverse	300.00	500.00
683. Ditto, Dragon & Phoenix on the reverse	300.00	500.00
684. Ditto, 10 Cash FD-2276	1200.00	2000.00

KANG XI REVERSE COINS

During the emperor Kang Xi's reign 21 mints were set operating. On the reverse of the coins were the names of the mints in both Han and Manchu script, with Han on the right and Manchu on the left. A verse was composed with 20 of the Han characters, five characters to a line, and rhyming aaba.

		VG	VF
a)	Tong — Da Tong mint, Shandong (province), No. 685.	FD-2252	$2.00
	Fu — Fujian mint, No. 686.	FD-2253	$2.00
	Ning — Ning Xia mint, Gansu, No. 687.	FD-2254	$2.00
	Dong — Shandong mint, No. 688.	FD-2255	$2.00
	Jiang — Jiang Ning mint, Jiangsu, No. 689.	FD-2256	$2.00
b)	Xuan — Xuan Fu mint, Zhili, No. 690.	FD-2257	$2.00
	Yuan — Taiyuan mint, Shanxi, No. 691.	FD-2258	$2.00
	Su — Suzhou mint, Jiangsu, No. 692.	FD-2259	$2.00
	Ji — Jizhiu mint, Zhili, No. 693.	FD-2260	$2.00
	Chang — Nanchang mint, Jiangxi No. 694.	FD-2261	$2.00
c)	Nan — Hunan mint, No. 695.	FD-2262	$10.00
	He — Henan mint, No. 696.	FD-2263	$2.00
	Lin — Linqing mint, Shandong, No. 697.	FD-2264	$2.00
	Guang — Guangdong (Canton) mint, No. 698.	FD-2265	$2.00
	Zhe — Zhejiang mint, No. 699.	FD-2266	$2.00
d)	Tai — Taiwan mint, No. 700.	FD-2267	$15.00
	Gui — Guangxi mint, No. 701.	FD-2268	$2.00
	Shaan — Shaanxi mint, No. 702.	FD-2269	$2.00
	Yun — Yunnan mint, No. 703.	FD-2270	$2.00
	Zhang — Zhangzhou mint, Fujian mint, No. 704.	FD-2271	$2.00

The original Taiwan coin was smaller than the rest, a larger version was later cast to match the others. The large Guangdong coins were of contemporary make. The coin with the character Gong is from the Gongchang mint, Gansu (No. 706). The coin with Xi on the reverse (No. 708) is said to be minted by Wu San Gui, Prince of Ping Xi.

	VG	VF
Guang, Large, No. 705.	$150.00	$300.00
Gong, FD-2272, No. 706.	$600.00	$1,200
Tai, Large, No. 707.	$60.00	$120.00
Xi, No. 708	$600.00	$1,200

685

686

687

688

689

690

691

692

693

694

695

696

697

698

699

700

701

702

703

704

705

706

707

708

Yong Zheng & Qian Long Coins

The 3rd emperor Yong Zheng (1723-36) was not so illustrious as his forebear nor were many nice words said about him, yet his coins maintained the standard of his father's, showing that the economy was still prospering. Due to a copper shortage, some mints were closed. The only varieties are those shown here, with the mint names in Manchu script on the reverse. The 2 cash coin from the Bao Qian mint (No. 710) is quite rare.

The 4th emperor Qian Long (1736-1796) was a greater scholar than his grandfather Kang Xi and the ablest administrator among the Manchu rulers. Many times he went around the kingdom in disguise to see for himself how things were going on. The empire reached its zenith during his reign, the most glorious one, second to only the Tang Dynasty. In the 1920's, a warlord ordered his soldiers to open up two of the Qing rulers' tombs, Qian Long's and that of the notorious empress Ci Xi. Of course, the latter yielded a rich haul of valuables, but in the first one only books, scrolls and chinaware was found. The looters were so frustrated that they torched and smashed everything inside the tomb. Qian Long loved the arts above worldly treasures.

The quantity of currency minted in Qian Long's time was much larger, but the size and weight had shrunk. After the suppression of the Zhun Ge Er region, mints were set operating in Xinjiang, bringing the total of mints to twenty-four. Red copper was used for the coins (No. 709). The 10 cash coins were not much different than the 1 cash in size and weight, and owing to the shortage of currency and the higher cost of living in that remote province, all 1 cash coins were used at the same value as the 10 cash. No. 710 is a commemorative. The wide rim of No. 711 bears some resemblance to the Korean Chang Ping Tong Bao coin, from which it derived its name.

709

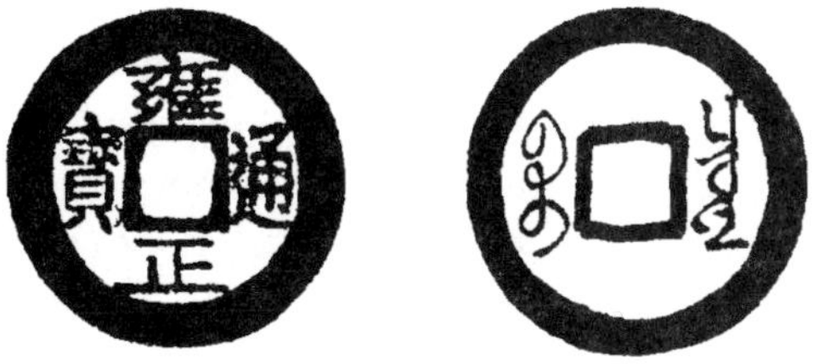

710

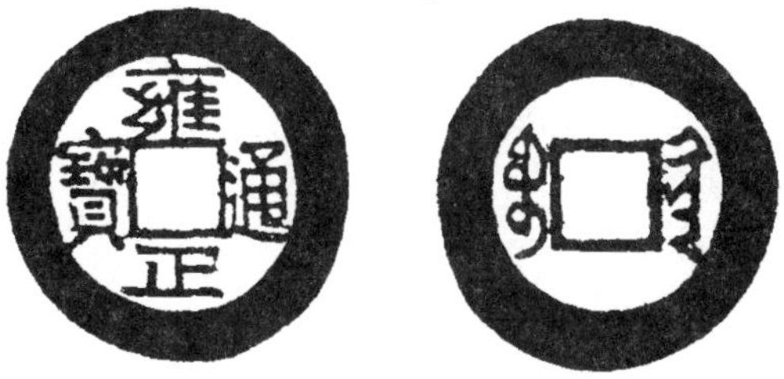

711

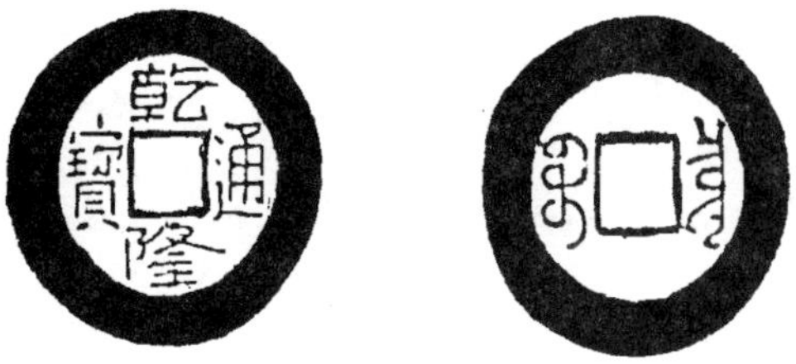

712

713

714

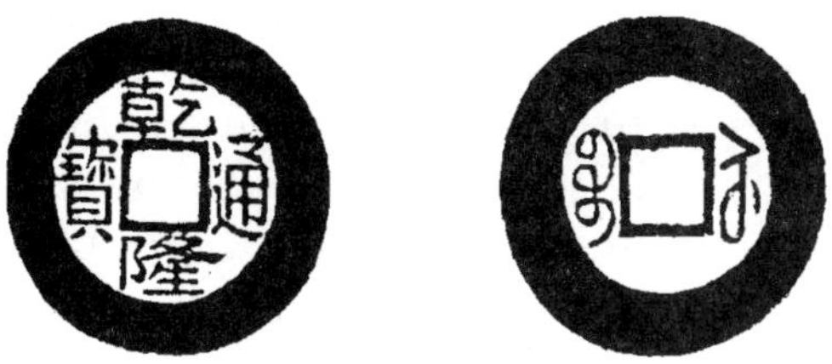

715

	VG	VF
709. Yong Zheng Tong Bao, Bao Quan Mint S-1464/FD-2277	1.00	3.00
710. Ditto, 2 Cash Bao Qian Mint, FD-2296	3500.00	5000.00
711. Qian Long Tong Bao, Bao Quan Mint S-1492/FD-2297	0.50	1.00
712. Ditto, 9 on top & Aksu Mint on two sides	15.00	30.00
713. Ditto, 10 Cash, Bao Quan Mint	800.00	1500.00
714. Ditto, Chang Ping style, Bao Su Mint	70.00	120.00
715. Ditto, Bao Zhe Mint, Wide rim	120.00	200.00

Jia Qing & Dao Guang Coins

Since Qian Long's time the currency was depreciating. It was getting worse with each succeeding ruler. The Qing Dynasty was on the decline, but the end was still a century away. During this time, large and heavy (!) cash were also issued; they were either trial pieces, patterns or palace coins to be presented to the Imperial Court at the end of each year.

- Jia Qing (1796-1821 A.D.) — Coins No. 715 & 716 are from the Guangxi mint. The character on the right is Gui, which stands for Guilin, a scenic city in Guangxi Province. The Gui on No. 715 is in Han script, both regular and running style, while that on No. 716 is in Han and Manchu scripts, possibly a trial piece. The nature of Nos. 716 & 717 has been mentioned in the above paragraph.

- Dao Guang (1821-51 A.D.) — During this emperor's reign, the currency production was dropping, and substandard coins were issued in large numbers. The imbalance of value between silver and copper was causing the mints to turn out currency at a loss. By 1824 the Fujian mint closed down, and several others had submitted petitions to follow suit. Coin No. 720 could be a pattern, not a regular issue.

From Qian Long to Tong Zhi, the 8th emperor, coins of the Chang Ping style appeared bearing the reign title of each successive ruler. Coins of this style also appeared in Guang Xu's time, but they were smaller than the rest. Legend has it that this variety was minted by a certain family in Jiangsu Province. For their several generations of meritorious service, they were awarded by the regime with the prestigious right to set up their own mint; from which came the Chang Ping coins (Nos. 711, 714, 717, 719, and 721), and considered legal tender.

716

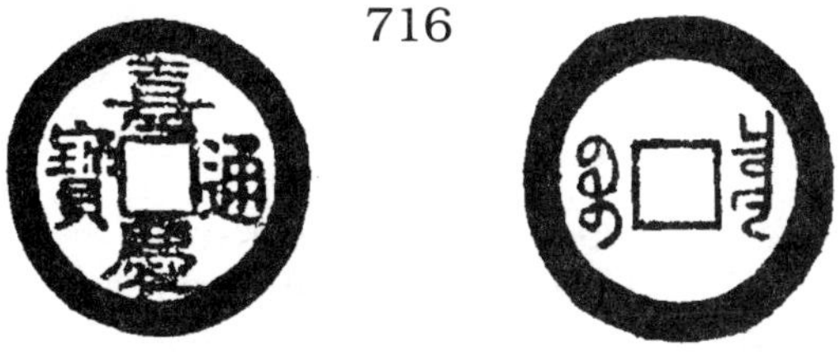

717

718

719

720

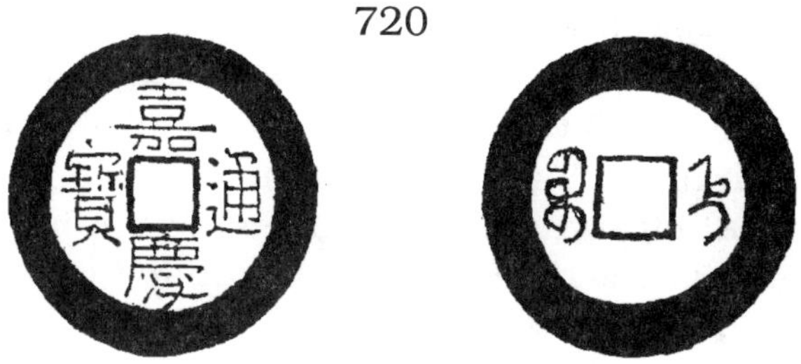

721

722

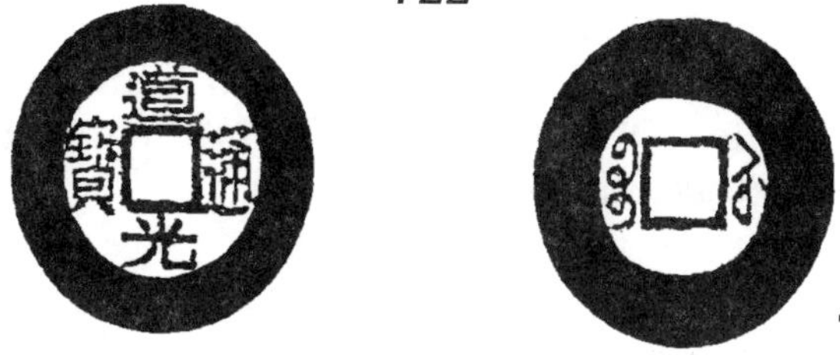

723

	VG	VF
716. Jia Qing Tong Bao S-1489 FD-2336	0.50	1.00
717. Ditto, Chang Ping style, Bao Su Mint	40.00	70.00
718. Ditto, Gui on reverse, Regular script on right & running script on the left FD-2360	100.00	200.00
719. Ditto, Gui in Han script on right & Manchu script on the left FD-2359	300.00	600.00
720. Ditto, Bao Zhi Mint, Large version	100.00	200.00
721. Dao Guang Tong Bao S-1512, FD-2348	0.50	1.00
722. Ditto, Chang Ping style, Bao Su Mint	40.00	70.00
723. Ditto, 2 Cash, Aksu Mint	350.00	700.00

Xian Feng Coins

1851-1861

In his time the Taiping rebellion was spreading like wildfire, engulfing half of the Middle Kingdom, cutting off the copper supply route over which supplies reached the imperial mints. To cope with the copper shortage and mounting military expenditure, the regime resorted to issuing paper money and coins of large denominations. Coins of various denominations and patterns poured forth from the provincial mints. There are over a thousand known varieties and new ones keep popping up every now and then, to the joy of collectors. Other good news for the collector is that the legends on many of the coins were written by renowned calligraphists of the times, sweeping away the stereotyped and lifeless legend writing tradition handed down from the Ming Dynasty through generations of emperors to Dao Guang's time, hence creating a diversity of writing, rendering many of Xian Feng's coins masterpieces of design, such as the coins No. 722 and 723, the legends said to be done by the great brushmaster Dai Chun-shi.

The coins No. 730, 732, 734 & 736 were from a semi-official mint run by Prince Qing Hui. He and others had contributed a large quantity of copper to the regime, and he was allowed to set up a mint. His petition to use a separate mint name other than the official names was not approved of; however, a compromise was reached whereby a moon and star was added on the reverse of his coins which would bear the mint name of the Board of Revenue. Prince Qing Hui's coins conform to minting standards and therefore accepted as official currency.

It is not surprising that among the enormous quantity of existing Xian Feng coins one may find dragons and fish jumbled together. The careful collector may chance upon a very rare engraved master coin or a coin pattern amid a heap of common issues, just the kind of situation that collectors are always dreaming about; one chance in a million.

724

725

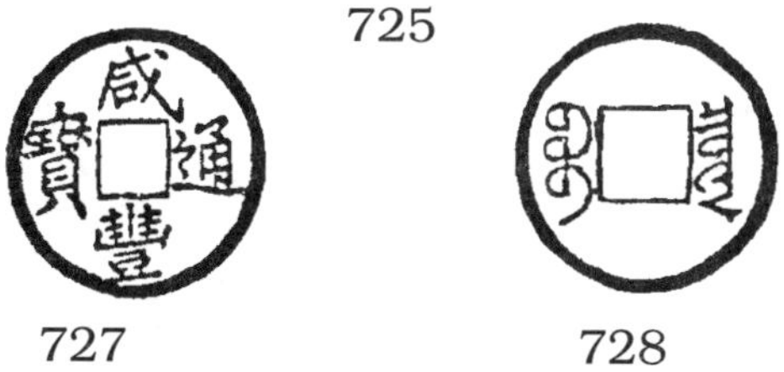

726

727

728

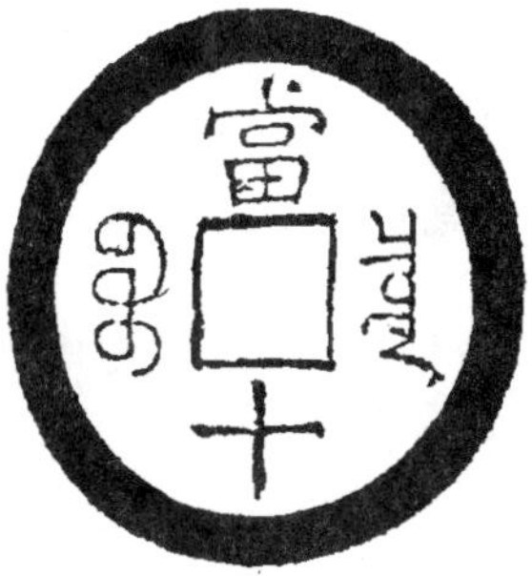

729

730

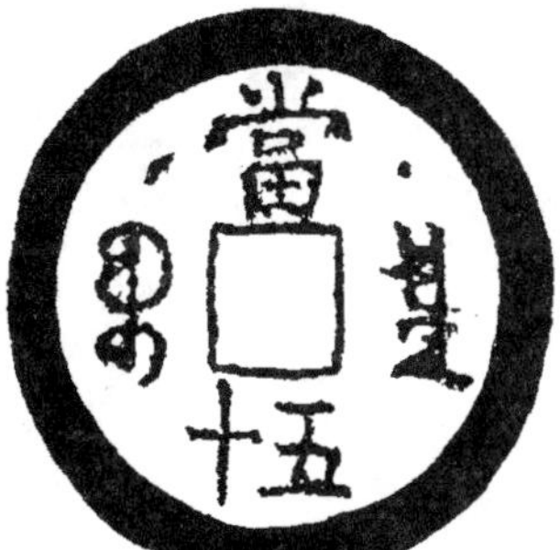

731

732

	VG	VF
724. Xian Feng Tong Bao, S-1534/FD-2411	0.50	1.00
725. Ditto, Dai script, Copper	400.00	800.00
Iron	15.00	30.00
726. Xian Feng Zhong Bao, Value 5, Dai script, FD-2417	1500.00	3000.00
727. Ditto, Value 10, Orthodox script FD-2424	600.00	1000.00
728. Ditto, 10 Cash, Regular script S-1592/FD-2421	5.00	10.00
729. Ditto, Value 50 FD-2427	10.00	20.00
730. Ditto, Value 50, Star & crescent on rev. FD-2429	10.00	20.00
731. Xian Feng Yuan Bao, Value 100 FD-2430	15.00	25.00
732. Ditto, Value 100, Star & crescent on rev. FD-2431	15.00	30.00

733

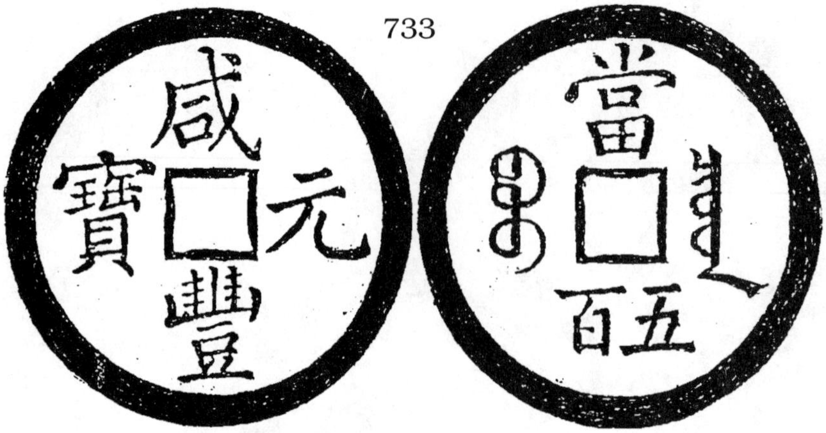

734

735

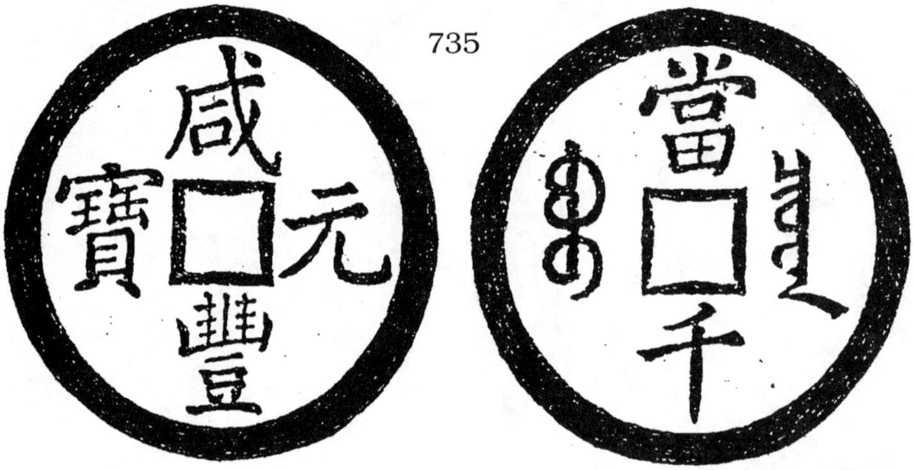

736

	VG	VF
733. Xian Feng Yuan Bao, Value 500. B of Rev. Mint, FD-2433	70.00	120.00
734. Ditto, Value 500, Prince Qing Hui Mint FD-2434	80.00	150.00
735. Ditto, Value 1,000, B of Rev. Mint FD-2435	100.00	200.00
736. Ditto, Value 1,000, Prince Qing Hui Mint, FD-2436	120.00	250.00

N.B. Prince Qing Hui & others made a large donation of copper to the government and petitioned for the rights to open a mint in their own name. The authorities decreed that their mint could only adopt a name already in use, but conceded that a star and crescent be imprinted on the reverse as their mint mark.

737

738

739

740

741

742

	VG	VF
737. Xian Feng Zhong Bao, Value 5, B of Works, FD-2440	15.00	20.00
738. Ditto, Value 10, B of Works, FD-2442	15.00	20.00
739. Ditto, Value 50, B of Works, FD-2443	15.00	25.00
740. Xian Feng Yuan Bao, Value 100, B of Works, FD-2445	15.00	25.00
741. Ditto, Value 500, B of Works, FD-2446	70.00	120.00
742. Ditto, Value 1,000, B of Works, FD-2447	100.00	200.00

Xian Feng 1 Cash Coins

Of the 31 mints in operation during the emperor Xian Feng's reign, 22 mints cast regular issues of copper 1 cash coins for circulation purposes. Two others: the Bao Zhi and Bao De mints issued only iron coins for circulation. The Bao Zhi copper coins (No. 745) are either mother coins or trial pieces; The one or two existing Bao De copper pieces are engraved master coins. (No. 747). The Bao Ji variety also exists. Three samples are presented to the public in the volume of Qing Dynasty coins of the <<Da Xi>> Encyclopedia.

Bao Quan (No. 743) — Board of Revenue.
Bao Yuan (No. 744) — Board of Works.
Bao Zhi (No. 745) — Zhili Province.
Bao Ji (No. 746) — Zhili Province.
Bao De (No. 747) — Dihua (Present day Urumqi), Xinjiang Autonomous Region.
Bao Shaan (No. 748) — Shaanxi Province.
Bao Gong (No. 749) — Gong Chang, Gansu Province.
Bao Chuan (No. 750) — Sichuan Province.
Bao He (No. 751) — Henan Province.
Bao Wu (No. 752) — Wuchang, Hubei Province.
Bao Su (No. 753) — Suzhou, Jiangsu Province.
Bao Zhe (No. 754) — Zhejiang Province.
Bao Fu (No. 755) — Fujian Province.

743

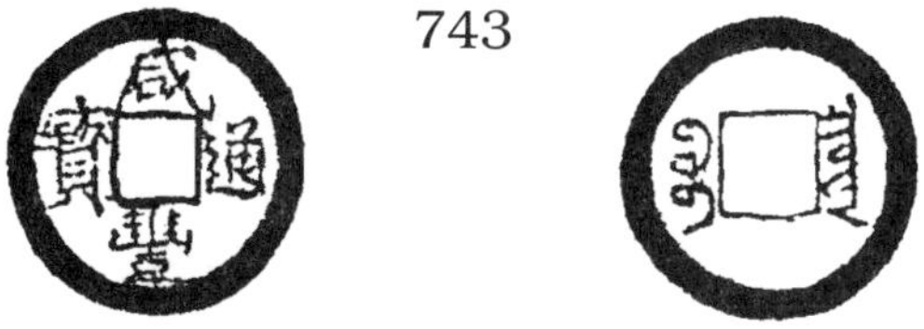

744

745

746

747

748

749

750

751

752

753

754

755

	VG	VF
743. Xian Feng Tong Bao, Dai script Mother coin, Board of Revenue FD-2415	400.00	800.00
Iron	15.00	30.00
744. Ditto, Bao Yuan Mint S-1535/FD-2437	0.50	1.00
745. Ditto, Bao Zhi Mint Copper Pattern	70.00	120.00
Iron	5.00	10.00
746. Ditto, Bao Ji Mint	300.00	600.00
747. Ditto, Bao De Mint Engraved Master coin	1500.00	3000.00
Iron	10.00	20.00
748. Ditto, Bao Shaan Mint S-1550/FD-2496	0.50	3.00
749. Ditto, Bao Gong Mint S-1542/FD-2536	0.50	3.00
750. Ditto, Bao Chuan Mint S-1540/FD-2549	0.50	3.00
751. Ditto, Bao He Mint	20.00	40.00
752. Ditto, Bao Wu Mint S-1539/FD-2470	1.00	3.00
753. Ditto, Bao Su Mint S-1536/FD-2462	1.00	3.00
754. Ditto, Bao Zhe Mint S-1538/FD-2475	0.50	1.00
755. Ditto, Bao Fu Mint S-1549/FD-2507	1.00	3.00

Bao Gui (No. 756) — Guilin, Guangxi Province.
Bao Chang (No. 757) — Nanchang, Jiagxi Province.
Bao Jin (No. 758) — The literary name for Shanxi Province.
Bao Qian (No. 759) — Guizhou Province.
Bao Dong (No. 760) — Dongchuan, Yunnan Province.
Bao Nan (No. 761) — Hunan Province.
Bao Guang (No. 762) — Guangdong Province.
Bao Yun (No. 763) — Yunnan Province.
Bao Tai (No. 764) — Taiwan Province.
Bao Yi (No. 765) — Yili, Xinjiang Province.
Bao Zhao (No. 766) — Local mint, Yunnan Province.
Bao Ji (No. 767) — Jinan, Shandong Province.
Bao Aksu (No. 768) — Aksu, Xinjiang Province.

The Guangdong, Taiwan, and Bao Zhou mints cast only 1 cash coins. The Aksu piece (No. 768) is a pattern. No regulars were issued. The Shandong Bao Ji mint issued very few 1 cash coins. The rubbing shown on the opposite page (No. 767) was provided by courtesy of the <<DA XI>> Editorial Department, Shanghai, China.

756 757 758 759

760 761 762 763

764 765 766 767 768

	VG	VF
756. Xian Feng Tong Bao, Bao Gui Mint, S-1551/FD-2546	0.50	1.00
757. Ditto, Bao Chang Mint S-1537, FD-2504	0.50	1.00
758. Ditto, Bao Jin Mint	1.00	3.00
759. Ditto, Bao Qian Mint FD-25441.00	3.00	
760. Ditto, Bao Dong Mint S-1547/FD-2553	0.50	1.00
761. Ditto, Bao Nan Mint S-1543/FD-2535	1.00	3.00
762. Ditto, Bao Guang Mint	15.00	30.00
763. Ditto, Bao Yun Mint S-1544/FD-2557	0.50	1.00
764. Ditto, Bao Tai Mint FD-2530	10.00	20.00
765. Ditto, Bao Yi Mint	25.00	50.00
766. Ditto, Bao Zhou Mint	15.00	30.00
767. Ditto. Bao Ji Mint	200.00	400.00
768. Ditto, Aksu Mint, Pattern FD-2567	150.00	300.00

769

770

771

772

773

774

	VG	VF
769. Xian Feng Zhong Bao, Value 50, Bao Zhi Mint FD-2452	10.00	20.00
770. Xian Feng Yuan Bao, Value 100, Bao Zhi Mint FD-2453	15.00	25.00
771. Xian Feng Zhong Bao, Value 10, Bao Ji Mint FD-2454	15.00	25.00
772. Ditto, Large version FD-2455	150.00	250.00
773. Ditto, Value 50 FD-2456	50.00	80.00
774. Xian Feng Yuan Bao, Value 100, Bao Ji Mint FD-2457	300.00	600.00

775

776

777

778

779

780

781

	VG	VF
775. Xian Feng Zhong Bao, Value 10, Bao Ji Mint FD-2448	250.00	400.00
776. Ditto, Value 50, Bao Ji Mint FD-2449	250.00	400.00
777. Xian Feng Yuan Bao, Value 100 FD-2450	300.00	600.00
778. Xian Feng Zhong Bao, Value 5, Bao De Mint FD-2531	800.00	1600.00
779. Ditto, Value 10, Iron FD-2532	20.00	40.00
780. Ditto, Value 50, Bao De Mint FD-2533	35.00	50.00
781. Xian Feng Yuan Bao, Value 100, Bao De Mint FD-2534	50.00	80.00

782

783

784

785

786

787

788

	VG	VF
782. Xian Feng Zhong Bao, Value 10, Bao Shaan Mint, FD-2497	2.00	4.00
783. Ditto, Shaan above & 10 below FD-2498	400.00	700.00
784. Xian Feng Yuan Bao, Value 500, Bao Shaan Mint FD-2501	600.00	1200.00
785. Ditto, Value 1000, Bao Shaan Mint FD-2503	700.00	1500.00
786. Xian Feng Zhong Bao, Value 5, Bao Gong Mint FD-2537	5.00	8.00
787. Ditto, Large version	100.00	150.00
788. Xian Feng Yuan Bao, Bao Gong Mint, Value 500 FD-2542	600.00	1200.00
789. Ditto, Value 1,000, Bao Gong Mint, FD-2543		

789

790

791

792

793

794

795

796

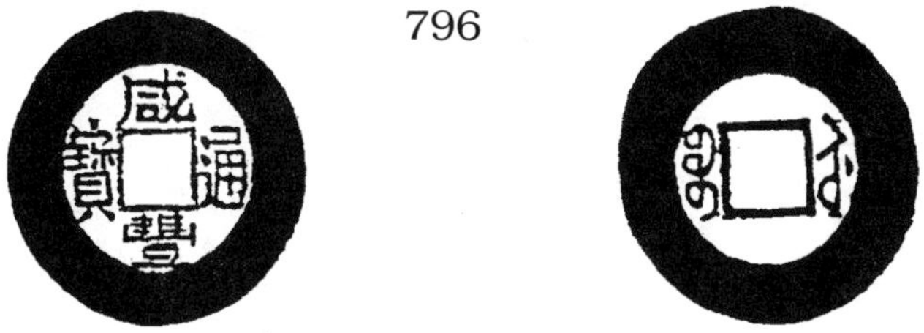

797

	VG	VF
790. Xian Feng Zhong Bao, Value 10, Bao He Mint FD-2491	2.00	5.00
791. Ditto, Value 50, Bao He Mint FD-2492	5.00	10.00
792. Xian Feng Yuan Bao, Value 100, Bao He Mint FD-2493	10.00	20.00
793. Xian Feng Zhong Bao, Value 10, Bao Wu Mint FD-2472	2.00	5.00
794. Ditto, Crescent beside the top character	7.00	14.00
795. Ditto, Value 50, Crescent beside the top character	40.00	80.00
796. Xian Feng Tong Bao, Chang Ping style, Bao Su Mint	50.00	100.00
797. Xian Feng Zhong Bao, Value 5, Bao Su Mint FD-2464	400.00	800.00

798

799

800

801

802

803

804

	VG	VF
798. Xian Feng Zhong Bao, Value 100, Bao Su Mint, S-1594/FD-2465	15.00	30.00
799. Ditto, Top character smaller	100.00	180.00
800. Ditto, Value 20 FD-2466	50.00	80.00
801. Ditto, Value, Top character smaller	300.00	500.00
802. Ditto, Value 50 FD-2468	10.00	20.00
803. Ditto, Legend done in different style	40.00	70.00
804. Ditto, Wide rim, Pattern	250.00	400.00

805

806

807

808

809

810

	VG	VF
805. Xian Feng Yuan Bao, Bao Su Mint FD-2469	12.00	25.00
806. Ditto, Wide rim, Pattern	300.00	500.00
807. Xian Feng Zhong Bao, Value 50, Bao Chuan Mint FD-2551	5.00	8.00
808. Xian Feng Yuan Bao, Value 100, Bao Chuan Mint FD-2552	5.00	10.00
809. Xian Feng Zhong Bao, Value 10, Bao Chang Mint FD-2505	2.00	5.00
810. Ditto, Value 50, Bao Chang Mint S-1590, FD-2506		

811

812

813

814

815

816

817

818

	VG	VF
811. Xian Feng Zhong Bao, Value 20, Bao Zhe Mint, Value above & 20 below FD-2479	1000.00	2000.00
812. Ditto, Value 30, Bao Zhe Mint FD-2481	—	—
813. Ditto, Value 40, Bao Zhe Mint FD-2483	—	—
814. Ditto, Value 50, Bao Zhe Mint FD-2485	—	—
815. Ditto, 100 on the top FD-2487	3500.00	—
816. Ditto, 10 on the top, VR	—	—
817. Xian Feng Zhong Bao, Value 10, Bao Fu Mint FD-2510	5.00	10.00
818. Ditto, Value 20 FD-2517	15.00	25.00

819

820

821

822

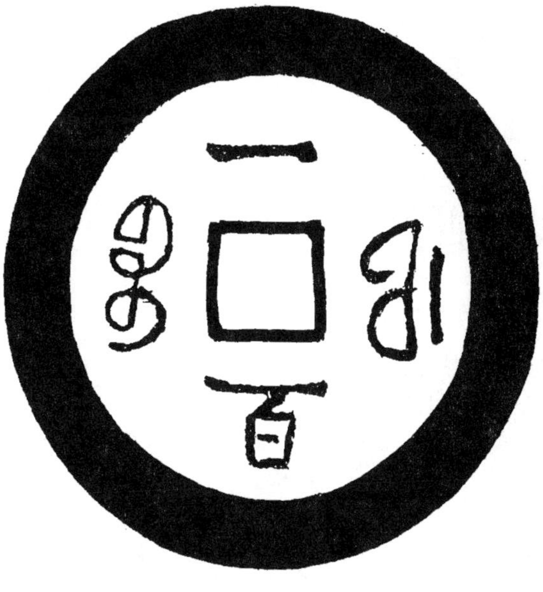

	VG	VF
819. Xian Feng Yuan Bao, Value 50, Fujian Mint FD-2523	50.00	100.00
820. Ditto, Value 100 S-1589/FD-2526	150.00	300.00
821. Ditto, Value 50, Different in size & style FD-2522	500.00	1000.00
822. Ditto, Value 100, Different in size & style FD-2527	700.00	1400.00

823

824

825

	VG	VF
823. Xian Feng Zhong Bao, Value 100 Fujian Mint FD-2528	300.00	600.00
824. Ditto, Value 5, Weight 2 Mace & 5 Candareens imprinted on the rim, FD-2509	1000.00	2000.00
825. Ditto, Value 100, Weight 5 Taels imprinted on the rim FD-2525	3500.00	—

826

827

828

829

830

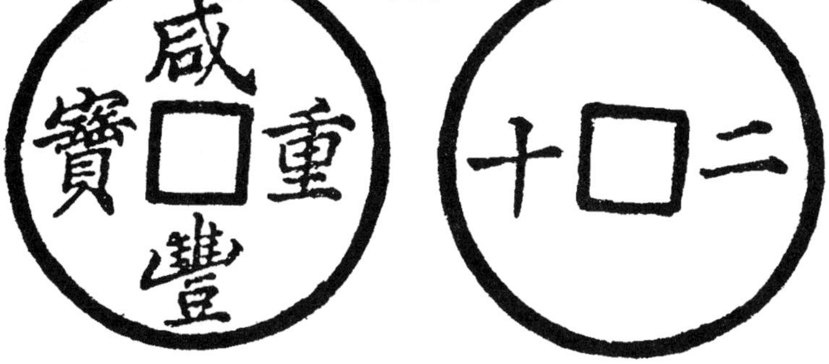

831

	VG	VF
826. Xian Feng Zhong Bao, Value 10, Weight 5 Mace on 4 corners of the field Fujian Mint FD-2515	700.00	1400.00
827. Ditto, Value 20, Weight 1 Tael on the field FD-2521	800.00	1600.00
828. Ditto, Weight 2 Taels & 5 Maca on the field FD-2524	1000.00	2000.00
829. Ditto, Value 100, Weight 5 Taels on the field, VR	—	—
830. Ditto, 20 on reverse	3500.00	—
831. Ditto, 5 Cash above, 3 Mace & 5 Candareens below	700.00	1400.00

832

833

834

835

836

837

	VG	VF
832. Xian Feng Zhong Bao, Value 50, Bao Gui Mint FD-2548	100.00	200.00
833. Ditto, Bao Di Mint, Value 10, Large FD-2564	50.00	80.00
Small	2.00	5.00
834. Ditto, Value 80	900.00	1800.00
835. Ditto, Value 4, Bao Yi Mint FD-2458	50.00	100.00
836. Ditto, Value 50 FD-2460	40.00	80.00
837. Xian Feng Yuan Bao, Value 100 Bao Yi Mint FD-2461	50.00	100.00

838

839

840

841

842

843

	VG	VF
838. Xian Feng Yuan Bao, Value 100, Aksu Mint FD-2574	30.00	60.00
839. Xian Feng Zhong Bao, Value 50, Kaxgar Mint FD-2565	120.00	200.00
840. Xian Feng Yuan Bao, Value 100, Kaxgar Mint FD-2566	120.00	200.00
841. Ditto, Value 100, Kuche Mint FD-2582	60.00	100.00
842. Xian Feng Zhong Bao, Value 50, Yarkant Mint FD-2576	60.00	120.00
843. Xian Feng Yuan Bao, Value 100, Yarkant Mint FD-2578	700.00	1400.00

The Qi Xiang & Tong Zhi Coins
Of Emperor Tong Zhi
1862-1875 A.D.

This emperor had two reign titles, Qi Xiang and Tong Zhi, the first given him by his father Xian Feng, and the other by his mother Ci Xi after she emerged the victor in the power struggle in 1861.

As the emperor Xian Feng lay dying, he entrusted his eitht-year-old son to his eight ministers, and decreed that the reign title was to be Qi Xiang — Good luck. Xian Feng died a few days later, in August, 1861. Meanwhile, coins bearing the reign title of Qi Xiang were being minted to be ready for the inaugural ceremonies scheduled for Lunar January of the coming year. This was not to happen, however, as three months later in November, Ci Xi staged a palace coup, did away with the eight ministers, and changed the reign title to Tong Zhi — To administer together (with Empress Ci An, wife of the emperor Xian Feng). Ci Xi was only a concubine at the time, but as the boy emperor-to-be's mother, she was empress dowager by right.

The Qi Xiang coins were already coming out of the mint, but orders came for them to be remelted for casting coins with the new reign title of Tong Zhi. Since the time of their existence was only three months and few escaped the furnace, they are very scarce today. Judging from the fact that the Qi Xiang coins are much larger and heavier than either the Xian Feng coins that came before and the Tong Zhi species that followed afterwards, they were probably intended to be commemoratives specially prepared for the inaugural ceremonies and not for general circulation.

Along with those listed here, two other interesting species were also cast by the official mint, a double-faced coin with the Qi Xiang legend on both sides of the coin, and the double legend variety with Qi Xiang Zhong Bao on one side and Tong Zhi Zhong Bao on the other. It is said that three years after the withdrawal of the Qi Xiang coins, some nobles presented a petition for some of the coins to be recast for souvenirs. Their request was granted, and that is how the two above-mentioned varieties came into being. They are recognized by numismatists and eagerly sought after as collectibles.

At the time the boy emperor Tong Zhi ascended the throne, the flames of the Taiping rebellion were still ablaze and the economy dislocated, the production of cash coins had decreased sharply. Of the mints still in operation some minted only small amounts of one cash coins. The larger denominations of the Henan and Shaanxi mints do not exist other than patterns or mother coins. Aside from the 10 cash coins issued by the Board of Revenue, Board of Works and the Gansu (Gongchang) mint, those from other mints are either mother coins or Board-issued patterns.

844

845

846

847

848

849

850

851

852

	VG	VF
844. Qi Xiang Tong Bao, Bao Quan Mint	800.00	1600.00
845. Ditto, Bao Yuan Mint, Large FD-2584	—	—
Small	600.00	1200.00
846. Ditto, Bao Gong Mint, VR	—	—
847. Ditto, Value 10, Bao Quan Mint FD-2588	1200.00	2400.00
848. Ditto, Bao Yuan Mint, Value 10 FD-2587	700.00	1500.00
849. Tong Zhi Tong Bao FD-2590	0.50	1.00
850. Ditto, Shun on reverse, Bao Zhou Mint	10.00	20.00
851. Ditto, Xin above & 10 below, Xinjiang	5.00	10.00
852. Ditto, Value 4, Bao Yi Mint, Pattern, FD-2596	400.00	800.00

Guang Xu Coins
1875-1908 A.D.

During his reign, machine-struck coins were appearing on the scene and circulating alongside the traditional mould-cast species. Western technology and machinery were introduced into China. The order of the day was changing, with coppers taking over the role of the square-holed cash coins. Surprisingly, in this period of transition the variety of design and artistry of the legend writing of the emperor Guang Xu's coins surpassed those of his predecessors. The brass mother coin from the Fujian mint, shown here, stands in elegance and forcefulness in comparison with those of the Song emperor Hui Zong.

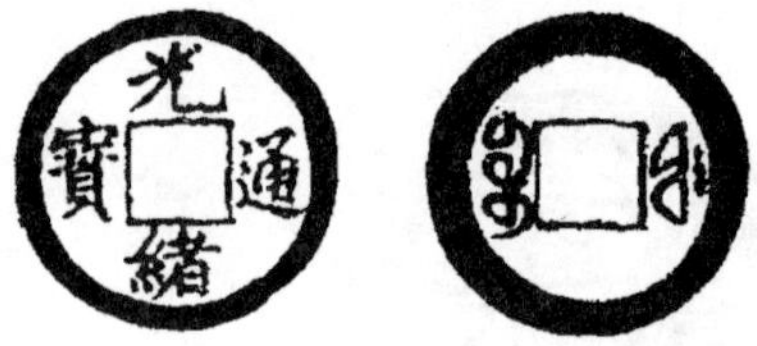

At that time, the minting of 10 cash was decreasing in amount and the issuing of coins of larger denominations had stopped altogether. Only 3 mints had cast regular issues of 10 cash — the Board of Revenue, Board of Works, and the Jiangsu mint. Of the others, only Board issued mother coins and patterns exist. The most commonly met machine-struck coins are from the following mints: Guangdong (No. 849), Fujian, Tianjin, Zhejiang and Zhangzhou. The coins minted by the Board of Revenue, Board of Works (No. 850), Jizhou, Zhili (No. 851) and Ningbo mints, and the Fengtian specie are trial pieces; and so is the "Long live the Emperor" coin from the Jiangnan mint (No. 853).

853

854

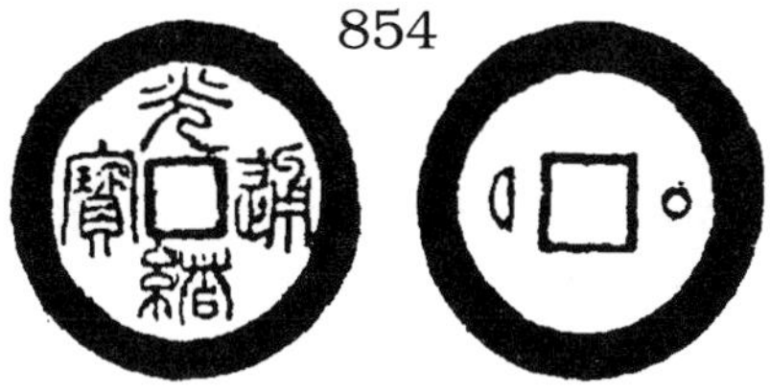

855

856

857

858

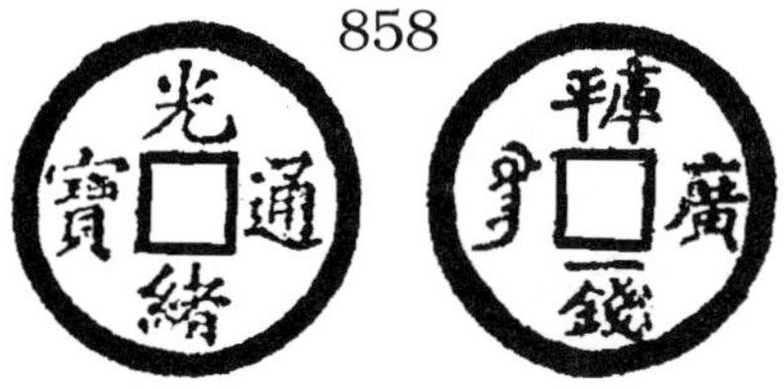

859

860

861

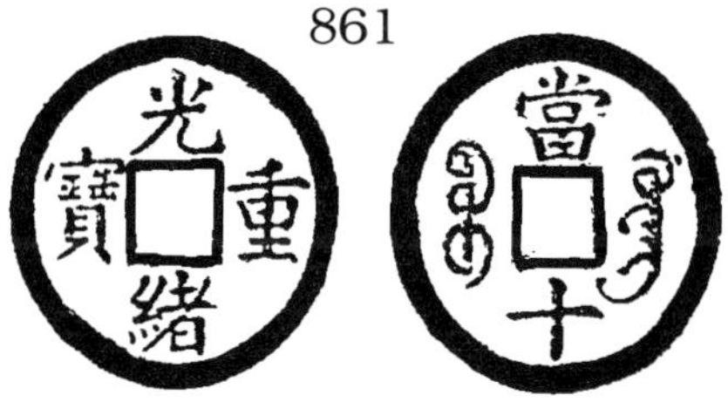

	VG	VF
853. Guang Xu Tong Bao FD-2615	0.50	1.00
854. Ditto, Seal script, Star & moon on reverse FD-2632	80.00	160.00
855. Ditto, Guang in Han & Manchu script on reverse	400.00	800.00
856. Ditto, Jin on top, Bao Yuan Mint	2.00	5.00
857. Ditto, Cun below, Bao Dong Mint FD-2625	20.00	35.00
858. Ditto, Ku Ping above & 1 Mace below, Machine-struck S-1588, FD-2631	0.50	1.00
859. Ditto, Bao Yuan Mint, struck coin	150.00	250.00
860. Ditto, Bao Zhi Mint, struck coin	100.00	200.00
861. Value 10, Bao Guang Mint, struck coin	250.00	500.00
862. Tian Zi Wan Nian, Jiang Nan Trial Minting & Value 10 on reverse	900.00	1500.00

862

Xuan Tong Coins
1908-11 A.D.

This ruler (a.k.a. Pu Yi), the last of Chinese emperors, experienced a dramatic change from emperor to citizen, all along living a colorful and secure life, no harm done to him by either the Guomindang Nationalists, Japanese or the Chinese Communists. By this time machine-struck coppers and silver dollars had taken over the role of the square-holed cash, and the few that were minted by the Board of Revenue played only a symbolic role, minted in consideration for the livelihood of the mint workers who would otherwise be left without a job (Nos. 854-5). The coins come in two sizes, the larger species preferred by collectors over the smaller ones. The Yunnan mint cast some 1 cash for circulation, and the Kuche mint in Xinjiang some 10 cash varieties. Some machine-struck coins were still being produced by the Guangdong and Fujian mints.

In the early years of the Republic of China, square-holed coins were still cast in Yunnan (Nos. 856-7) and Fujian (Nos. 858-9), but it was not until 1945 that the last square-holed coin passed away into oblivion in Annam after the founding of the Vietnam Republic.

863

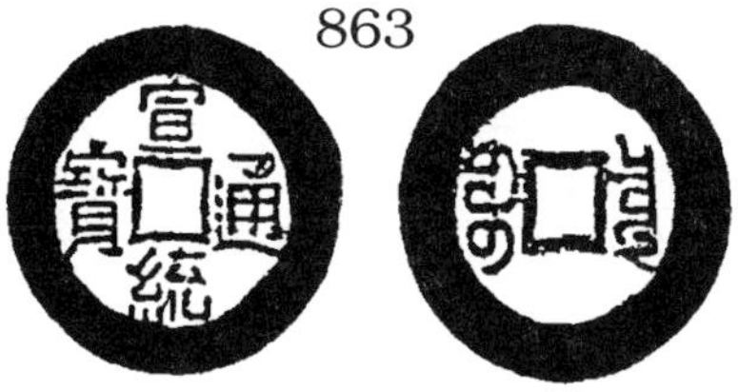

864

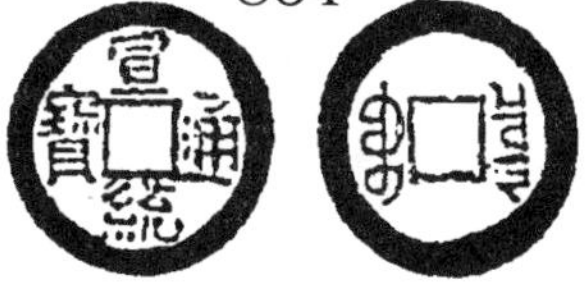

865

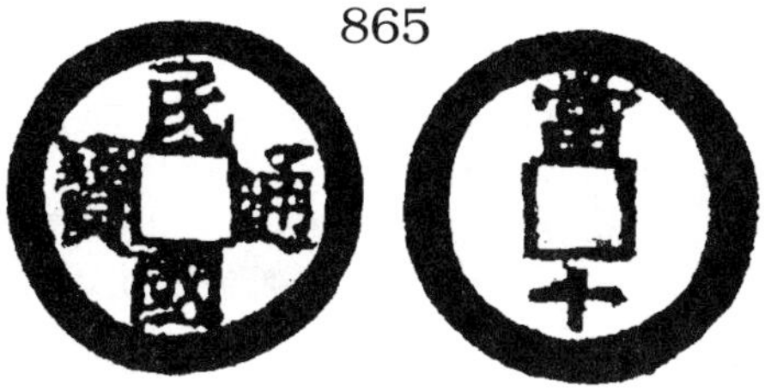

866

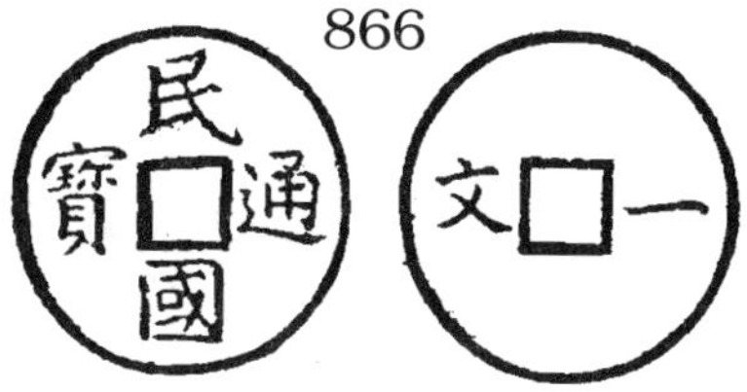

867

868

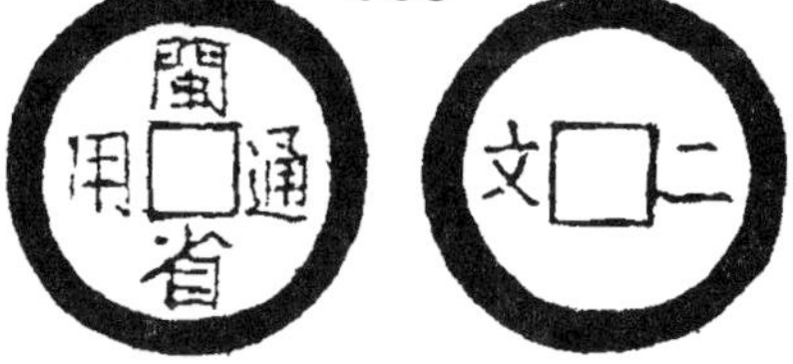

	VG	VF
863. Xuan Tong Tong Bao, Bao Quan Mint FD-2662	15.00	30.00
864. Ditto, Small version FD-2663	2.00	5.00
865. Min Guo Tong Bao, Value 10 on reverse	10.00	20.00
866. Ditto, 1 Cash on reverse	100.00	200.00
867. Fujian Province Mintage, 2 Cash on reverse	600.00	1200.00
868. Province of Min Currency, 2 Cash on reverse	600.00	1200.00

- The Min Guo Zhong Bao 10 cash shown here is a new specie discovered quite recently. It is not yet rated.

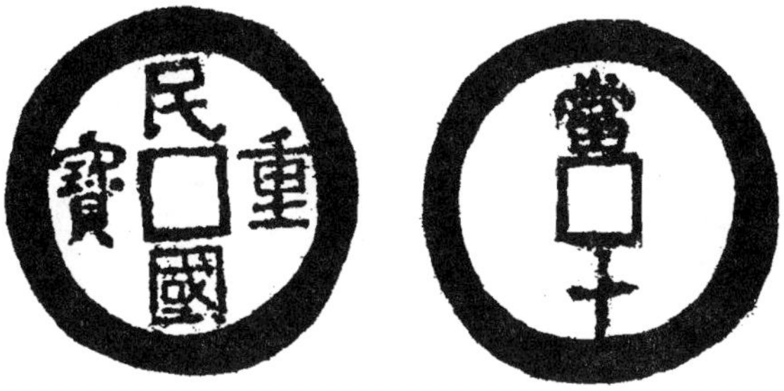

TAIPING REBEL COINS
1851-64 A.D.

The Taiping rebellion could have been a success story for its leader Hong Xiu-quan, an adherent of Christianity and advocate of equal rights among men and women. The area south of the Yangtze River had fallen into his hands. He had only to cross the river and strike while the iron was still hot, and the Qing empire would be no more. Instead, he settled down in Nanjing, set up his capital, and went about granting titles and favors to his generals, stirring up contention and causing the rebel ranks to split up, opening a gap through which the Qing troops wedged in and terminated the Heavenly Kingdom.

The coins of the Taipings come in many varieties, as the central government did not issue standardized patterns to the local levels, they took matters into their own hands and cast coins following their own inclinations. Coin No. .D.; together with the coin No. 879, the two are quite rare and interesting. The rarest of the Taiping coins is possibly Coin No. 876 with the simplified form of Bao (the character to the left of the center hole).

Of the Taiping coins, three sets deserve special mention:

- The legend done in Song script, with Sheng Bao on the reverse (Nos. 860-63).
- The legend cast in uneven relief, that is, some parts of the surface of the characters are higher and some lower (Nos. 866-69).
- The coins with wide rims, and the legend done in regular script (Nos. 872-74).

869

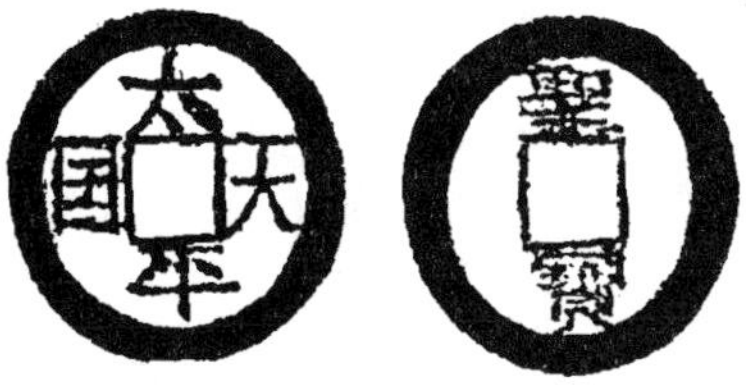

870

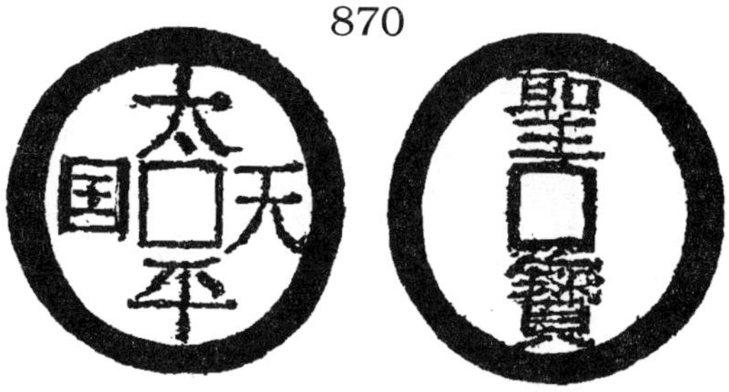

871

872

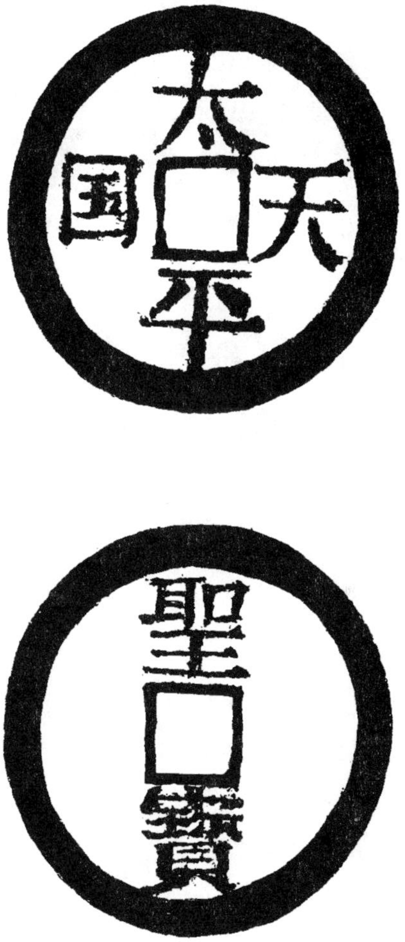

873

874

	VG	VF
869. Tai Ping Tian Guo, Legend in Song script, FD-2669, Sheng Bao on reverse.	40.00	80.00
870. Ditto, The 2nd in this set in Song script, FD-2673	100.00	200.00
871. Ditto, The 3rd in the set FD-2676	200.00	400.00
872. Ditto, The 4th in the set FD-2689	350.00	700.00
873. Tian Guo, Tong Bao on reverse, R	4000.00	—
874. Ditto, Sheng Bao on reverse S-1608/FD-2685	50.00	100.00

875

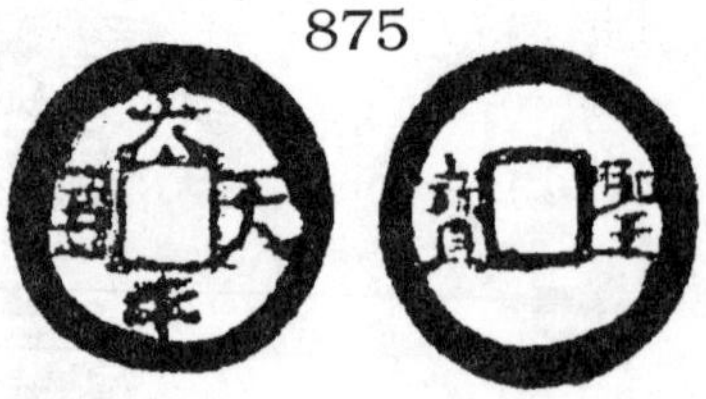

876

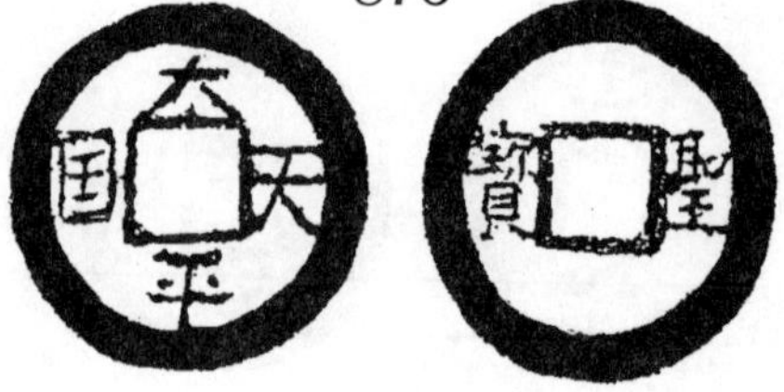

877

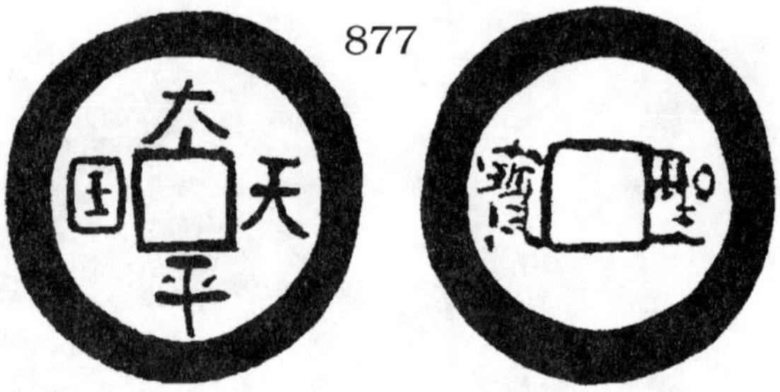

878

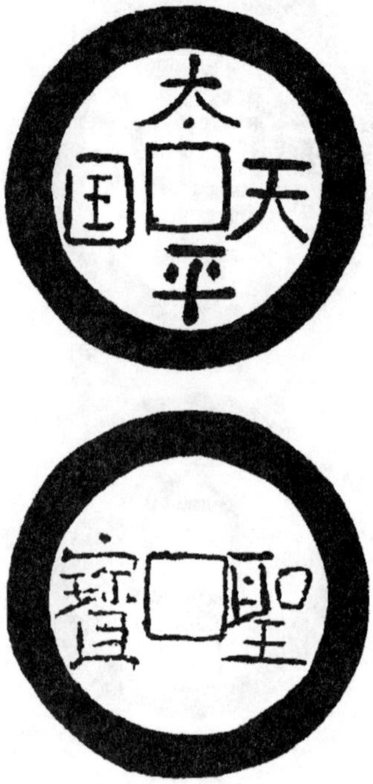

879

880

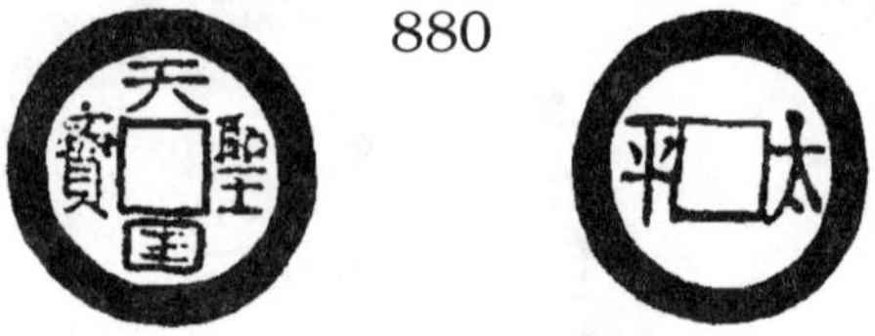

	VG	VF
875. Tai Ping Tian Guo, Sheng Bao on reverse, Legend cast in uneven relief S-1606	200.00	400.00
876. Ditto, The 2nd in this set of 4 in uneven relief FD-2671	70.00	140.00
877. Ditto, The 3rd in the set FD-2675	120.00	240.00
878. Ditto, The 4th in the set FD-2677	450.00	800.00
879. Tian Guo Tai Ping, Sheng Bao on reverse, Legend in Song script	1200.00	2400.00
880. Tian Guo Sheng Bao, Tai Ping on reverse, FD-2679	30.00	60.00

881

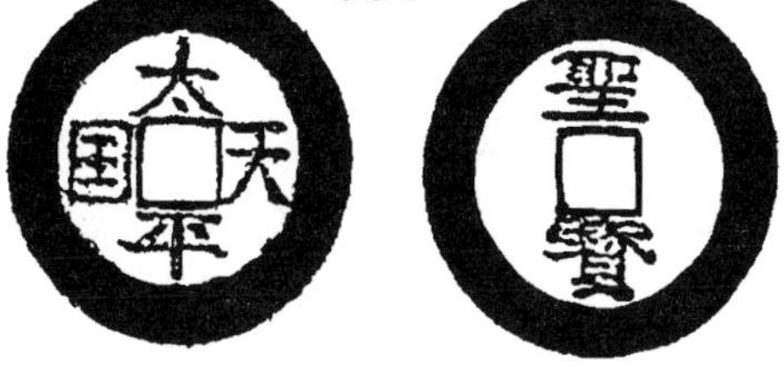

882

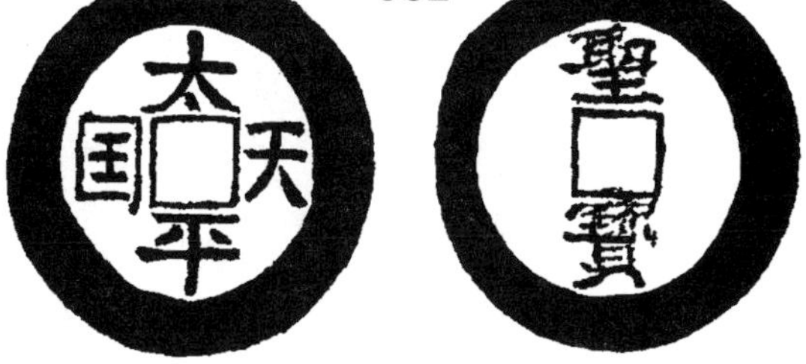

883

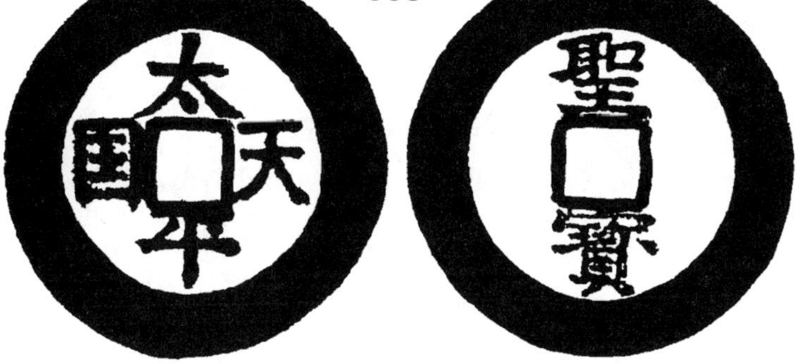

884

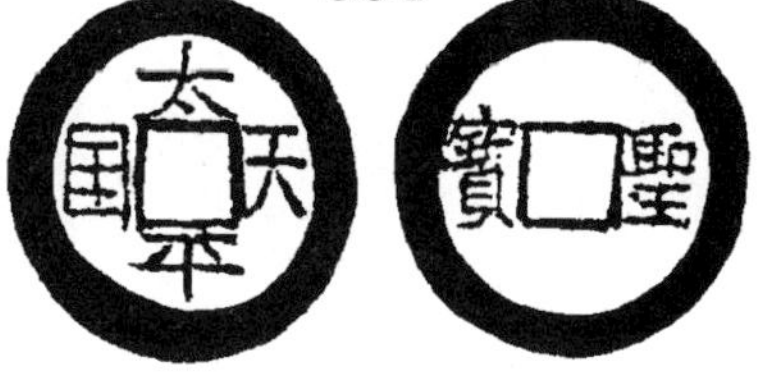

885

886

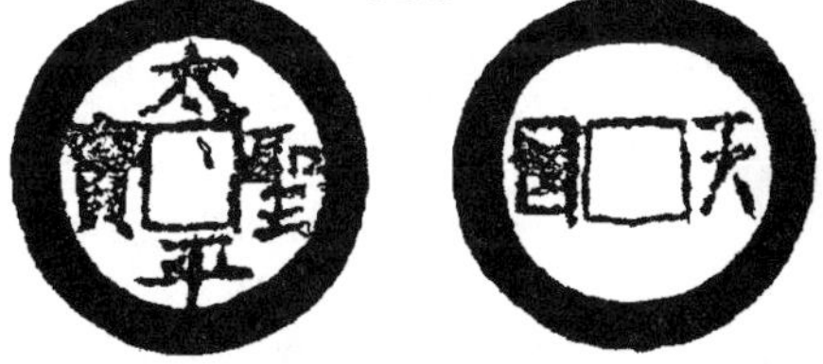

887

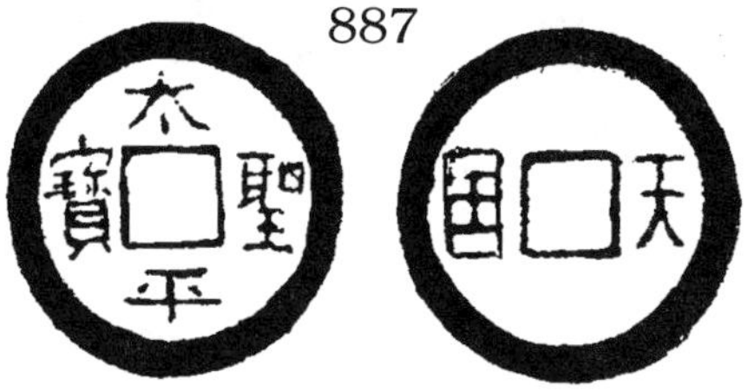

888

	VG	VF
881. Tai Ping Tian Guo, Sheng Bao on reverse, The 2nd of this wide-rimmed set in regular script FD-2672	35.00	70.00
882. Ditto, The 3rd in the set FD-2674	90.00	180.00
883. Ditto, The 4th in the set FD-2688	150.00	300.00
884. Tai Ping Tian Guo, Sheng Bao on reverse, FD-2684	15.00	30.00
885. Tai Ping Sheng Bao, Tian Guo on reverse, Bao in simplified form FD-2668	1500.00	3000.00
886. Ditto, Bao in orthodox script FD-2687	20.00	40.00
887. Ditto, Different style	40.00	80.00
888. Tian Guo, Sheng Bao on reverse FD-2683	500.00	1000.00

OTHER REBEL COINAGE AND TOKENS

After the Opium War of 1840, increased taxation led to peasant revolts. With the Taiping movement as example and mainstay, many factions sprang up overnight, some with their own regimes and monies.

• Chen Kai & Li Wen-mao — They formed the Triads in Guangxi Province, setting up the Da Cheng Kingdom in 1854 and cast the coin No. 891. After Chen's death in 1855, Li issued the Ping Jing series (Nos. 880-83). His faction is a branch of the Heaven & Earth Society.

• Heaven & Earth Society — The society operated mainly in Zhejiang and Fujian Province, issuing coins Nos. 884-9. The legend means Heavenly Court, and those on coins No. 885-7 Emperor.

• Shanghai Dagger Society — Founded by Liu Li Chuan in 1883. Its members carried daggers and occupied Shanghai by stealth in 1854, setting up the Da Ming Heavenly Kingdom. Their coins read the same as the Tai Ping Tong Baos of the Song Dynasty, but cast with a different alloy: yellow copper, not bronze. The first issue had a plain reverse; later issues had a sun and moon or the character Ming on the reverse, an indication of their objective — to chase away the Manchus and restore the Ming Dynasty, which the character and the symbols stand for.

• The Hao Army — Minted by Zhang Bao-shan in Guizhou Province in 1860.

• Wei Wu Zhi Zhu — The Heaven & Earth Society issued these to their leaders as a reminder for secrecy (Nos. 901-2). The legend means: Only I know; that is enough. This piece is interesting for its unique design. Each of the four characters has a box for one of its components. The center hole makes up for the boxes; thus the Wei is placed on the right side of the hole, the Wu on top, the Zhi to the left, and Zhu below the hole. Some contend that this coin to be just an amulet, with no political meaning. The legend can be read as: I am satisfied, and happy.

• Shui Lu Ping An — Some numismatists contend that this coin was minted by the Boxer rebels in 1900, while others say that it was a charm used by merchants; anyway, it is an interesting piece. The legend means safe passage by land and sea. On the reverse is one of the eight trigrams and weapons used by the boxers.

• Yi Ji Jin Qian — Minted by the Golden Coin Society, a faction of the Heaven & Earth Society (Nos. 904-6). These coins, minted around 1861, served as IDs and were issued to the leaders.

The coins minted by the peasant rebels occupy an important place in Chinese numismatics, as the rebels were fighting for their rights of survival and freedom from oppression. Their short duration, narrow sphere of circulation, historic significance and scanty numbers have always diffused their charms as collectibles.

889

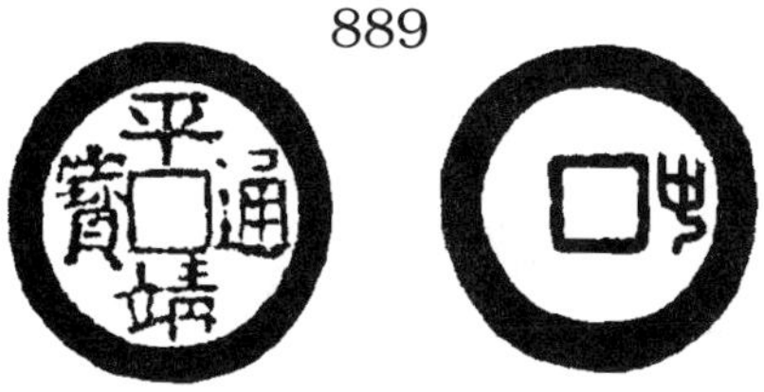

890

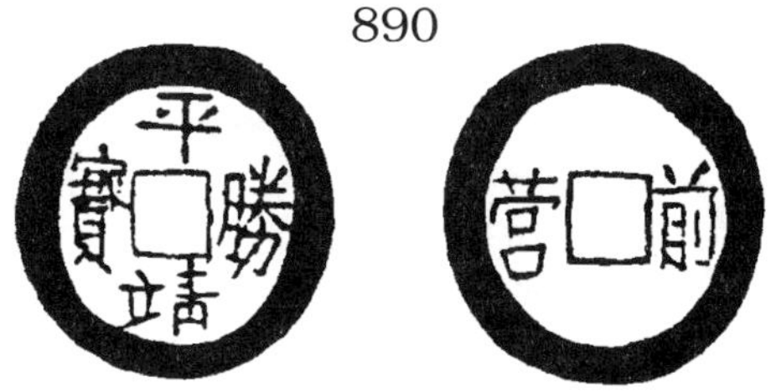

891

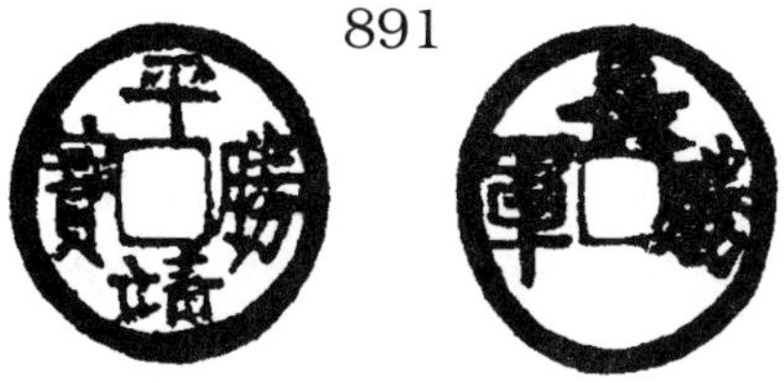

892

893

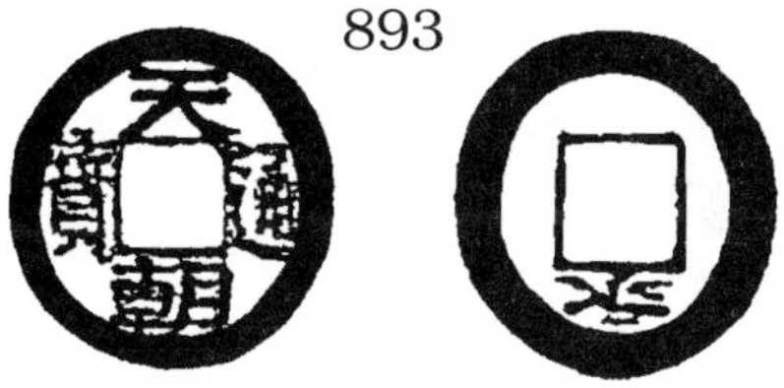

894

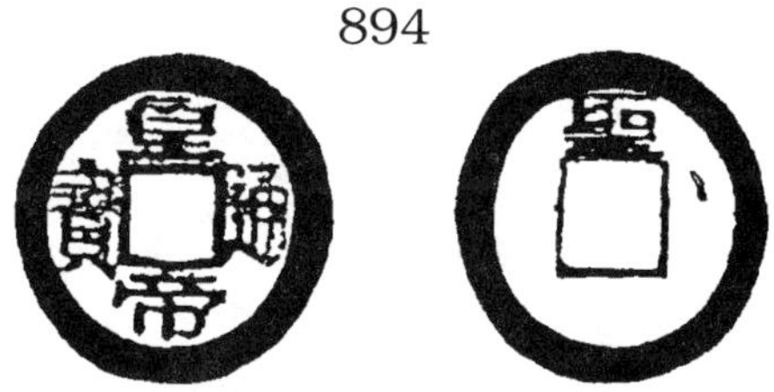

	VG	VF
889. Ping Jing Tong Bao, Zhong on reverse, FD-2691	250.00	500.00
890. Ping Jing Sheng Bao, Qian Ying on reverse, FD-2692	—	—
891. Ditto, Chang Sheng Jun on reverse FD-2699	450.00	900.00
892. Tai Ping Tong Bao, Crescent above & Ming below	100.00	200.00
893. Tian Chao Tong Bao, Inverted Yong on reverse FD-2704	200.00	400.00
894. Huang Di Tong Bao, Sheng on reverse, FD-2707	450.00	900.00

895

896

897

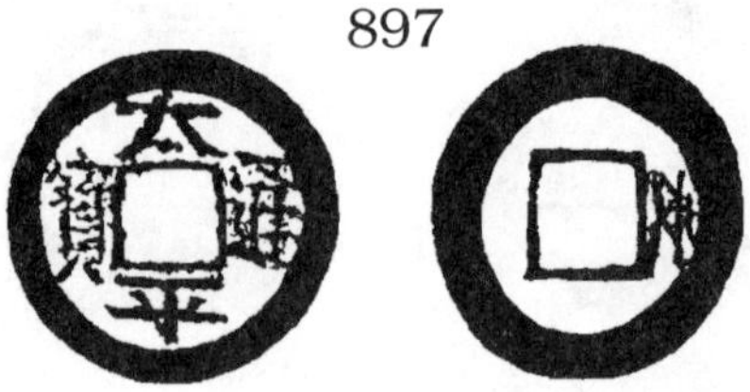

898

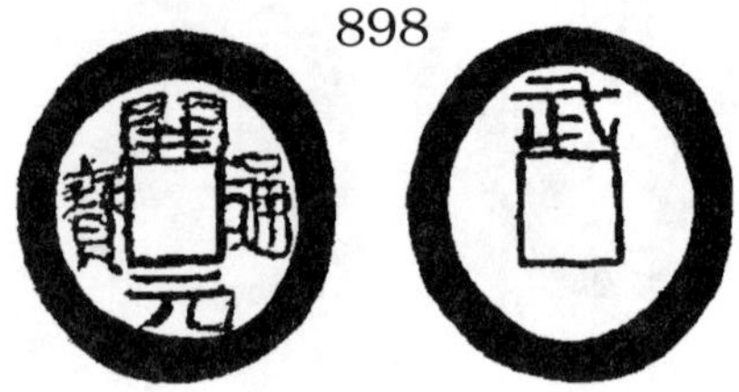

899

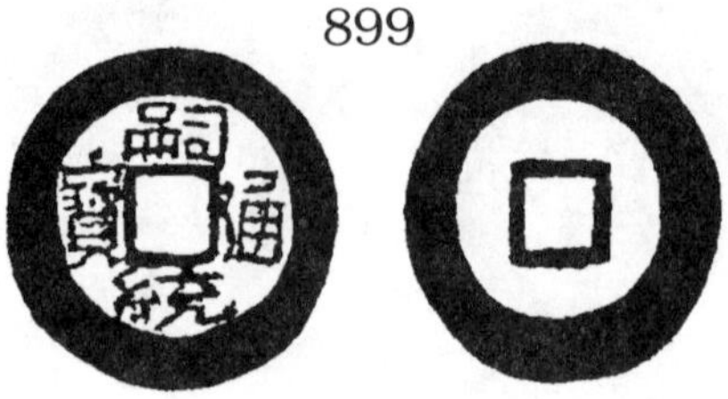

900

	VG	VF
895. Huang Di Tong Bao, Zhe on reverse, FD-2705	150.00	300.00
896. Ditto, small version S-1611	70.00	150.00
897. Tai Ping Tong Bao, Wen on reverse	100.00	200.00
898. Kai Yuan Tong Bao, Wu on reverse, FD-2703	300.00	600.00
899. Si Tong Tong Bao FD-3123	200.00	400.00
900. Ming Dao Tong Bao, Tian on reverse FD-3124	300.00	600.00

901

902

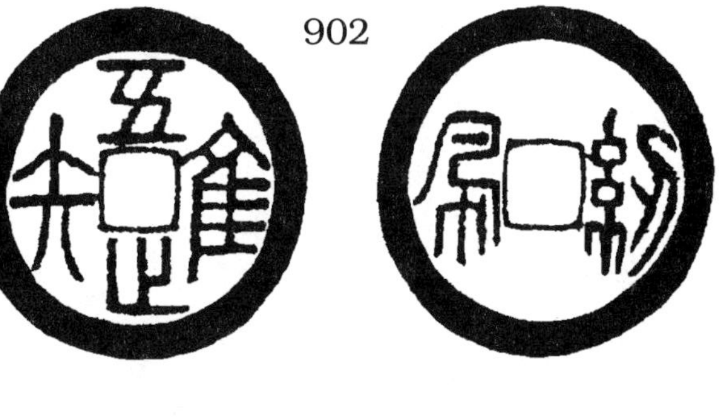

903

904

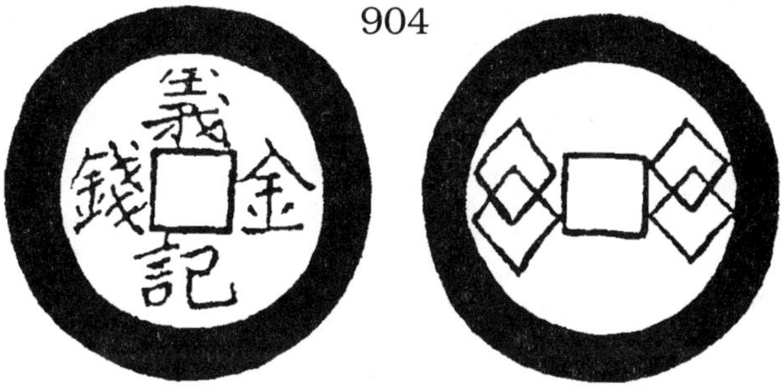

905

906

	VG	VF
901. Wei Wu Zhi Zhu, Regular script	300.00	600.00
902. Ditto, Seal script	150.00	300.00
903. Shui Lu Ping An, Seal script	30.00	60.00
904. Yi Ji Jin Qian	100.00	200.00
905. Ditto, Zhen Zhong Tuan Lian on reverse	1500.00	3000.00
906. Ditto, Tian on reverse	300.00	600.00

OTHER COINAGE

XINJIANG COINAGE

In the Han Dynasty (206 B.C.-221 A.D.), the imperial court sent Zhang Qian as emissary to the Western Region, and through his efforts relations were established with the local tribes. Along the route he traversed the Wu Zhu coins of the Han Dynasty flowed in, and soon local mints were turning out imitations made of red copper, which was plentiful in that region. Some tribes or kingdoms produced Wu Zhu coins displaying symbols or characters from their own cultures.

• Lou Lan Wu Zhu (No. 907) — This coin was unearthed from the ruins of the Lou Lan Kingdom (Kroraimna), which ceased to exist around A.D. 300. The style of the legend dates the coin from the Eastern Han Dynasty (25-221 A.D.). The largeness of the center hole, the red copper, and its size (26.5 mm) sets it apart from the Han Wu Zhu.

• Ba Chu Wu Zhu (No. 908) — This coin from the Ba Chu region is devoid of any legend.

• Yu Tian Wu Zhu (No. 909) — This coin is striking for its rectangular center hole, minted probably during the Eastern Han Dynasty (25-221 A.D.). In ancient times Yutian was also named Khotan (Khotamna). The character on the left is interpreted as the Chinese character Yu, the Yu of Yutian; the one on the right to be Yuan, presumed to stand for currency. Interestingly, the character Yu was also struck on the Kushan drachma, which implies that the two coins were in circulation at about the same time period.

• Kharosthi Wu Zhu (No. 910) — In Chinese, Qiu Ci is the name for this kingdom, which had already established formal relations with the Western Han Dynasty during the emperor Wu Di's reign (141-87 B.C.). Some Chinese numismatists claim the symbol above the center hole stands for 50 in the Kharosthi language and 0 for one tenth of a Zhu; the two symbols together denote the amount of 5 Zhu, which in the Han language reads Wu Zhu. The four varieties are listed here in time order, the last to be minted being the blank coin No. 913.

907

908

909

910

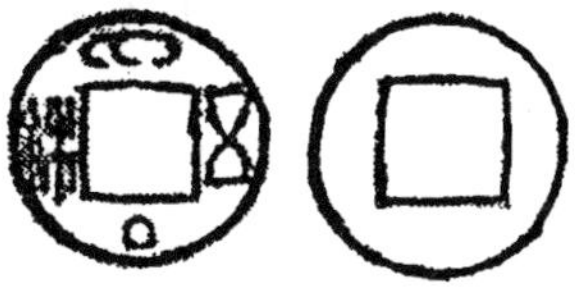

911

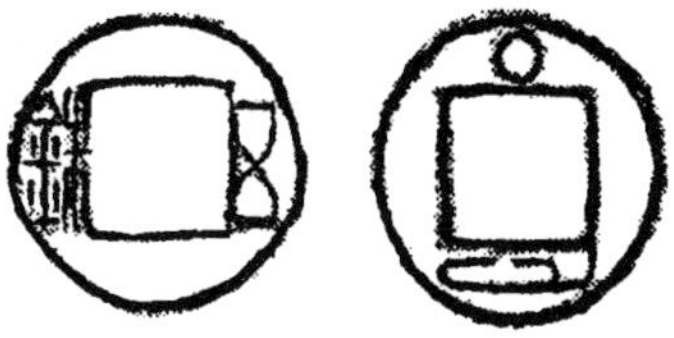

912

913

	VG	VF
907. Lou Lan Wu Zhu	10.00	20.00
908. Wu Zhu, Xinjiang make, No legend	2.00	5.00
909. Yu Tian Rectangular hole Wu Zhu, VR	—	—
910. Kharosthi Wu Zhu, Symbols on obverse	200.00	400.00
911. Ditto, Symbols on reverse	80.00	160.00
912. Ditto, Only symbols, No legend	100.00	200.00
913. Ditto, Blank coin, No legend	5.00	10.00

• Da Li & Jian Zhong coins (Nos. 914-17) — Confronted with the onslaught of the Tufans (Ancient Tibetans) and cut off from their home base, the Tang garrisons stationed in the Western Region started minting their own currency. To express their loyalty to the Tang regime and determination to stand their ground, they used the then current reign titles Da Li and Jian Zhong for the coin legends. As all such coins were made with red copper and few have surfaced outside Xinjiang, it is reasonable to say that the coins were local issues intended for use by the military. The coin No. 916 is the simplified form for Da Li Tong Bao and coin No. 917 for Jian Zhong.

• Gao Chang Ji Li (No. 918) — The Gao Chang Kingdom was founded in A.D. 460 and exterminated by the Tang Dynasty in A.D. 641. One of its kings married a Tang princess and adopted Tang customs, which explains why the coin legend was written in the Han script. The coin is much larger and heavier than regular currency, hence it must be a commemorative.

914

915

916

917

918

	VG	VF
914. Da Li Yuan Bao FD-702	60.00	100.00
915. Jian Zhong Tong Bao FD-704	150.00	250.00
Small	70.00	120.00
916. Da on obverse, Plain reverse	120.00	200.00
917. Zhong on obverse, Plain reverse	150.00	250.00
918. Gao Chang Ji Li FD-1819	400.00	800.00

CENTRAL ASIAN COINS

The coins listed here were unearthed both in Central Asia and Xinjiang, China. In the mid 600s, Chinese expeditions to the Silk Road cities in Central Asia resulted in the incorporation of this region into the map of the Tang Dynasty in 658 A.D. Under the influence of Tang coin culture, Sogdiana produced a series of square-holed coins patterned after the Kai Yuan Tong Bao coins of the Tang Dynasty (Nos. 916-19). Four types are presented below:

1. Sogdian Kai Yuan Tong Bao coin (No. 916) — This specie was first discovered in Pendjikent, Russian Uzbekstan, in the Qing Dynasty. It was first minted in Bukhara and then in Samarkand in the 7th century. The tamga on the right side of the reverse stands for "Almighty (Armuzda)", synonymous with Sultan, or Khaqan. The tamga on the left, according to Smyrnova, the Russian specialist on Central Asian numismatics, originated from the left-hand character on the Wang Mang value 500 knife coin of the Han Dynasty, which in Chinese reads "Dao", meaning knife or sword.

2. Sogdian SySpr MLK' coin (No. 917) — Probably minted around 637-658, or 658-696 A.D.: the khaqan who minted this coin has yet to be identified. The legend reads: Shishpir, Supreme Ruler of Sogdia. The tamga on the left-hand side of the reverse is the clan emblem of the Sogdian royal family in Samarkand, and the one on the right is that of a powerful family in Bactria; the other two have not been identified yet.

3. Sogdian coin (No. 918) — Minted c.698-700. The two tamgas on the coin are the same as those on the aforesaid one. The legend is in Sogdian script.

4. Sogdian coin (No. 919) — Minted 8th-9th century. Sogdian legend/tamga.

916

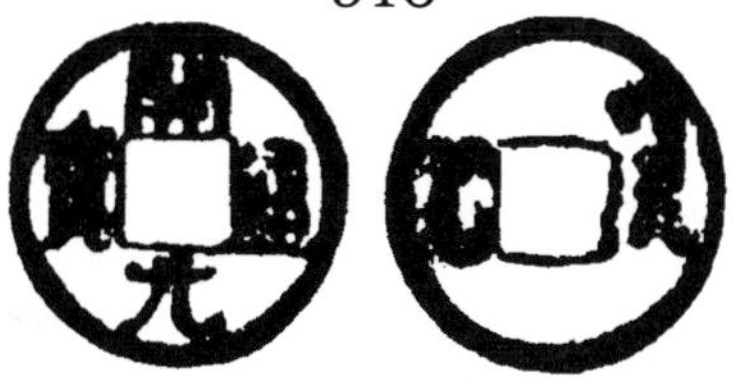

917

918

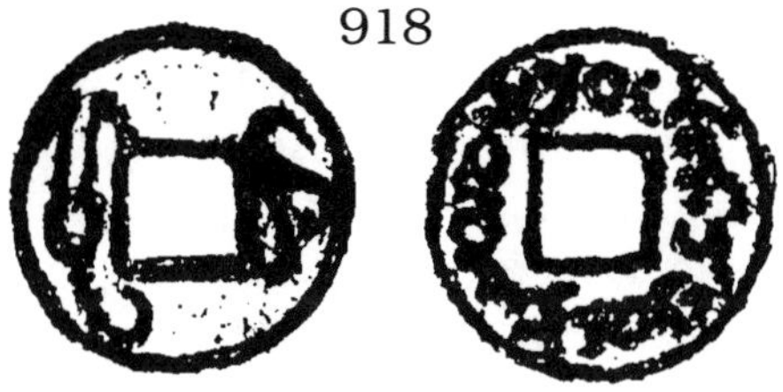

919

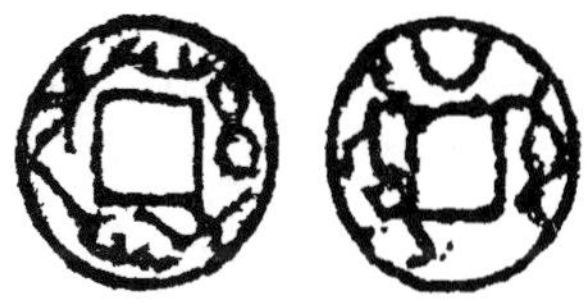

	VG	VF
916. Sogdian Kai Yuan Tong Bao coin	—	—
917. Sogdian coin	—	—
918. Ditto	—	—
919. Ditto	—	—

N.B. These coins have not yet been listed in Chinese catalogs. However, some similar to these were listed in Dmitry Markov's Mail Bid Auction #6, 1998.

TURGIS COINAGE

The Turgis people who minted the coin shown here (No. 920) belonged to one of the collateral branches of the Western Turks. After the collapse of the latter, they settled in the Sujab and Yili valleys in modern northwestern Xinjiang, China. Towards the end of the 7th century, their leader Wu-Che-Lo gained actual control of the 10 clans and the former territories of the Western Turks. The title of Commander of Yao-Chi was conferred on him by the empress Wu Ze Tian of the Tang Dynasty regime. In 706 A.D., the Turgis people set up their own khanate and gained recognition from the Tang court, which conferred titles on their successive khaqans (khans).

920

The Sogdian legend on the obverse may be read as: Currency of the Mighty Turgis Khaqan. The tamga on the reverse, according to some sources, is the clan emblem of the Black Clan.

It was quite improbable that Wu-he-Lo issued the coin, since he did not proclaim himself khaqan and for the fact that the word khaqan was inscribed on it. Although his son So-Ko established the Turgis Kingdom in 706 A.D. and received the title of khaqan from the Tang court in 719 A.D., he was still not a very influential person in the Western Region, and therefore not in the position to mint this coin, which, judging from archaeological findings, was distributed over a rather wide area. After his assassination, a clan chieftain Su-Lu brought together the remnants of his followers, and gradually established his supremacy in the Western Region. The title of khaqan was conferred on him by the Tang court in 719 A.D. Trade flourished in the region during his rule, increasing the demand for hard cash. It was quite reasonable that quantities of the Turgis coins were cast in those times. The tamga on the reverse stands as the emblem of the Black Clan, of which he was a member. That the coin was minted by him is now gaining general recognition.

This coin was first discovered by Mannerheim of Finland in Khotan, Xinjiang, in 1938. It was also discovered by Bernstein in Russian territory. It is listed in Chinese catalogs but with no price grading.

UIGHUR COINS

Before Xinjiang became a province of the Qing Dynasty, it was a vast stage on which numerous empires rose and fell. Among them was the Gaochang Kingdom of the Uighurs, which existed from the 9th to the 14th century. Two coins are identified as currency of this regime. From the different inscriptions on the two coins, it is presumed that the first one was minted in the early years of the khanate and the second one in later years.

921

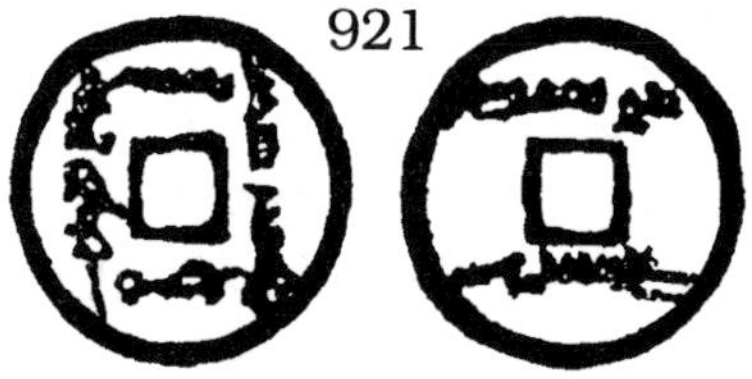

• Uighur Khagan coin (No. 921) — The legend on the obverse reads: Prestigious and divine Uighur Khagan. The reverse reads: circulated by order of Turmis (The Khagan). This coin was unearthed at Beiting (Bekdalish), the kingdom's summer capital. The Uighur script was created around the 8th century, but it was not till the 9th century when the Uighurs moved westward and set up their ethnic kingdom that their script came into general use. In the early years of the khanate, the ruler was called Khagan. In the 12th and 13th centuries, the nomenclature was changed to Yiduhu, and Khagan passed out of use. From inscriptions on wooden artifacts of that period mentioning the khagan's name, the minting date of the coin may be set in the 10th century, before 947 A.D.

922

• Yiduhu coin (No. 922) — The word Yiduhu appears in the legend of this coin, placing the date of its mintage after the 12th century, when it replaced the word Khagan. This coin, therefore, must have been minted 200 years later than the coin No. 921.

The two coins have not yet been listed in Chinese catalogs.

XINJIANG RED COINS

After the suppression of the Junggar Mongols in Xinjiang in the 20th year of the emperor Qian Long (1756 A.D.), the name of the region was changed to Yili, and in 1756 the first Xinjiang mints went into operation, collectively called the Yili mint. The mint drew on the local resources of red copper, and as the coin products were red in color, they were called Xinjiang Red Coins (Nos. 923-5). The coin No. 925 bears the mint name of Zhejiang on the reverse, but in fact it was minted in Xinjiang, the workmanship coarse and the copper red in color were common features of the red coins.

The red coins with the numeral 10 inscribed on the reverse in the shape of a cross (No. 926) were first issued in the 8th year of Dao Guang (1828). They were intended to be Pul coins, worth 10 cash, the Pul long being the currency used by the Junggar Mongols in that area. The early issues were 27-27.2mm and 5.2-5.4g in weight, but they shrank in size to that of a common 1 cash coin soon afterwards; and the local Muslim people accepted them only as such in the marketplace, the authorities passing over the matter in silence.

The coin in question is shown here. The top character on the reverse is the numeral 8, standing for the 8th year of Dao Guang; at the two sides is Akdu mint in Manchu script, and at the bottom is the numeral 10 in the shape of a cross. With the passing of time, the cross (Numeral 10) had to be inscribed on all cash coins issued, as a mark of guarantee, implying that they were government issues, not counterfeits! After the quelling of Yakub beg in 1878, the Aksu and Kuche mints renewed the casting of red coins, but without the cross (Numeral 10) on the reverse. It was not long, however, that the cross appeared on the coins again.

• Hui (Muslim) coin (No. 926) — This coin was minted by the Hui minorities of the Chinese Northwest when they rose up in revolt and issued currency in the Islamic language. The faulty administration of the Qing authorities from within and foreign separatist influence from outside had created unrest among the Muslim population in the Northwest region, and when the peasants in Xinjiang revolted, the Hui people in Gansu and Yunnan followed suit. They maintained their power until 1873, when they were suppressed by local Qing generals, and the invader Yakub Beg by the new governor-general of Xinjiang, Zuo Zhongtang.

• Rashdin coin (Nos. 927-8) — In 1864 the Xinjiang peasants revolted, overthrew the local Qing authorities and set up their own government. Rashdin, a member of the upper religious circles, seized control of the government, proclaimed himself Khan, and issued the coins No. 927 & 928. The legend on the obverse reads: Seyyid Ghazi Rashdin Khan; and on the reverse: minted in the Capital, Kuche. He was slain by the invader Yakub Beg in 1867 A.D.

923

924

925

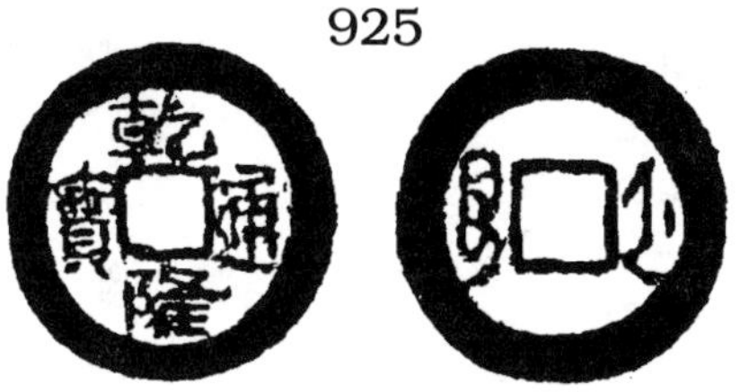

926

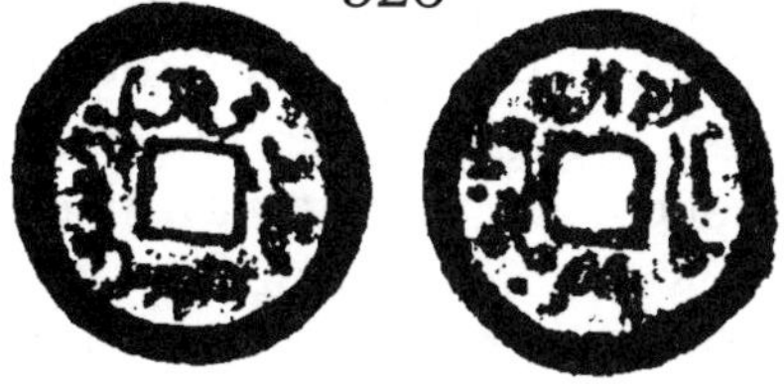

927

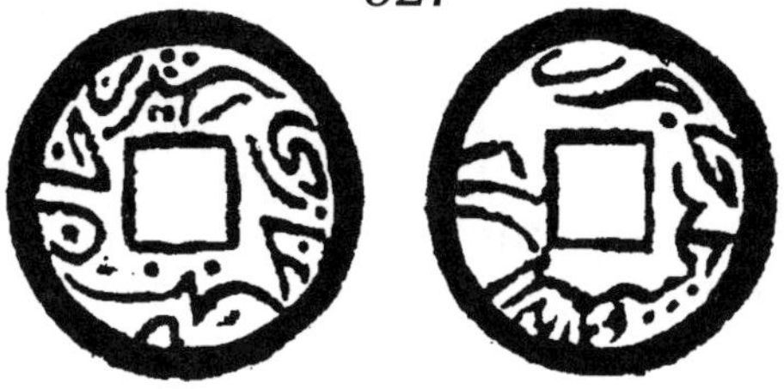

928

	VG	VF
923. Qian Long Tong Bao, Yili Mint	5.00	10.00
924. Ditto, Value 10, Kashgar above & 10 below	5.00	10.00
925. Ditto, Bao Zhe Mint (Xinjiang make)	15.00	30.00
926. Hui (Muslim) coin	—	—
927. Rashdin coin, Large version	20.00	40.00
928. Ditto, Small version	5.00	10.00

TO BE HUNG BY THE HEELS
Coin Politics

People are used to the fact that insurgent regimes issue their own coinage as an extension of politics. There is nothing unusual about this, as they are using the coins inside their own territory, and one may see at a glance who minted the coins. There is, however, an unusual case in which the rebels are invisible, and the coins they minted were used right inside enemy territory, under the noses of the enemy without their suspecting that there was something in the air. The coin shown here is a Tong Zhi Tong Bao specimen. On closer look one sees that the reign title Tong Zhi was placed upside down, Tong at the bottom and Zhi at the top, both facing towards the sky, just like a person hung by the heels. It is not a mint error. Viewing history in retrospect, it was in Tong Zhi's time that the Taiping rebellion was suppressed. The rebellion had been an ethnic war between the oppressed Han people and the overlording Manchus. This coin provided an outlet for the masses to vent their suppressed anger, passing from hand to hand with a tacit message. The war was lost, but the embers smouldered on, to resurge with a vengeance in 1911 and topple the Manchu empire.

Tong Zhi himself was not fated to be hung by the heels; this, however, is exactly what happened to the dictator Mussolini at the end of World War II.

The mint name on the reverse is Zhejiang, the heartland where the flames of the rebellion raged most furiously, the cradle of many secret organizations like the Heaven & Earth Society and the Shanghai Triads (Dagger Society).

SECTION II

Varieties & Variants

This section deals with the variants of certain species that appeared in Section I, some of which exist in several versions, and provide an inexhaustible source of entertainment to collectors. Not all variants are listed, though, for the simple reason that there are so many of them, and not all of them have been made public. To cite an instance: The coin varieties issued by the Qing emperor Xian Feng run into the thousands, and though comprehensive catalogs have been compiled by Chinese and Japanese numismatists on the subject, many serious collectors of Xian Feng coins actually possess this or that specimen not listed in the catalogs.

DESCRIPTION

I. Varieties, Variants & Variations

Varieties — Coins with different legends are varieties.

Variants — When the legend is the same but written in a different style, such a coin is a variant.

Variations — A coin is the same in legend and style as the norm, but minute differences in the treatment of the brushstrokes gives it a different profile. In Section VI the standard Da Guan Tong Bao is shown along with several variations.

II. Calligraphic styles

Upon acquiring a new coin, one compares the legend on it with the corresponding rubbing in the catalog, brushstroke by brushstroke. The legend on the coin is written in one of six different styles of script: regular, seal, Li, running, scribbling or Song.

Regular — This is the kind of script now used in China in everyday correspondence and printed matter. It was used extensively for coin legends during the Song Dynasty. Some superb samples are the Chong Ning No. 275, Da Guan No. 282, Xian Feng No. 743, and Xian Feng No. 1637.

Li — Evolving from the Small Seal Script of the Han Dynasty, this style is dignified and elegant, composed of thin straight lines with no enlargement or tapering at the two ends, except for the long horizontal lines and hooks, which taper upwards at the right tip; cf. Shun Tian Yuan Bao (No. 176).

Seal — The brushstrokes bend and turn, forming circular patterns. There are two kinds of Seal script: the Large Seal and the Small. The former was initiated during the Zhou Dynasty by the historian Zhou; the latter by Shi Huang Di's minister Li Si during the Quin Dynasty. The Large Seal script was used on the ancient knife and spade coins; for the Small Seal script, cf. the Qin Ban Liangs No. 43-46, Wu Zhu No. 57, Wang's coins No. 68-90, Yong Tong Wan Guo (No. 136), and Tai He Zhong Bao (No. 409).

Running — Some of the brushstrokes run into each other and the characters are somewhat simplified. This style is usually used in hurried writing to save time. Chinese calligraphists have brought into play its linear qualities and out of it was created an exotic art form of exquisite beauty; cf. Yuan You Tong Bao 3 cash (Nos. 1509 & 1512).

Scribbling — This is a cipherlike variation of the running script; the characters are further simplified and so distorted that only a person with some training can recognize them, which arouses a reminder of the shorthand used by stenographers. Not only the strokes but the characters run into each other as they race down the paper. Compare the Zhi He Yuan Bao in Running script (No. 204) with the one in Scribbling script (No. 206).

Song — As presented on pp. 74

IRON COINS OF THE SOUTHERN SONG REGIME

When the Jins occupied the Song territory north of the Yangtse river and led away the two Song emperors as hostages, the remnants of the royal family fled across the river and set up the Southern Song Dynasty. The two regimes stood facing each other in a deadlock, the Jins without the military might to advance any further, and treason filling the air at the Song court. The iron coins of the Southern Song was a product of the currency war that ensued.

Being alerted that the Jins were sneaking Song coins across the river for their own use, the Song regime ordered all mints bordering the river to mint and circulate iron coins. This proved a bonanza to the Jins, who were in short supply of iron to forge their weapons. This time the Songs countermanded by adding zinc to the iron, making it too soft for military use. Listed here are the names and locations of 34 of the mints; not all of them had their names imprinted on the reverse of the coins.

春 Chun — Quchun mint, Hubei.
同 Tong — Tongan mint, Anhui.
邛 Qiung — Huimin mint, Sichuan.
利 Li — Lizhou mint, Sichuan.
漢 Han — Hanyang mint, Hubei.
雅 Ya — Baizhang mint, Sichuan.
嘉 Jia — Fengyuan mint, Sichuan.
泉 Quan — Shenquan mint, Zhejiang.
川 Chuan — Chengdu mint, Sichuan.
定 Ding — Fengyuan mint, Sichuan.
惠 Hui — Huimin mint, Sichuan.
光 Guang — Guangzhou mint, Henan.
松 Song — Shusong mint, Anhui.
舒 Shu — Shusong mint, Anhui.
豐 Feng — Fengyu mint, Jiangxi.
永 Yong — Yongping mint, Jiangxi.
裕 Yu — Yuguo mint, Jiangxi.
冶 Ye — Daye mint, Jiangxi.
廣 Guang — Guangning mint, Jiangxi.
安 An — Qian mint, Hubei.

西. Xi — Huimin mint, Sichuan.
當 Dang — Ditto.
復 Fu — Ditto.
行 Xing — Ditto.
使 Shi — Ditto.
直 Zhi — Ditto.
慶 Qing — Ditto.
用 Yong — Ditto.
通 Tong — Ditto.
正 Zheng — Ditto.
准 Zhun — Ditto.
寶 Bao — Ditto.
權 Quan — Ditto.
信 Xing — Ditto.

The Chinese numerals:

	Ordinary style	Orthodox style
1.	一	壹 弌
2.	二	貳 弍
3.	三	叁 弎
4.	四	肆
5.	五	伍
6.	六	陆
7.	七	柒
8.	八	捌
9.	九	玖
10.	十	拾

	Ordinary style	Orthodox style
20	廿	貳拾
30	卅	叁拾
47	七四	肆柒
53	三五	伍叁
61	六一	陆壹

	Ordinary style	Orthodox style
100	百	佰
1,000	千	仟
10,000	万	萬

Spade Coins

929

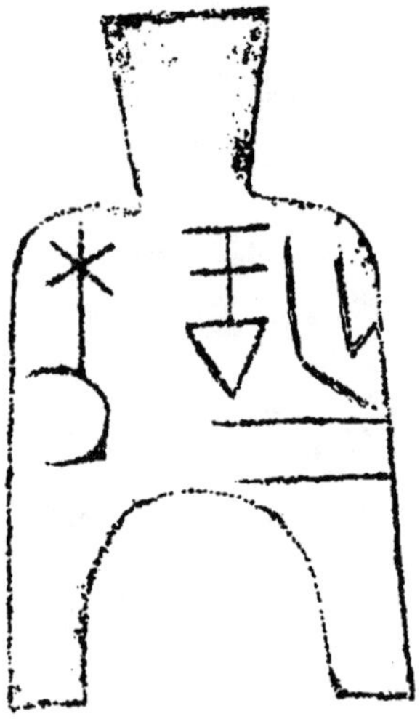

930

931

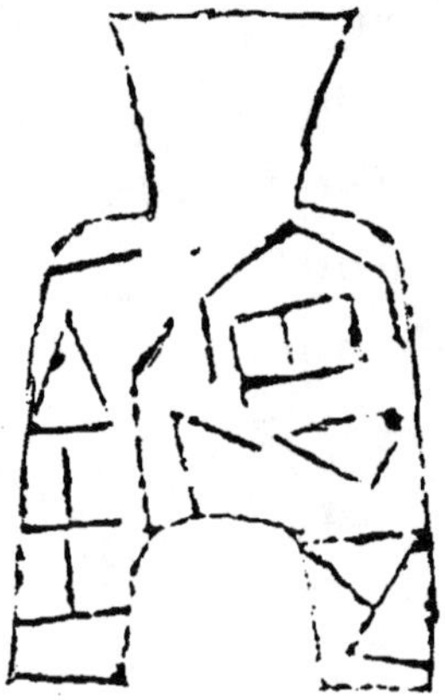

932

933

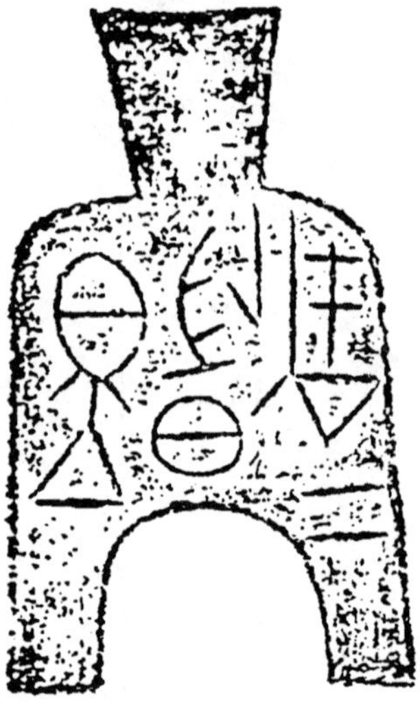

934

935

936

	VG	VF
929. Liang Er Jin Spade FD-275	1500.00	3000.00
930. Liang Ban Jin Spade FD-273	500.00	1000.00
931. An Yi Yi Jin Spade FD-300	100.00	200.00
932. An Yi Ban Jin Spade FD-298	800.00	1600.00
933. Jin Yang Er Jin Spade FD-271	1500.00	3000.00
934. Jin Ban Jin Spade FD-269, R	3500.00	—
935. Liang Zheng Shang Jin Dang Lie FD-305	100.00	200.00
936. Liang Dan Shang Er Jin (Bai — 100) Dang Lie, FD-303	2000.00	4000.00

937

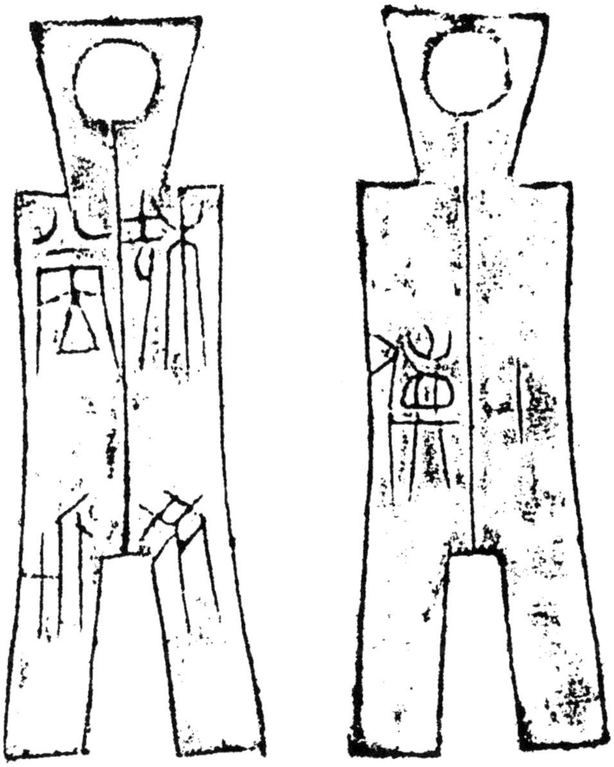

938

939

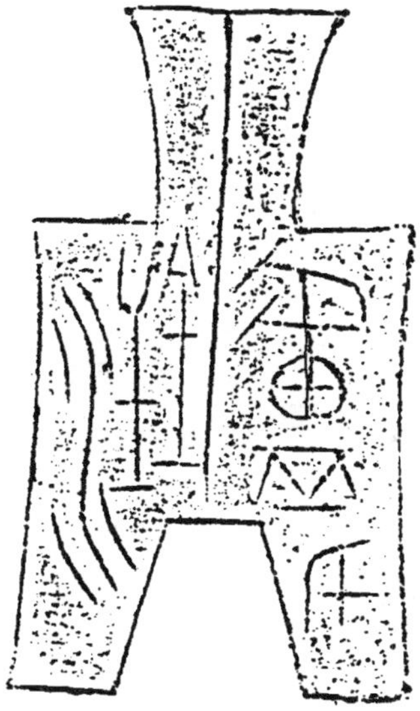

	VG	VF
937. Shu Bu Dang Jin FD-289, Shi Huo on reverse	300.00	600.00
938. Si Bu Dang Jin FD-287	400.00	800.00
939. Lu Shi Jin Bi FD-285	550.00	1100.00
940. Gong Spade FD-283	40.00	80.00

940

941

942

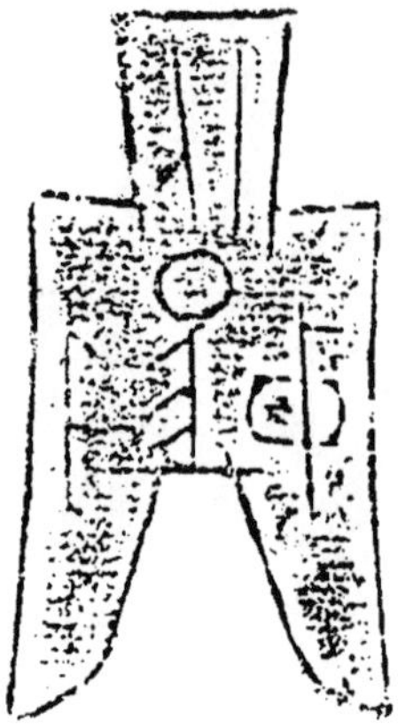

943

944

945

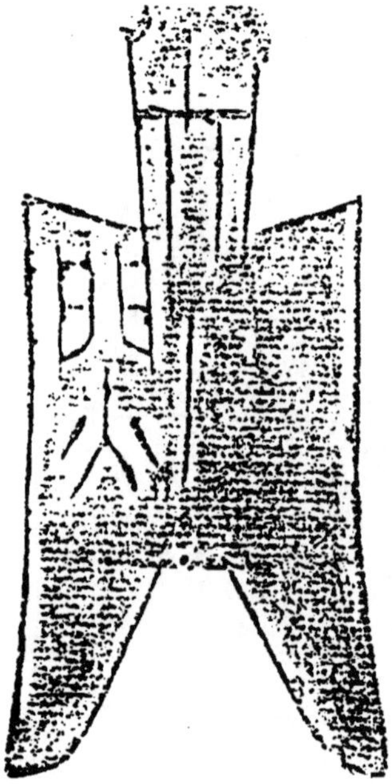

946

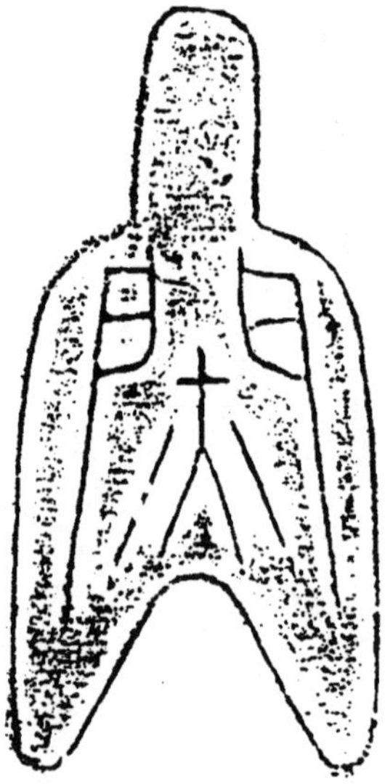

947

948

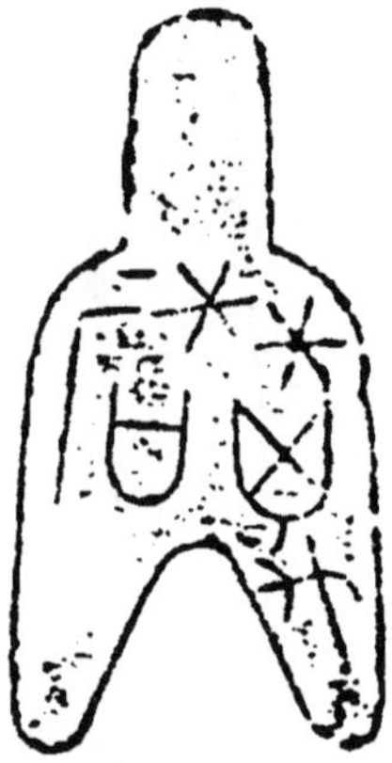

949

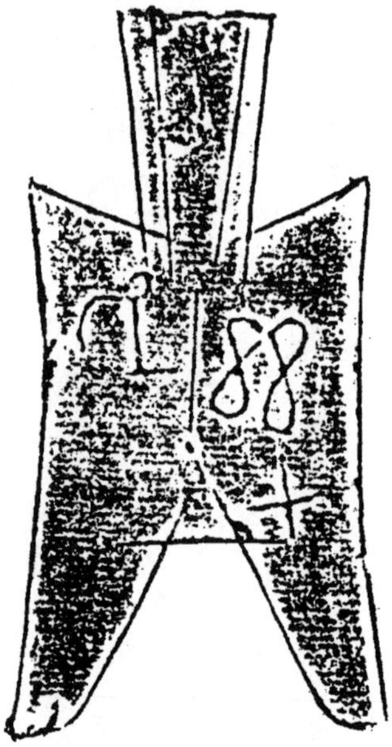

	VG	VF
941. Ling Ban Spade FD-137	50.00	100.00
942. Zhong Yang Spade FD-130	80.00	160.00
943. Wu An Spade FD-148	30.00	60.00
944. Shang Shui Spade	150.00	300.00
945. Ling Spade FD-138	150.00	300.00
946. Ling FD-321	250.00	500.00
947. Ling FD-320	250.00	500.00
948. Li Shi FD-317	500.00	1000.00
949. Zi Shi Spade FD-127	300.00	600.00

950

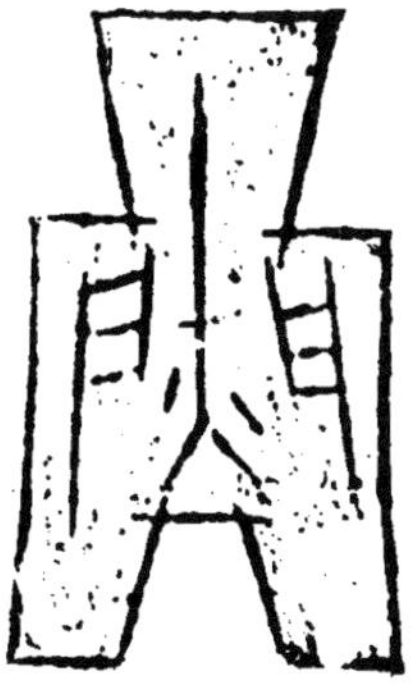

951

952

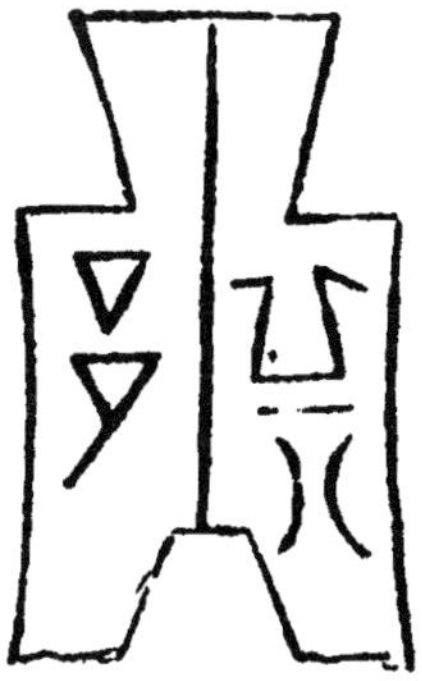

953

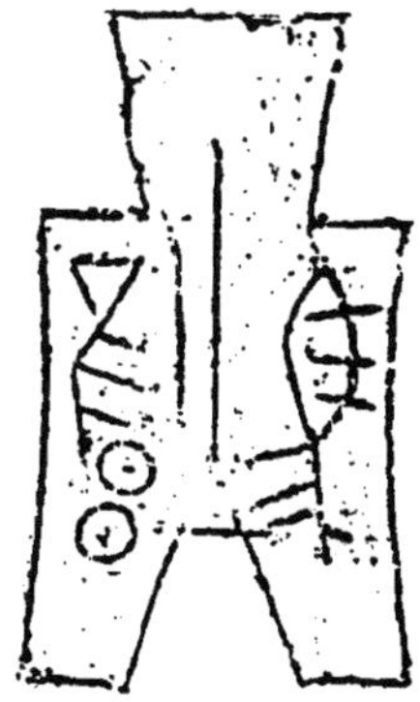

954

955

956

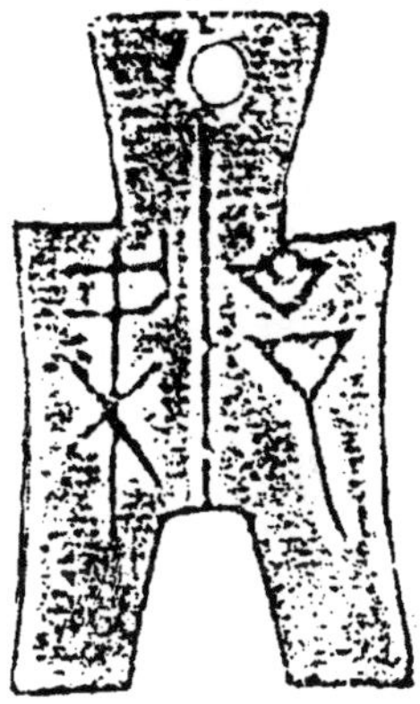

957

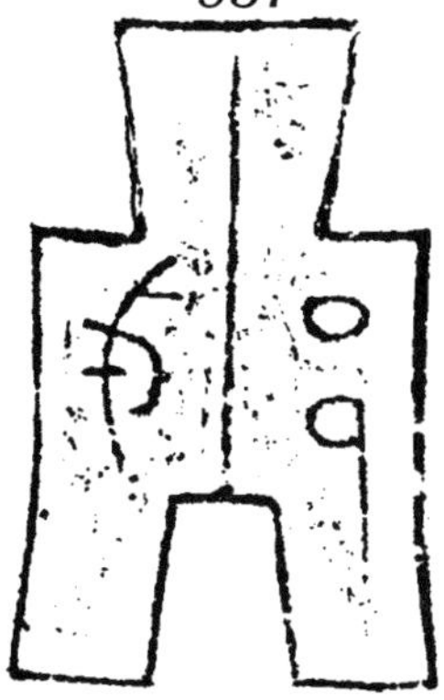

958

959

	VG	VF
950. Lin Spade FD-246	30.00	60.00
951. An (Tao) Yang Spade FD-167	15.00	25.00
952. Gong Spade FD-219	35.00	70.00
953. Ma Yong Spade	35.00	70.00
954. Qi Bei Spade FD-230	20.00	40.00
955. Gao Du Spade FD-243	30.00	60.00
956. Liang Yi Spade FD-184	30.00	60.00
957. Ge Yi Spade FD-188	35.00	70.00
958. Dong Zhou Spade	300.00	600.00
959. You Min Xin Ye Spade	300.00	600.00

Knife Coins

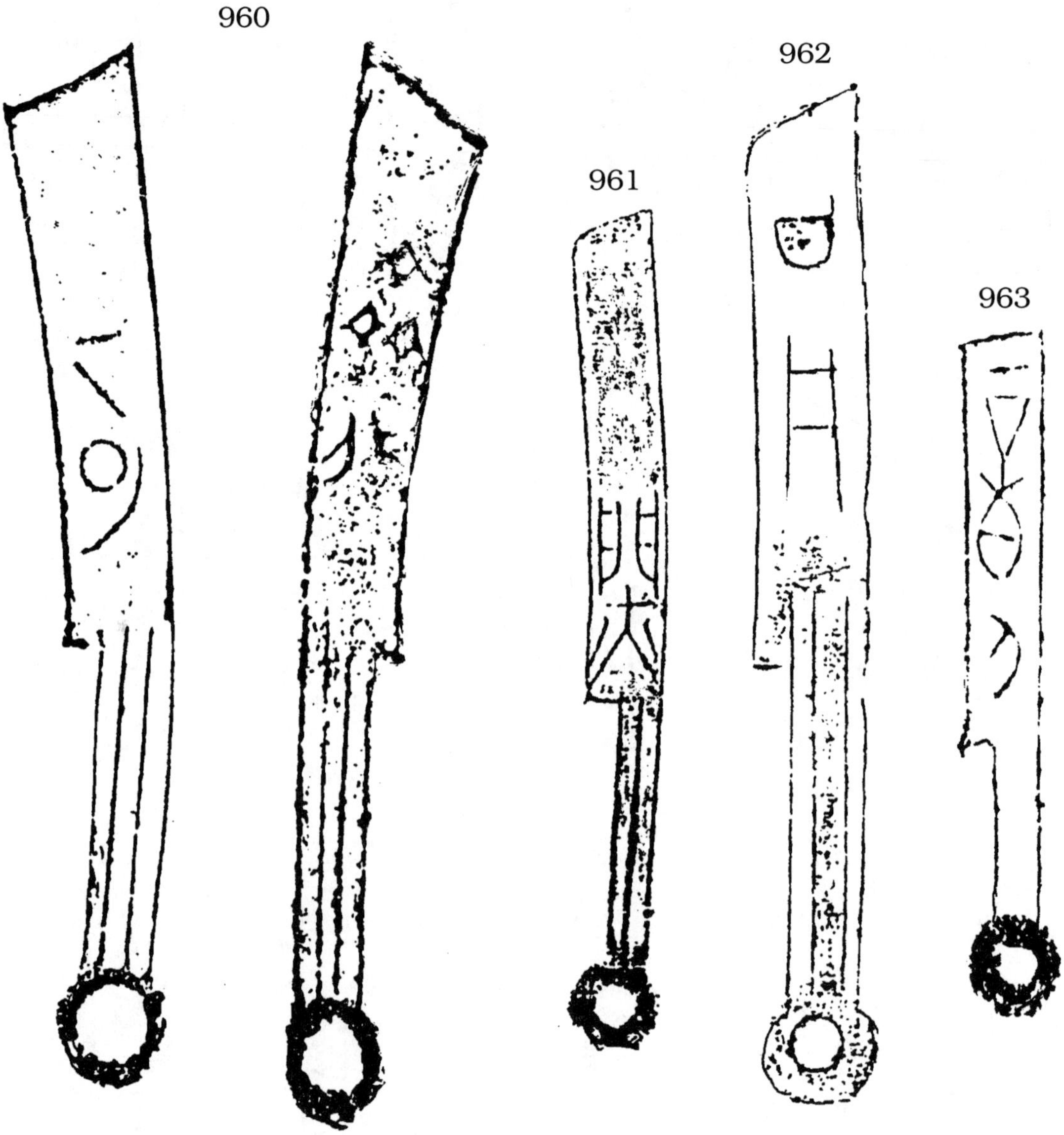

	VG	VF
960. Ming Knife, Qi Hua on reverse FD-340	1500.00	3000.00
961. Straight-blade Knife, Lin on obverse FD-347	3500.00	—
962. Ditto, Gan Dan on obverse FD-345	40.00	70.00
963. Ditto, Jin Hua on obverse	1200.00	2400.00

964

965

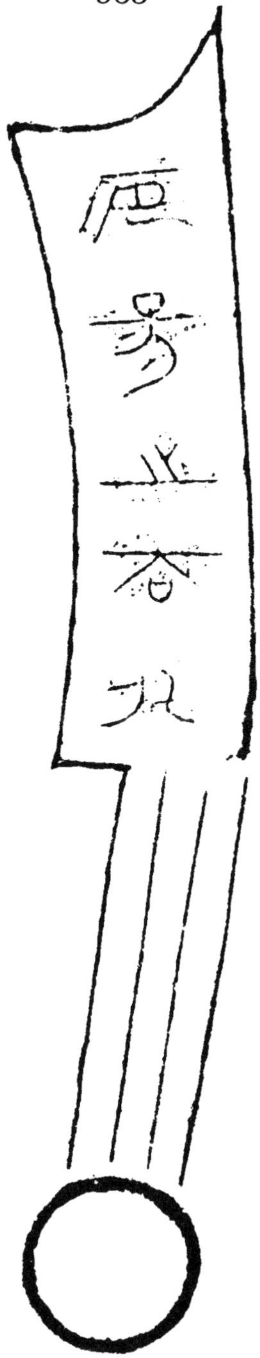

966

967

	VG	VF
964. 5-Character Knife — Jie Me Zhi Fa Hua FD-354	450.00	900.00
965. 5-Character Knife — An Yang Zhi Fa Hua FD-356	400.00	800.00
966. 4-Character Knife — Jie Me Fa Hua FD-355	400.00	800.00
967. 6-Character Knife — Qi Fan Bang Chang Fa Hua, F-350	1500.00	3000.00

Round Coins

968

969

970

971

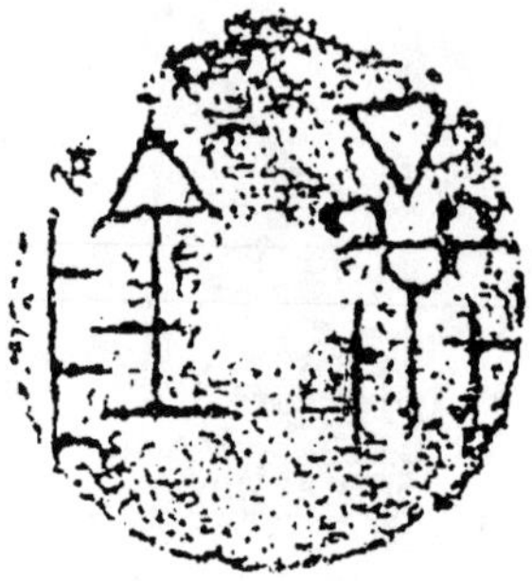

972

973

974

975

976

977

978

	VG	VF
968. Round-holed Coin — Li Shi FD-372	2000.00	4000.00
969. Round-holed Coin — Gong Tun Chi Jin FD-360	2000.00	4000.00
970. Round-holed Coin — Xi Zhou FD-10	1500.00	3000.00
971. Round-holed Coin — Ji Yin FD-366	450.00	900.00
972. Round-holed Coin — An Zang FD-363	1200.00	2400.00
973. Round-holed Coin — Zhu Zhong Yi Liang Shi Er FD-390	1000.00	2000.00
974, Square-holed Coin — Yi Huo FD-438	80.00	160.00
975. Square-holed Coin — Yi Si Huo FD-439	35.00	70.00
976. Ant-nose Money	5.00	10.00
977. Ant-nose Money	5.00	10.00
978. Ant-nose Money	150.00	300.00

Qin Dynasty Ban Liang Varieties

979

980

981

982

983

984

985

986

987

988

989

990

	VG	VF
979. Ban Liang, 38mm, 26g	120.00	240.00
980. Ban Liang, 37mm, 16g	60.00	120.00
981. Ban Liang, Special-purpose coin	800.00	1600.00
982. Ban Liang, Reversed Legend	60.00	120.00
983. Ban Liang, Reversed Legend, Liang inverted	75.00	140.00
984. Ban Liang, With Outer Rim	70.00	140.00
985. Ban Liang, Two Bars on top	20.00	35.00
986. Ban Liang, With Spiral Patterns	70.00	140.00
987. Ban Liang, With Two Characters: Shang Wen	100.00	200.00
988. Mini Ban Liang	20.00	35.00
989. Ban-liang Style coin	20.00	40.00
990. Snake-eye Ban Liang, Legend on same level as Outer Rim	20.00	40.00

Wu Zhu Varieties

991

992

993

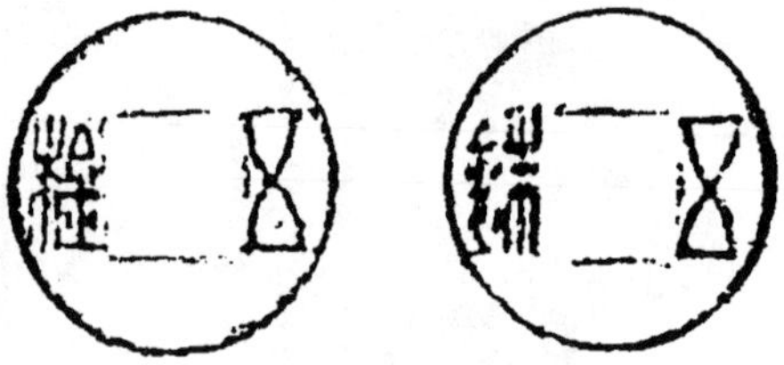

994

995

996

997

998

999

	VG	VF
991. Wu Zhu, Double Zhu	160.00	300.00
992. Ditto, Double Wu	10.00	20.00
993. Ditto, Same Legend on both sides, Zhu reversed on the obverse	100.00	200.00
994. Ditto, Sunken outer rim	20.00	40.00
995. Ditto, with inner rim	15.00	30.00
996. Trident Wu Zhu (Zhu radical with Long Center Stroke)	20.00	40.00
997. Ditto, Cashew Wu Zhu (Four Dots Shaped Like Cashew Nuts)	20.00	40.00
998. Wu Zhu, Wu Separated in Middle	30.00	50.00
999. Chicken-eye Wu Zhu	10.00	20.00

1000

1001

1002

1003

1004

1005

1006

1007

1008

1009

1010

1011

	VG	VF
1000. Wu Zhu, Large Size	80.00	150.00
1001. Ditto, Legend in vertical position	350.00	700.00
1002. Ditto, Switched Legend position	100.00	200.00
1003. Ditto, Pattern	50.00	100.00
1004. Ditto, Reversed Legend	5.00	10.00
1005. Ditto, With Character Ping	25.00	50.00
1006. Ditto, the Right Radical of the Zhu Missing	60.00	120.00
1007. Ditto, with Da Ji Added	150.00	300.00
1008. Ditto, Wu in top position	50.00	90.00
1009. Ditto, Three Wus	100.00	150.00
1010. Ditto, Wu Zhu with additional Wu	60.00	100.00
1011. Ditto, Atypical Wu	40.00	70.00

1012 1013 1014 1015

1016 1017 1018 1019 1020

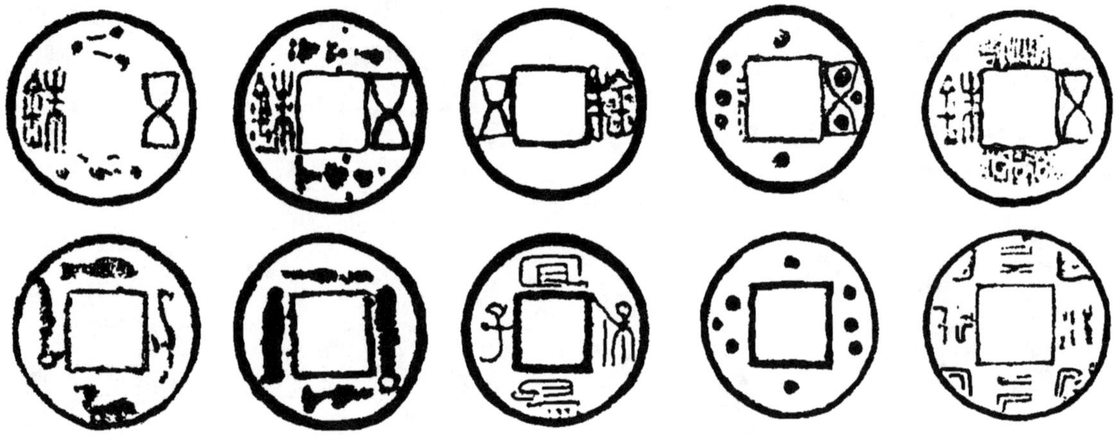

	VG	VF
1012. Wu Zhu, Marks symbolizing Ten Thousand	150.00	300.00
1013. Ditto, Two circles	70.00	150.00
1014. Ditto, Good luck symbols on both sides	200.00	400.00
1015. Ditto, Good luck inscription Jun Yi Hou Wang	300.00	600.00
1016. Ditto, Good luck symbols on both sides	250.00	500.00
1017. Ditto, Symbols & figures on both sides	300.00	600.00
1018. Ditto, Good luck inscription on reverse	100.00	200.00
1019. Ditto, Dots (Stars) on both sides	80.00	150.00
1020. Ditto, Geometrical pattern on reverse	80.00	150.00

N.B. Coin charms dating from before the Tang and Song Dynasties have an added vintage value.

1021

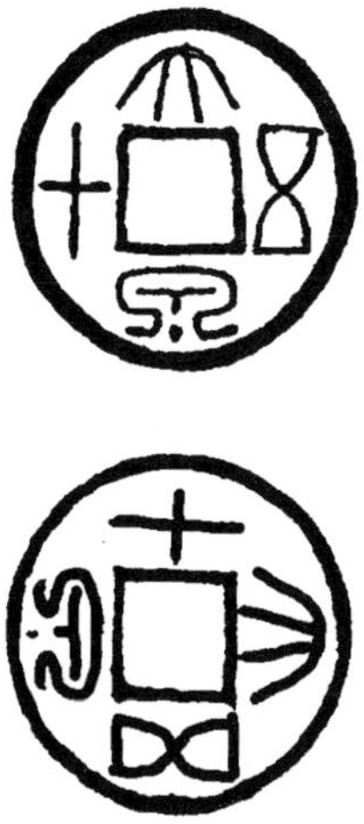

1022

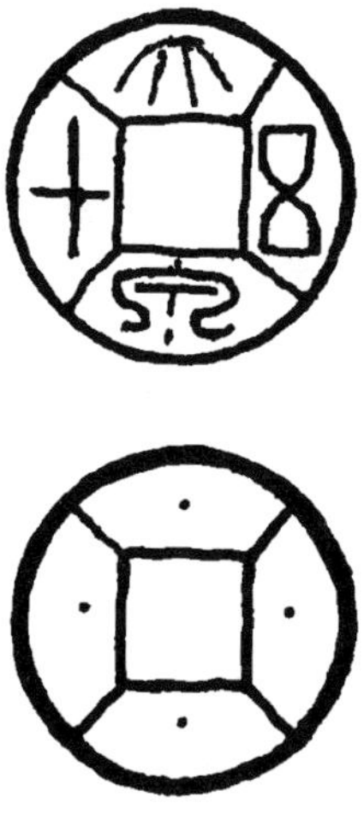

1023

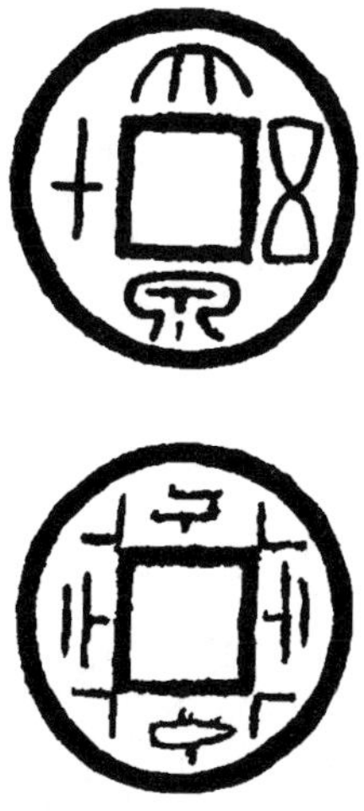

1024

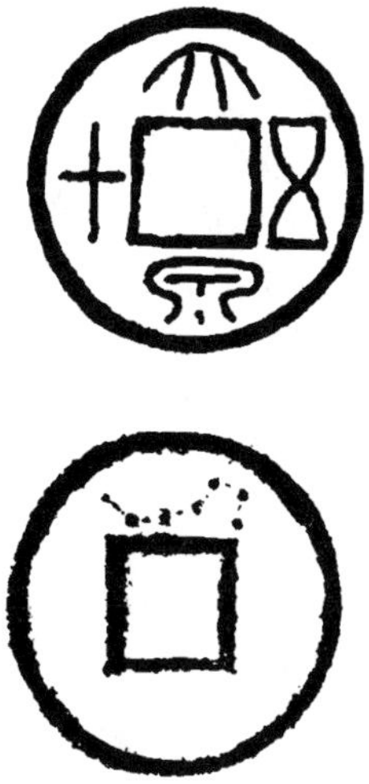

1025

1026

1027

1028

	VG	VF
1021. Da Quan Wu Shi, 3 o'clock legend on rev. S-135	30.00	60.00
1022. Ditto, Radiating strokes on both sides	80.00	150.00
1023. Ditto, Geometrical pattern on reverse	100.00	200.00
1024. Ditto, dipper on reverse	300.00	600.00
1025. Ditto, Characters on the two sides reversed, S-136/FD-420	20.00	40.00
1026. Double outer rim S-122/FD-449	30.00	50.00
1027. Ditto, Extra large	150.00	300.00
1028. Ditto, Midget S-127/FD-446	5.00	10.00

1029

1030

1031

1032

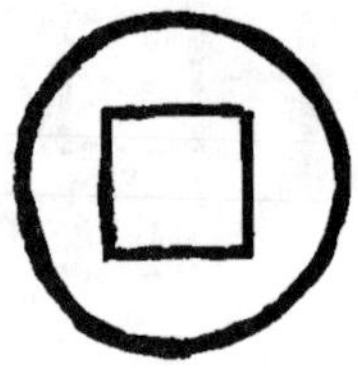

1033

1034

1035

1036

1037

1038

1039

1040

	VG	VF
1029. Huo Quan, Rectangular-shaped right radical, FD-489	150.00	300.00
1030. Ditto, Legend reversed FD-495	20.00	40.00
1031. Ditto, Unorthodox script	30.00	50.00
1032. Ditto, No legend S-173	15.00	25.00
1033. Ditto, Two characters Wu Da appended FD-670	120.00	240.00
1034. Ditto, Two characters Da Yuan appended	100.00	200.00
1035. Ditto, Four rays on obverse	20.00	40.00
1036. Ditto, Double legend	100.00	200.00
1037. Ditto, Four rays on reverse FD-491	20.00	40.00
1038. Ditto, Star & moon on reverse	40.00	70.00
1039. Ditto, Two fish on obverse	50.00	100.00
1040. Ditto, Good luck inscription Yi Guan Ci Ji and Pattern on reverse	120.00	240.00

Three Kingdoms & Six Dynasties Varieties

1041

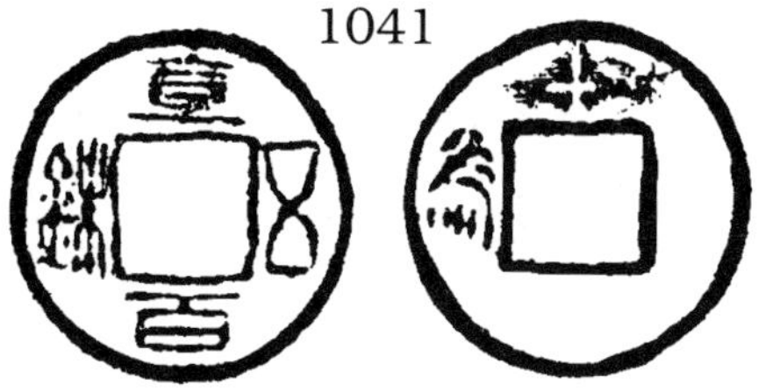

1042

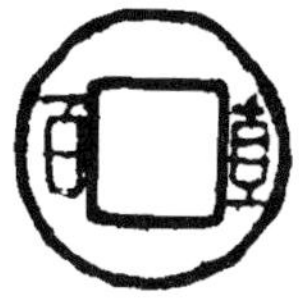

1043

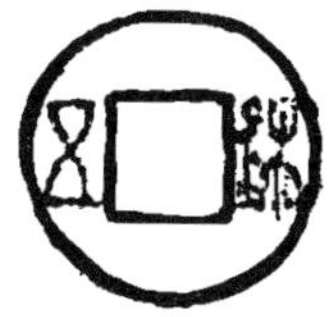

1044

1045

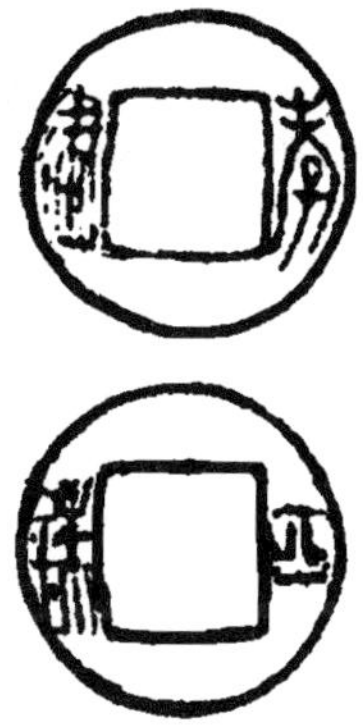

1046

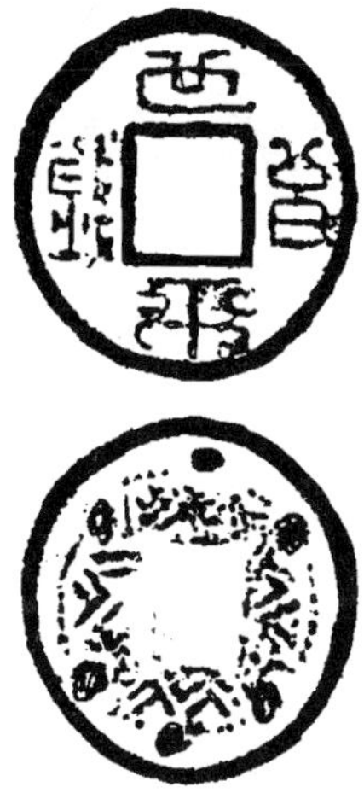

1047

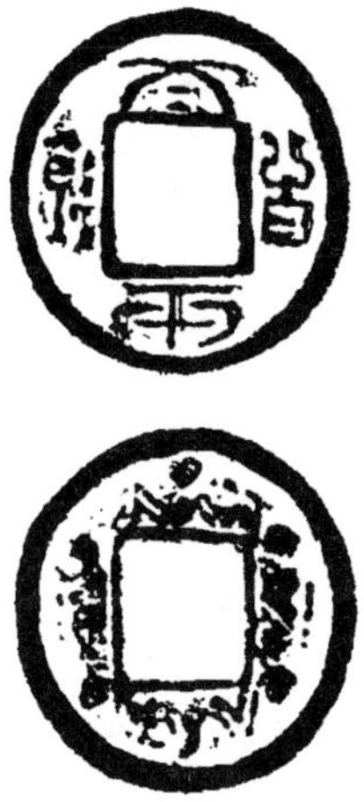

1048

	VG	VF
1041. Zhi Bai Wu Zhu, Character Wei on reverse S-185	20.00	40.00
1042. Zhi Bai S-188/FD-522	10.00	20.00
1043. Wu Zhu, Read from left to right FD-527	50.00	80.00
1044. Da Quan Dang Qian, Extra-large size	2000.00	4000.00
1045. Xiao Jian, Si Zhu on reverse S-218/FD-567	20.00	40.00
1046. Shi Ping Bai Qian, in folding script FD-541	300.00	500.00
1047. Tai Ping Bai Qian, Stars & pattern on reverse	30.00	50.00
1048. Tai Qing Feng Le FD-666	350.00	600.00

Tang Dynasty Varieties

1049

1050

1051

1052

1053

1054

1055

1056

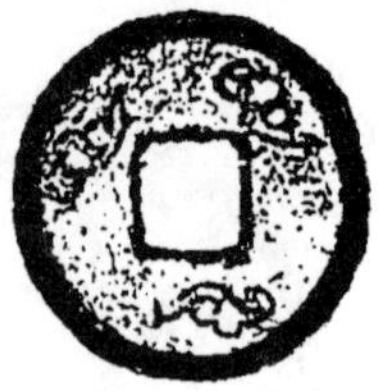

1057

1058

1059

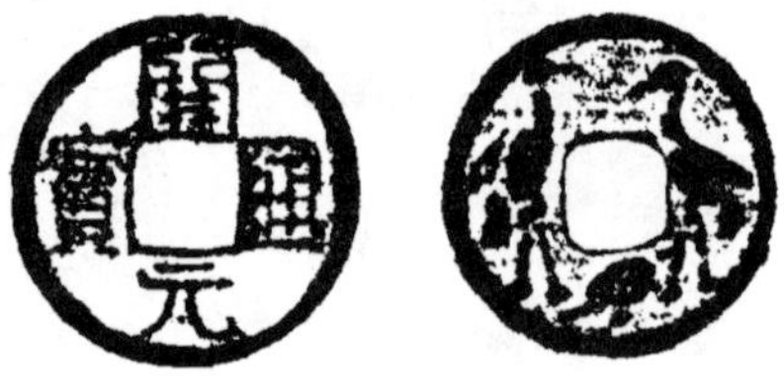

	VG	VF
1049. Kai Yuan Tong Bao, 2nd stroke of bottom character tilting upward at right end S-314/FD-673	5.00	10.00
1050. Ditto, 2nd stroke of bottom character tilting upward at both ends FD-674	5.00	10.00
1051. Ditto, Crescent on reverse S-315	2.00	5.00
1052. Ditto, Double crescent on reverse S-335	2.00	5.00
1053. Ditto, Crescent & Star on reverse S-344/FD-680	5.00	10.00
1054. Ditto, Star above & Crescent below FD-681	5.00	10.00
1055. Ditto, Knot above & Crescent below on reverse	100.00	200.00
1056. Ditto, Three clouds on reverse	100.00	200.00
1057. Ditto, Gigantic Kai	20.00	40.00
1058. Ditto, Weak Countenance, Large Characters	250.00	500.00
1059. Ditto, Two Cranes & Turtle on reverse	80.00	150.00

KAI YUAN TONG BAO - HUI CHANG KAI YUAN
(Local mint names on reverse)

1060

1061

1062

1063

1064

1065

1066

1067

1068

1069

1070

1071

	VG	VF
1060. Chang — Yangzhou S-366/FD-709	2.00	5.00
1061. Yi — Xichuan, S-372/FD-711	5.00	10.00
1062. Jing — Jingzhao Fu, Jin reversed FD-708	25.00	50.00
1063. Le — Leyang S-370/FD-710	2.00	5.00
1064. Lan — Lantian S-373/FD-716	2.00	5.00
1065. Xiang — Xiangzhou S-380/FD-712	2.00	5.00
1066. Jing — Jiangling S-382/FD-714	2.00	5.00
1067. Yue — Yuezhou S-383/FD-717	2.00	5.00
1068. Xuan — Xuanzhou S-384/FD-718	5.00	10.00
1069. Hong — Jiangxi S-385/FD-719	5.00	10.00
1070. Tan — Hunan S-390/FD-723	5.00	10.00
1071. Dui — Duizhou S-392/FD-724	5.00	10.00

1072

1073

1074

1075

1076

1077

1078

1079

1080

1081

1082

	VG	VF
1072. Run — Zhexi S-393/FD-725	2.00	5.00
1073. E — Ezhou S-395/FD-726	5.00	10.00
1074. Ping — Pingzhou S-396/FD-727	20.00	40.00
1075. Xing — Xingyuan Fu S-398/FD-729	2.00	5.00
1076. Liang — Liangzhou S-399/FD-730	5.00	10.00
1077. Guang — Guangzhou S-400/FD-732	5.00	10.00
1078. Zi — Dongchuan S-402/FD-737	5.00	10.00
1079. Fu — Fuzhou FD-738	25.00	50.00
Fu on the right side	150.00	300.00
1080. Dạn — Danzhou, S-404/FD-740	25.00	50.00
1081. Gui — Binzhou, Guiyang FD-734	20.00	40.00
1082. Yong — Jiangnan Prefecture, Yongzhou, FD-735	150.00	350.00

1083

1084

1085

1086

1087

1088

1089

1090

1091

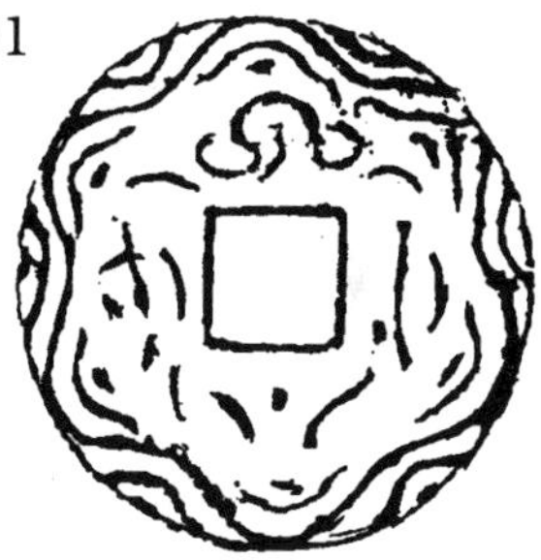

	VG	VF
1083. Qian Yuan Zhong Bao, Cloud on rev. S-358/FD-696	50.00	100.00
1084. Ditto, 4 stars on reverse FD-695	200.00	400.00
1085. Ditto, Sun on reverse	80.00	150.00
1086. Ditto, Numeral 10 on reverse (10 cash)	1000.00	2000.00
1087. Ditto, Bird on reverse FD-690	150.00	300.00
1088. Ditto, Character Hong on reverse FD-719	250.00	400.00
1089. Ditto, Numeral 2 on reverse (2 cash)	1500.00	2500.00
1090. De Yi Yuan Bao, 4 Clouds on reverse	300.00	600.00
1091. Shun Tian Yuan Bao, patterns on both sides	350.00	700.00

Five Dynasties Varieties

1092

1093

1094

1095

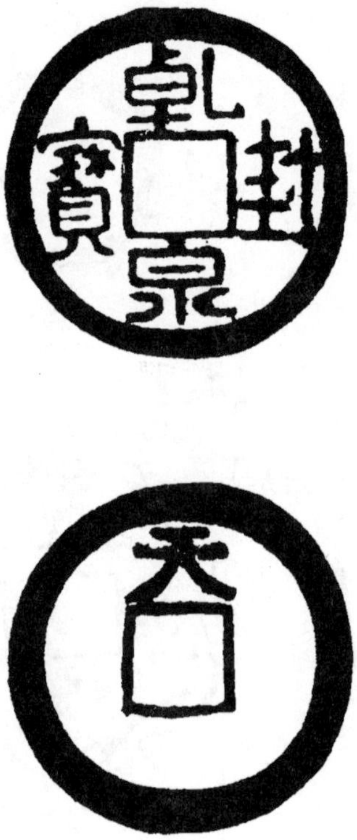

1096

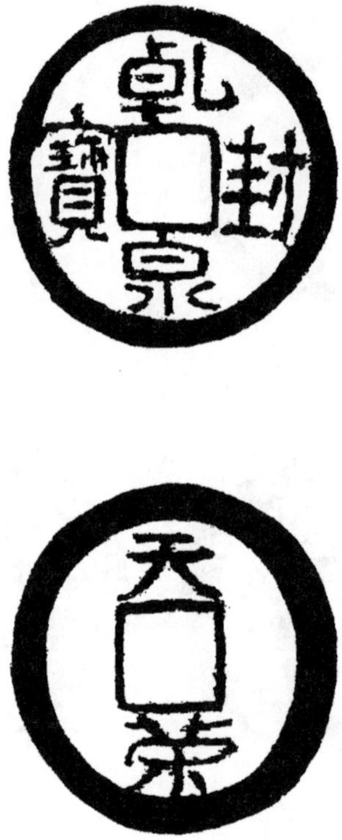

1097

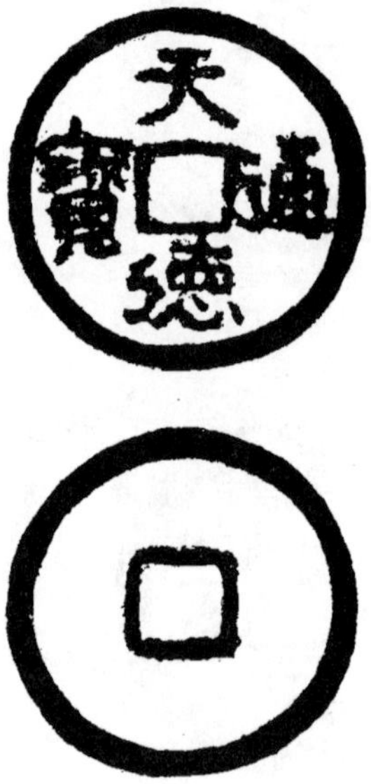

	VG	VF
1092. Kai Yuan Tong Bao (Lead) — Min on reverse FD-777	20.00	40.00
1093. Ditto, Fu on reverse	10.00	20.00
1094. Ditto, Yin on reverse	450.00	800.00
1095. Qian Feng Quan Bao — Tian on rev. S-448/FD-791, VR	—	—
Iron FD-796	60.00	120.00
1096. Qian Feng Quan Bao — Tian Ce on reverse, Iron FD-799	200.00	400.00
1097. Tian De Tong Bao FD-784, ER	—	—

N.B. The three lead Kai Yuan coins were issued by the Kingdom of Min of the Five Dynasties.

1098

1099

1100

1101

1102

1103

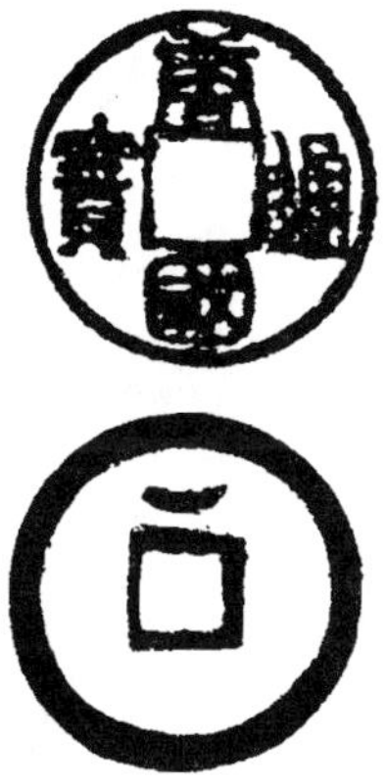

1104

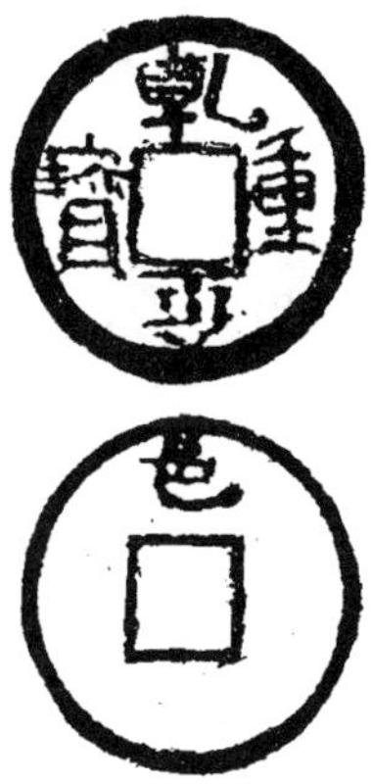

1105

	VG	VF
1098. Yong Tong Quan Huo, Seal script FD-808	1500.00	3000.00
1099. Kai Yuan Tong Bao, Wide rim	5.00	10.00
1100. Ditto, Extra-large	20.00	40.00
1101. Tang Guo Tong Bao, Seal script, Large star on reverse FD-816	50.00	100.00
1102. Ditto, Li script	30.00	60.00
1103. Ditto, Large seal script	600.00	1000.00
1104. Qian Heng Zhong Bao, Yong on reverse (Lead) FD-828	5.00	10.00
1105. Yong An Yi Qian FD-839	1200.00	2400.00
Iron FD-841	150.00	300.00

N.B. The two Kai Yuan coins were minted by the Southern Tang Kingdom of the Five Dynasties.

Northern Song Varieties & Variants

1106

1107

1108

1109

1110

1111

1112

	VG	VF
1106. Chun Hua Yuan Bao, Li script, Three dots crowded together FD-866	350.00	700.00
1107. Xian Ping Yuan Bao, Wide rim, FD-879	200.00	350.00
1108. Ditto, 4 rays on reverse	200.00	350.00
1109. Xiang Fu Tong Bao, large star on reverse FD-884	40.00	70.00
1110. Ditto, Star & crescent on reverse FD-885	50.00	80.00
1111. Zhi Ping Yuan Bao, 4 rays on reverse	40.00	70.00
1112. Huang Song Tong Bao, 2 Cash, Seal script FD-908	1500.00	3000.00

1113

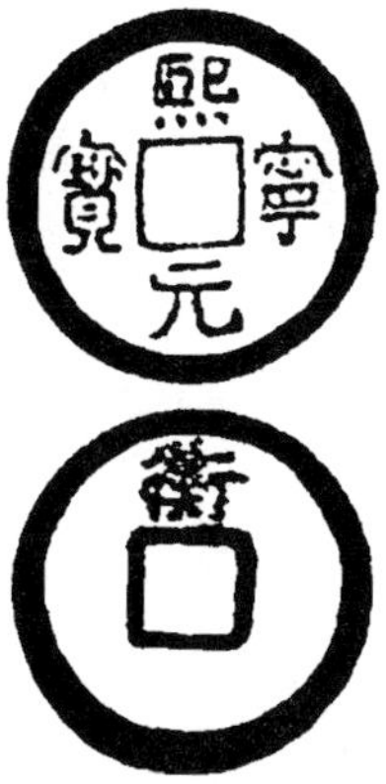

1114

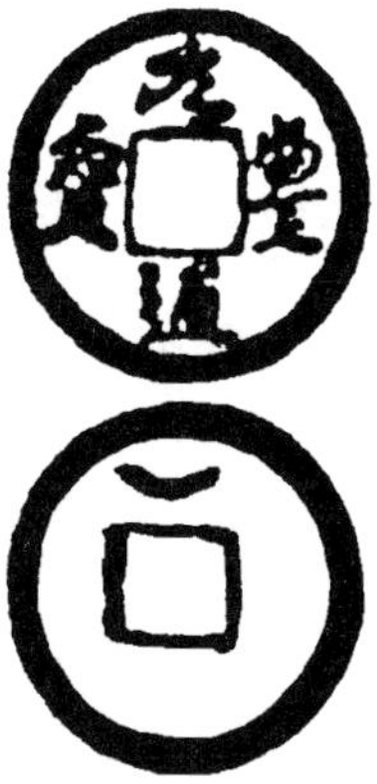

1115

1116

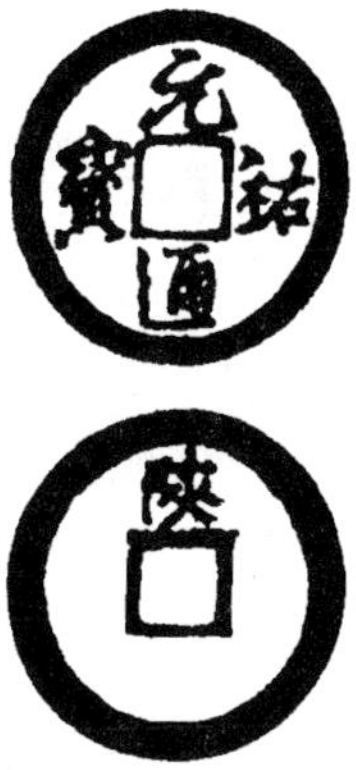

1117

1118

1119

1120

	VG	VF
1113. Xi Ning Yuan Bao, Heng on reverse, FD-954	40.00	80.00
1114. Yuan Feng Tong Bao, Large crescent on reverse FD-965	40.00	80.00
1115. Yuan You Tong Bao, Shaan on reverse, Seal script FD-981	450.00	800.00
1116. Ditto, Running script FD-982	450.00	800.00
1117. Yuan Feng Tong Bao, 3 Cash, Star on reverse, Running script, Iron	10.00	20.00
1118. Ditto, Crescent on reverse, Seal script, Iron	10.00	20.00
1119. Ditto, 1 Cash, Li script, Small characters	15.00	25.00
1120. Shao Sheng Yuan Bao, Li script FD-994	1500.00	3000.00

1121

1122

1123

1124

1125

1126

1127

1128

1129

1130

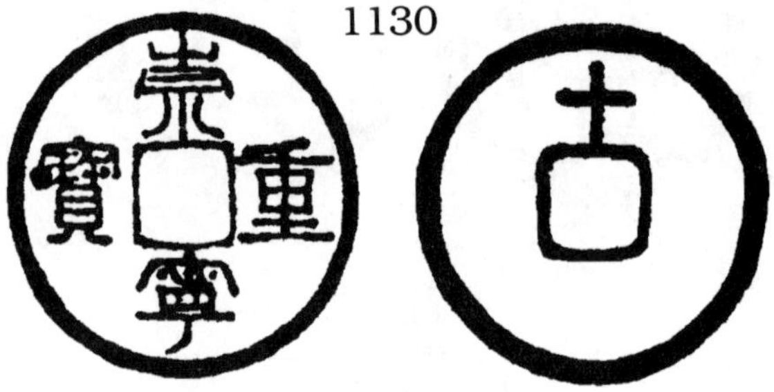

	VG	VF
1121. Jian Guo Tong Bao, Regular script, ER	—	—
1122. Ditto, Seal script	—	—
1123. Sheng Song Yuan Bao, Running script FD-1019	1000.00	2000.00
1124. Ditto, Seal script FD-1020	2000.00	4000.00
1125. Ditto, Seal script, Weakly done Yuan FD-1023	80.00	150.00
1126. Ditto, Song with two outspreading strokes FD-1024	150.00	300.00
1127. Chong Ning Tong Bao, Large characters FD-1037	30.00	60.00
1128. Ditto, Tall Chong, Elegant style	350.00	600.00
1129. Ditto, 10 Cash, Large characters FD-1042	350.00	600.00
1130. Ditto, Numeral 10 on reverse, Li script FD-1051	150.00	250.00

Southern Song Varieties

1131

1132

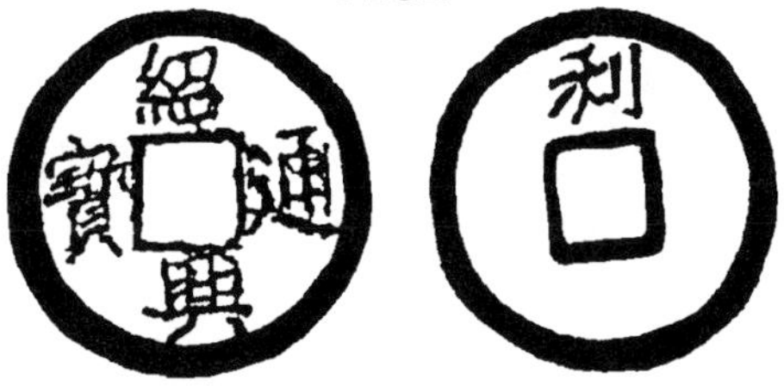

1133

1134

1135

1136

1137

1138

1139

	VG	VF
1131. Jian Yan Tong Bao, Simplified Bao S-673, FD-1142	2.00	5.00
1132. Shao Xing Tong Bao, Li on reverse, Iron, S-693/FD-1171	5.00	10.00
1133. Long Xing Yuan Bao, Seal script, Iron	25.00	40.00
1134. Long Xing Tong Bao, 2 Cash Iron	10.00	20.00
1135. Long Xing Yuan Bao, 2 Cash, Iron FD-1179	10.00	20.00
1136. Qian Dao Yuan Bao, Shong on reverse, Iron	5.00	10.00
1137. Ditto, 2 Cash, Zheng on reverse, Iron FD-1184	25.00	50.00
1138. Ditto, Tong on reverse, Iron	5.00	10.00
1139. Ditto, Chun on reverse, Iron	5.00	10.00

N.B. The legends on the Southern Song coins were mostly written in the Song script, a variation of the regular script, and which later developed into a branch of art lettering used with preference on ads and documents.

1140

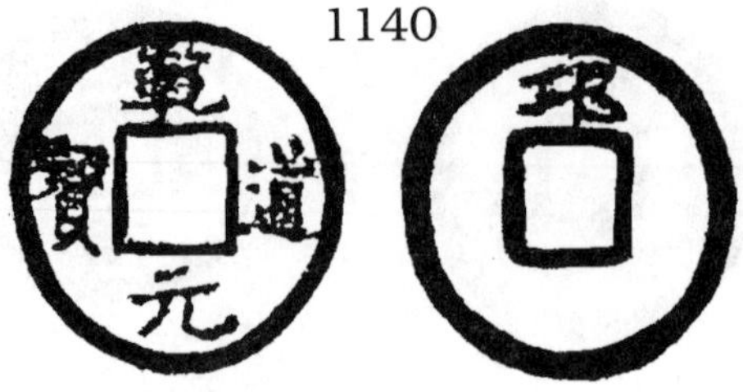

1141

1142

1143

1144

1145

1146

1147

1148

	VG	VF
1140. Qian Dao Yuan Bao, Qiong on reverse 2 Cash, Iron S-713/FD-1194	10.00	20.00
1141. Ditto, Yu on reverse	40.00	70.00
1142. Ditto, An on reverse	150.00	300.00
1143. Chun Xi Yuan Bao, Crescent embracing star on reverse, Seal script	70.00	120.00
1144. Ditto, Song script, Crescent on reverse	1.00	2.00
1145. Ditto, Numeral 10 on reverse	1.00	2.00
1146. Ditto, Numeral 16 on reverse	1.00	2.00
1147. Ditto, 7 in orthodox script S-715/FD-1199	1.00	2.00
1148. Ditto, Seal script, Large characters, Iron, Chun & 7 on reverse	50.00	80.00

N.B. Starting from the 7th year of Chun Xi, numerals began to appear on the reverse of the coins denoting the year of mintage. The Chun Xi coins are dated from the 7th year and ended in the 11th year.

1149

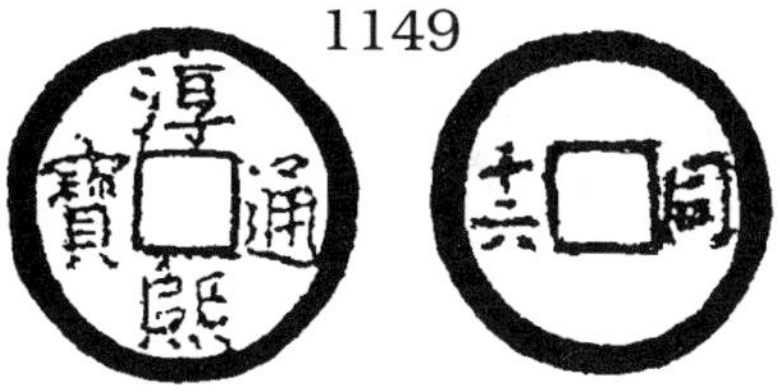

1150

1151

1152

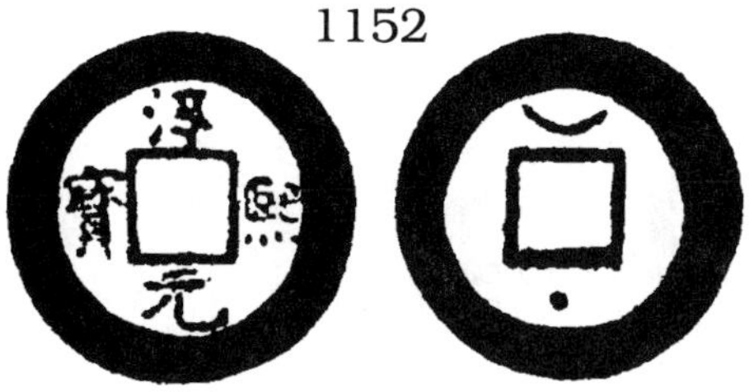

1153

1154

1155

1156

1157

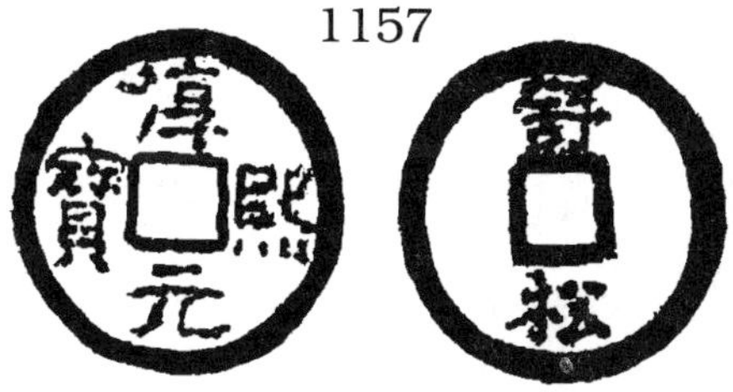

	VG	VF
1149. Chun Xi Tong Bao, Tong on right & 16 on the left	20.00	40.00
1150. Ditto, Shong on reverse, Iron	20.00	40.00
1151. Ditto, Large crescent on reverse *, Iron	2500.00	5000.00
1152. Chun Xi Yuan Bao, 2 Cash, Crescent & Star on reverse	2.00	5.00
1153. Ditto, Quan on reverse FD-1209	10.00	20.00
1154. Ditto, Numeral 7 in orthodox script FD-1205	2.00	5.00
1155. Ditto, Numeral 12 on reverse	2.00	5.00
1156. Chun Xi Yuan Bao, Large Characters in seal script, Iron	5.00	10.00
1157. Ditto, Song script, Shu & Shong on reverse, Iron	10.00	20.00

* In Section 3 is shown the mother coin of this specimen.

1158

1159

1160

1161

1162

1163

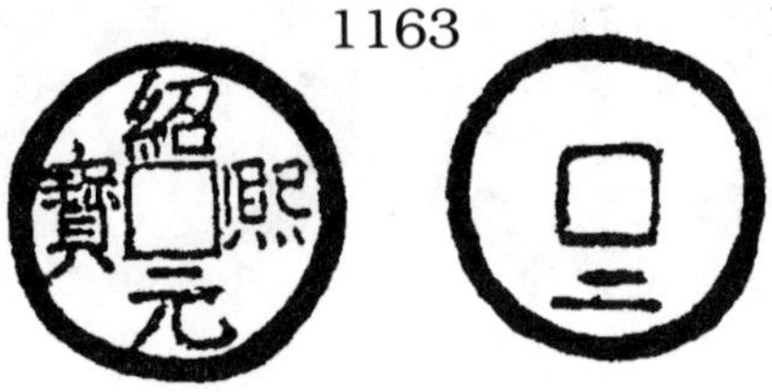

1164

1165

1166

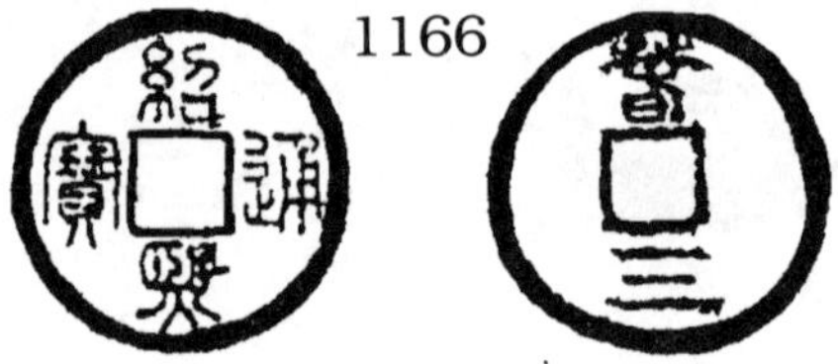

	VG	VF
1158. Chun Xi Tong Bao, 2 Cash, Chun above & Numeral 13 below, Iron	2.00	5.00
1159. Ditto, Li on reverse, Iron	15.00	30.00
1160. Ditto, Qiong on reverse, Iron	15.00	30.00
1161. Ditto, Tong on right & 16 on the left, Iron FD-1221	2.00	5.00
1162. Ditto, Feng on reverse, Iron	50.00	100.00
1163. Shao Xi Yuan Bao, 1 Cash, Numeral 2 on reverse, S-759	1.00	2.00
1164. Ditto, Tong on right & Numeral 2 on the left	1.00	2.00
1165. Ditto, Chun above & Numeral 5 below, Iron	1.00	2.00
1166. Ditto, Seal script, Chun above & 3 below, Iron	30.00	60.00

N.B. The Shao Xi coins are dated from the 1st year through the 5th.

1167

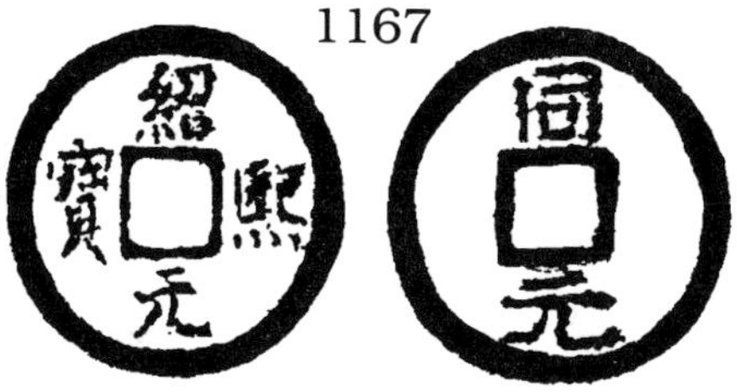

1168

1169

1170

1171

1172

1173

1174

1175

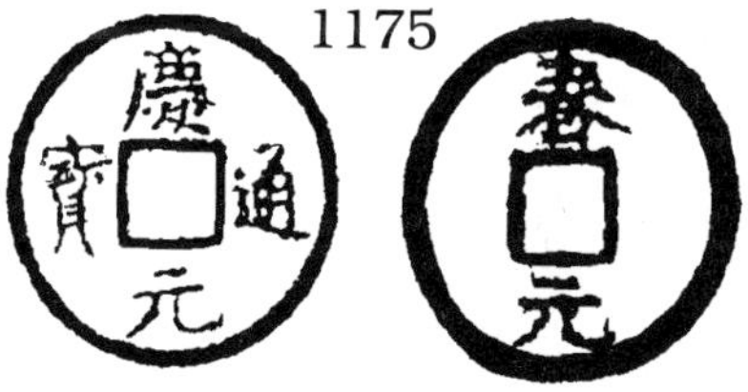

	VG	VF
1167. Shao Xi Yuan Bao, Tong above & Yuan (Numeral 1) below, Iron S-773	2.00	5.00
1168. Ditto, Guang on right & 1 on the left	100.00	200.00
1169. Ditto, Chun above & 2 below	15.00	30.00
1170. Ditto, Chun above & 3 below S-775/FD-1241	2.00	5.00
1171. Ditto, Tong above & 3 below, Iron FD-1242	2.00	5.00
1172. Ditto, Chun above & 3 below, Seal script, S-752/FD-1241, (This & the above are Tong Bao coins)	20.00	40.00
1173. Ditto, Crescent above, Numerals 4 on right & 7 on the left, Iron S-785	5.00	10.00
1174. Qing Yuan Tong Bao, 6 on reverse S-793/FD-1244	1.00	2.00
1175. Ditto, Chun above & Yuan (Numeral 1) below, S-808/FD-1252	2.00	5.00

N.B. The Qing Yuan coins are dated from the 1st year through the 7th.

1176

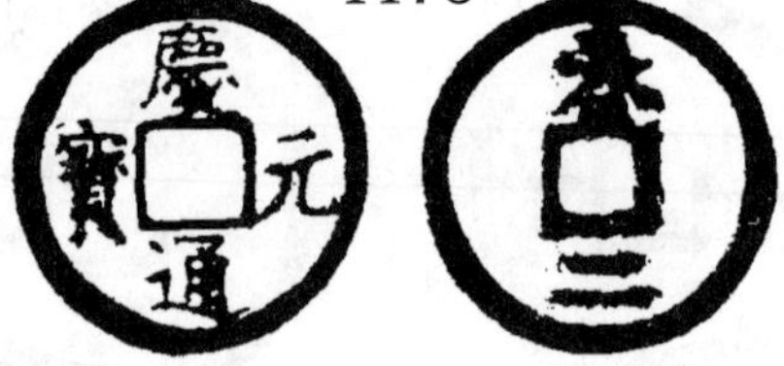

1177

1178

1179

1180

1181

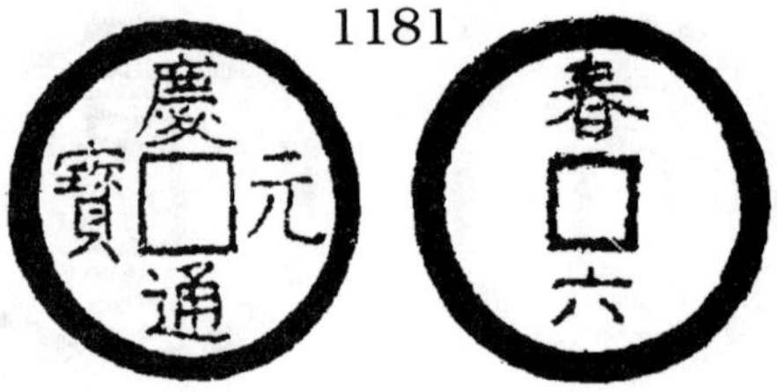

1182

1183

1184

1185

	VG	VF
1176. Qing Yuan Tong Bao, Chun & 2 on reverse, Iron, FD-1253	2.00	5.00
1177. Ditto, Chun & 3 on reverse, Iron S-805/FD-1255	2.00	5.00
1178. Ditto, Chun & 7 on reverse, Iron	40.00	70.00
1179. Ditto, Tong & 6, Iron S-804/FD-1263	2.00	5.00
1180. Ditto, Han & Yuan (Numeral 1) FD-1264	2.00	5.00
1181. Ditto, Legend read clockwise, 2 Cash, Chun & 6 on reverse S-816/FD-1272	2.00	5.00
1182. Ditto, Chun & 7 on reverse, Iron FD-1273	10.00	20.00
1183. Ditto, Tong & 6, Iron S-812/FD-1278	2.00	5.00
1184. Ditto, Tong & 7 on reverse, Iron	2.00	5.00
1185. Ditto, Han & 6 on reverse, Iron S-820/FD-1284	2.00	5.00

N.B. Qing Yuan coins are dated from the 1st year through the 7th.

1186

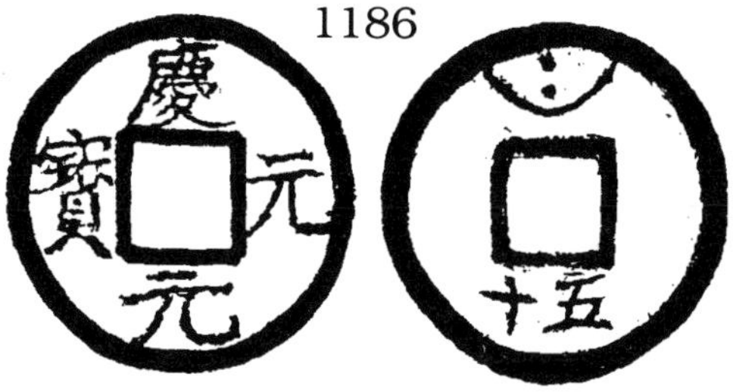

1187

1188

1189

1190

1191

1192

1193

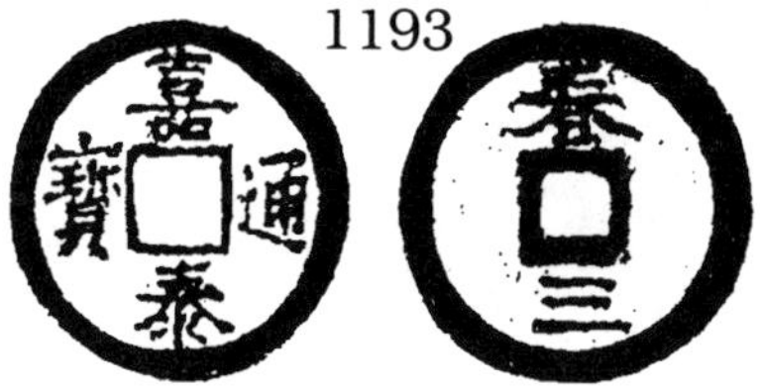

	VG	VF
1186. Qing Yuan Yuan Bao, Crescent & 2 stars above and 50 below, Iron FD-1294	5.00	10.00
1187. Ditto, Crescent & 2 stars above and 56 below	5.00	10.00
1188. Ditto, Chuan above, Numeral 30 on right & 5 on the left, Iron	5.00	10.00
1189. Ditto, Li & 6 above and 56 below, Iron S-834	5.00	10.00
1190. Jia Tai Tong Bao, Yuan (Numeral 1) S-835/FD-1301	1.00	2.00
1191. Ditto, Numeral 2 on reverse S-836	1.00	2.00
1192. Jia Tai Yuan Bao, Tong above & Yuan below, Iron FD-1310	5.00	10.00
1193. Jia Tai Tong Bao, Chun above & 3 below, Iron	2.00	5.00

N.B. The Jia Tai coins are dated from the 1st year through the 4th.

1194

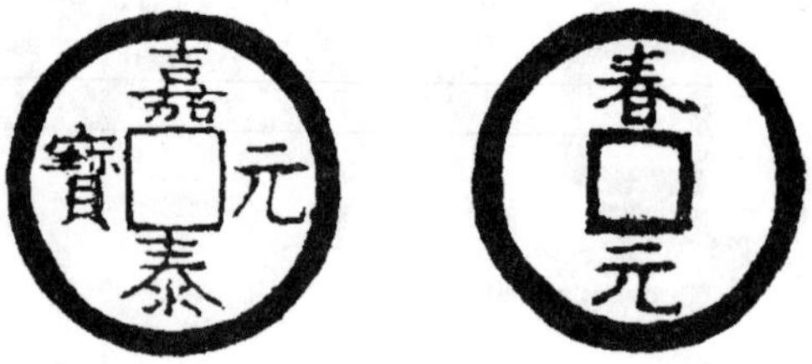

1195

1196

1197

1198

1199

1200

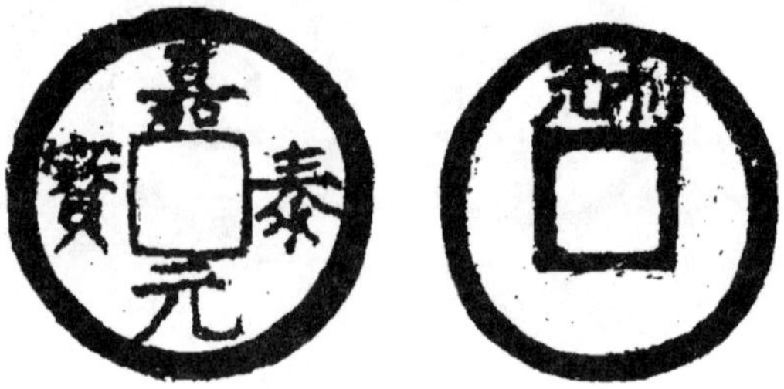

1201

1202

	VG	VF
1194. Jia Tai Yuan Bao, 2 Cash, Chun above & Yuan below, Iron S-844	2.00	5.00
1195. Ditto, Tong above & Yuan below, Iron	2.00	5.00
1196. Ditto, Han above & Yuan below, Iron S-845	2.00	5.00
1197. Jia Tai Tong Bao, 2 Cash, Tong above & Yuan below, Iron	2.00	5.00
1198. Ditto, Chun above & 2 below, Iron S-848	2.00	5.00
1199. Ditto, Li above & 60 below, Iron	2.00	5.00
1200. Jia Tai Yuan Bao, 3 Cash, Li & Yuan on reverse, Iron	2.00	5.00
1201. Ditto, Chuan & 1 above & 38 below, Iron S-854	5.00	10.00
1202. Ditto, Chuan & 3 above and 41 below, Iron	5.00	10.00

1203

1204

1205

1206

1207

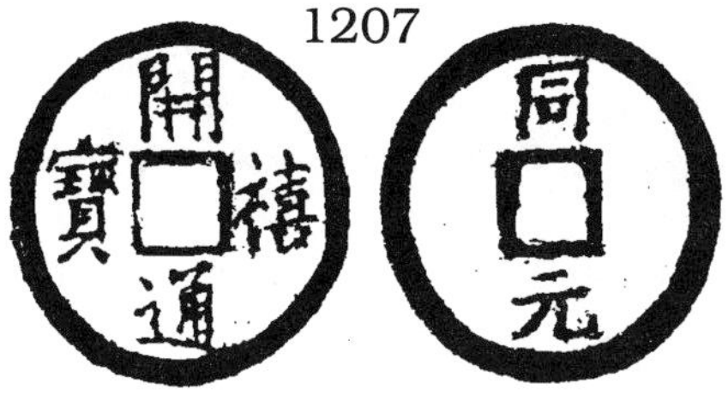

1208

1209

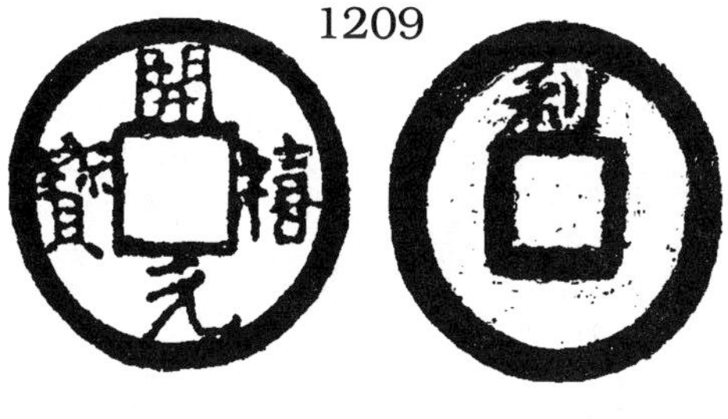

1210

1211

	VG	VF
1203. Kai Xi Tong Bao, 3 on reverse S-859/FD-1331	2.00	5.00
1204. Ditto, Iron, Chun above & Yuan below	2.00	5.00
1205. Ditto, Tong above & 2 below, Iron FD-1336	2.00	5.00
1206. Ditto, Chun above & 2 below, Iron	2.00	5.00
1207. Ditto, 2 Cash, Tong above & Yuan below S-863	5.00	10.00
1208. Ditto, Han above & Yuan below, Iron S-866	5.00	10.00
1209. Kai Xi Yuan Bao, 3 Cash, Li on reverse, Iron	2.00	5.00
1210. Ditto, Han above & 2 below, Iron	2.00	5.00
1211. Ditto, Chun above & 3 below, Iron	2.00	5.00

N.B. The Kai Xi coins are dated from the 1st year through the 3rd.

1212

1213

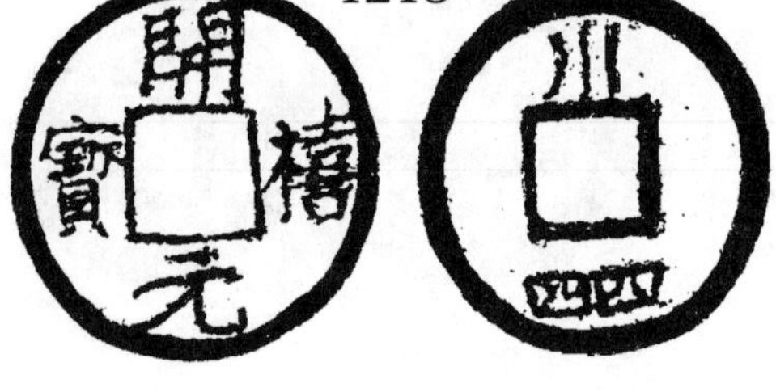

1214

1215

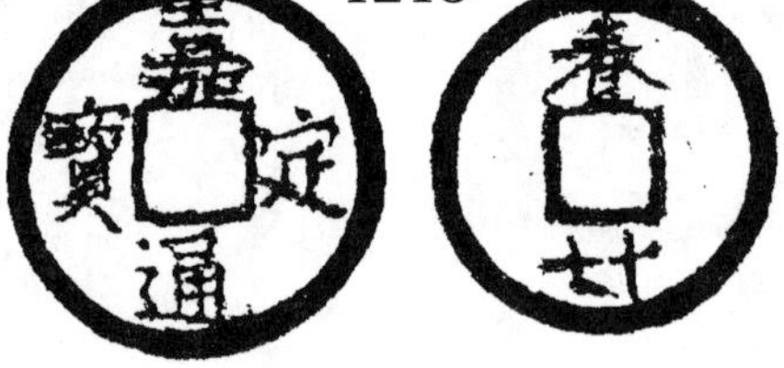

1216

1217

1218

	VG	VF
1212. Kai Xi Yuan Bao, Numeral 3 & Chuan above and 42 below, Iron S-873	5.00	10.00
1213. Ditto, Chuan & 3 above and 44 below, Iron	5.00	10.00
1214. Jia Ding Tong Bao, 14 on reverse S-889/FD-1361	2.00	5.00
1215. Ditto, Chun above & 17 below, Iron	2.00	5.00
1216. Ditto, Han above & 15 below, Iron	2.00	5.00
1217. Ditto, 3 Cash, Yong above & 5 below FD-1410	5.00	10.00
1218. Ditto, Xing above & 5 below, Iron FD-1411, (The numeral 5 is in orthodox script).	5.00	10.00

N.B. The Jia Ding coins are dated from the 1st year through the 14th.

1219

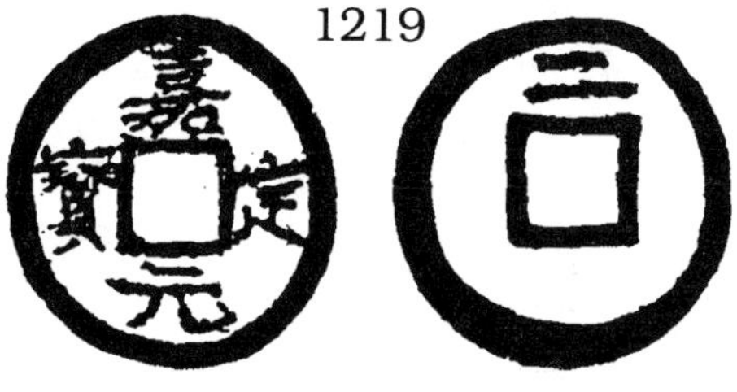

1220

1221

1222

1223

1224

1225

1226

	VG	VF
1219. Jia Ding Yuan Bao, Numeral 2 on reverse, Iron S-905/FD-1418	2.00	5.00
1220. Ditto, 3 Cash, Li Zhou above & 3 below S-933	2.00	5.00
1221. Ditto, Li & 2 (Orthodox script) above & 5 below, 5 Cash, Iron	5.00	10.00
1222. Ditto, 5 Cash, Li & 1 (Orthodox script) above and 5 (Seal script) below, Iron F-1422	5.00	10.00
1223. Ditto, Yong above & 5 below, Iron FD-1425	5.00	10.00
1224. Ditto, Seal script, 3 above & below S-932/FD-1421	25.00	50.00
1225. Jia Ding Chong Bao, Crescent & 2 stars on reverse FD-1428	15.00	30.00
1226. Jia Ding Quan Bao, 3 on reverse, Iron FD-1429	15.00	30.00

1227

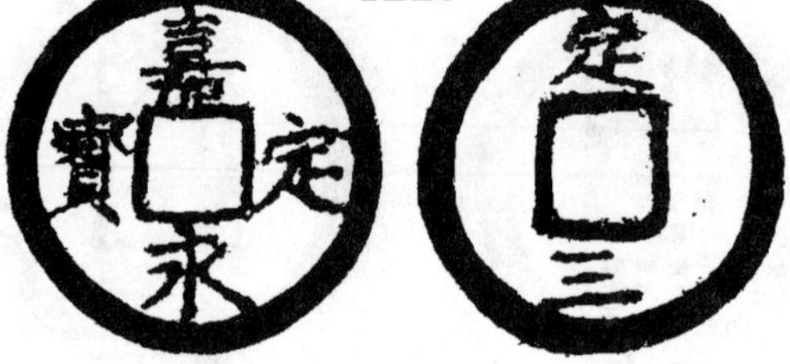

1228

1229

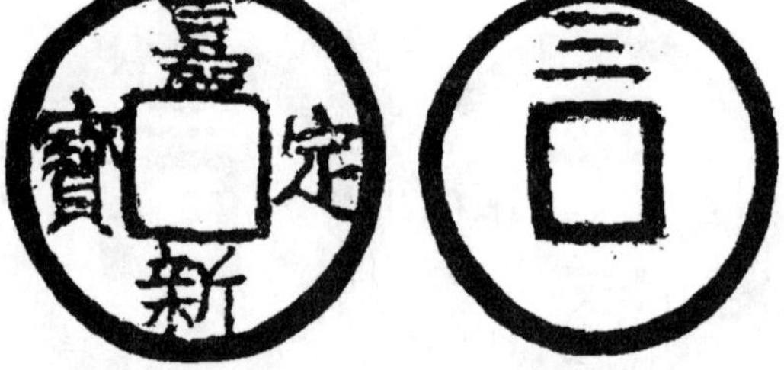

1230

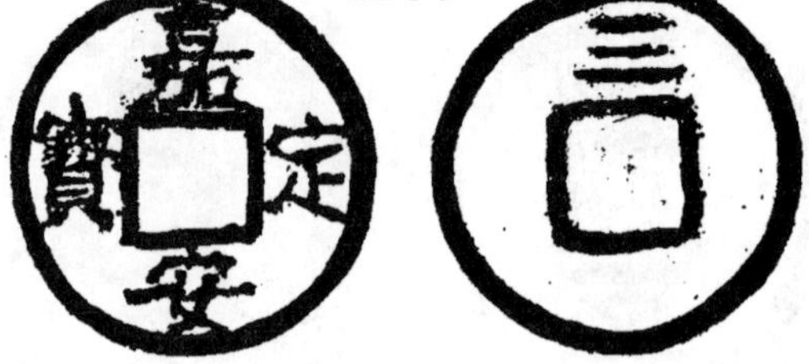

1231

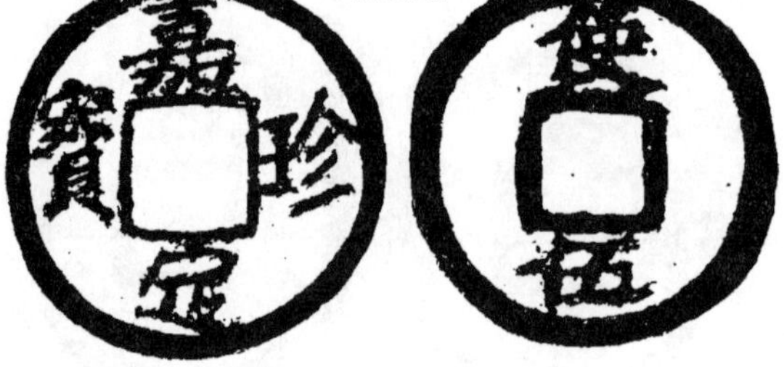

1232

	VG	VF
1227. Jia Ding Yong Bao, Ding above & 3 below, Iron FD-1433	10.00	20.00
1228. Jia Ding Zhen Bao, Crescent & 2 stars on reverse, Iron S-937/FD-1434	10.00	20.00
1229. Jia Ding Xin Bao, 3 on reverse, Iron FD-1435	15.00	30.00
1230. Jia Ding An Bao, 3 on reverse, Iron FD-1436	25.00	50.00
1231. Jia Ding Zhen Bao, Shi above & 5 (Orthodox script) below, Iron FD-1437	35.00	70.00
1232. Jia Ding Long Bao, 3 on reverse, Iron, FD-1438	70.00	140.00

1233

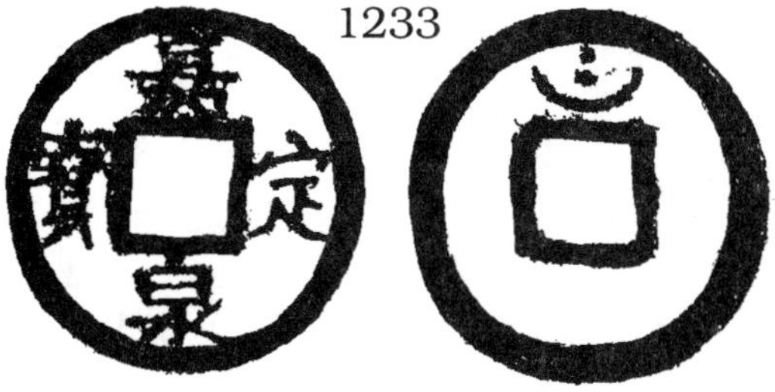

1234

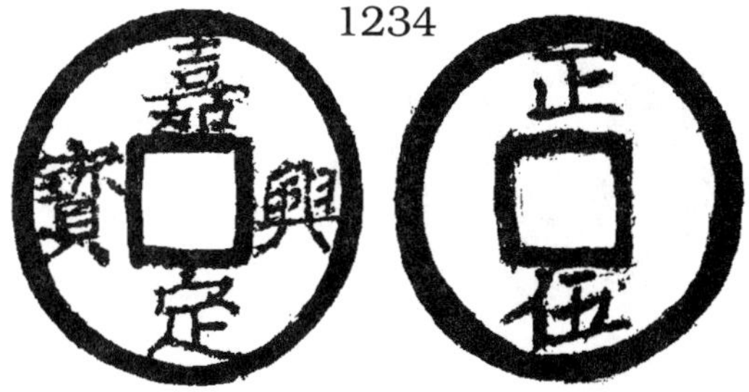

1235

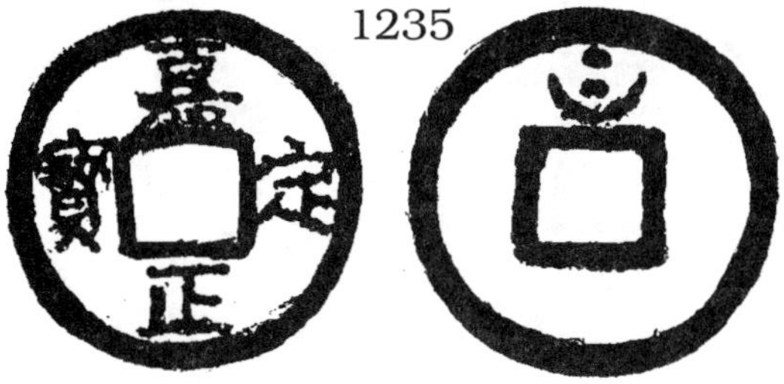

1236

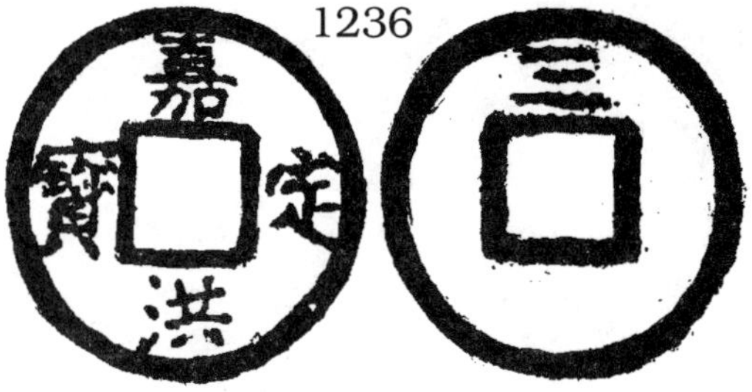

1237

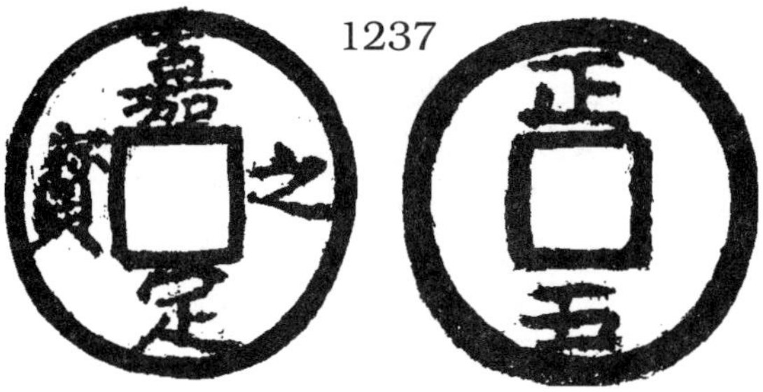

1238

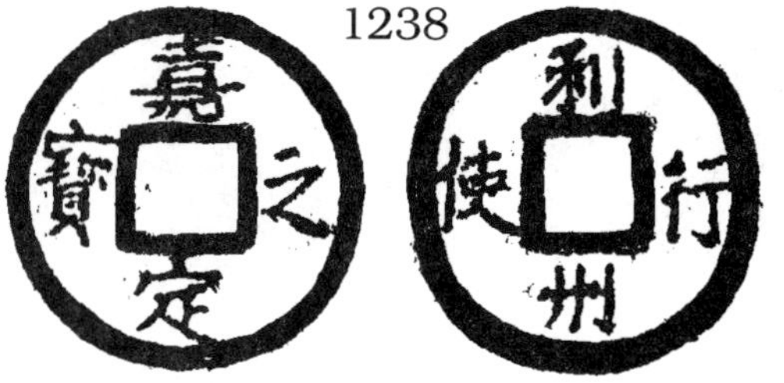

	VG	VF
1233. Jia Ding Quan Bao, Crescent & 2 stars on reverse, Iron FD-1439	45.00	90.00
1234. Jia Ding Xing Bao, Zheng above & 5 below, Iron, S-953/FD-1440	15.00	30.00
1235. Jia Ding Zheng Bao, Crescent & 2 stars on reverse, Iron FD-1441	10.00	20.00
1236. Jia Ding Hong Bao, 3 on reverse, Iron FD-1442	35.00	70.00
1237. Jia Ding Zhi Bao, Zheng above & 5 below, Iron S-954/FD-1443	5.00	10.00
1238. Jia Ding Zhi Bao, 3 Cash, Li Zhou (Top to bottom), & Xing Shi (read from right to left), Iron S-940/FD-1444	5.00	10.00

1239

1240

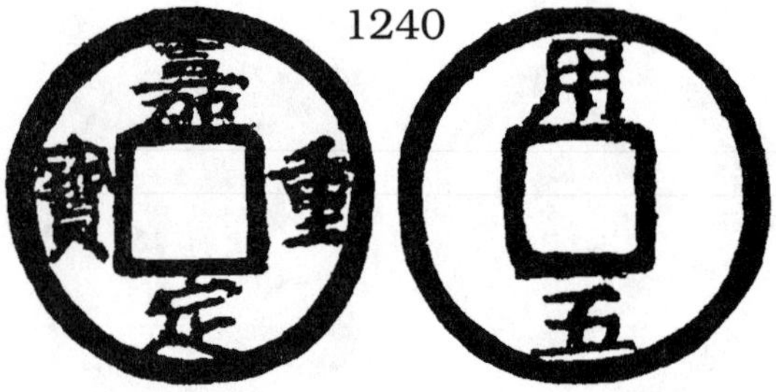

1241

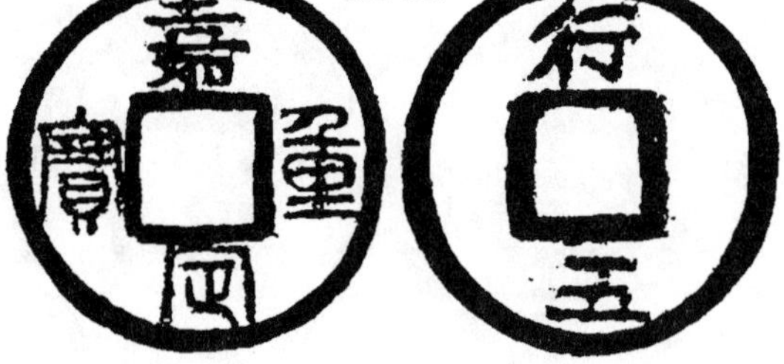

1242

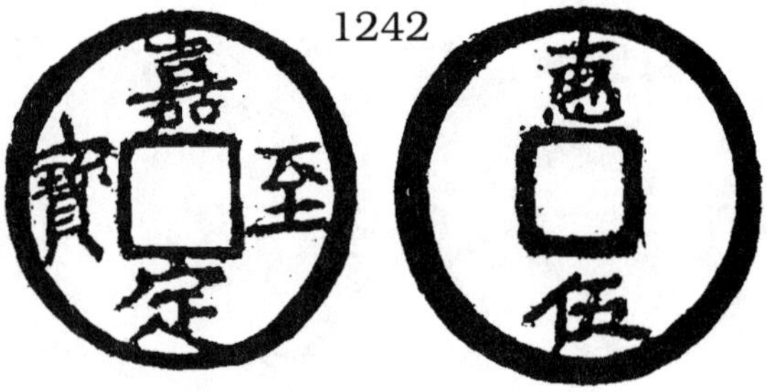

1243

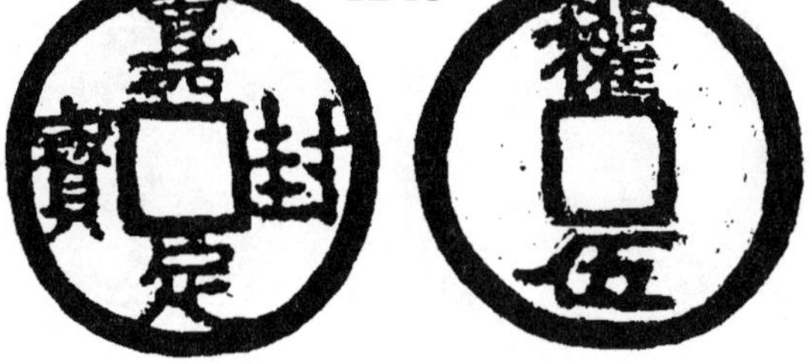

	VG	VF
1239. Jia Ding Wan Bao, Plain reverse, Iron, S-938/FD-1445	10.00	20.00
1240. Jia Ding Zhong Bao, Yong above & 5 below, Iron FD-1446	5.00	10.00
1241. Ditto, Seal script, Xing above & 5 below, Iron S-950/FD-1447	5.00	10.00
1242. Jia Ding Zhi Bao, Hui above & 5 below, Iron S-955/FD-1448	10.00	20.00
1243. Jia Ding Feng Bao, Quan above & 5 below, Iron FD-1449	120.00	240.00

N.B. The Jia Ding coins are dated from the 1st year through the 14th.

1244

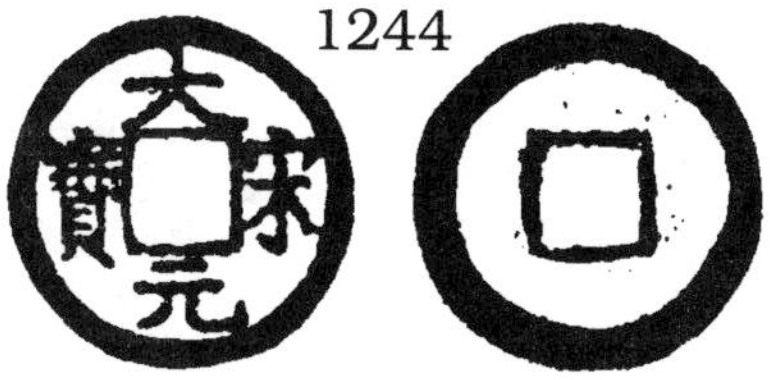

1245

1246

1247

1248

1249

1250

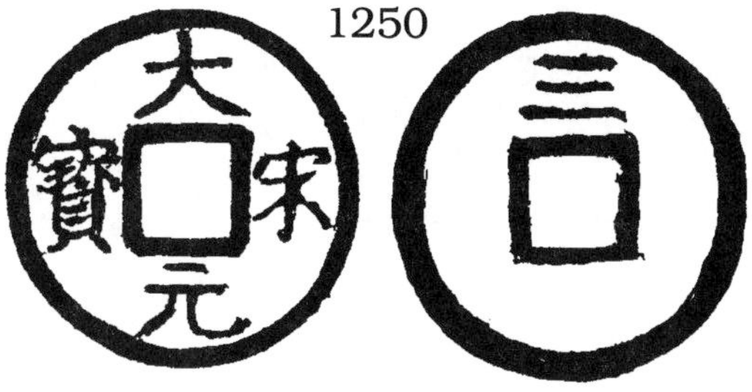

1251

1252

	VG	VF
1244. Da Song Yuan Bao, Plain reverse FD-1455	20.00	35.00
1245. Ditto, Yuan on reverse S-959/FD-1456	5.00	10.00
1246. Ditto, Numeral 3 on reverse S-960/FD-1458	5.00	10.00
1247. Ditto, Chun above & 3 below, Iron	5.00	10.00
1248. Ditto, Han above & crescent below, Iron	5.00	10.00
1249. Da Song Tong Bao, Han above & 3 below, Iron	10.00	20.00
1250. Da Song Yuan Bao, 3 Cash, Iron FD-1162	10.00	20.00
1251. Ditto, Xi above & 3 below FD-1464, Iron	10.00	20.00
1252. Ditto, Quan above & 3 below, Iron S-964, FD-1465	10.00	20.00

N.B. The Da Song coins are dated from the 1st year through the 3rd.

1253

1254

1255

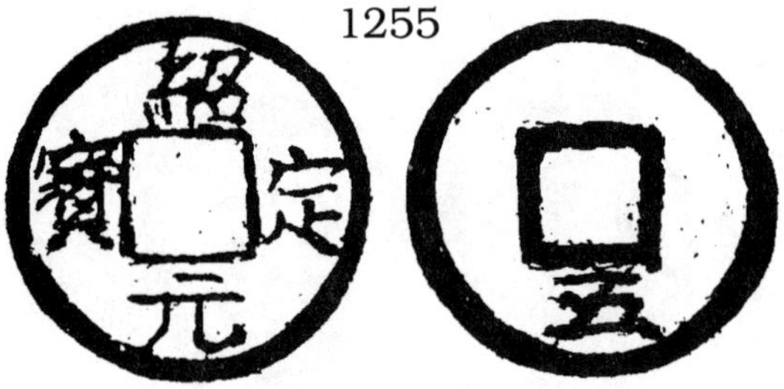

1256

1257

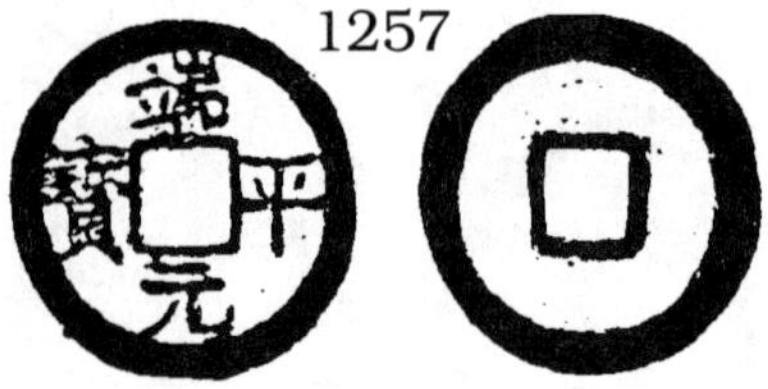

1258

	VG	VF
1253. Shao Ding Tong Bao, Numeral 4 on reverse, S-970/FD-1473	2.00	5.00
1254. Ditto, Chun above & 3 below, Iron S-980	5.00	10.00
1255. Shao Ding Yuan Bao, 5 Cash, Numeral 5 on reverse, Iron	15.00	30.00
1256. Duan Ping Yuan Bao, Yuan on reverse (Numeral 1) S-981/FD-1487	15.00	25.00
1257. Ditto, Plain reverse	35.00	70.00
1258. Duan Ping Tong Bao, Chun above & Yuan below, Iron	40.00	80.00

N.B. The Shao Ding coins are dated from the 1st year through the 6th; Duan Ping coins are dated only the 1st year.

1259

1260

1261

1262

1263

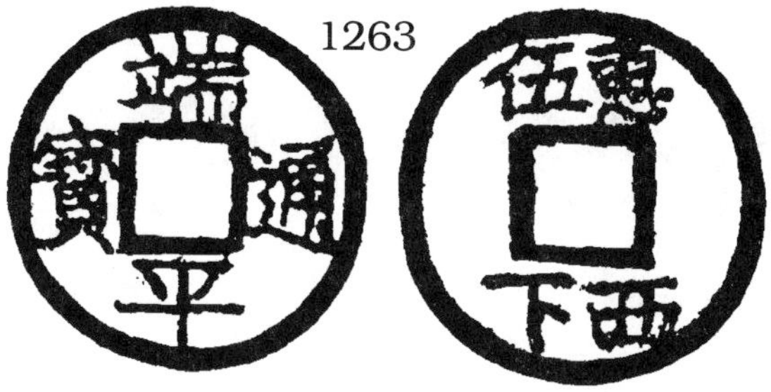

1264

1265

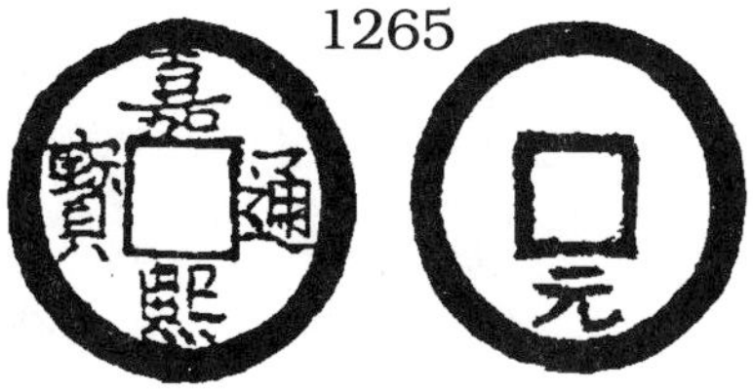

1266

	VG	VF
1259. Duan Ping Yuan Bao, Qiong above & 5 below, 5 Cash, Iron S-985	10.00	20.00
1260. Ditto, Ding & 5 above, Bei & Zhong below, Iron	10.00	20.00
1261. Ditto, Dong & Zhong above, and 5 below, Iron	10.00	20.00
1262. Ditto, Bei & Shang above, and 5 below, Iron	10.00	20.00
1263. Duan Ping Tong Bao, Hui & 5 above, and Xi & Xia below, Iron	10.00	20.00
1264. Ditto, Hui & 5 above, Xi & Shang below S-988	10.00	20.00
1265. Jia Xi Tong Bao, Yuan on reverse S-992/FD-1505	2.00	5.00
1266. Ditto, 5 Cash, 5 above, and Dong & Zhong below, Iron FD-1514	30.00	60.00

N.B. The Jia Xi coins are dated from the 1st year through the 4th.

1267

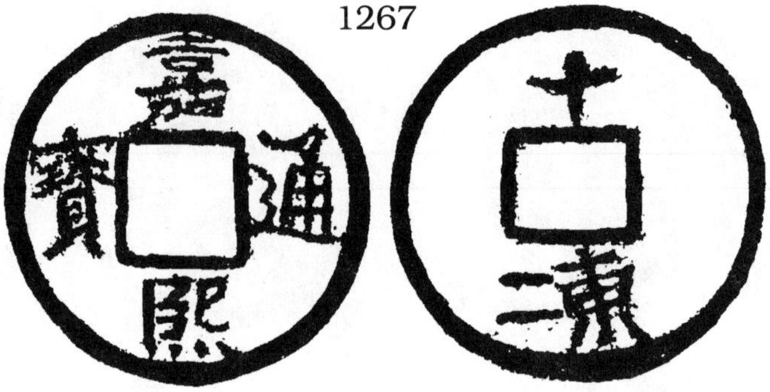

1268

1269

1270

1271

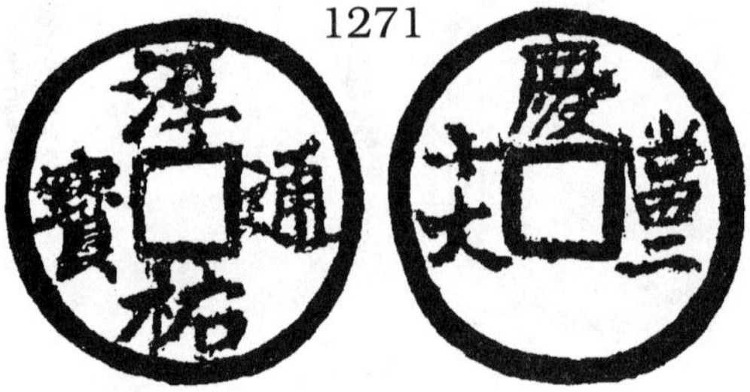

1272

	VG	VF
1267. Jia Xi Tong Bao, 10 above & Dong and 2 below, Iron	300.00	600.00
1268. Chun You Yuan Bao, 10 on reverse S-1008/FD-1528	2.00	5.00
1269. Ditto, 11 on reverse S-1009/FD-1529	20.00	40.00
1270. Ditto, 12 on reverse S-1010/FD-1530	5.00	10.00
1271. Chun You Tong Bao, Qing above, Value 2 on right & 10 Cash on the left, Iron FD-1556	500.00	800.00
1272. Chun You Tong Bao, Value 100 FD-1558	70.00	140.00

N.B. The Chun You coins are dated from the 1st year through the 12th.

Yuan Dynasty Varieties

1273

1274

1275

1276

1277

1278

1279

1280

1281

1282

1283

	VG	VF
1273. Da Ding Tong Bao, Shen on rev. S-1488/FD-1642	2.00	5.00
1274. Ditto, You on reverse S-1489/FD-1643	2.00	5.00
1275. Ditto, 2 Cash FD-1646	120.00	240.00
1276. Chong Qing Tong Bao, FD-1664, VR	—	—
1277. Zheng Guan Bao Qian, Tangut script, R	3500.00	—
1278. Qian You Yuan Bao, Tangut script FD-1685	250.00	500.00
1279. Tian Qing Yuan Bao, Tangut script FD-1690	250.00	500.00
1280. Da Chao Jin He FD-1697	500.00	1000.00
1281. Zhi Da Yuan Bao FD-1723	80.00	150.00
1282. Zhi Da Yuan Bao, 2 Cash FD-1727	700.00	1400.00
1283. Zhi Zheng Tong Bao, 10 Cash, Mao above (Mongol script) & 10 below FD-1809	150.00	300.00

Ming Dynasty Varieties

1284

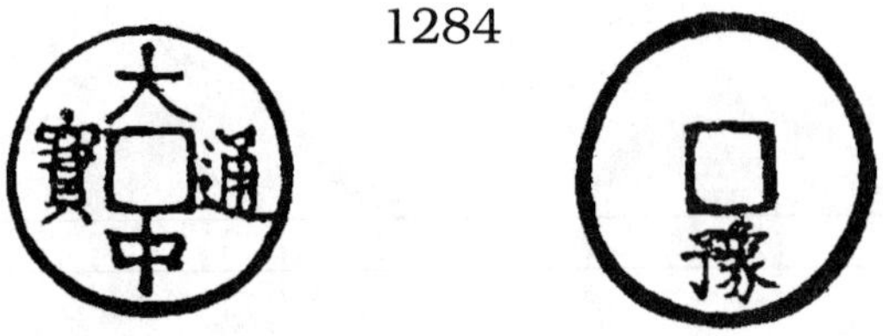

1285

1286

1287

1288

1289

1290

1291

1292

1293

	VG	VF
1284. Da Zhong Tong Bao, Yu on reverse FD-1851	15.00	30.00
1285. Ditto, Zhe on reverse FD-1847	1000.00	2000.00
1286. Ditto, Gui above & 1 below FD-1849	50.00	100.00
1287. Ditto, 2 Cash, Beiping on reverse FD-1855	300.00	600.00
1288. Ditto, Jing on reverse FD-1857	1000.00	2000.00
1289. Ditto, Ji on reverse FD-1859	1000.00	2000.00
1290. Ditto, E on reverse FD-1856	1000.00	2000.00
1291. Ditto, Yu on reverse FD-1862	40.00	80.00
1292. Ditto, 2 above & Fu below FD-1861	300.00	600.00
1293. Ditto, Guang on right, and 2 on the left FD-1863	450.00	900.00

1294

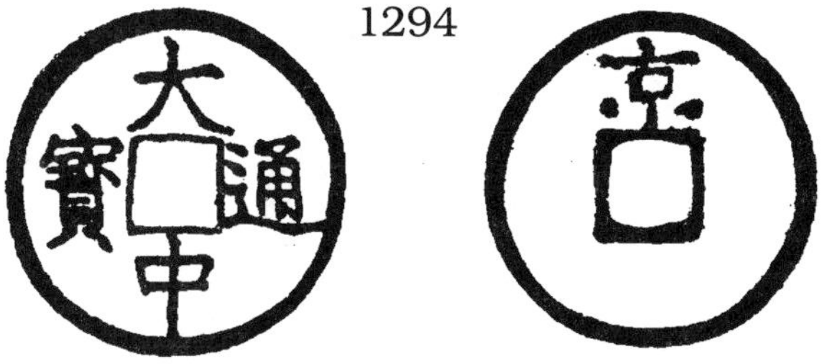

1295

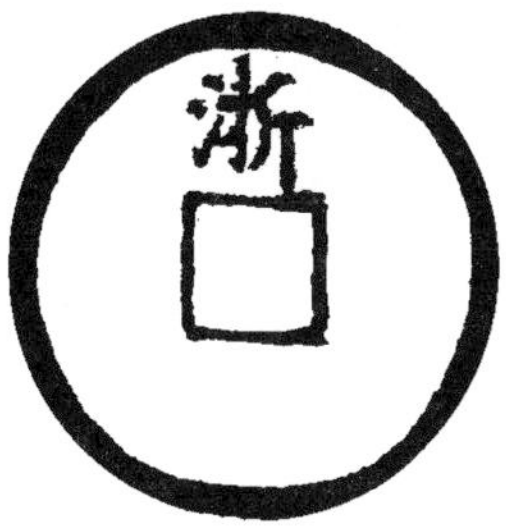

1296

1297

1298

1299

1300

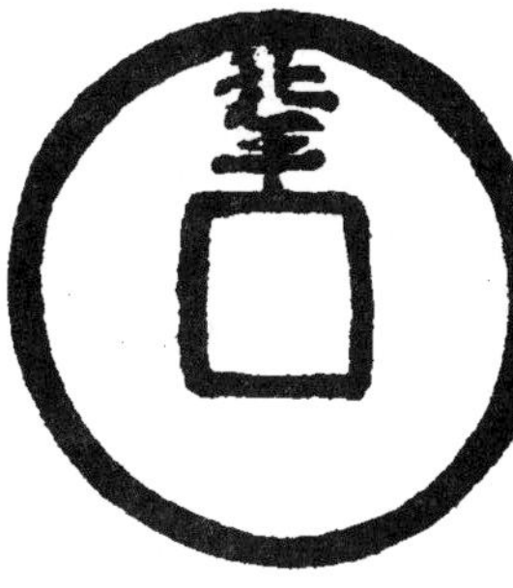

1301

1302

1303

	VG	VF
1294. Da Zhong Tong Bao, 3 Cash, Jing on reverse, FD-1867	450.00	900.00
1295. Ditto, Zhe on reverse FD-1868	30.00	60.00
1296. Ditto, 3 above & Fu below FD-1871	1000.00	2000.00
1297. Ditto, Yu on reverse; FD-1872	50.00	100.00
1298. Ditto, Guang on right & 3 on the left FD-1873	1000.00	3000.00
1299. Ditto, 5 Cash, Jing on reverse FD-1877	700.00	1400.00
1300. Ditto, Beiping on reverse FD-1875	400.00	800.00
1301. Ditto, Gui above & 5 below FD-1880	100.00	2000.00
1302. Ditto, 5 above & Fu below FD-1881	350.00	700.00
1303. Ditto, Guang on right, and 5 on the left, FD-1883		

1304

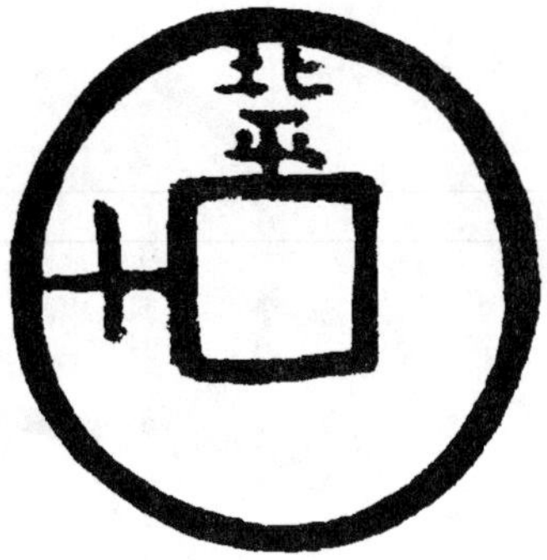

1305

1306

1307

1308

1309

	VG	VF
1304. Da Zhong Tong Bao, 10 Cash, Beiping above & 10 on the left FD-1885	50.00	100.00
1305. Ditto, E above & 10 below, FD-1887	50.00	100.00
1306. Ditto, Ji above & 10 below, S-1136/FD-1890	35.00	70.00
1307. Ditto, Gui above & 10 below, FD-1891	90.00	180.00
1308. Ditto, 10 above & Yu below, FD-1892	25.00	50.00
1309. Ditto, 10 above & Zhe below, S-1135/FD-1894	25.00	50.00

1310

1311

1312

1313

1314

1315

1316

1317

1318

1319

	VG	VF
1310. Hong Wu Tong Bao, 1 Mace on reverse (1 Cash), S-1142/FD-1896	1.00	3.00
1311. Ditto, Gui on reverse FD-1902	2.00	5.00
1312. Ditto, Gui above & 1 below FD-1903	65.00	130.00
1313. Ditto, Yu on reverse FD-1906	15.00	30.00
1314. Ditto, Fu on reverse S-1148/FD-1904	5.00	10.00
1315. Hong Wu Tong Bao, 2 Cash, 2 Mace on reverse, FD-1909	5.00	10.00
1316. Ditto, Plain on reverse FD-1912	300.00	600.00
1317. Ditto, Ji on reverse FD-1914	1200.00	2400.00
1318. Ditto, Gui above & 2 below FD-1915	1000.00	2000.00
1319. Ditto, Guang on right & 2 on the left, FD-1918	1200.00	2400.00

1320

1321

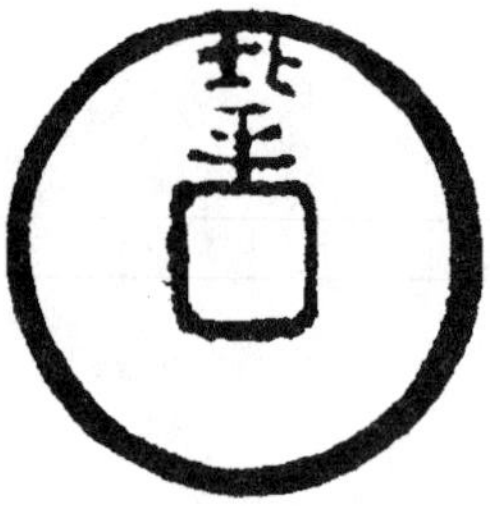

1322

1323

1324

1325

1326

	VG	VF
1320. Hong Wu Tong Bao, 3 Cash, 3 Mace on reverse S-1155/FD-1922	5.00	10.00
1321. Ditto, Beiping on reverse, FD-1923	200.00	400.00
1322. Ditto, Jing on reverse FD-1925	650.00	1300.00
1323. Ditto, Yu on reverse FD-1930	35.00	70.00
1324. Ditto, E on reverse FD-1924	1200.00	2400.00
1325. Ditto, 3 above & Fu below FD-1929	250.00	500.00
1326. Ditto, Guang on right & 3 on the left FD-1931	—	—
1327. Ditto, Hong Wu Tong Bao, 5 Cash, 5 on reverse FD-1933	450.00	900.00

1327

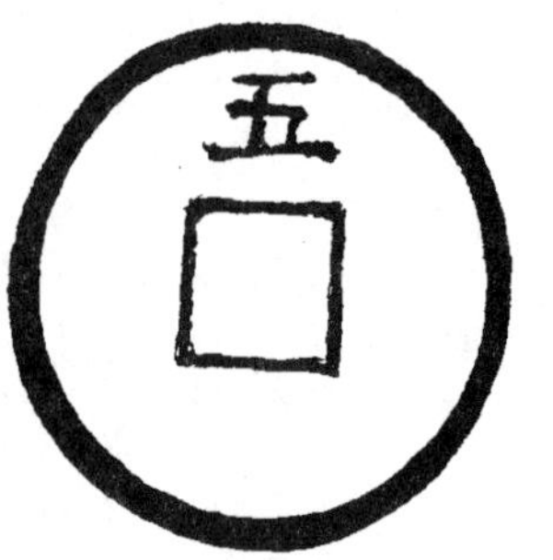

1328

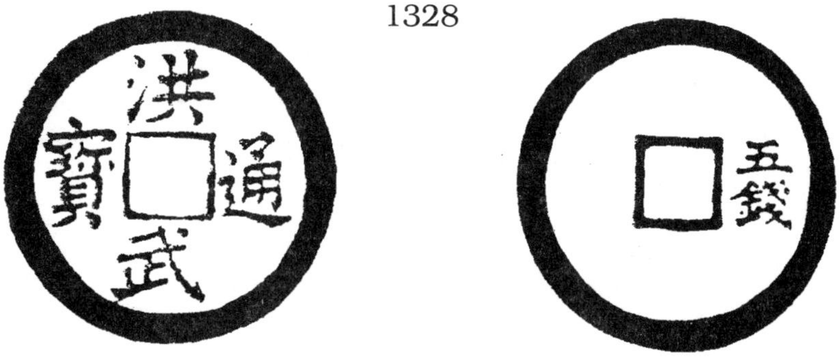

1329

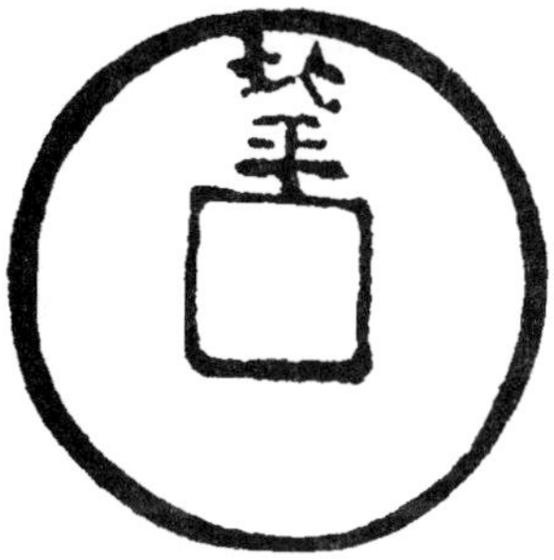

1330

1331

1332

1333

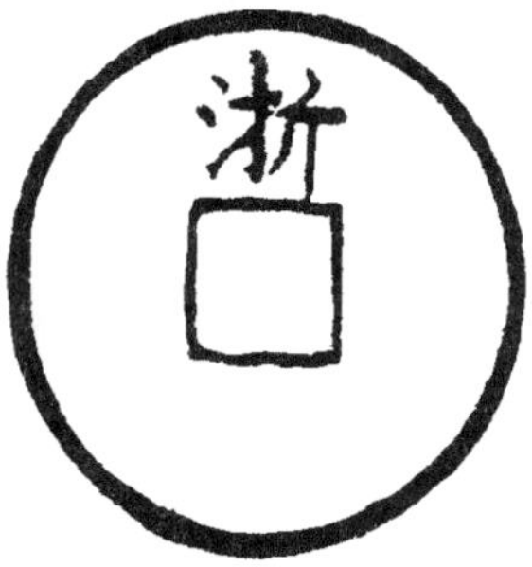

1334

	VG	VF
1328. Hong Wu Tong Bao, 5 Cash, 5 Mace on reverse S-1157/FD-1934	60.00	120.00
1329. Ditto, Beiping on reverse, FD-1935	200.00	400.00
1330. Ditto, Jing on reverse FD-1937	600.00	1200.00
1331. Ditto, E on reverse FD-1936	1200.00	2400.00
1332. Ditto, Ji on reverse FD-1939	1000.00	2000.00
1333. Ditto, Zhe on reverse FD-1938	50.00	100.00
1334. Ditto, Guang on right & 5 on the left FD-1944	1200.00	2400.00

1335

1336

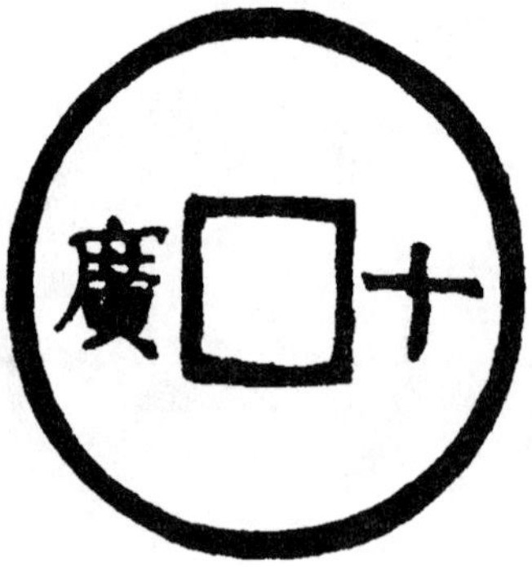

1337

1338

1339

1340

	VG	VF
1335. Hong Wu Tong Bao, 10 Cash, Beiping above & 10 on the right S-1161/FD-1947	45.00	90.00
1336. Ditto, 10 on right & Guang on the left FD-1949	450.00	900.00
1337. Ditto, Ji above & 10 below, FD-1951	45.00	90.00
1338. Ditto, 10 above & Yu below, S-1160/FD-1953	30.00	60.00
1339. Ditto, 10 above & Fu below, S-1163/FD-1954	25.00	50.00
1340. Ditto, 10 above & Zhe below, S-1162/FD-1957	25.00	50.00

1341

1342

1343

1344

1345

1346

1347

1348

1349

1350

	VG	VF
1341. Yong Le Tong Bao, 3 Cash, 3 Mace on reverse, ER	—	—
1342. Hong Xi Tong Bao, ER	—	—
1343. Hong Zhi Tong Bao, 10 Cash, ER	—	—
1344. Jia Jing Tong Bao, 10 Cash, ER	—	—
1345. Wan Li Tong Bao, Crescent on reverse, FD-1973	65.00	120.00
1346. Ditto, Tian on reverse FD-1977	35.00	60.00
1347. Ditto, Gong on reverse S-1189/FD-1976	25.00	50.00
1348. Ditto, Zheng on reverse FD-1975	120.00	200.00
1349. Ditto, Gong on reverse FD-1974	8.00	15.00
1350. Ditto, Dragon pattern on reverse	350.00	650.00

1351

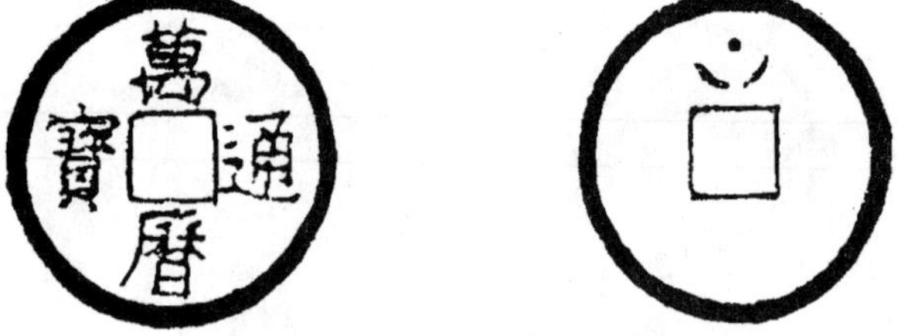

1352

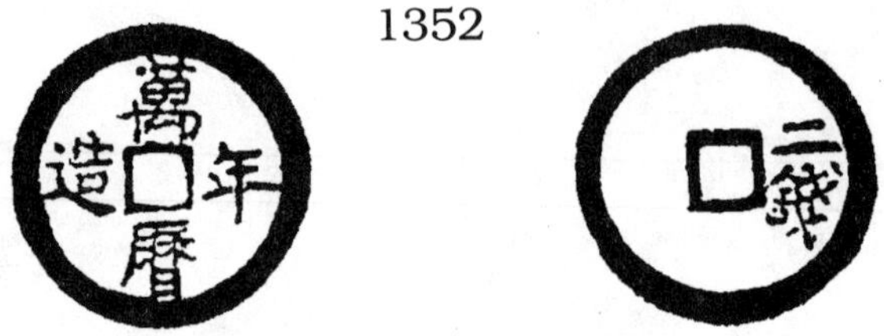

1353

1354

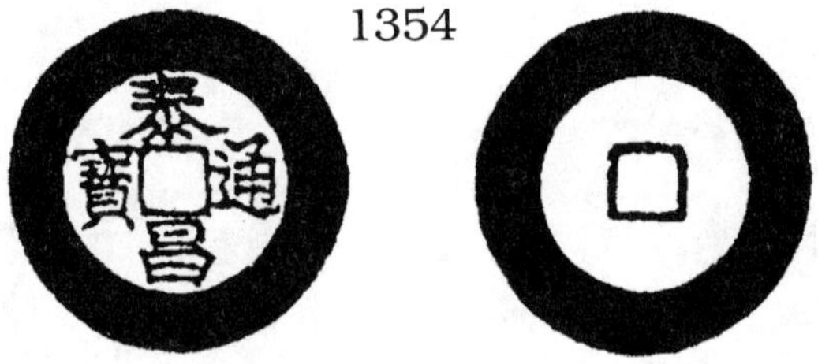

1355

1356

1357

	VG	VF
1351. Wan Li Tong Bao, Crescent & star on reverse, FD-1981	200.00	350.00
1352. Wan Li read from top to bottom & Year of Make from right to left, 2 Mace on rev. Silver, VR	—	—
1353. Tai Chang Tong Bao, Wan Li Tong Bao on reverse FD-1987	55.00	100.00
1354. Tai Chang Tong Bao, 2 Cash	500.00	900.00
1355. Tian Qi Tong Bao, Star on reverse	6.00	10.00
1356. Ditto, Hu on reverse S-1207/FD-1990	2.00	5.00
1357. Ditto, Zhen on reverse FD-2004	50.00	90.00

1358

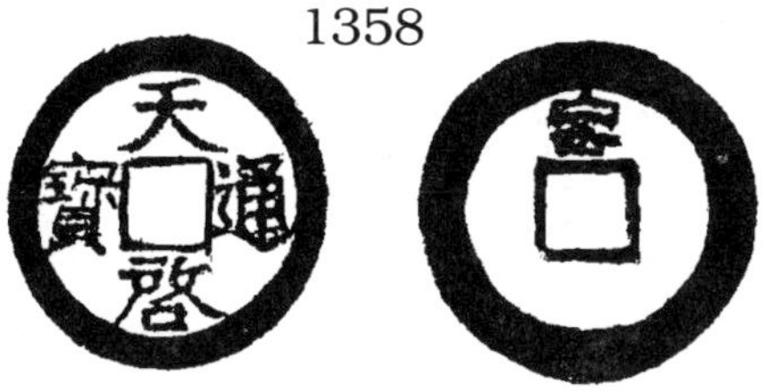

1359

1360

1361

1362

1363

1364

1365

1366

1367

	VG	VF
1358. Tian Qi Tong Bao, Mi on reverse, FD-2001	90.00	180.00
1359. Ditto, 2 Cash, 2 on rev. Silver, VR	—	—
1360. Chong Zhen Tong Bao, Gong on reverse, S-1251/FD-2048	1.00	2.00
1361. Ditto, Hu on reverse S-1249/FD-2046	2.00	5.00
1362. Ditto, Jing on reverse	400.00	800.00
1363. Ditto, Jia on reverse S-1236/FD-2038	5.00	10.00
1364. Ditto, Bing on reverse S-1238/FD-2040	10.00	20.00
1365. Ditto, Ding on reverse FD-2041	50.00	100.00
1366. Ditto, Wu on reverse S-1239/FD-2042	2.00	5.00
1367. Ditto, Ji on reverse S-1240/FD-2043	4.00	8.00

1368

1369

1370

1371

1372

1373

1374

1375

1376

1377

1378

1379

	VG	VF
1368. Chong Zhen Tong Bao, Guan above & crescent below S-1256/FD-2062	5.00	10.00
1369. Ditto, Gui on reverse S-1269/FD-2070	1.00	2.00
1370. Ditto, Jiang on reverse S-1258/FD-2052	2.00	5.00
1371. Ditto, Ju on reverse S-1254/FD-2063	2.00	5.00
1372. Ditto, Zhong on reverse S-1266/FD-2065	10.00	20.00
1373. Ditto, Ning on reverse FD-2068	70.00	140.00
1374. Ditto, Guang on reverse S-1270/FD-2072	10.00	20.00
1375. Ditto, Gong on reverse FD-2067	30.00	60.00
1376. Ditto, Zhi on reverse FD-2076	100.00	200.00
1377. Ditto, Ying on reverse S-1267/FD-2071	2.00	5.00
1378. Ditto, Qing above & Zhong below, FD-2066	10.00	20.00
1379. Ditto, Tai Ping on reverse S-1271, FD-2078	10.00	20.00

1380

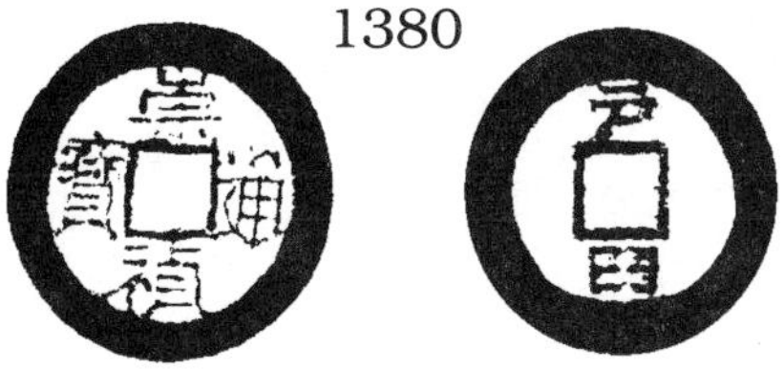

1381

1382

1383

1384

1385

1386

1387

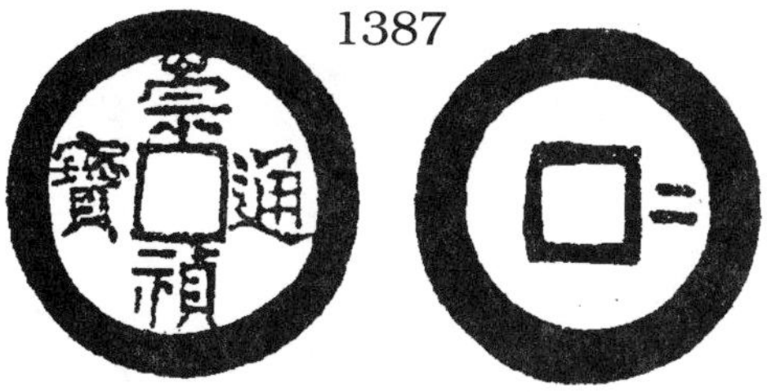

1388

1389

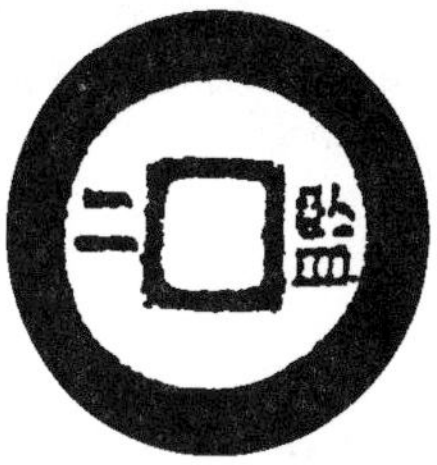

	VG	**VF**
1380. Chong Zhen Tong Bao, Hu above & Jiu below, S-1250/FD-2047	5.00	10.00
1381. Ditto, Jiu on reverse FD-2055	80.00	160.00
1382. Ditto, Xin on reverse S-1257/FD-2053	2.00	5.00
1383. Ditto, Qing on reverse FD-2064	3.00	6.00
1384. Ditto, Chong above & star below FD-2056	5.00	10.00
1385. Chong Zhen Tong Bao, 2 Cash, Gong above & 2 below S-1281/FD-2088	20.00	40.00
1386. Ditto, Ju on right & 2 on the left FD-2087	40.00	80.00
1387. Ditto, 2 on reverse S-1283/FD-2091	2.00	6.00
1388. Ditto, Hu on right & 2 on the left FD-2084	10.00	20.00
1389. Ditto, Jian on right & 2 on the left FD-2092	40.00	80.00

Southern Ming Varieties

1390

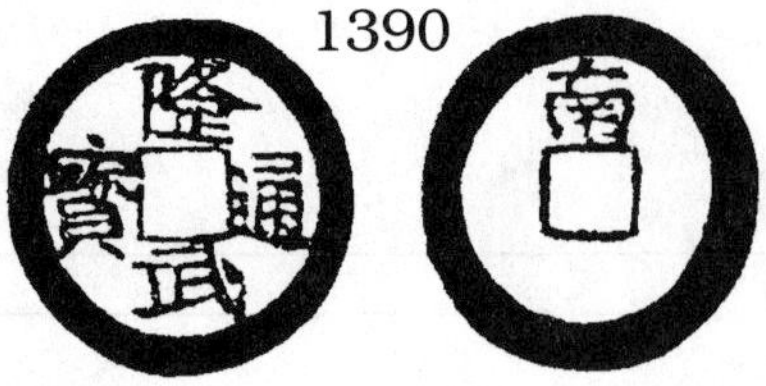

1391

1392

1393

1394

1395

1396

1397

1398

	VG	VF
1390. Long Wu Tong Bao, Nan on reverse	500.00	1000.00
1391. Yong Li Tong Bao, 2 above & Li below S-1314/FD-2127	5.00	10.00
1392. Ditto, Yu on reverse FD-2119	35.00	70.00
1393. Ditto, Du on reverse	5.00	10.00
1394. Ditto, Bu on reverse FD-2123	60.00	120.00
1395. Ditto, Fu on reverse	750.00	1500.00
1396. Ditto, Liu on reverse S-1305	5.00	10.00
1397. Ditto, Yue on reverse S-1306/FD-2121	10.00	20.00
1398. Ditto, Fu on reverse S-1307/FD-2118	8.00	16.00

Qing Dynasty Varieties & Variants

1399

1400

1401

1402

1403

1404

1405

1406

1407

1408

1409

	VG	VF
1399. Shun Zhi Tong Bao, Board of Revenue in Manchu script S-1405/FD-2178	1.00	2.00
1400. Ditto, Board of Works S-1406/FD-2179	1.00	2.00
1401. Ditto, Chang on rev. in Han script S-1376/FD-2203	20.00	40.00
1402. Ditto, Yuan on reverse S-1371/FD-2212	10.00	20.00
1403. Ditto, Ning on reverse S-1377/FD-2205	5.00	10.00
1404. Ditto, He on reverse S-1364/FD-2184	5.00	10.00
1405. Ditto, Yun on reverse S-1373/FD-2199	5.00	10.00
1406. Ditto, Xuan on right & 1 Cash on the left, FD-2225	8.00	16.00
1407. Ditto, Yuan & 1 Cash on rev. S-1397/FD-2223	8.00	16.00
1408. Ditto, Ning & 1 Cash on rev. S-1403/FD-2230	2.00	5.00
1409. Ditto, Lin & 1 Cash on rev. S-1396/FD-2222	2.00	5.00

1410

1411

1412

1413

1414

1415

1416

1417

1418

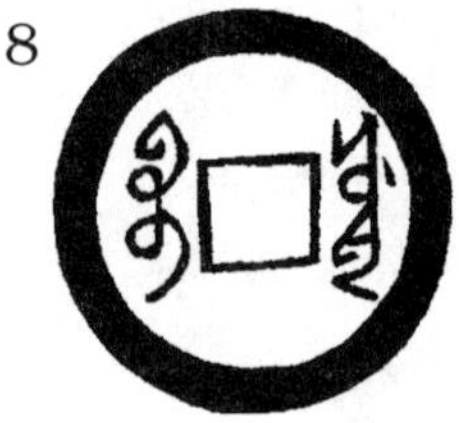

	VG	VF
1410. Shun Zhi Tong Bao, Hu & 1 Cash on reverse, S-1390/FD-2216	1.00	2.00
1411. Ditto, Chang & 1 Cash on rev. S-1401/FD-2228	1.00	2.00
1412. Ditto, Zhe & 1 Cash on rev. S-1393/FD-2219	1.00	2.00
1413. Ditto, He & 1 Cash on rev. S-1400/FD-2227	1.00	2.00
1414. Ditto, Fu & 1 Cash on rev. S-1394/FD-2220	8.00	16.00
1415. Ditto, Shaan & 1 Cash on rev. S-1402/FD-2229	5.00	10.00
1416. Ditto, Yun & 1 Cash on rev. S-1404/FD-2232	2.00	5.00
1417. Kang Xi Tong Bao, Crescent & star, and Nan in both Han & Manchu script on reverse S-1447	100.00	200.00
1418. Yong Zheng Tong Bao, Board of Works in Manchu script on reverse S-1453/FD-2278	2.00	5.00

1419

1420

1421

1422

1423

1424

1425

1426

1427

1428

	VG	VF
1419. Yong Zheng Tong Bao, Bao An on rev. S-1458/ FD-2286	2.00	5.00
1420. Ditto, Bao Nan mint	45.00	90.00
1421. Ditto, Bao Chuan mint FD-2294	20.00	40.00
1422. Qian Long Tong Bao, Yili mint FD-2327	2.00	4.00
1423. Ditto, Wushi mint FD-2329	2.00	4.00
1424. Ditto, Aksu mint FD-2328	2.00	4.00
1425. Ditto, Aksu above & 10 below	2.00	4.00
1426. Ditto, Kaxgar above & 10 below	2.00	4.00
1427. Ditto, Kuche above & 10 below	1.00	2.00
1428. Ditto, Yarkant mint FD-2330	2.00	4.00

1429

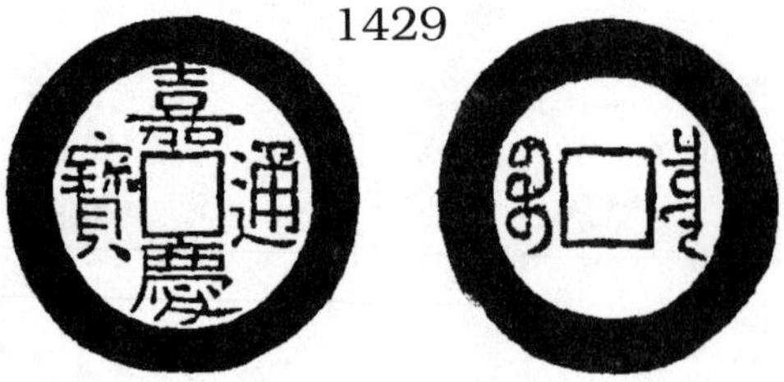

1430

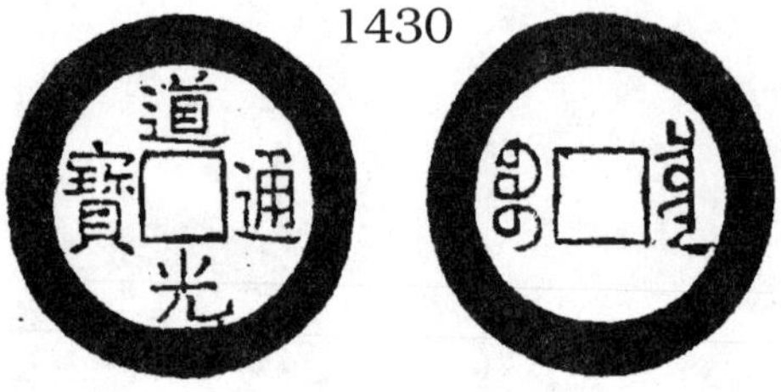

1431

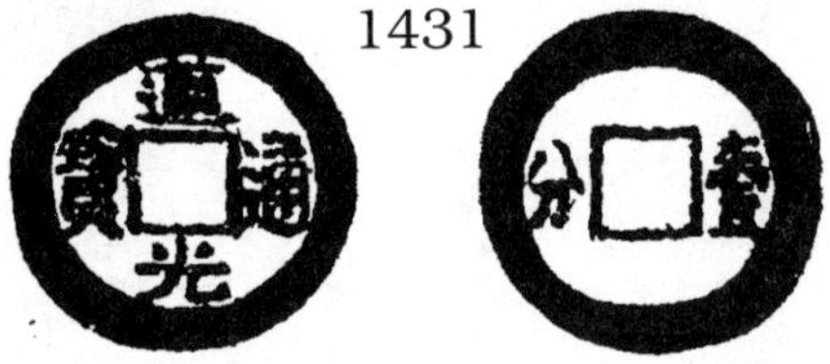

1432

1433

1434

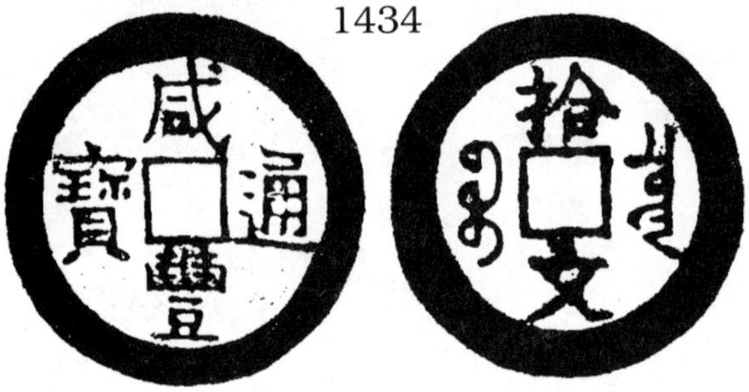

1435

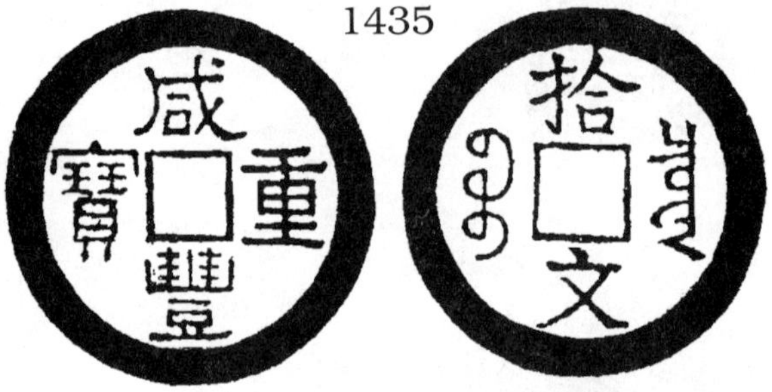

1436

	VG	VF
1429. Jia Qing Tong Bao, Large, Board of Revenue	5.00	10.00
1430. Dao Guang Tong Bao, Large, Board of Revenue	5.00	10.00
1431. Dao Guang Tong Bao, 1 Candareen on reverse FD-2410	60.00	180.00
1432. Ditto, 8th year above & 5 below, 5 Cash, Aksu mint FD-2408	5.00	10.00
1433. Ditto, 10 Cash, Aksu above & 10 below, Aksu in Manchu script	80.00	160.00
1434. Xian Feng Tong Bao, 10 Cash, 10 above & Cash below, Board of Revenue FD-2424	600.00	1200.00
1435. Xian Feng Zhong Bao, 10 above & Cash below FD-2426	1200.00	2400.00
1436. Ditto, 50 Cash, Crescent & star on field FD-2429	8.00	16.00

1437

1438

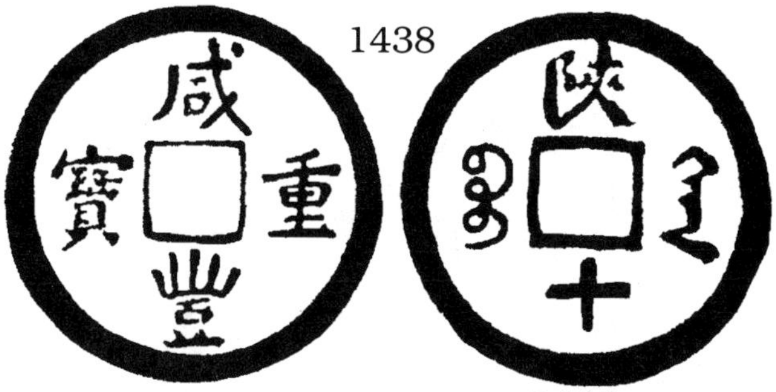

1443

1439

1440

1441

1442

1444

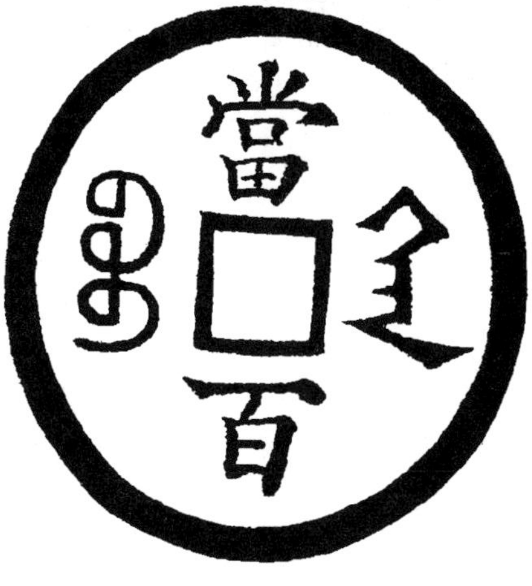

	VG	VF
1437. Xian Feng Zhong Bao, Value 10 Jinan mint	350.00	700.00
1438. Ditto, Shaan above & 10 below, Shaanxi mint	450.00	900.00
1439. Ditto, Value 10, Gongchang mint, FD-2541	90.00	180.00
1440. Ditto, Small size	2.00	5.00
1441. Ditto, Value 50, Gongchang mint	10.00	20.00
1442. Xian Feng Yuan Bao, Value 100, Gongchang mint	10.00	20.00
1443. Xian Feng Zhong Bao, Value 50, Shaanxi mint FD-2499	10.00	20.00
1444. Xian Feng Yuan Bao, Value 100, Shaanxi mint FD-2500	10.00	20.00

1445

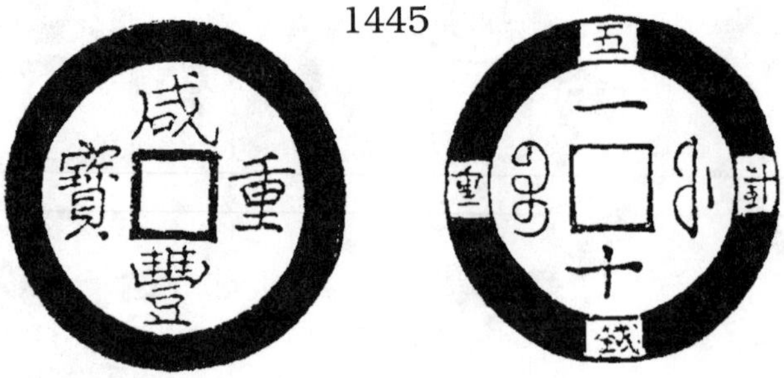

1446

1447

1448

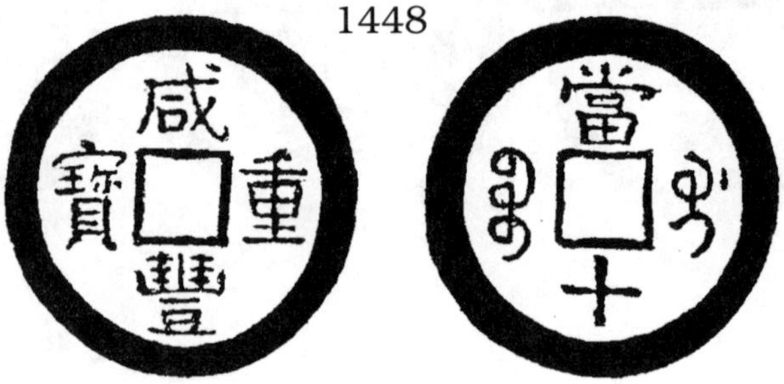

1449

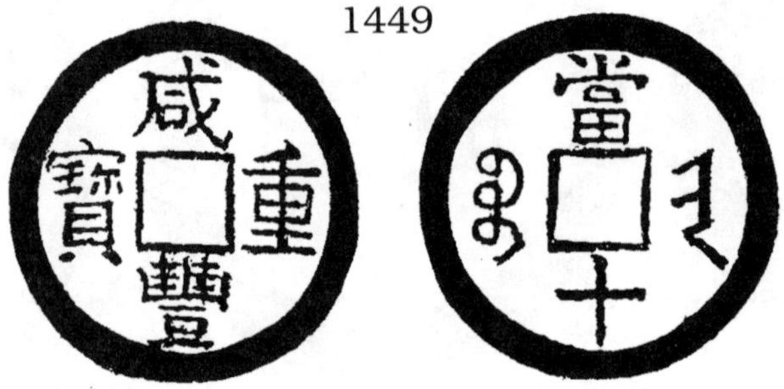

	VG	VF
1445. Xian Feng Zhong Bao, 10 Cash and Fujian mint on reverse, Weight 5 Mace on rim FD-2514	10.00	20.00
1446. Ditto, 20 Cash & Fujian mint on reverse, Weight 1 Tael on rim S-1591/FD-2520	15.00	30.00
1447. Ditto, 50 Cash & Fujian mint on reverse, 2 Taels & 5 Mace on rim FD-2525	150.00	300.00
1448. Xian Feng Zhong Bao, Value 10 & Guilin mint on reverse FD-2547	2.00	5.00
1449. Xiang Feng Zhong Bao, Value 10 & Bao Jin (Shanxi) mint on reverse	2.00	5.00

1450

1451

1452

1453

1454

1455

1456

1457

1458

		VG	VF
1450.	Xian Feng Zhong Bao, Value 10, Bao Qian (Guizhou) mint FD-2545	2.00	5.00
1451.	Ditto, Value 10, Yunnan mint FD-2558	2.00	5.00
1452.	Ditto, Value 10, Bao Dong (Yunnan) mint, S-1596/FD-2555	5.00	10.00
1453.	Ditto, Value 8, Bao Di (Dihua) mint, FD-2563	2.00	5.00
1454.	Ditto, Value 4, Yili mint FD-2458	50.00	100.00
1455.	Ditto, Value 10, Yili mint FD-2459	50.00	100.00
1456.	Xian Feng Tong Bao,Value 5 & Aksu mint on reverse FD-2568	1.00	2.00
1457.	Ditto, Value 10 & Aksu on reverse FD-2569	1.00	2.00
1458.	Xian Feng Zhong Bao, Value 50 & Aksu on reverse FD-2571	30.00	60.00

1459

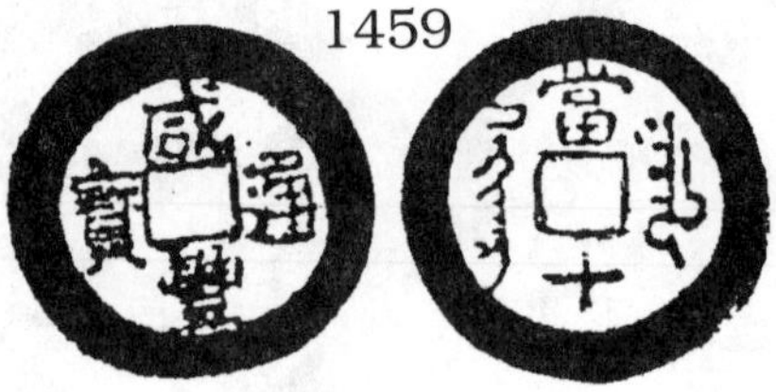

1460

1461

1462

1463

1464

1465

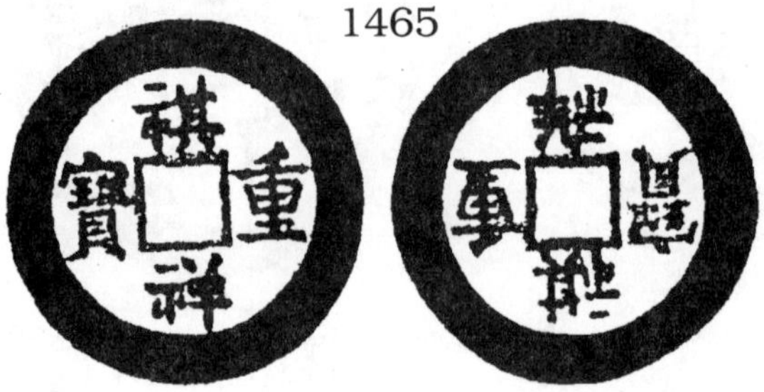

1466

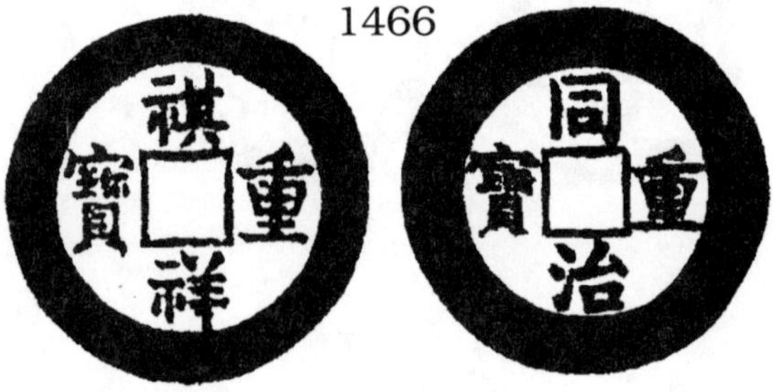

	VG	VF
1459. Xian Feng Tong Bao, Value 10 & Kaxgar on reverse	1.00	2.00
1460. Ditto, Value 5 & Kuche on reverse FD-2579	1.00	2.00
1461. Ditto, Value 10 & Kuche on reverse FD-2580	25.00	50.00
1462. Xian Feng Zhong Bao, Value 50 & Kuche on reverse	10.00	20.00
1463. Xian Feng Tong Bao, Value 10 & Yarkant on reverse FD-2575	1.00	2.00
1464. Qi Xiang Tong Bao, Bao Gong (Gansu) mint, VR	—	—
1465. Qi Xiang Zhong Bao, Double face FD-2589	1000.00	2000.00
1466. Ditto, Double legend, Tong Zhi Zhong Bao on reverse	1000.00	2000.00

1467

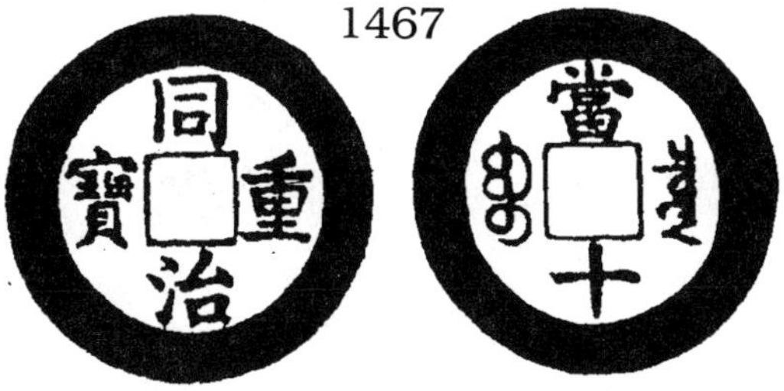

1468

1469

1470

1471

1472

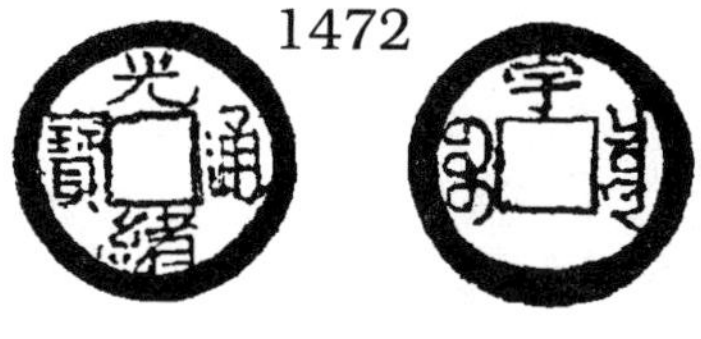

1473

1474

1475

1476

1477

	VG	VF
1467. Tong Zhi Zhong Bao, Value 10, B of R, S-1601/FD-2601	3.00	6.00
1468. Ditto, 10 Cash, B of W S-1600/FD-2598	3.00	6.00
1469. Ditto, 10 Cash, Gongchang mint S-1602/FD-2609	7.00	14.00
1470. Tong Zhi Tong Bao, 5 Cash, Kuche mint	2.00	5.00
1471. Tong Zhi Zhong Bao, 10 Cash Aksu mint	2.00	5.00
1472. Guang Xu Tong Bao, Yu above hole on reverse	2.00	5.00
1473. Ditto, Zhou above hole	1.00	2.00
1474. Ditto, Ri above hole	1.00	2.00
1475. Ditto, Lie above hole	1.00	2.00
1476. Ditto, Lai above hole	1.00	2.00
1477. Ditto, Wang above hole	1.00	2.00

1478

1479

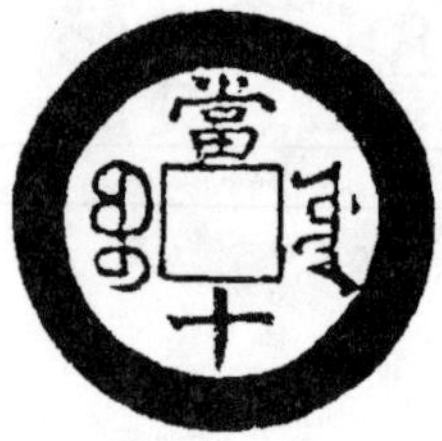

1480

1481

1482

1483

1484

1485

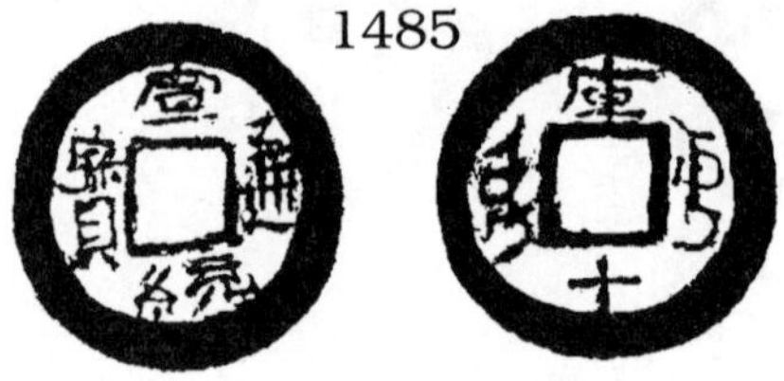

	VG	VF
1478. Guang Xu Zhong Bao, Value 10, B of R, S-1603/FD-2640	2.00	5.00
1479. Ditto, 10 Cash, B of W FD-2637	2.00	5.00
1480. Ditto, Xin-(jiang) above & 10 below FD-2630	3.00	6.00
1481. Guang Xu Tong Bao, Gui in Han script on right and Manchu script on the left	50.00	100.00
1482. Ditto, Official Mint above & 4 Candareens below, Fengtian mint, Machine struck trial piece, FD-2626	200.00	350.00
1483. Xuan Tong Tong Bao, Guangdong mint, Machine struck FD-2664	2.00	4.00
1484. Ditto, Fujian mint, Machine struck	3.00	6.00
1485. Ditto, Ku above & 10 below, Wushi mint	20.00	40.00

1486

1487

1488

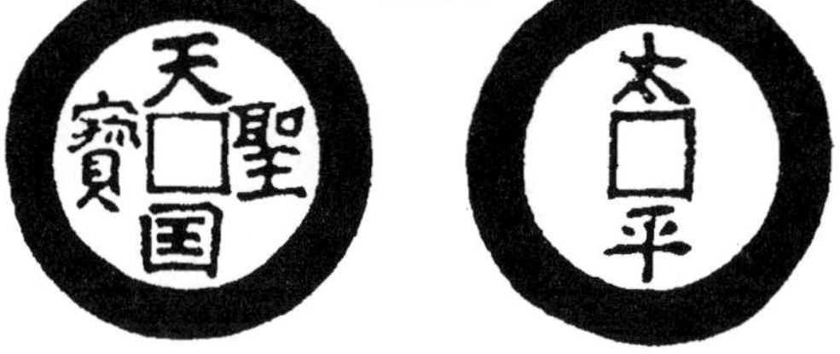

1489

1490

1491

	VG	VF
1486. Tai Ping Tian Guo, Sheng Bao on reverse, S-1606/FD-2684	5.00	10.00
1487. Tian Guo Tai Ping, Sheng Bao on rev. FD-2670	15.00	30.00
1488. Tian Guo Sheng Bao, Tai Ping on rev. 5 Cash, R	2500.00	—
1489. Ping Jing Sheng Bao, Yu Lin Jun on rev. Yu above, Lin on right & Jun on the left FD-2698	450.00	900.00
1490. Tai Ping Tong Bao, Wen on reverse FD-2701	250.00	500.00
1491. Fu Jian Tong Bao, 2 Cash & Provincial Make on reverse (Read first vertically, then horizontally)	700.00	1400.00

SECTION III

Seeds Patterns & Trial Pieces

Engraved Master Coin	EM
Mother Coins	M
Patterns	P
Trial Pieces	TP

Price Listing

The prices for seed coins and patterns are in a way rather consistent, an engraved master coin fetching $1,500 for the 1 cash pieces, $2,000 for the 10 cash, $400 for mother coins, and $200 for patterns or trial pieces. However, This is not always the case, as some varieties are rarer than others, and of course, the fluctuation factor is always present.

A value grading system is adopted to help the reader have some idea of the value of certain items as compared with other ones in this section. Sinces the comparative prices have been quoted above, there would be no need to refer to the prices listed on p. vi.

DESCRIPTION

Mothers coins are the seeds for minting regular currency. They attract the attention of numismatists for their exquisite beauty and superb workmanship, as well as their rarity. The first known mother coins date from the Tang Dynasty (618-907 AD), and master coins from the Ming Dynasty (1368-1644 AD). Only till the Republic years did it become evident that the use of these coins for minting purposes was an established system in the Qing Dynasty.

After a new cash design had been decided upon, a coin model is carved from ivory and presented to the Emperor for approval. Upon approval, a master coin is engraved from quality copper and again presented for inspection and approval. The square hole in the center is left unfinished; only a small hole is bored, called "Gold Mouth". When a master coin is selected for use, the "Gold Mouth" is "Opened", that is, the center hole is processed into the commonly seen square hole. The master coin is then used to imprint molds for casting the mother coins, which are then used to make molds for the regular issues. Pattern coins are those selected from the first batch of regular issues to be presented to the authorities for inspection, Some of them could be distributed to the local mints, after which they design their own currency.

Trial pieces fall into two catagories, those that were cast to test their practibility and those cast to test the quality of the molds. Into the first category fall the large coins cast by the early emperors of the Qing Dynasty, which were minted but not put into official circulation; Trial pieces of the Song Dynasty fall into the second one. At that time, mold testing was the customary practice in the casting of iron coins. Copper was used for the tests, but only iron coins were cast for official circulation; so when one comes upon a copper coin identical with an iron coin, it is certain to be a trial piece, hence a prized collectible.

Mother coins may also be categorized into two groups: one used in making molds for casting iron coins, and the other for copper. The mother coins of the Song Dynasty belong mostly to the first kind while those of the Qing Dynasty to the second.

Master coins are identified by their superb workmanship. Engraved by hand, the marks of the engraver's knife are clearly visible, the copper golden yellow in color, the fields between the characters raised like mounds, and the coin surface very smooth, with a mirror-like finish. The mother coins, cast from molds, look quite different. Though some knife marks are still visible, tiny grains of copper show up on the coin field, the mark of the cast coin: the copper is of a lighter hue. On the patterns, the brush-strokes are decidedly thicker, with more specks on the field, and the quality of the workmanship coarser, yet markedly superior to that of those minted for general circulation.

1492

1493

1494

1495

1496

1497

1498

1499

1500

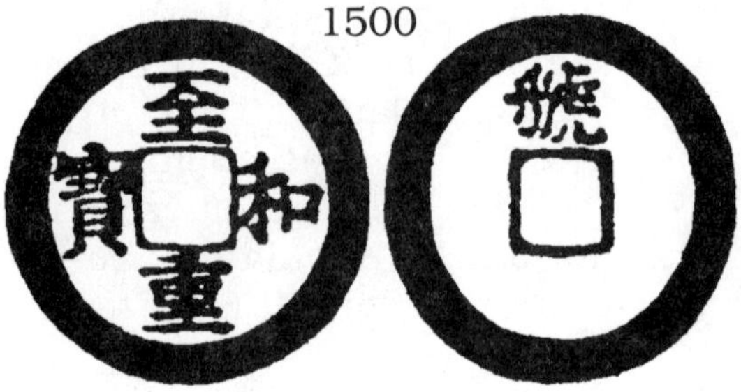

1501

1502

1492. Song Yuan Tong Bao M, FD-855	G-S
1493. Ditto TP, FD-856	G-3
1494. Tai Ping Tong Bao 10 Cash M, FD-864	G-2
1495. Ditto M-FD-865	G-VR
1496. Chun Hua Yuan Bao M	G-R
1497. Xiang Fu Yuan Bao M	G-R
1498. Ditto M, FD-888	G-R
1499. Ditto, 10 Cash M	G-VR
1500. Zhi He Zhong Bao, Guo on reverse, M, FD-929	G-R
1501. Ditto, Fang on reverse M, FD-931	G-R
1502. Qing Li Zhong Bao M	G-S

N.B. M — mother coin.
TP — trial piece.

1503

1504

1505

1506

1507

1508

1509

1510

1511

1512

1503. Xi Ning Tong Bao M, FD-959	G-S
1504. Ditto M, FD-960	G-1
1505. Yuan Feng Zhong Bao, Seal script, Trial pattern	G-R
1506. Ditto, Running script M, FD-974	G-1
1507. Ditto, Seal script M, FD-973	G-1
1508. Ditto M	G-S
1509. Yuan You Tong Bao, Running script M, FD-986	G-1
1510. Ditto, Seal script M, FD-985	G-1
1511. Ditto, Large & heavy characters, M	G-1
1512. Ditto, 3 Cash TP	G-R

1513

1514

1515

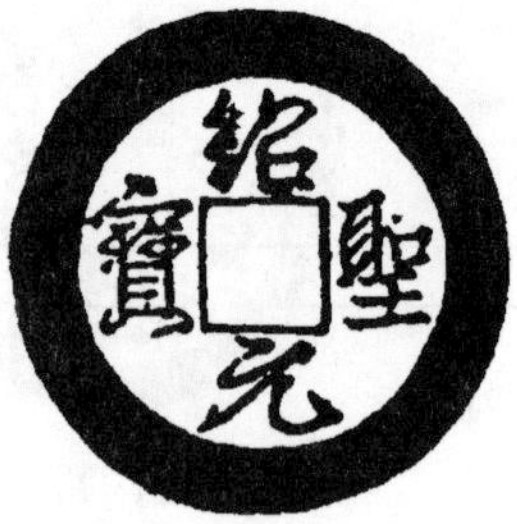

1516

1517

1518

1519

1520

1521

1522

1523

1524

1513. Shao Sheng Yuan Bao, Running script M	G-R
1514. Shao Sheng Tong Bao, Li script M	G-1
1515. Shao Sheng Yuan Bao, 3 Cash, Running script M	G-1
1516. Ditto, 3 Cash, Seal script M	G-1
1517. Yuan Fu Tong Bao, Li script M, FD-1006	G-S
1518. Ditto, 3 Cash M, FD-1011	G-S
1519. Sheng Song Tong Bao M, FD-1034	G-S
1520. Sheng Song Yuan Bao, Running script M	G-S
1521. Ditto, 3 Cash, Li script M	G-S
1522. Chong Ning Yuan Bao, Li script M, FD-1953	G-R
1523. Chong Ning Tong Bao, 2 Cash, Slender Gold style M, FD-1044	G-2
1524. Chong Ning Zhong Bao, 3 Cash, Li script M	G-2

1525

1526

1527

1528

1529

1530

1531

1532

1533

1534

1525. Da Guan Tong Bao, Slender Gold style, Pattern	G-1
1526. Ditto, Running script M, FD-1056	G-S
1527. Ditto, 2 Cash, Slender Gold style M	G-2
1528. Ditto, 3 Cash M	G-2
1529. Zheng He Tong Bao, 3 Cash, Seal script M, FD-1080	G-2
1530. Ditto, 3 Cash, Li script M, FD-1083	G-2
1531. Ditto, 1 Cash, Seal script M	G-R
1532. Ditto, 2 Cash, Seal script, wide rim M	G-2
1533. Ditto, 3 Cash, Seal script M	G-S
1534. Zheng He Zhong Bao, 2 Cash M, FD-1091	G-S

1535

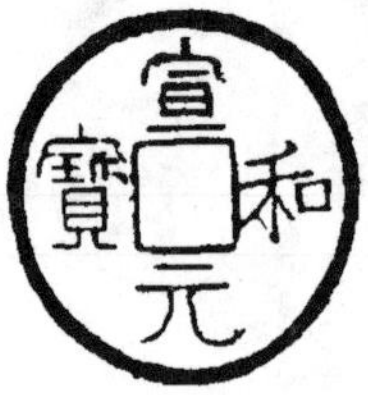

1536

1537

1538

1539

1540

1541

1542

1543

1544

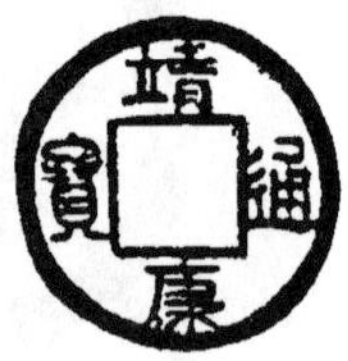

1545

1535. Xuan He Yuan Bao, Li script P	G-2
1536. Ditto, Seal script P	G-2
1537. Xuan He Tong Bao, Li script, Brass P	G-5
1538. Ditto, Li Script, Brass P	G-5
1539. Ditto, Shaan on reverse, Slender Gold style M	G-3
1540. Ditto, Seal script M	G-S
1541. Ditto, Li script M	G-S
1542. Ditto, 2 Cash M	G-3
1543. Ditto, 3 Cash M	G-3
1544. Jing Kang Tong Bao, Li script M	G-R
1545. Ditto, Seal script M	G-R

1546

1547

1548

1549

1550

1551

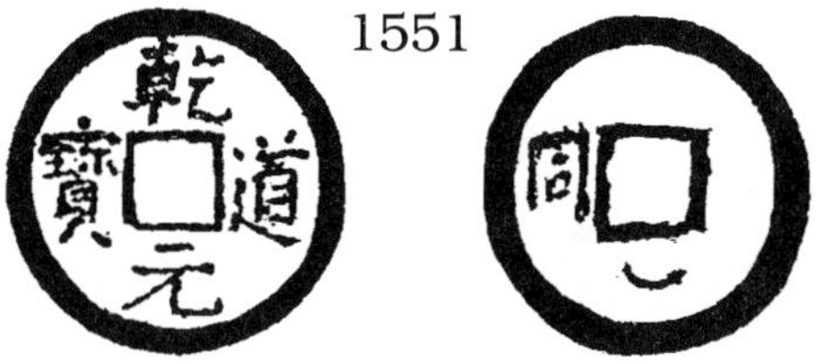

1552

1553

1554

1546. Jian Yan Tong Bao, Li script M, FD-1145	G-S
1547. Ditto, Seal script M	G-S
1548. Shao Xing Tong Bao, Song script M, FD-1165	G-2
1549. Ditto, 3 Cash M	G-1
1550. Qian Dao Yuan Bao, Zheng on reverse M	G-S
1551. Ditto, Tong on reverse M, FD-1191	G-S
1552. Chun Xi Yuan Bao, Plain reverse M	G-S
1553. Ditto, Seal script, Crescent on reverse M or TP	G-R
1554. Ditto, Li script TP	G-S

1555

1556

1557

1558

1559

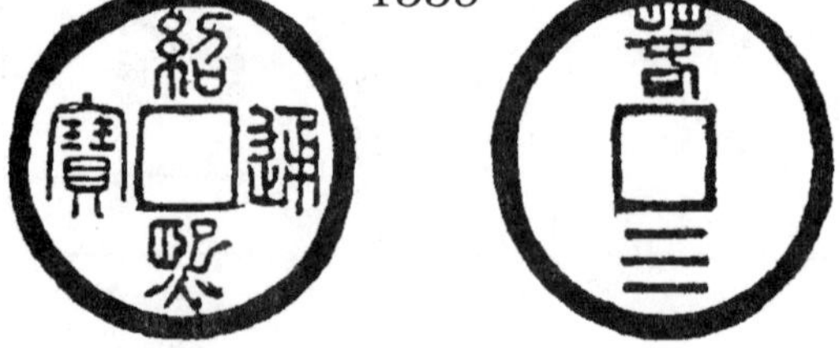

1560

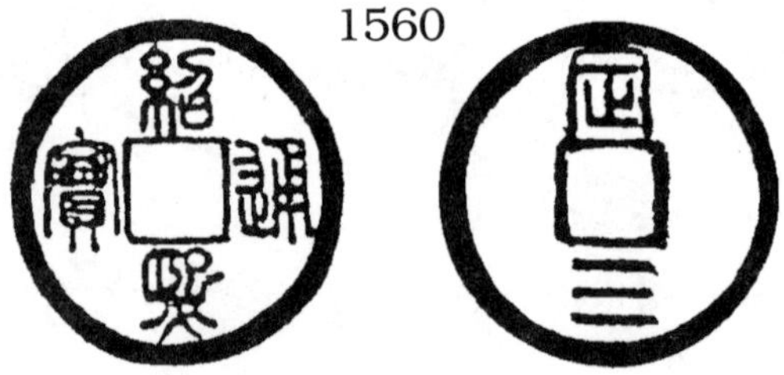

1555. Chun Xi Yuan Bao, 2 Cash, Tong on reverse M, FD-1212	G-S
1556. Ditto, Seal script, Li on reverse M, FD-1213	G-S
1557. Ditto, 3 Cash, Song script, Crescent & stars on reverse M	G-S
1558. Shao Xi Yuan Bao, 1 Cash, Chun & Yuan on reverse TP	G-S
1559. Ditto, 2 Cash, Seal script, Chun & 3 on reverse M	G-S
1560. Ditto, Ding & 3 on reverse	G-S

1561

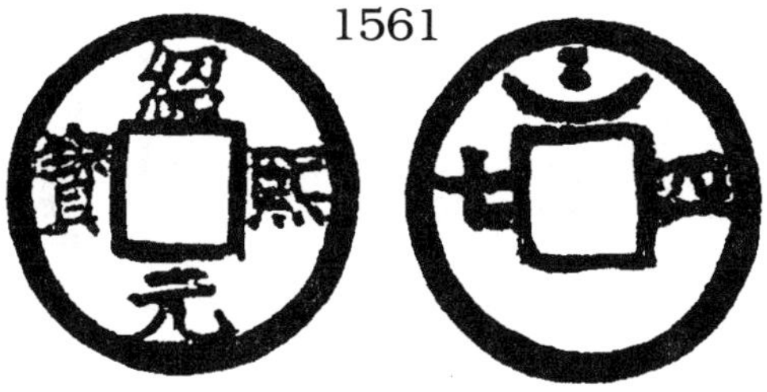

1562

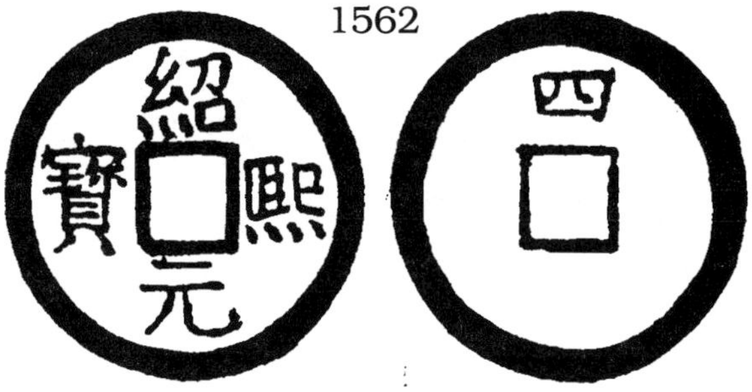

1563

1564

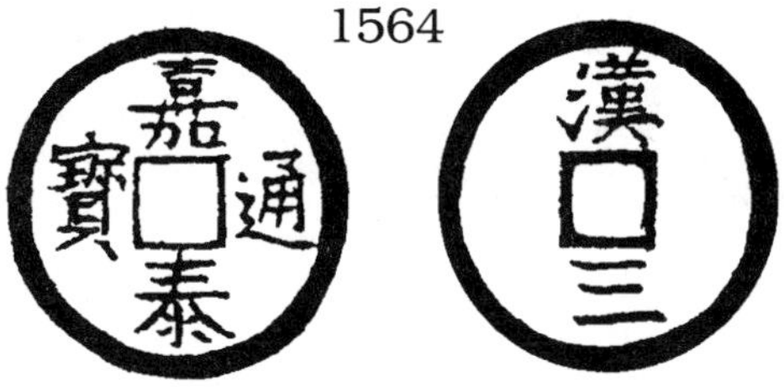

1565

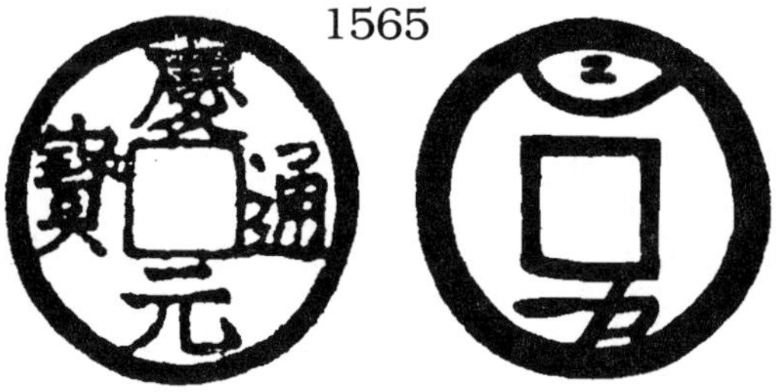

1566

1561. Shao Xi Yuan Bao, 2 Cash, Crescent with 2 stars & 47 on reverse (4 on right & 7 on the left) M	G-S
1562. Ditto, 5 Cash, 4 on reverse TP	G-VR
1563. Jia Tai Yuan Bao, Chuan & 2 above, and 39 below, 3 Cash M	G-R
1564. Ditto, 2 Cash, Han & 3 on reverse M	G-S
1565. Qing Yuan Tong Bao, 3 Cash, Crescent with 2 stars above, and 51 below M	G-S
1566. Ditto, 3 Cash, Yong on reverse M, FD-1250	G-R

N.B. The crescent with 2 stars may be interpreted as the numeral 3 in orthodox script.

1567

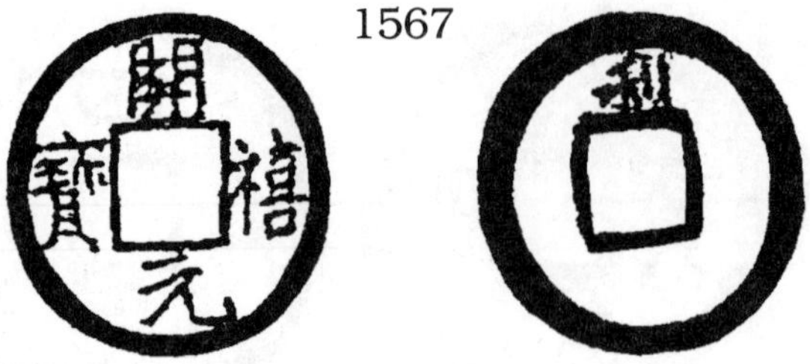

1568

1570

1569

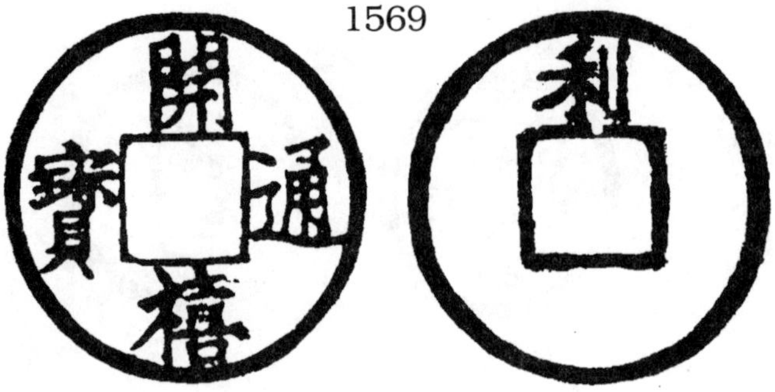

1571

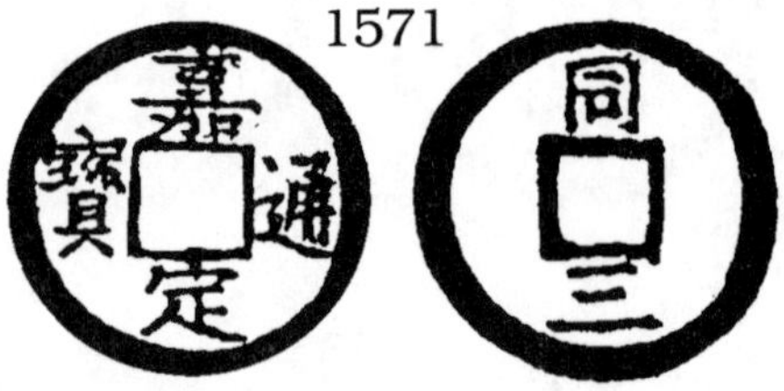

1572

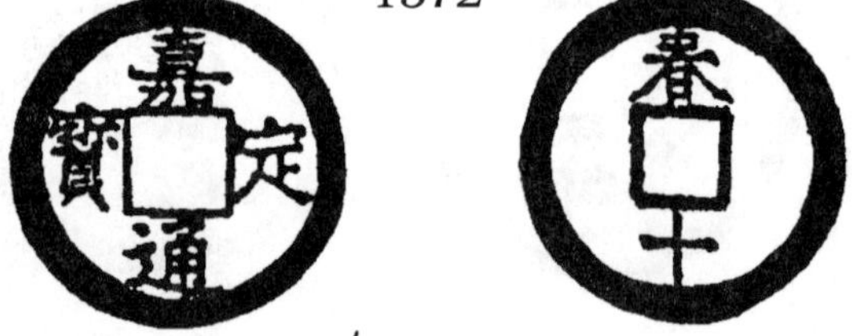

1573

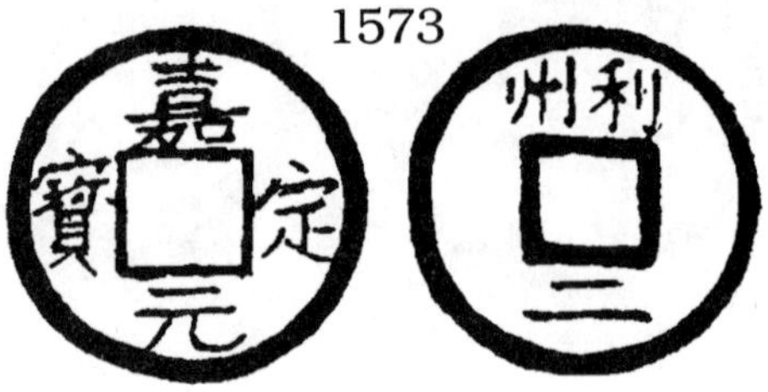

1567. Kai Xi Yuan Bao, 3 Cash, Li on reverse M	G-R
1568. Ditto 1 Cash, Tong & 2 on reverse M, FD-1335	G-S
1569. Ditto, 10 Cash, Li on reverse	G-VR
1570. Jia Ding Yuan Bao, Lizhou and 1 on reverse M FD-1413	G-1
1571. Jia Ding Tong Bao, Tong and 3 on reverse, 2 Cash, M, FD-1377	G-S
1572. Ditto, Chun & 10 on reverse M, FD-1378	G-S
1573. Jia Ding Yuan Bao, Lizhou and 2 on reverse M, FD-1415	G-S

1574

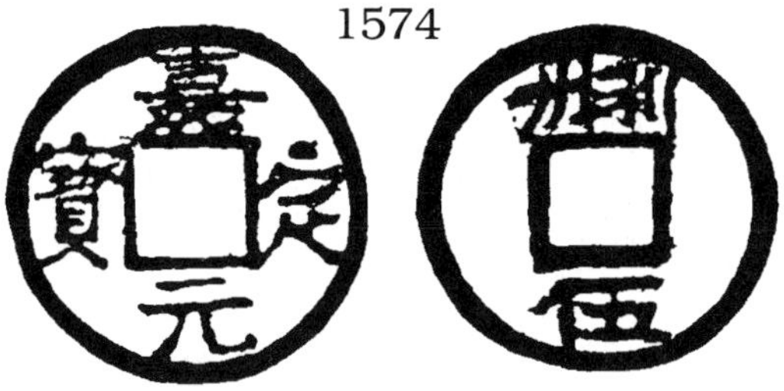

1575

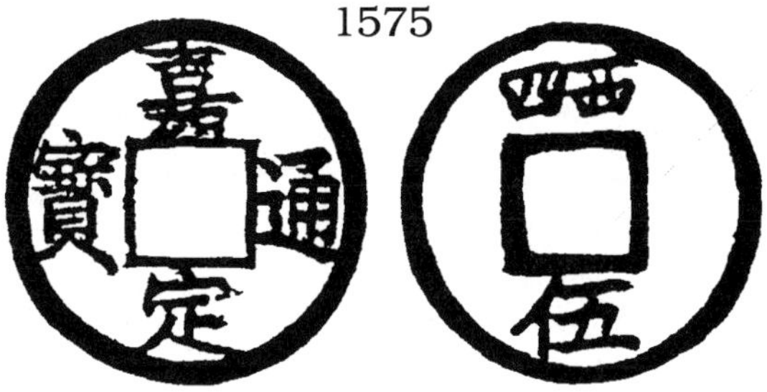

1576

1577

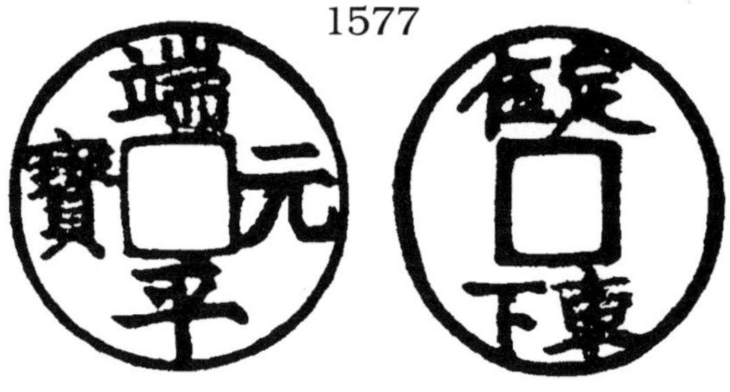

1578

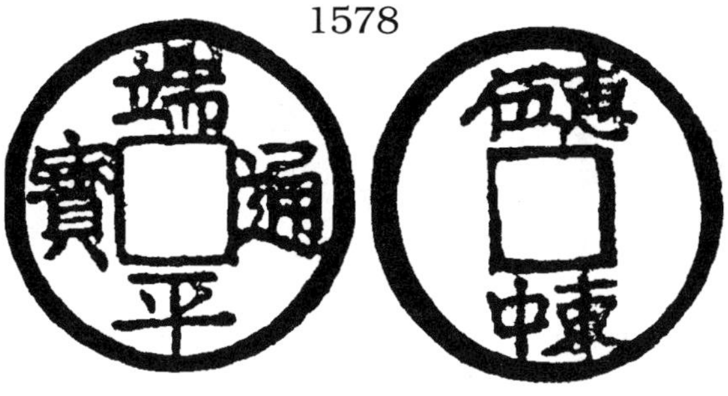

1579

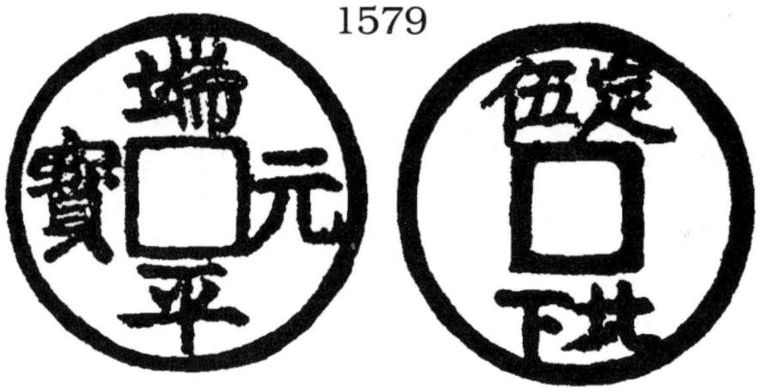

1574. Jia Ding Yuan Bao, 3 Cash, Lizhou & 5 on reverse M	G-S
1575. Jia Ding Tong Bao, 5 Cash, Xi (West) 4 & 5 on reverse M	G-R
1576. Duan Ping Tong Bao, 1 Cash, Chun & Yuan on reverse M	G-R
1577. Duan Ping Yuan Bao, Ding & 5 above, and Dong (East) & Xia (Down) below M, FD-1496	G-S
1578. Duan Ping Tong Bao, Hui & 5 above, and Dong (East) & Zhong (Central) below M, FD-1499	G-R
1579. Duan Ping Yuan Bao, Ding & 5 above, and Bei (North) & Xia (Down) below M	G-R

1580

1581

1582

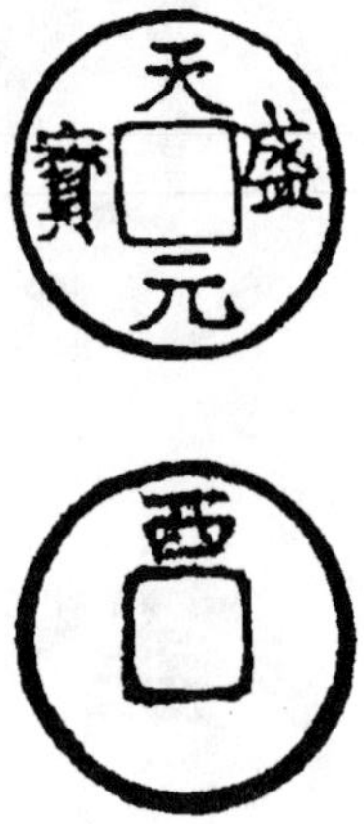

1583

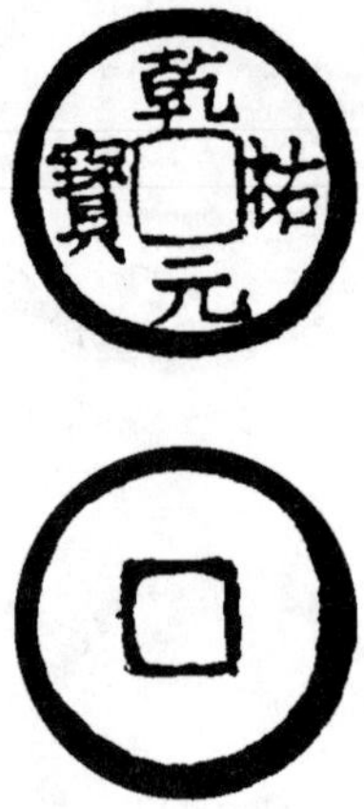

1584

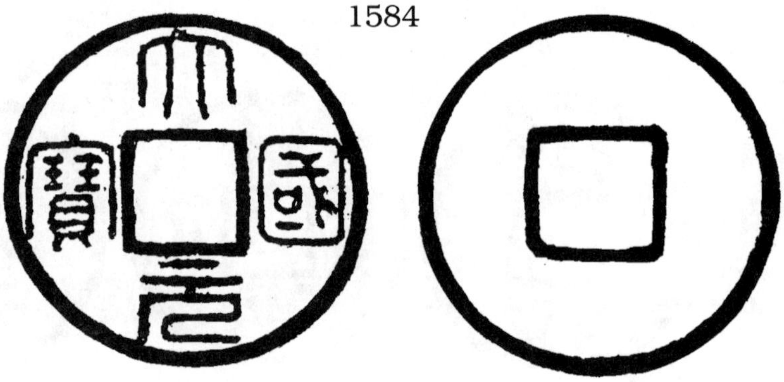

1580. Da Liao Tian Qing, Vault Amulet, FD-1635	G-VR
1581. Tai He Zhong Bao, 3 Cash TP	G-S
1582. Tian Sheng Yuan Bao, Xi on reverse M	G-R
1583. Qian You Yuan Bao M, FD-1687	G-2
1584. Da Yuan Guo Bao, Lead EM	G-R

1585

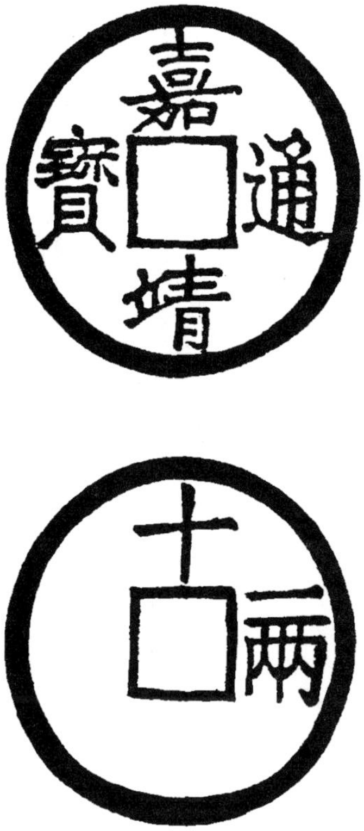

1586

1587

1588

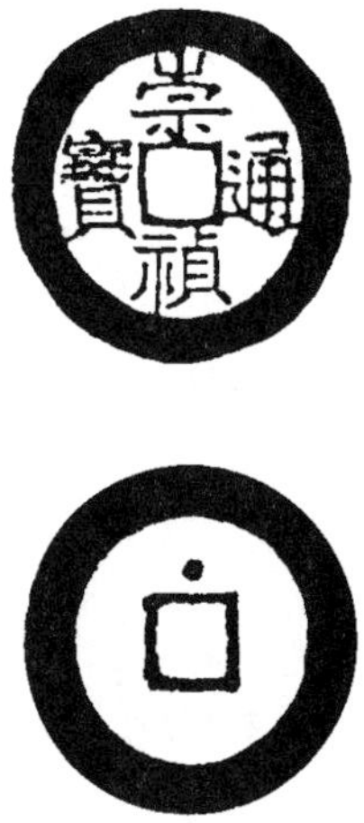

1589

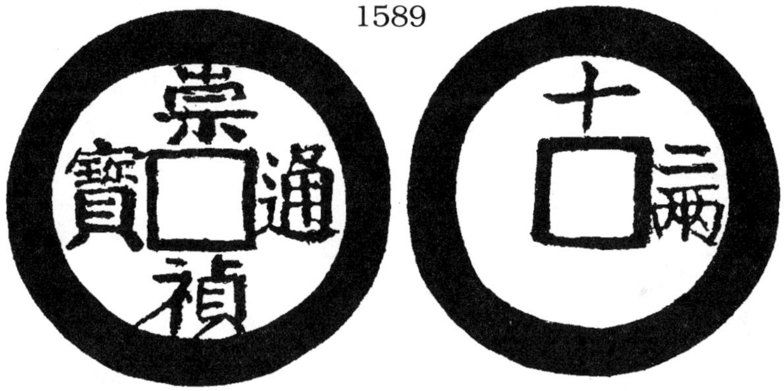

1585. Jia Jing Tong Bao, 10 on top, and 1 Tael on the right EM	G-ER
1586. Tian Qi Tong Bao, Brass M	G-S
1587. Ditto, 2 & star on reverse P	G-1
1588. Chong Zhen tong Bao, star on reverse P	G-1
1589. Ditto, 10 on top & 2 Taels on the right TP, FD-2097	G-R

1590

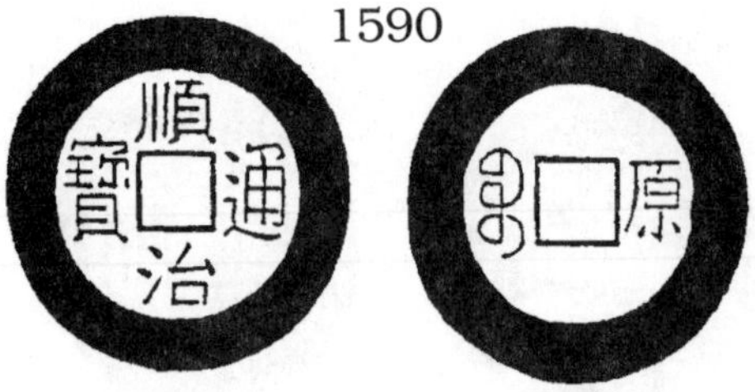

1591

1592

1593

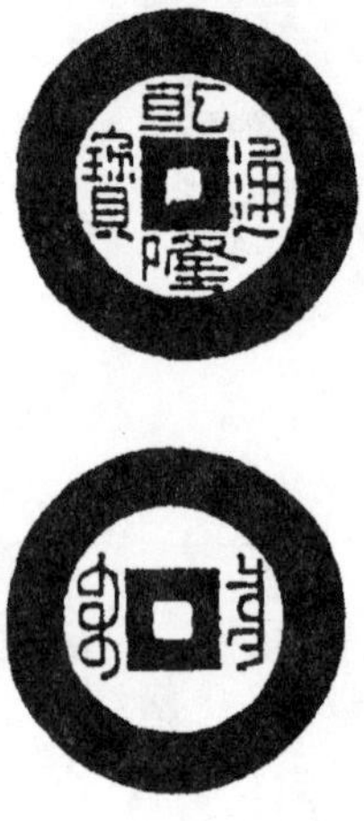

1594

1595

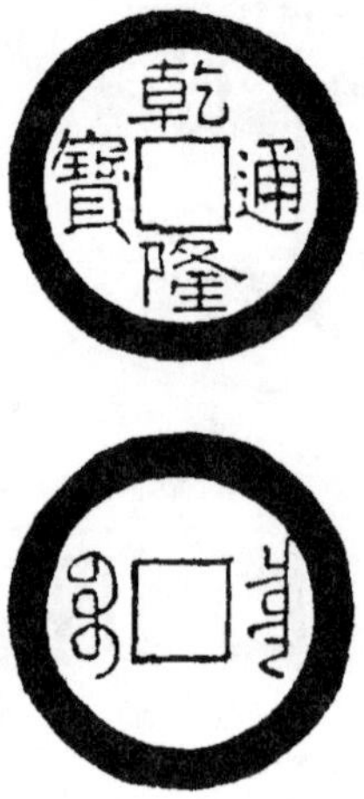

1596

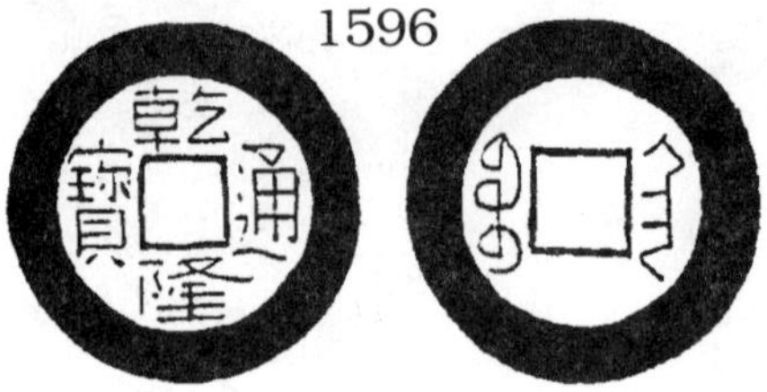

1597

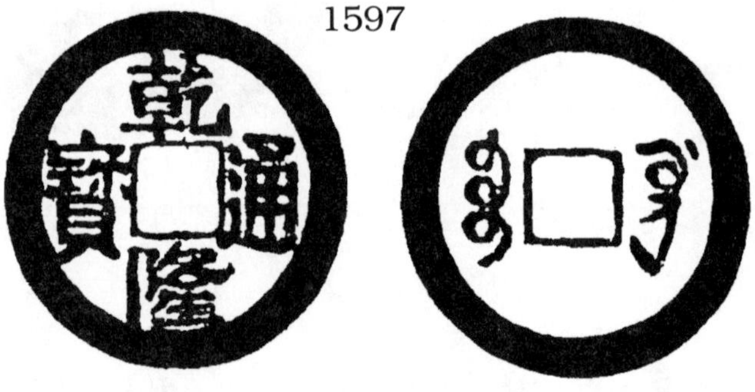

1590. Shun Zhi Tong Bao, Yuan in Han script on the right EM	G-R
1591. Yong Zheng Tong Bao B of Rev EM	G-R
1592. Ditto, B of W EM	G-R
1593. Qian Long Tong Bao, B of Rev EM	G-1
1594. Ditto EM	G-1
1595. Ditto M	G-2
1596. Ditto, Shaanxi mint EM	G-S
1597. Ditto, Gongchang (Gansu) mint TP	G-S

1598 1599 1600 1601

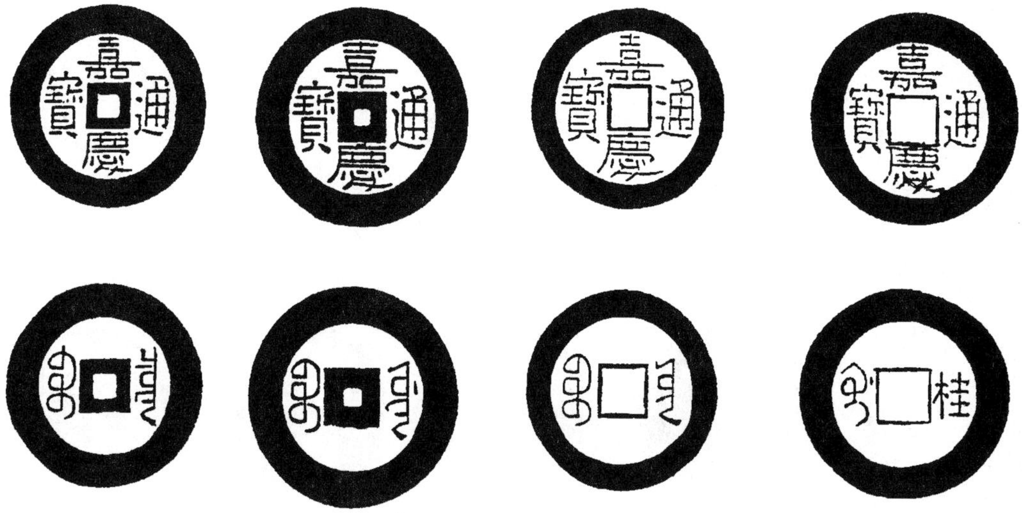

1602 1603 1604 1605

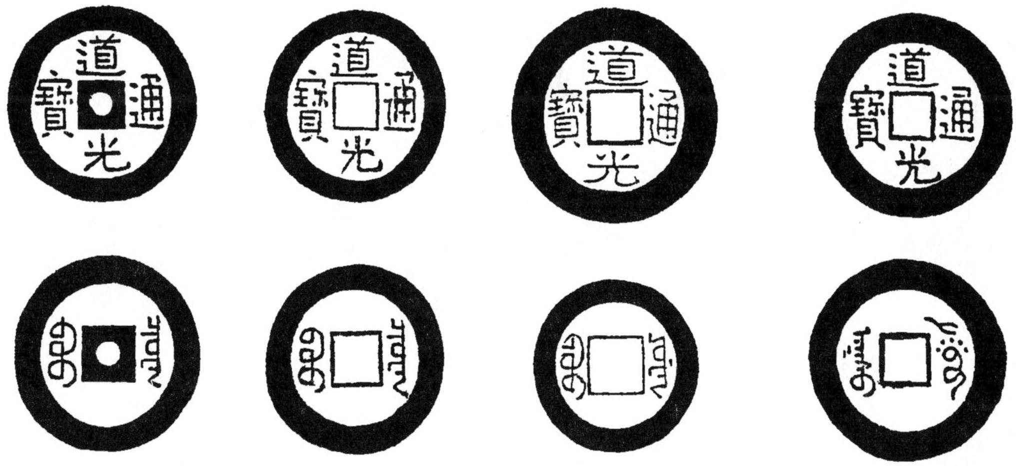

1598. Jia Qing tong Bao, B of Rev EM	G-1
1599. Ditto, B of Works EM	G-1
1600. Ditto, Yunnan mint EM	G-1
1601. Ditto, Gui (Guangxi mint) in both Han & Manchu script on reverse TP	G-3
1602. Dao Guang Tong Bao, B of Rev EM	G-1
1603. Ditto, B of Rev M	G-3
1604. Ditto, B of Works mint EM	G-S
1605. Ditto, Aksu mint P, FD-2407	G-3

1606

1607

1608

1609

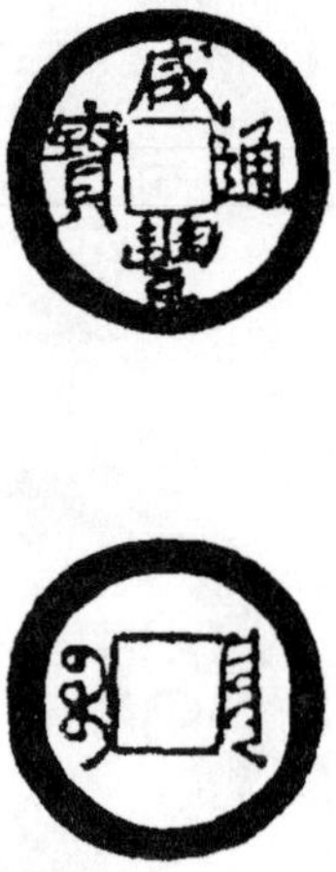

1610

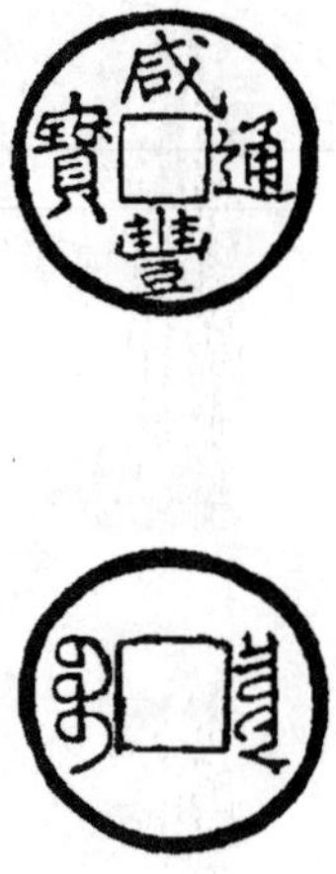

1611

1612

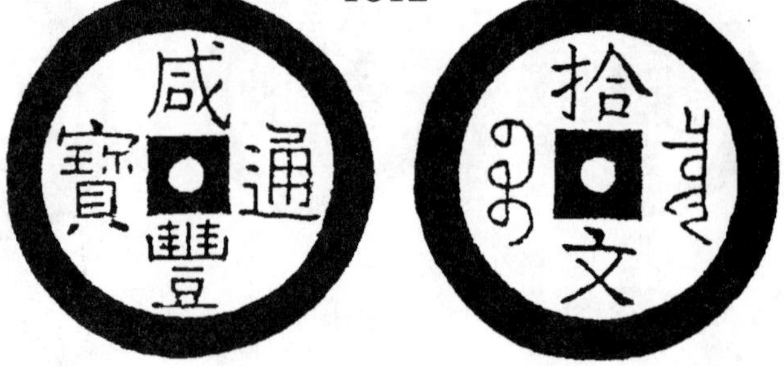

1606. Xian Feng Tong Bao, B of Rev M	G-2
1607. Ditto EM, FD-2412	G-1
1608. Ditto M	G-3
1609. Ditto M, FD-2415	G-2
1610. Ditto M	G-2
1611. Xian Feng Tong Bao, 5 Cash, B of Rev EM, FD-2418	G-S
1612. Ditto, 10 Cash, B of Rev EM, FD-2425	G-R

1613

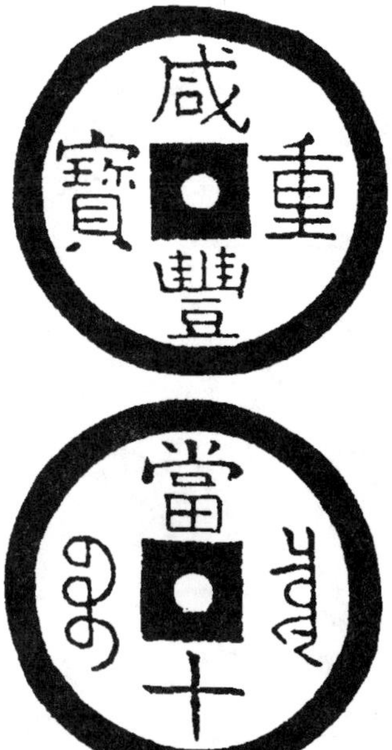

1614

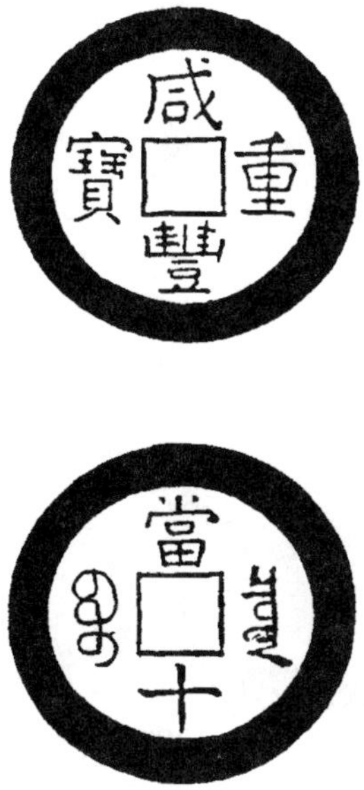

1615

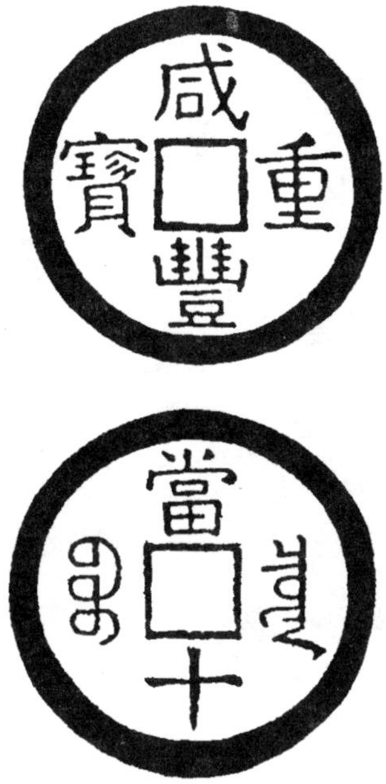

1616

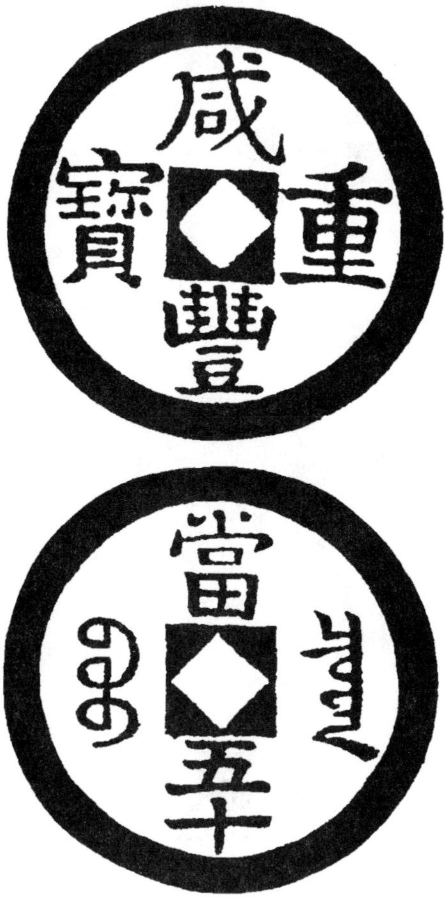

1617

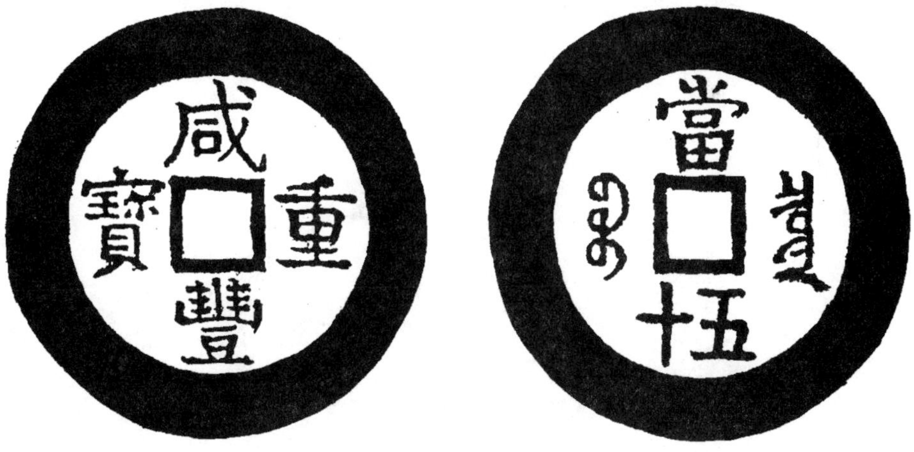

1613. Xian Feng Zhong Bao, B of Rev, 10 Cash EM, FD-2423	G-S
1614. Ditto EM	G-1
1615. Ditto M, FD-2422	G-2
1616. Ditto, 50 Cash EM, FD-2428	G-R
1617. Ditto, 50 Cash P	G-1

1618

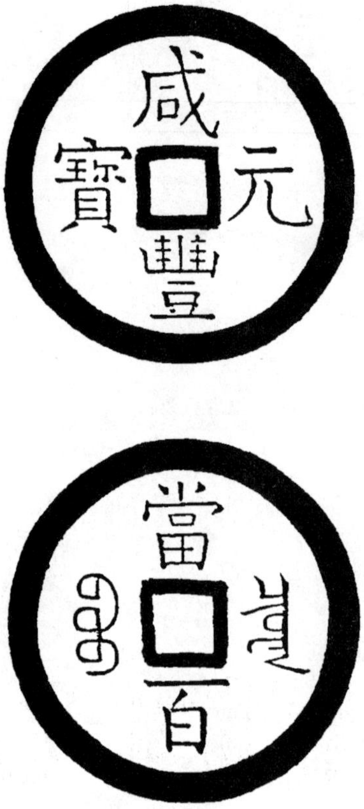

1619

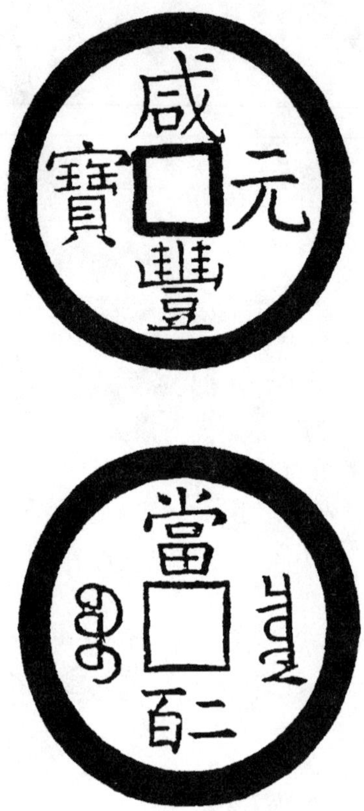

1620

1621

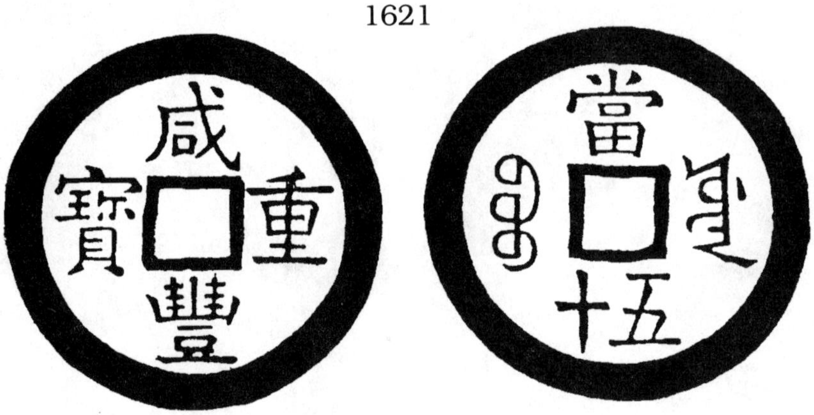

1618. Xian Feng Yuan Bao, 100 Cash, B of Rev EM — G-S

1619. Ditto, 200 Cash TP, FD-2432 — G-R

1620. Ditto, 300 Cash TP — G-ER

1621. Ditto, 50 Cash, B of W P — G-3

1622

1623

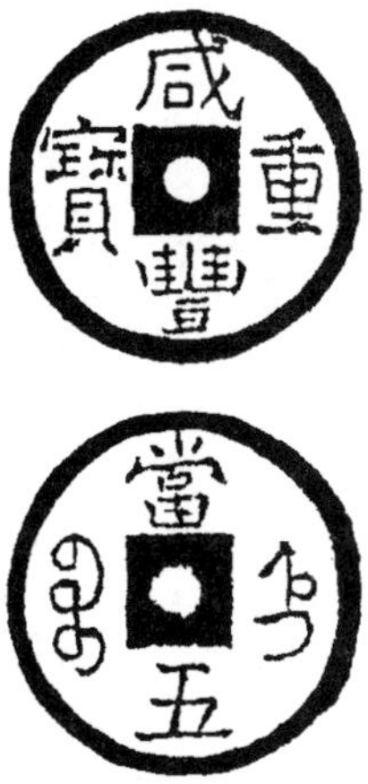

1624

1625

1626

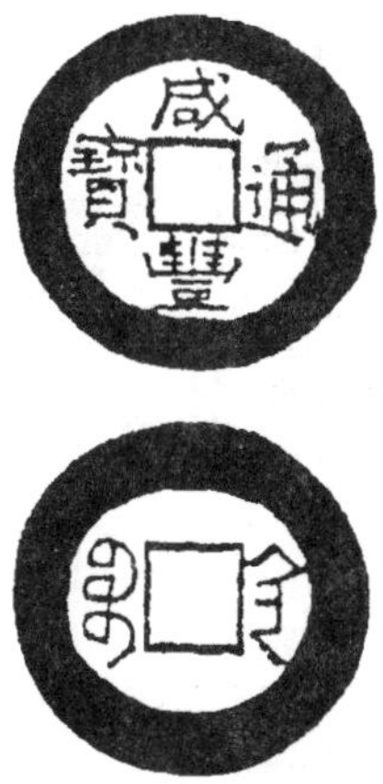

1627

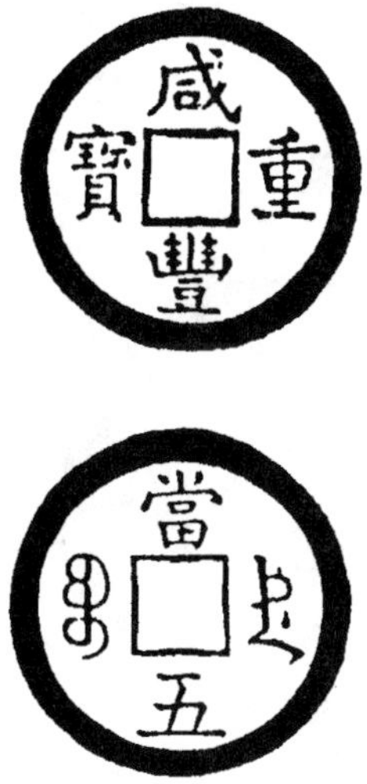

1628

1629

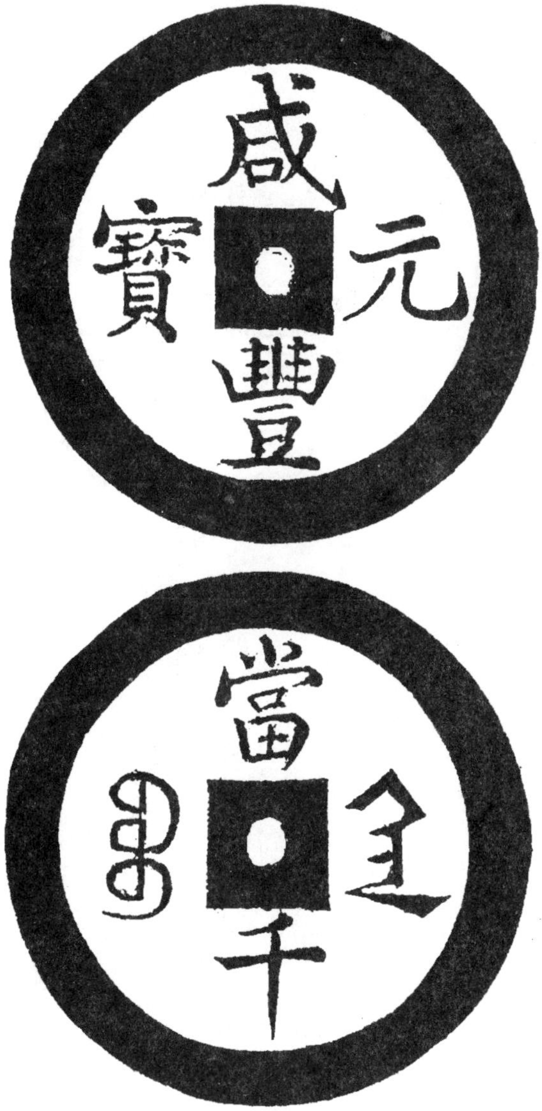

1622. Xian Feng Tong Bao, Zhili mint M	G-2
1623. Ditto, 5 Cash EM	G-S
1624. Xian Feng Zhong Bao, 5 Cash, Jizhou (Hebei) mint M	G-S
1625. Xian Feng Tong Bao, Bao De Jehol mint EM	G-S
1626. Ditto, Shaanxi mint P	G-3
1627. Xian Feng Zhong Bao, Jehol mint, 5 Cash M	G-1
1628. Ditto, 10 Cash, Sichuan mint M	G-2
1629. Xian Feng Yuan Bao, 1,000 Cash, Shaanxi mint EM	G-ER

1630

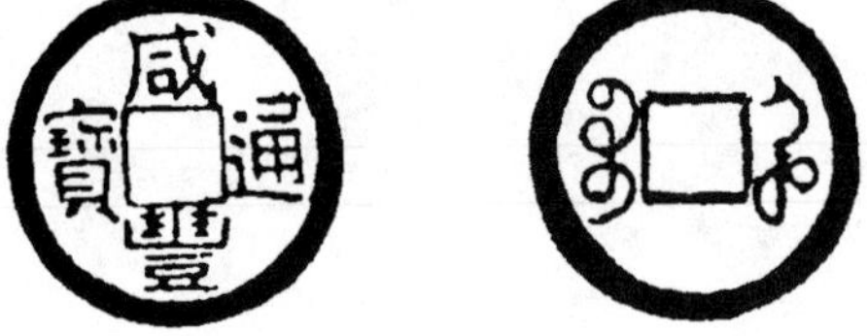

1631

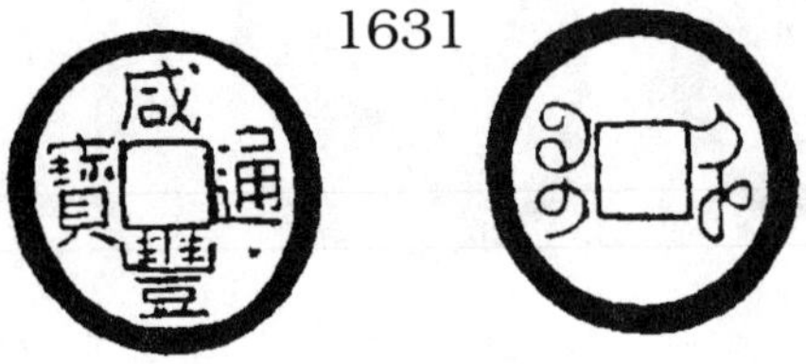

1633

1632

1634

1630. Xian Feng Tong Bao, Henan mint, EM FD-2490	G-S
1631. Ditto M	G-2
1632. Ditto M	G-2
1633. Xian Feng Zhong Bao, 10 Cash, Henan mint EM	G-S
1634. Ditto, 50 Cash, Coin model, Carved from ivory	G-VR

1635

1636

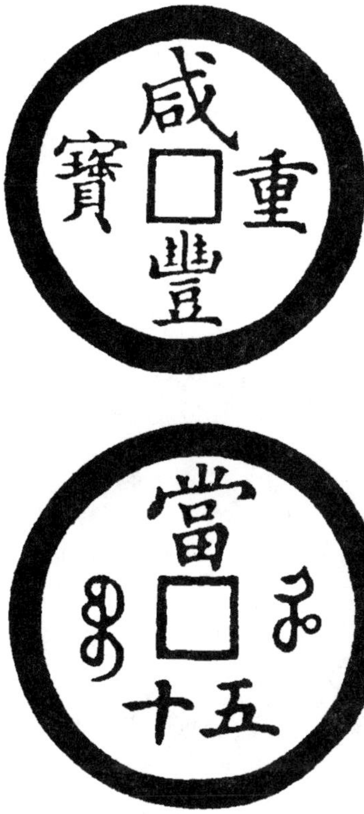

1637

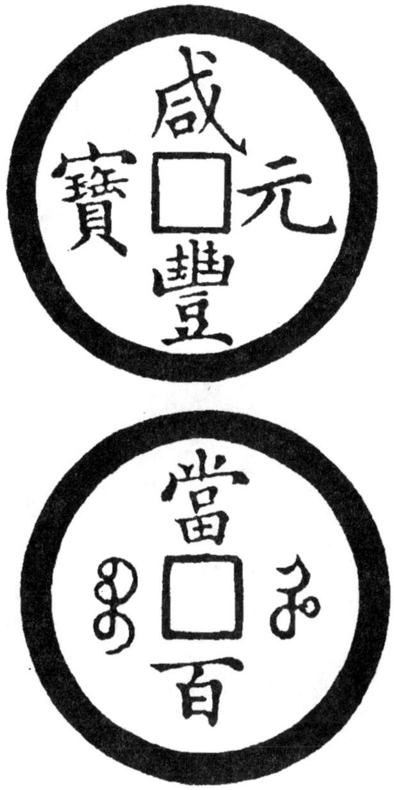

1638

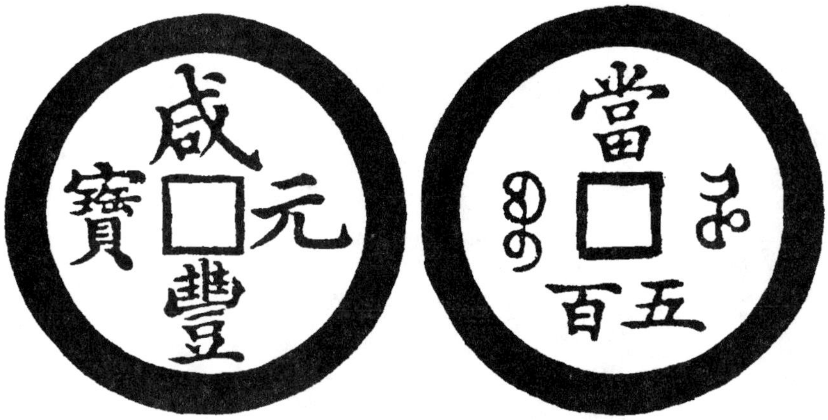

1639

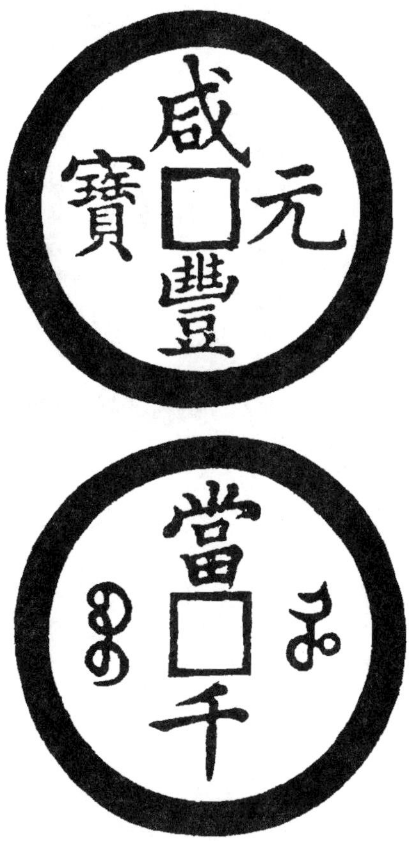

1635. Xian Feng Zhong Bao, 10 Cash, Henan mint TP — G-S
1636. Ditto, 50 Cash TP — G-S
1637. Xian Feng Yuan Bao, 100 Cash, Henan mint TP — G-S
1638. Ditto, 500 Cast TP — G-S
1639. Ditto, 1,000 Cast TP — G-S

1640

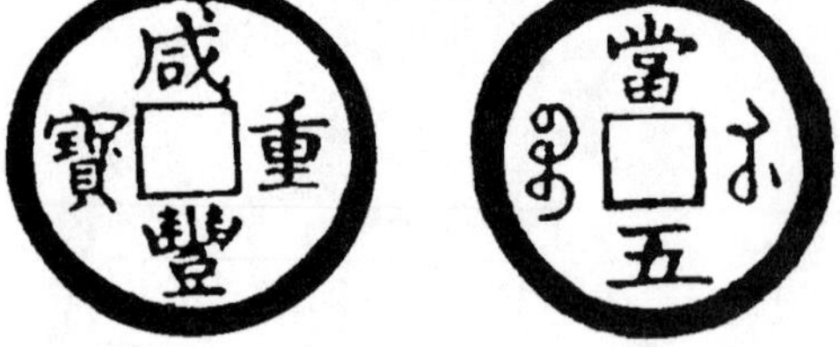

1641

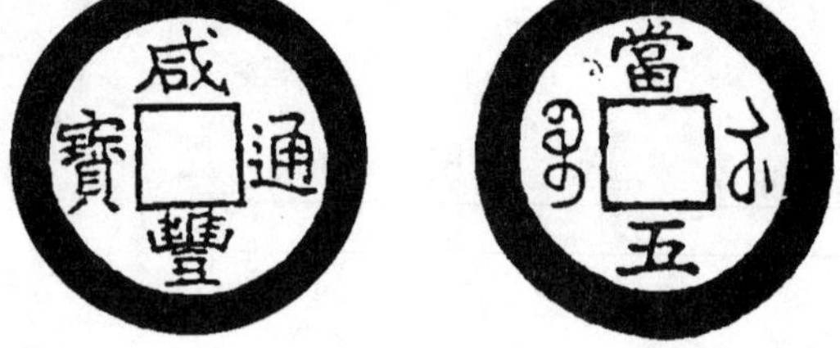

1642

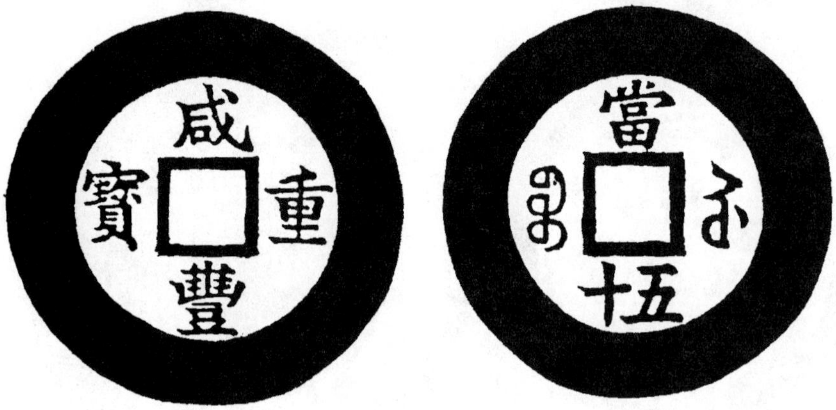

1643

1644

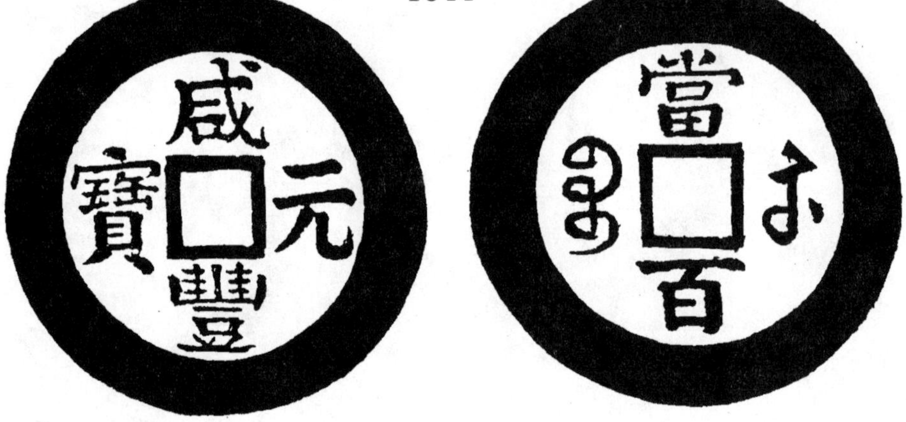

1640. Xian Feng Zhong Bao, 5 Cash, Jiangsu mint M, FD-2464 G-1
1641. Ditto, 5 Cash M G-2
1642. Ditto, 50 Cash TP G-1
1643. Ditto, 50 Cash TP G-2
1644. Xian Feng Yuan Bao, 100 Cash TP G-2

1645

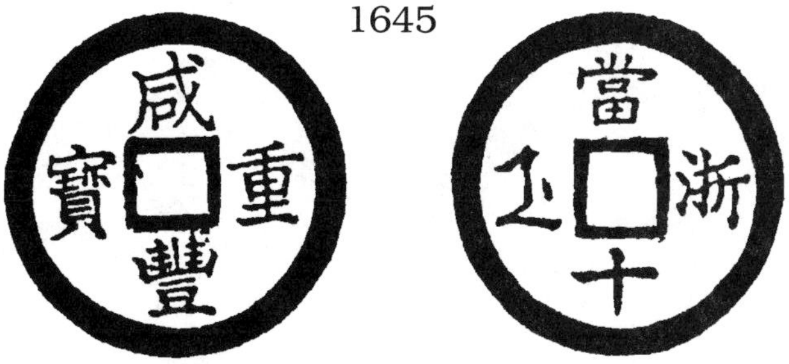

1646

1647

1648

1649

1650

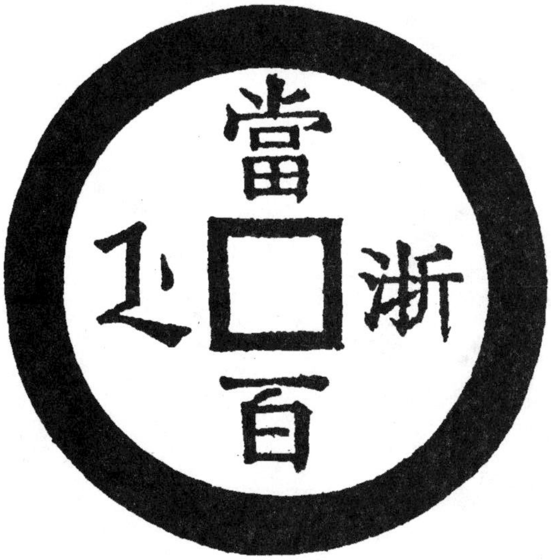

1645. Xian Feng Zhong Bao TP, 10 Cash, Zhejiang mint, FD-2477 G-2
1646. Ditto, 20 Cash TP, FD-2480 G-2
1647. Ditto, 30 Cash TP, FD-2482 G-2
1648. Ditto, 40 Cash TP, FD-2484 G-2
1649. Ditto, 50 Cash TP, FD-2486 G-2
1650. Ditto, 100 Cash TP, FD-2488 G-2

1651

1652

1653

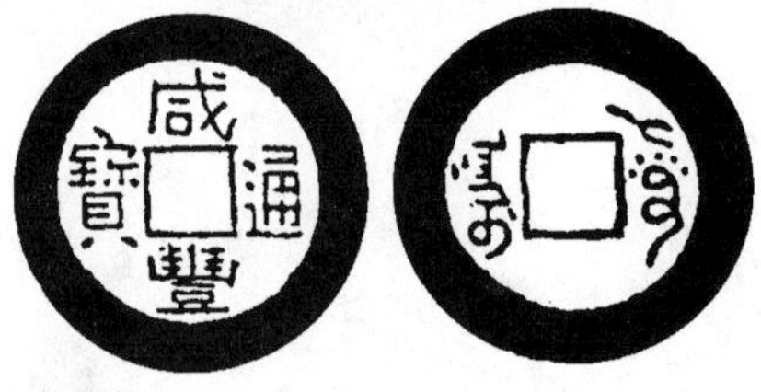

1654

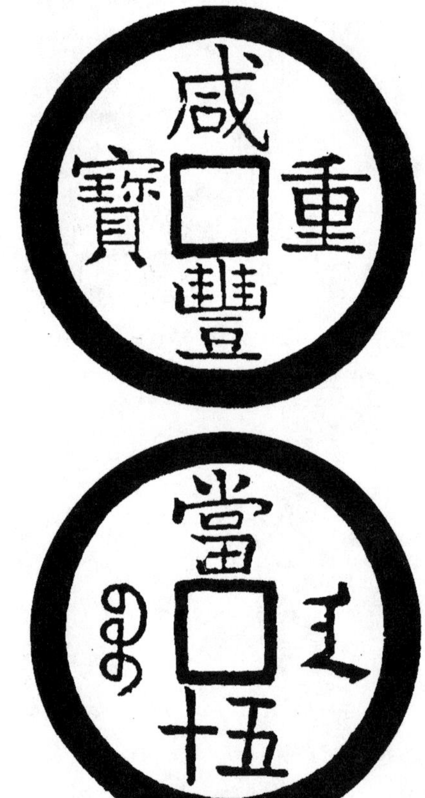

1655

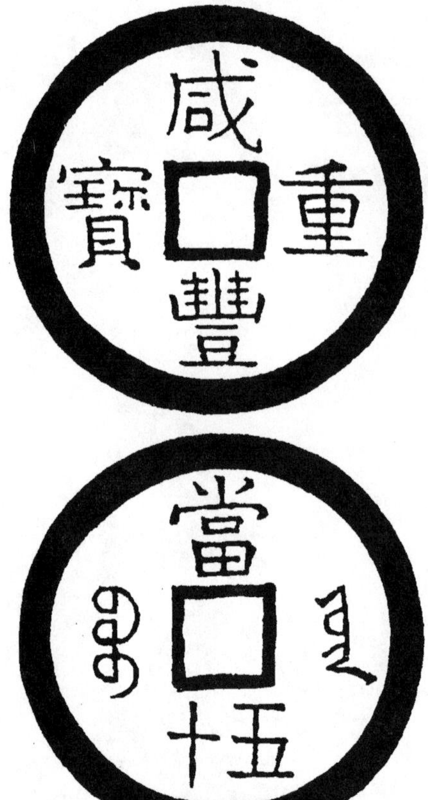

1651. Xian Feng Tong Bao, 20 Cash, Fujian mint TP	G-2
1652. Ditto, 1 Cash, Hunan mint P	G-3
1653. Ditto, Aksu mint P	G-3
1654. Xian Feng Zhong Bao, 50 Cash, Anhui mint P	G-S
1655. Ditto, 50 Cash, Yunnan mint M	G-S

1656

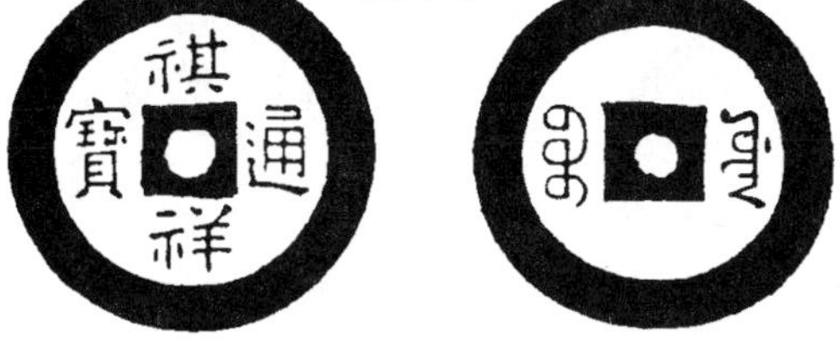

1657

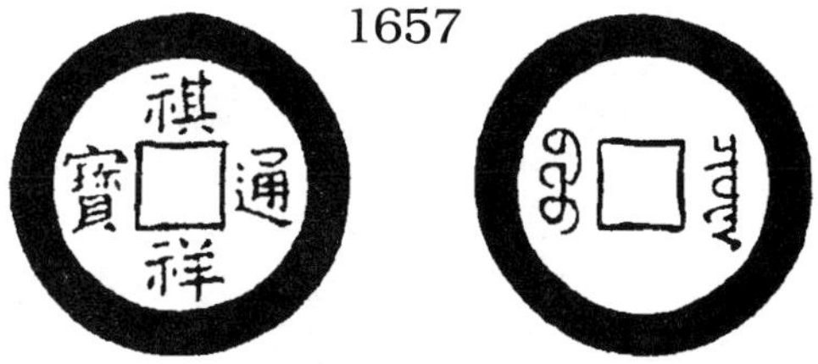

1658

1659

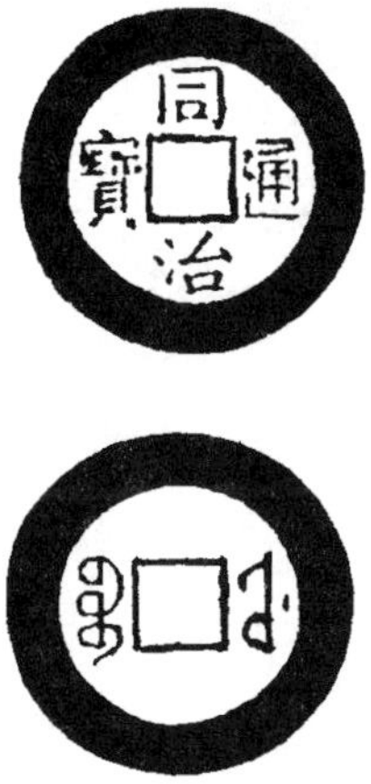

1660

1661

1656. Qi Xiang Tong Bao, B of W EM	G-R
1657. Ditto, B of Rev M	G-S
1658. Tong Zhi Tong Bao, B of Rev EM	G-S
1659. Ditto, Fujian mint M	G-1
1660. Ditto, Sichuan mint M	G-1
1661. Ditto, Zhili mint M	G-2

1662

1663

1664

1665

1666

1667

1668

1669

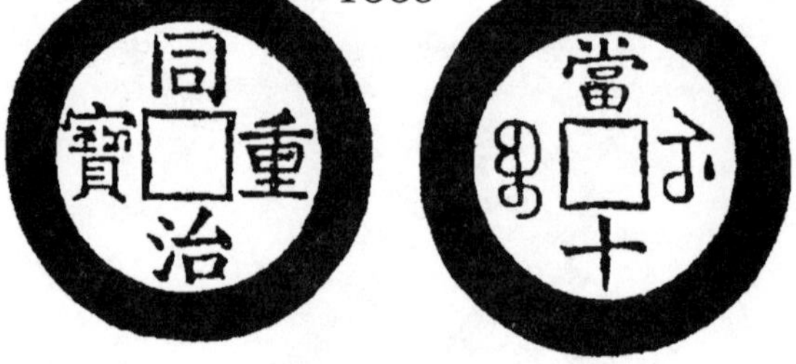

1670

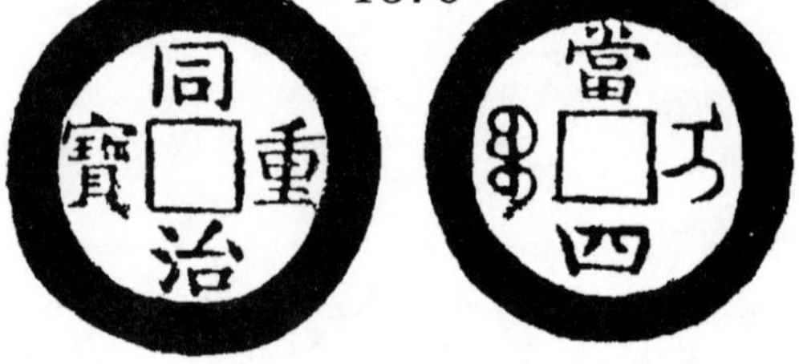

1662. Tong Zhi Tong Bao, Fujian mint P	G-3
1663. Ditto, Shaanxi mint P	G-3
1664. Ditto, Hunan mint P	G-3
1665. Ditto, Hubei mint P	G-3
1666. Ditto, Guangdong mint P	G-3
1667. Ditto, Shanxi mint P	G-3
1668. Ditto, Aksu mint P	G-3
1669. Tong Zhi Zhong Bao, 10 Cash, Jiangsu mint P	G-3
1670. Ditto, 4 Cash, Yili mint P	G-3

1671

1672

1673

1674

1675

1676

1677

1678

1679

1680

1681

1682

1671. Tong Zhi Zhong Bao, 10 Cash, Zhejiang mint P	G-2
1672. Ditto, Sichuan mint P	G-2
1673. Ditto, Hubei mint P	G-2
1674. Ditto, Shanxi mint P	G-2
1675. Ditto, Jiangxi mint P	G-2
1676. Ditto, Fujian mint P	G-2
1677. Ditto, Shaanxi mint P	G-2
1678. Ditto, Zhili mint P	G-2
1679. Ditto, Guangxi mint P	G-2
1680. Ditto, Hunan mint P	G-2
1681. Ditto, Aksu mint P	G-2
1682. Ditto, Yili mint P	G-2

1683

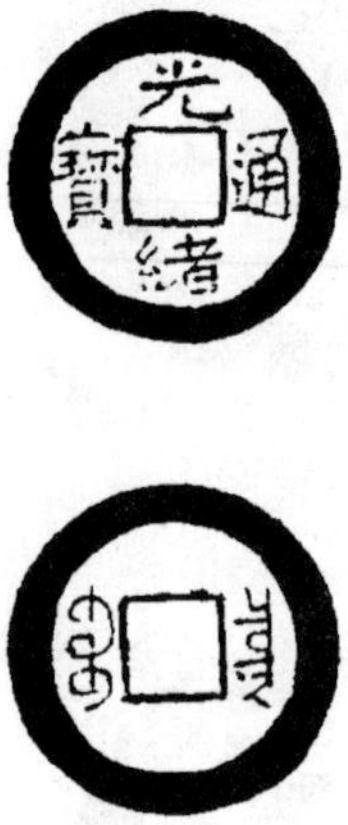

1684

1685

1686

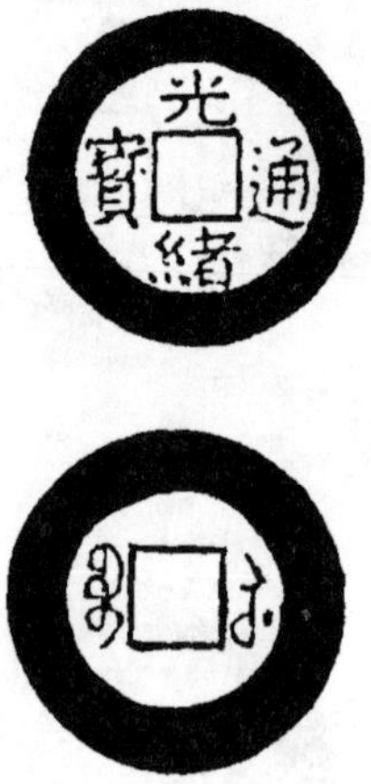

1687

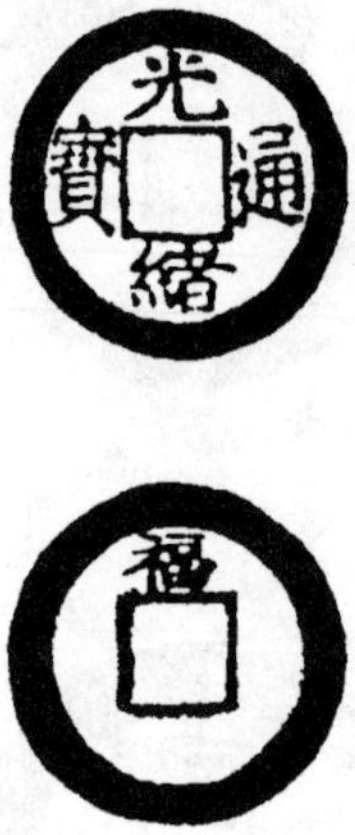

1688

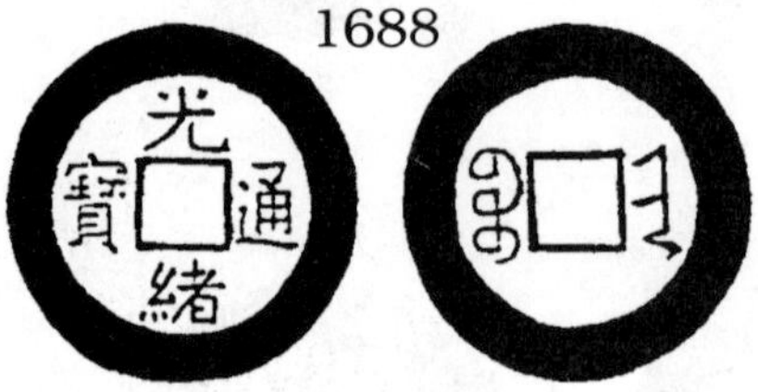

1689

1690

1691

1692

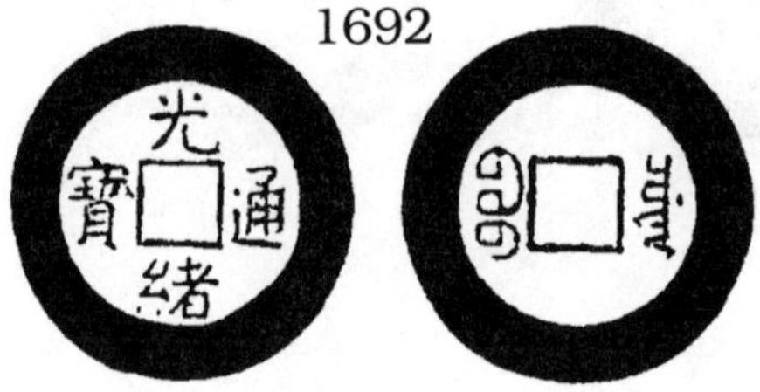

1683. Guang Xu Tong Bao, B of Rev EM	G-1
1684. Ditto, B of W mint EM	G-1
1685. Ditto, Fujian mint M	G-2
1686. Ditto, Jiangsu mint M	G-3
1687. Ditto, Fu (Fujian) in Han script on reverse P	G-3
1688. Ditto, Shanxi mint P	G-3
1689. Ditto, Yunnan mint P	G-3
1690. Ditto, Yili mint P	G-3
1691. Ditto, Aksu mint P	G-3
1692. Ditto, Sichuan mint P	G-3

1693

1694

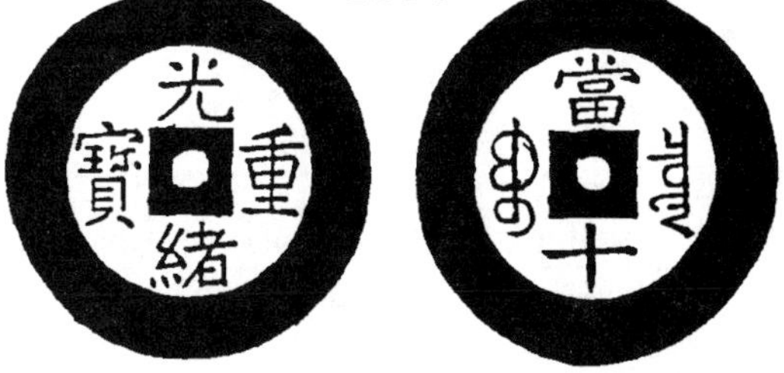

1695

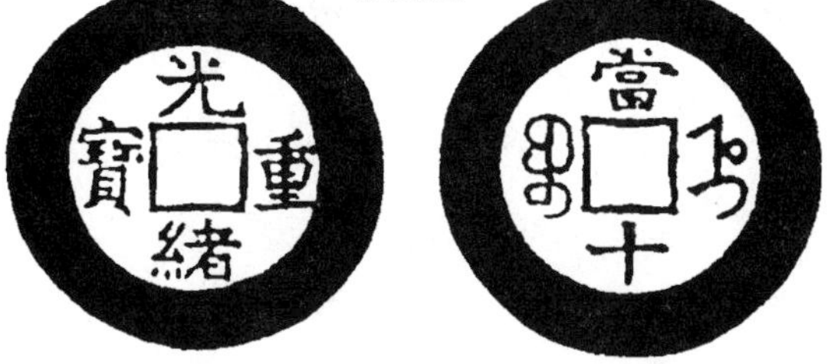

1696

1697

1698

1699

1700

1701

1702

1703

1704

1705

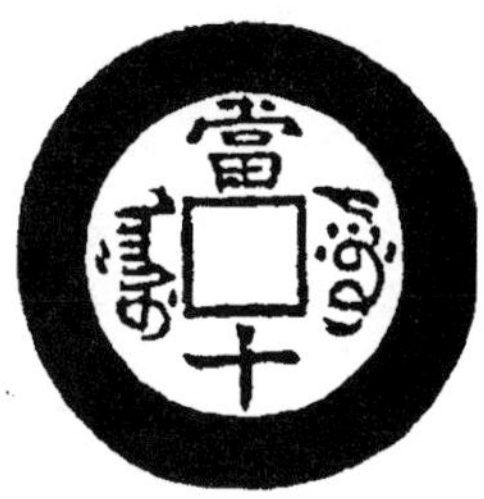

1693. Guang Xu Zhong Bao, 10 Cash, Ivory Model, B of Rev, FD-2643	G-VR
1694. Ditto, 10 Cash EM, FD-2642	G-S
1695. Ditto, Zhili mint P, FD-2644	G-3
1696. Ditto, Jiangsu mint P, FD-2645	G-3
1697. Ditto, Guangdon mint P, FD-2654	G-3
1698. Ditto, Fujian mint P, FD-2648	G-3
1699. Ditto, Hunan mint P, FD-2650	G-3
1700. Ditto, Shanxi mint P, FD-2651	G-3
1701. Ditto, Shaanxi mint P, FD-2652	G-3
1702. Ditto, Guangxi mint P, FD-2655	G-3
1703. Ditto, Yunnan mint P, FD-2656	G-3
1704. Ditto, Guizhou mint P, FD-2657	G-3
1705. Ditto, Aksu mint P, FD-2659	G-3

1706

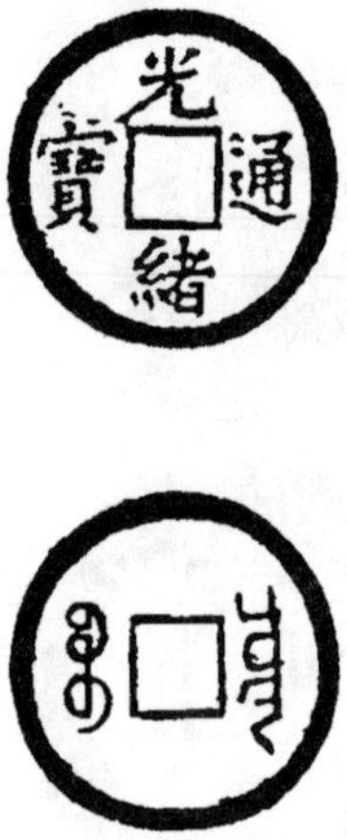

1707

1708

1709

1710

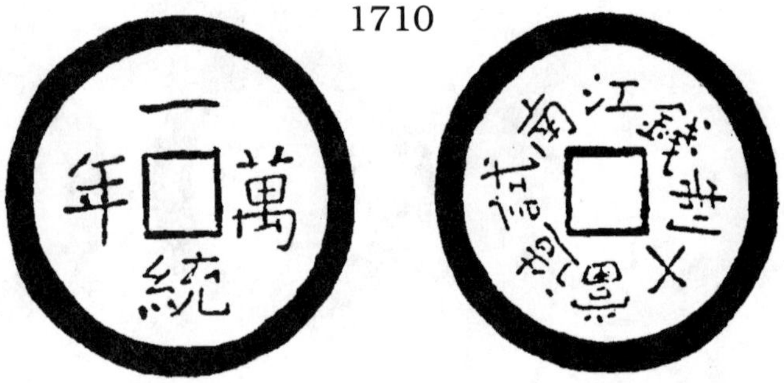

1711

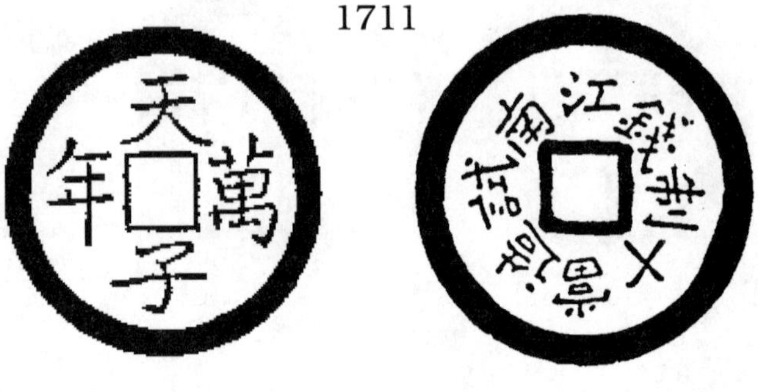

1706. Guang Xu Tong Bao, B of Rev, Machine-struck Pattern — G-3
1707. Ditto, Zhili MSP — G-3
1708. Ditto, Official Currency above, and 4 candareens below MSP, FD-2626 — G-3
1709. Guang Xu Zhong Bao, 10 Cash, Guangdong mint MSP — G-2
1710. Unity Everlasting, 10 Cash, Jiangnan Trial Piece on reverse FD-2665 — G-1
1711. Long Live the Emperor, 10 Cash, Jiangnan Trial Piece on reverse — G-1

1712

1713

1714

1712.	Unity Everlasting, Good Luck on the reverse TP	G-3
1713.	Xuan Tong Tong Bao, B of Rev EM	G-S
1714.	Heavenly Kingdom on obverse, Imperial Currency on reverse (Taiping Heavenly Kingdom) M	G-S

N.B. The mother coins of certain periods have certain marked features: The alloy of mother coins of the Northern Song is usually of a whitish color (Brass), and the superb workmanship sets them apart from the regular issues; their thickness usually reaches 2mm and over. They are either identical to their iron counterparts or bronze coins that are smaller and thinner.

Mothers coins of the Southern Song are most easily identified, as the inscriptions on the reverse are identical with those of their iron couterparts.

The mother coins of the Qing Dynasty are cast with quality copper of a yellowish-golden color. The sides of the coins and center hole taper outward forming a fish-back shape, making it easier for their removal from the sand molds.

The mother coin of the Taiping rebels shown here is larger and more exquisitely done than those cast for circulation; the sides and centerhole were filed into the same tapering shape as the mother coins of the Qing regime.

SECTION IV
APPENDICES

IDENTIFYING VARIANT CASH COINS

The identification of variant cash coins is a most productive task, which for their numbers and the difficulties involved, offers great potential for study, recreation and treasure hunting. Variants is a loose term for coins that have legends done a little different from the major issues appearing in Section I of this catalog. Just imagine the thrill experienced upon resolving the background or value of a certain coin that has been on one's hands for some time, or wading through a vast sea of coins at a dealer, outwitting that unsuspecting person and acquiring a precious item at a trifling price. It's a gratifying experience, tackling variants!

The three groups of coins in this section were selected to demonstrate how identification work is carried out. In the first group of Wu Zhu coins, solving the identity of a Wu Zhu coin and relating it to its proper lineage is the main objective. In the second group of Kai Yuan Tong Bao coins, the problem is tracing them to the emperor who issued them. This is an impossible task, as almost all emperors of the Tang Dynasty adopted the same Kai Yuan legend for their coinage, thus attempting to pinpoint which of the twenty-three rulers minted which variety would be a futile undertaking. Narrowing the scope, however, to the first seven emperors would be a credible and interesting venture. Firstly, excavation findings are available to the researcher for a starting point; secondly, the existing evidence allows ample room to fill in certain gaps through justifiable inferencing. Looking back on history, during the period of the first seven emperors, the Tang Dynasty developed into the most glorious of Chinese feudal dynasties. For one hundred and twenty years its economy maintained a steady upward surge, a phenomena never again witnessed, even to this day.

Of the seven monarchs, three were legendary figures, one of whom was the one and only woman emperor in Chinese history, and for her courage, brilliance and achievements, deserves to be ranked among the greatest women of all time.

At first glance, all Kai Yuan coins look quite the same in appearance; however, a closer scrutiny may reveal to the interested inquirer the existence of certain clues which can serve as a guide in the identification process.

The third group of Northern Song coins attracts the most attention from collectors, scholars and dealers for its diverse artistic varieties designed during the reign of the Emperor Hui Zong, himself a brushmaster of the first degree, and who wrote some of the legends of the coins in this group in his own hand.

IDENTIFYING WU ZHU COINS

JUN GUO WU ZHU

The legend is casually written and the workmanship crude. The earliest issues were larger than normal and began shrinking in size with the passing of time. The edges were unfiled and there were splashes of copper around the edges. The head of the Zhu radical is angular, which feature is found on all Western Wu Zhu varieties, a distinguishing feature that sets it apart from the Eastern Han Wu Zhus on which the head had been modified to a rounded one. Three samples of the Jun Guo Wu Zhu are given here, The first one may be termed a primitive Wu Zhu, as it is larger than normal, the legend not done neatly, and the workmanship of inferior quality — Part of the sprue is still attached to the coin, the sides unfiled, and the four dots of the leftmost radical not visible. The second one is in better shape, with the sides filed and the size about the norm; the legend is still in a rather sloppy form and there is a bar under the center hole. The coin's 3.5mm thickness is unusual for its size, which averages 1.5-2mm on most species. The third one stands out for its nicely written Wu character. The two crossing strokes of the Wu character are straight as compared with the slightly curved ones on other varieties, a feature highly prized by collectors of Wu Zhu coins.

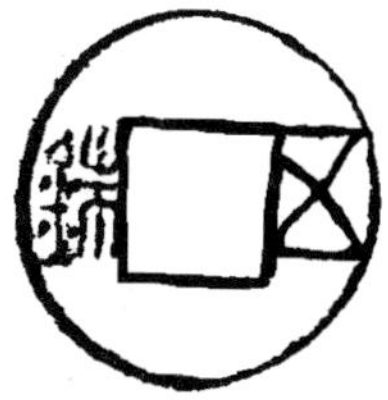

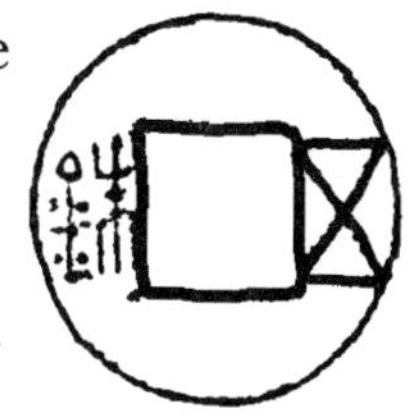

CHI ZE WU ZHU

The legend and workmanship were both finely executed to prevent counterfeiting; the size is larger and weight heavier than its predecessor the Jun Guo Wu Zhu, and the San Guan Wu Zhu that came after it. The standard size must have been upwards of 2.55mm and the weight 4g and over. The first one is the largest of the three shown here. It is listed in Section I as No. 64. The word Chi means "red" and Ze "side", indicating that after undergoing the process of filing, the sides reveal a reddish color. Although no proven Chi Ze Wu Zhus have turned up in actual excavation finds, it is generally agreed that the specimens found in Prince Liu Sheng's innermost burial chamber belong to this category. The second and third specimens shown here are from that collection.

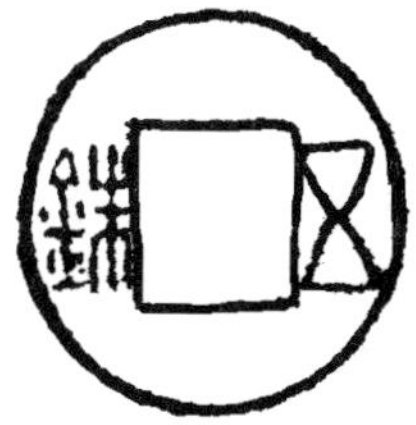

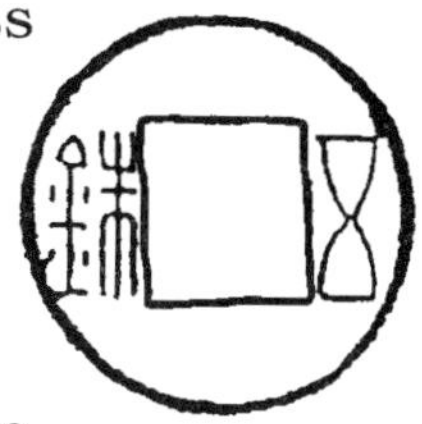

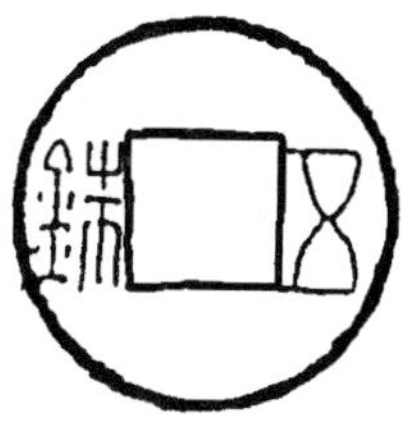

SAN GUAN WU ZHU

These were minted by the three central minting authorities to replace the Chi Ze Wu Zhu. They are a bit smaller than the Chi Ze, and there is a horizontal bar above the center hole, which appears on all later western Han varieties. San means "Three" and Guan is "Authority", hence its name San Guan Wu Zhu. The size and weight of this issue set the standard for all subsequent ones.

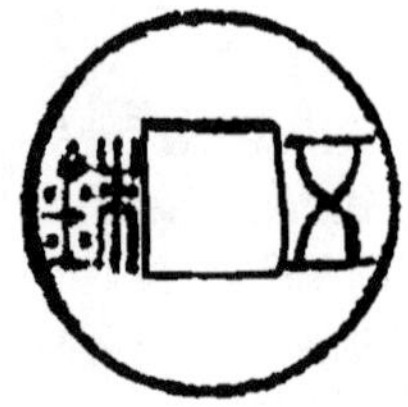

ZHAO DI WU ZHU

This variety was issued by the Emperor Zhao Di. The character Wu on the right is shaped like two triangles linked by a rim in the middle, resembling a pair of glasses.

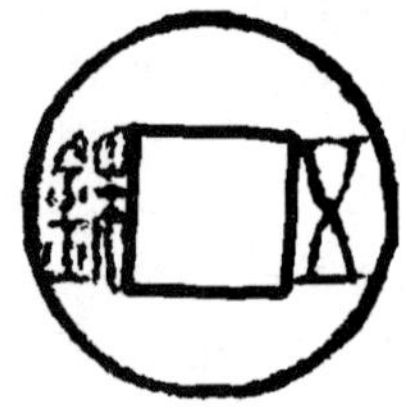

XUAN DI WU ZHU

Zhao Di's successor Xuan Di made a slight change in Zhao Di's Wu Zhu design, and the result was that the character Wu took on the shape of two cannon shells joined tip to tip.

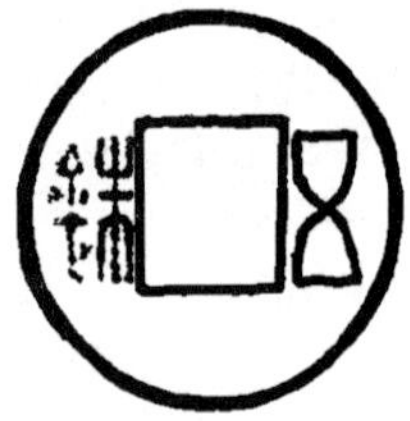

WANG MANG WU ZHU

The usurper Wang Mang spared no cost in the making of his Wu Zhu coins, which were unusually large and heavy, exceeding 25mm in diameter and 4.2g in weight. The legend is in low relief while the outer rim rises high, a feature of his coins. Both the outer and inner rims on the reverse are higher and wider than other Wu Zhu varieties, much like the Da Quan 50 Cash he put into circulation.

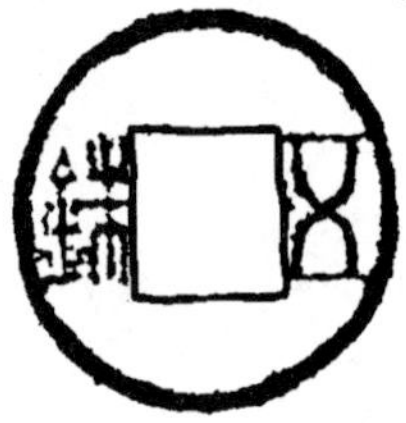

GENG SHI WU ZHU

The coin is thinner and the center hole larger than other Western Han Wu Zhu varieties, and the outer rim a bit wider. The head of the Jin radical to the left of the center hole is small and shaped like an equilateral triangle. The Zhu head is rounded, setting the pattern for the Eastern Han Wu Zhu.

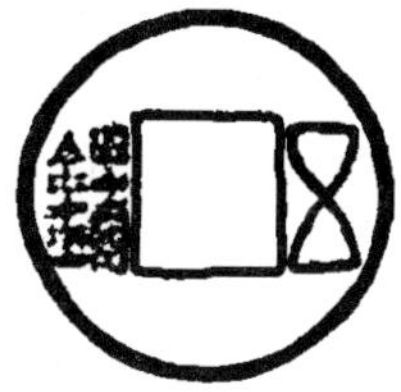

GONG SUN SHU WU ZHU

His are iron coins, the legend fashioned after the Western Han Wu Zhu.

EASTERN HAN WU ZHU

The head of the Zhu radical is rounded, a feature that sets it apart from the Western Han Wu Zhu. The early issues are larger than the above Geng Shi variety. On the whole, Eastern Han Wu Zhus are thinner and lighter than their Western Han counterparts, and the rims and legend are in low relief, as compared with the high relief of the Western Han varieties.

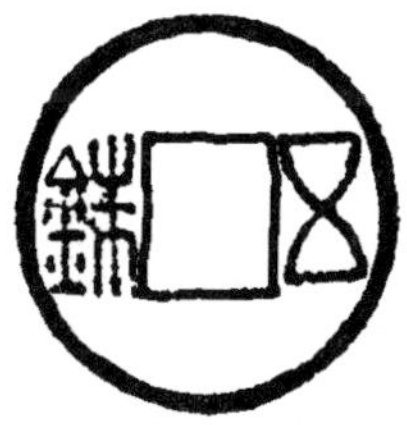

LING DI WU ZHU

The legend is in the style of the above Wu Zhu. On the reverse are four rays spreading out from the center hole.

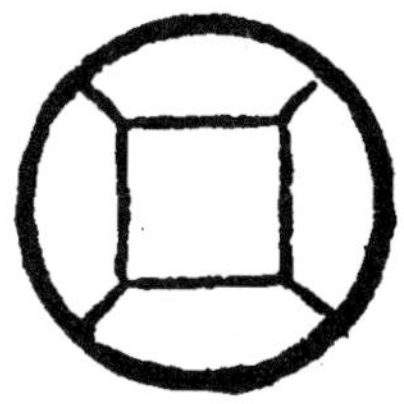

DONG ZHUO WU ZHU

The coin is small and plain, with no legend on it.

YUAN SHAO WU ZHU

The Wu Zhu legend is reversed, with Wu on the left and Zhu on the right. There are four rays on the reverse radiating from the center hole. The coin is thin and the legend in low relief.

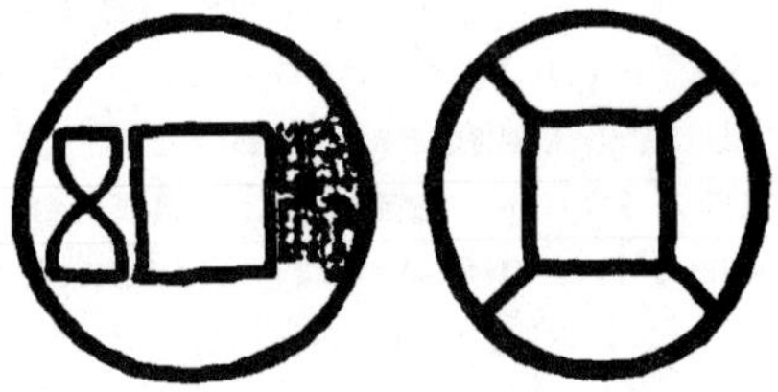

SHU WU ZHU

The coin is small in size. There is a rim around the center hole. As many of these coins were unearthed in Gansu Province, some authorities contend that the coin was minted by the Posterior Liang regime.

WEI WU ZHU

Two varieties of Wu Zhu are considered minted by the Wei regime, one large and one small. The long perpendicular stroke of the Zhu radical is broken off in the middle, breaking up the Zhu radical into three sections. The coin is thin and the legend in low relief. Recent archaeological findings have confirmed the smaller one to be of Wei issuance. The four outer corners of the two characters are joined to the outer rim, and the center hole is larger than other coins that approach this one in size. The workmanship is crude, leaving the sides unfiled.

SHEN LANG WU ZHU

The left radical of Zhu is missing, and the workmanship of coarse quality.

TWO PILLAR WU ZHU

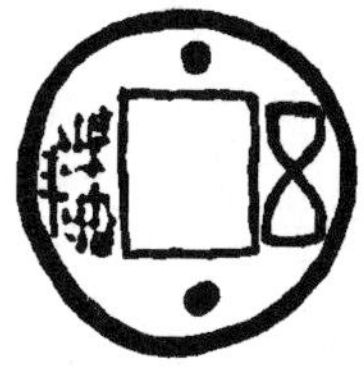

The name of this coin came from the two dots on the obverse, which in the chronicles were called "Pillars". There is another variety named Four Pillar Wu Zhu, as there were two dots on the obverse and another two on the reverse.

YONG PING WU ZHU

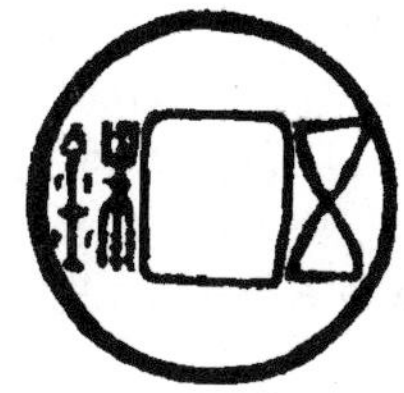

The coin was minted during the Yong Ping years of the Emperor Xuan Wu Di, hence its name. The two characters are longer than those of the Han Dynasty and beautifully written. The two crossing strokes of the character Wu are slightly and gracefully curved.

CHEN WU ZHU

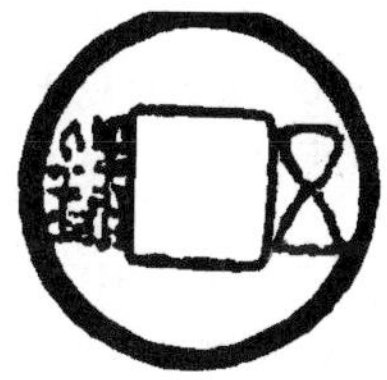

The two characters, though small, are gracefully written. The outer rim is slightly wider than those of other varieties. Like most currencies of this period, the weight and quality of the coin is substandard.

WESTERN WEI WU ZHU

The crossing strokes of the character Wu are straight and there is a vertical bar on its left side. The arrowhead of the Zhu character is long and its point slants toward the right. The rim is wide and the coin heavy, averaging 3.7g.

SUI WU ZHU

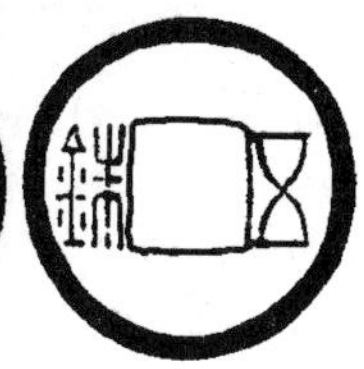

It is generally said that three varieties of Wu Zhus were issued in this dynasty. The large one is identical to the Western Wei variety in appearance, only that it is lighter in weight, averaging around 3g. So far, no Wu Zhus of this description have been unearthed from any Sui Dynasty tombs to verify its identity. One of the smaller species may be regarded as its shrunken version. The coin at the lower right was circulated towards the last years of the Sui Dynasty. The crossing strokes of the character Wu are slightly curved and the alloy is of a whitish color, for which reason it is commonly called "White Cash Wu Zhu".

DETERMINING THE PEDIGREE OF EARLY KAI YUAN COINS

The Kai Yuan Tong Bao coins of this period share some common features — the alloy is of a whitish color; the first stroke of the bottom character is short, commonly called "Short-stroke Yuan"; the reverse is plain, but some have a slender crescent with sharp tips at both ends imprinted on the reverse, different in style from the plump crescents of the Middle Tang period.

Searching for the coins cast by the first Emperor Gao Zhu, one bears in mind that the coin legend was written by the great calligraphist Ou Yang-Xiu, and that the emperor had decreed the coins to be two Zhu and four Lei in weight, nowadays roughly four grams. The coin shown below comes closest to featuring the characteristics of the original version, the legend starting clockwise from the uppermost character:

Kai — Rather slender in shape.
Tong — The uppermost stroke of the head is rather long and curves a bit upward at the left end; the three dots on the left have long sharp tails trailing to the left.
Yuan — First stroke (uppermost) short.
Bao — Small, which grew in size on later varieties.

The coin shown here meets the above descriptions, coming closest to Ou Yang's style — Lean and vigorous, at the same time graceful and poised; the characters seemingly plain and neat, yet full of subtle twists. The weight is up to standard: 4 grams.

Diameter: 23.45mm.
Weight: 4.175 g.

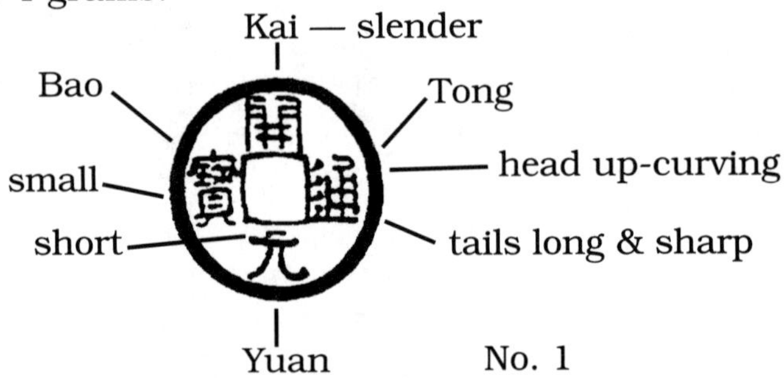

No. 1

As the first issue of Kai Yuan coins came out in the Wu De years of the first Emperor Gao Zhu, they are commonly called Wu De Kai Yuans. The early Tang period relates to the seven emperors, and the coins they issued are as follows:

1. Wu De Kai Yuan — Wu De is the reign title of the first emperor of the Tang Dynasty. So far, no coins from tombs of that period have been unearthed. However, from the tomb of Princess Chang Le, the emperor's favorite daughter, five Kai Yuan coins were earthed (<<Da Xi>> Nos. 54-58) which may be regarded as Wu De Kai Yuans, as they look very much like the coin shown above (No.1), but quite different from Tai Zong's (<<Da Xi>> No. 59); furthermore, the Chinese do not bury their dead with the belongings of living persons.

Three of the five are shown here, Nos. 54, 55 and 56. They are all around 24mm in diameter and over 4 grams in weight.

2

3

4

2. Zhen Guan Kai Yuan — Zhen Guan is the reign title of the second Emperor Tai Zong (a.k.a. Li Shi Min). Coin No. 5 was found in a tomb dated the 21st year of Zhen Guan (<<Da Xi>> No. 59). Compared with the Wu De species, this one has a wider rim, and the brushstrokes thicker and harsher; the Kai is wider, the left leg of Yuan stiffer and stretched out farther, and the two topmost strokes of the Kai thicker, like a pair of commanding eyebrows, a faint hint of the emperor's macho taste. The coin profile is quite in keeping with him, the actual founder of the new dynasty, who for 10 years had fought north & south on horseback, creating a new empire on the ruins of the former one. In 23 years he had brought stability and prosperity to the Middle Kingdom, and deserves to go down in history as one of its greatest leaders. His coins are, on the whole, larger than those of his predecessor's, in direct proportion to the growing economy; and prices were going down, a trend that was to continue for 120 years.

5

3. Gao Zong Kai Yuan — Two lots of coins were found with persons buried during his reign, the first consisting of one coin dated the 5th year of Yong Hui (654 AD), and the second consisting of two and a half coins dated the 1st year of Lin De (664 AD).

1) Yong Hui Kai Yuan — On this coin the original style of Ou Yang-Xiu is still preserved, but some subtle retouches are apparent: the two boxes on the upper part of the Kai are smaller and set wider apart than those of the Wu De Kai Yuans; the two legs of the number sign within the Kai are longer, either touching or almost touching the inner rim right below, and the Bao is smaller than later varieties. (No. 6).

6

2) Lin De Kai Yuan — Three coins were found in a tomb dating from this period, one of them broken, only one half remaining. The styles of the three are each different from the other.

a) Spread-legged Kai Yuan — The two legs of Yuan are spread wider apart than those of other types; the Tong head is tilted upward and rising higher than the inner rim and the Kai is wider than usual (No. 7).

7

b) Weak-profile Kai Yuan — The name was given by Japanese numismatists for its homely looks (No. 8). The basic style had been changed, taking on a rather reserved look. The left leg was pulled in, almost parallel with the right one, which makes the Yuan stand at attention rather than at ease; hence the name "Stiff-legged Kai Yuan" given it by the Chinese. Were there a beauty contest, this specie could not compete against the other early Kai Yuans, not to say the contestant making its debut below (No. 9).

8

c) Shrunken-legend Kai Yuan — The distance between the legend and the outer rim had widened due to the shrinking of the characters: the uppermost stroke of the Tong head is shorter and does not curl upward at the left tip as did those of its predecessors and companions (No. 9). This treatment of the original Ou Yang design tends to lend a more effeminate grace to the legend, in a way toning down the macho of the Zhen Guan variety (No. 5). This half piece, if restored, could have looked like the following one (No. 10), taking into consideration the closeness of size and style. The design is a msterstroke and the workmanship excellent.

9

4. Wu Ze Tian Kai Yuan — Wu Ze Tian was the emperor Tai Zong's teen-age concubine. Exiled to a nunnery before Tai Zong's death, she was recalled by his son, the new Emperor Gao Zong, in the 5th year of his reign (654 AD), and made empress the following year. Gao Zong was an indecisive ruler and often troubled with headaches, whereupon he passed on the examining and approval of all State papers to his empress, who then took an active part in politics. The ministers were no match for the strong-willed and resourceful Wu Ze Tian, and by 656 AD all power had fallen into her hands. She and her husband sat side by side as they held court, an occasion publicly dubbed the "rule of the two emperors". After her husband's death and the dethronement of her two sons 28 years later, she proclaimed herself emperor, the one and only female emperor in Chinese history. For 50 years, first as regent and then as emperor, she held an iron sway over the empire, raising the economy to a new high; a girl-power success story setting a role model for generations of wannabes to strive for achievement. The few excavation finds dated from her time do not provide a direct answer as to what coins she actually issued; they can only serve as a starting point for us to find the answer for ourselves.

1) Wu Ze Tian as empress — It may be not without reason to presume that the three aforesaid Lin De coins (Nos. 7-9) were still in circulation at the time of the deceased person's burial in 664 AD, and that their circulation continued for some time afterwards. Empress

10

Wu's regency was to last another 20 years. Over the years, the two coins No. 7 & 8 could have been withdrawn in favor of coin No. 10 for its dignity and charm, quite befitting the empress, a woman of extraordinary caliber and beauty. Judging from excavation finds and market information, coin No. 7 is the scarcest of the three. Although more plentiful than this one, coin No. 8 showed little change in size or weight. Coin No. 10 showed the greatest change, its size varying from 24.4mm to 25.6mm, and the weight from 3.74g to 4.64g, an indication that it was issued over a long period of time.

11

24.4mm, 4.435g.

12

25mm, 4.406g.

13

25.3mm, 4.529g.

14

25.6mm, 4.638g.

The three coins numbered 7, 8, & 9 were quite consistent in specifications. Had the larger ones numbered 12 to 14 been available, they might in all probability have been preferred over the smaller ones to accompany the deceased. The productive power at that time was just recovering from a setback due to the rise of corrupt influences in the court circles before Wu was recalled. It was some years later, after she had overcome a monetary cries that the economy began a steady upward surge, providing the basis for issuing currency in larger specifications

The presumption that this type of coin was issued over a long period of time, during and even after Wu Ze Tian';s reign, may hold good by the fact that from a tomb dated 706 AD, the second year after she yielded the throne to her son Zhong Zong, a coin was discovered (No. 15) resembling Coin No. 14 in that the distance between the rim and the characters at the top, bottom and left-hand side are characteristics of the Shrunken-legend type.

15

14

Some changes are apparent, though, as evident in the elongation of the characters Bao and Kai; yet the upward curving Tong head reminds one of Coin No. 5. Anway, the coin is proof that the Shrunken-legend variety was still in circulation at the time, forty years after the first of the species appeared on the scene (No. 9), and that it had grown in direct proportion to the growth of the economy.

2) Wu Ze Tian as emperor — Three hoards of Kai Yuan coins were found at burial sites dated within the period of her

reign. Of the 38 coins discovered in the tombs, rubbings of only three of them are known to have been made public (Nos. 16-18). Although all three were strictly in the Wu De Kai Yuan style, two of them were substandard (Nos. 17-18), around 23mm in diameter and not quite 3g in weight, which marks them as counterfeits. The three hoards may provide the reader with the following facts:

16

a) Since no other varieties were published, the other 35 coins are all presumed to be of the Wu De type.

b) In the second hoard, all three were well below standard, thus defined as counterfeits.

17

c) Among the 25 coins in the third hoard, five were counterfeits.

d) The coin from the first hoard (No. 16) is larger than the early Wu De Kai Yuans and it retains their original Ou Yang calligraphic style. The outer horizontal and perpendicular strokes of the Kai meet at right angles, retaining the majestic air, but the thickset and vigorous eyebrows of the Zhen Guan species (No. 5) have thinned out, so have all the other strokes and the outer rim. One gets the impression that the original design had undergone a careful facelifting, resulting in a better balanced image; but the abandon of the master and the macho of the second emperor is there no more. During the fifty years of her rule, from empress to regent to emperor, she had consolidated the stability and prosperity handed down from the second Emperor Tai Zong, and furthermore, laid down the foundation for her grandson Xuan Zong to advance the empire to its zenith, to become the most glorious of China's feudal Dynasties.

18

Across a span of 120 years, from the first Emperor Gao Zhu through the Kai Yuan years of the 7th Emperor Xuan Zong, the currency maintained an appreciation trend parallel to the economic growth. The currency issued by her son Zhong Zong, both before he was displaced and after his resuming the throne, met regular standards; therefore, the coins she issued should not have retracted from the above monetary pattern, thus the counterfeits must have been isolated cases. Regarding the scissors difference between the coins and the economy as the norm may not be setting us on the right track.

To complicate matters further, Wu Ze Tian changed the dynastic name to Zhou five years after she proclaimed herself emperor. It was a very sensitive issue, as all her subjects regarded themselves as loyal to the House of Li, the royal family of the Tang Dynasty. That no coins bearing her reign title were issued and to revert to the established Kai Yuan pattern would seem a reasonable move under the circumstances of those times. Whether this surmise be tenable or irrational, further excavation evidence is needed for corroboration.

5. Zhong Zong Kai Yuan — Zhong Zong became ruler upon his father Gao Zong's death. He was twice seated on the throne, the first time displaced six weeks by his mother the Empress Wu, and the second time after his mother's abdication 20 years later. For the first term he used the reign title Si Sheng and for the second, Sheng Long.

1) Si Sheng Kai Yuan — The size, weight & workmanship all reached previous standards. The Kai is obviously wider than the other varieties that came before it; while the outer rim is in higher relief than the legend on other species, they are on a par in the case of this one; the outer rim is thickset, as are the brushstrokes (No. 19).

19

2) Sheng Long Kai Yuan — At first glance, this (No. 20) and the one above appear to be quite the same; looking closer, however, minute differences are discernable. The Sheng Long coins are in fact retouched versions of the Si Sheng type issued two decades earlier. The two boxes face each other squarely in the face, their horizontal lines more parallel and straighter than their corresponding parts on the Si Sheng variety; the left leg of the character Yuan at the bottom is straighter and more dynamic; the two short strokes on the two sides of the radical forming the topmost part of the Bao on the left side of the center hole are symmetrical more or less, while those on the Si Shengs are visibly asymmetrical. In the twenty years' time he had matured quite a bit, and so had his coins.

20

6. Rui Zong Kai Yuan — Rui Zong and Zhong Zong were two brothers. Like his brother, Rui Zong was also seated twice on the throne. No documentation is available concerning the currency that he issued, so we have to start out from inference. Among the early Kai Yuans there is a specie, which from the quantity in existence, place it as a distinct type (No. 20). The coin is large, the first stroke of Yuan short, and the alloy of a whitish color, all characteristics of the early Kai Yuans. The style of the legend, though a continuation of the Ou Yang pattern, is a far cry from the vigorous and well-knit original. The characters are large and heavy, but somewhat sloppily written. The most prominent feature is the bent leg of Yuan, soft and flabby. The second time he mounted the throne, the economy was still gaining momentum, providing the conditions for him to mint full-value currency. Times, however, had changed. Immersed in peace and plenty, he had acquired a mentality different from that of his grandsires'. The

21

fullness of the characters and the softness of the bent leg fit in finely with his personality, a vivid portrait of his state of mind.

7. Xuan Zong Kai Yuan — During Xuan Zong's reign, the empire reached the summit of its glory. Prices were at an all-time low and the currency an all-time large. His coins were an enlarged version of Gao Zong's weak countenance Kai Yuan, with a little retouching (No. 21). To combat pirateering, he decreed that the mints increase the size of the coins to 26mm. After 29 years of vigorous work, he decided to take it easy, changed the reign title from Kai Yuan to Tian Bao, and started on a new life with his favorite concubine Yang Gui Fei (a.k.a. Yang Yu Huan). During this period crescents appeared on the reverse of his Kai Yuan coins, said to be nailmarks imprinted by his Precious Dear Concubine Yang on the wax coin samples. True or not, it makes an interesting story.

22

23

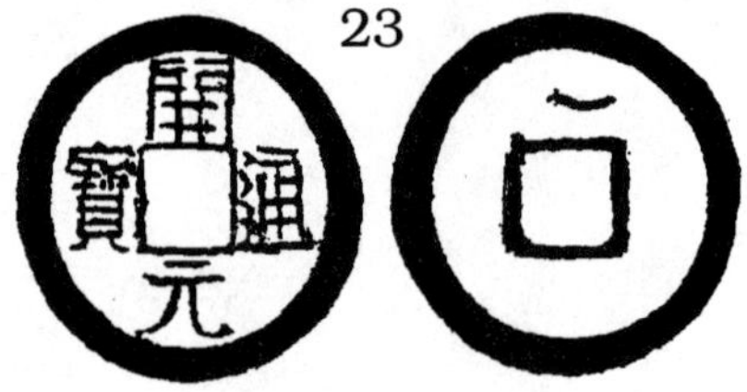

And so ends the cash history of the early period of the Tang Dynasty. The coins of this period were superb in artistic merit, quality and workmanship. The evolution of the Kai Yuan Tong Bao coin with its sustained appreciation over a span of 120 years had never been witnessed before and perhaps never to happen again in Chinese history. The reader may proceed to the study of the Kai Yuans of the Middle and Late Tang periods, all of which used the same reign title — Kai Yuan Tong Bao, another unparalleled phenomena in Chinese monetary history.

DA GUAN TONG BAO VARIETIES

Standard Pattern

The handwriting best resembles that on the large 10 Cash coin, done by the Emperor Hui Zong himself. As the Tong is quite small, it is also named Small Tong.

G-9

Wide Guan

The character Guan is wider than the one on the standard version. The two boxes protrude much further to the left than usual.

G-8

Raised Tong

The Tong rises above the upper rim of the center hole, while on other varieties the Tong is level with the rim.

G-8

Declining Tong

The Tong drops below the upper rim of the center hole. This variety is not much favored by some collectors.

G-12

Receding Da

The character Da is not placed in center position, but somewhat to the right, a characteristic setting it aside from other varieties.

G-8

Trailing Tail

The right leg of the Da seems bent and trailing behind, and the other characters seem to be leaning back and gazing upwards.

G-8

The legend on this specie was written by the Emperor Hui Zong, one of the greatest of Chinese brushmasters. Together with the Chong Ning Zhong Bao, the two varieties serve as superb examples of his penmanship, also known as the Slender Gold Style — beautiful, skinny, yet full of vitality. Over 30 varieties of Da Guan Tong Bao exist. Both Chinese and Japanese numismatists have contributed to the nomenclature of these coins, nice figurative names in the original language, but quite naive when rendered into English.

Stretching Tong

The top crosswise stroke of the Guan stretches to the left longer than usual, and lower part of Tong resembles an animal stretching its body in a yawn.

G-9

Broad Da

The Da is wide and flat. It is also known as Large Letter Tong in regular script, as the bottom stroke of the Tong does not protrude as far out to the left as other varieties.

G-3

Large Tong

The Tong head is located farther to the right than those of other species, its right side on a vertical line with the right side of the radical below it, lending the Tong a smart and erect look.

G-S

Running Script

This is a variant of the norm in regular script, also in the emperor's own hand. The bronze coin is a mother coin, the iron ones regular issues. The two must not be confused.

Bronze G-R
Iron G-7

Level-head Tong

The upper stroke of the Tong head is long and level. It is also called Tong with remote dot for the dot being farther apart from the bottom part than usual.

G-3

Dipping Guan

The box on the left side of Guan is in the shape of an inverted triangle and lower than the one beside it. This coin is also called small letter Tong in regular script.

G-8

Wide Rim

The outer rim is wider than average. There are other wide rimmed varieties, all of which are not often available.

G-6

Large Version

Collectors take a liking to Da Guan 1 cash coins over 26mm in diameter, which fetch good prices in the market. Coins this size are scarce (26.8mm).

G-S

ZHENG HE TONG BAO VARIETIES

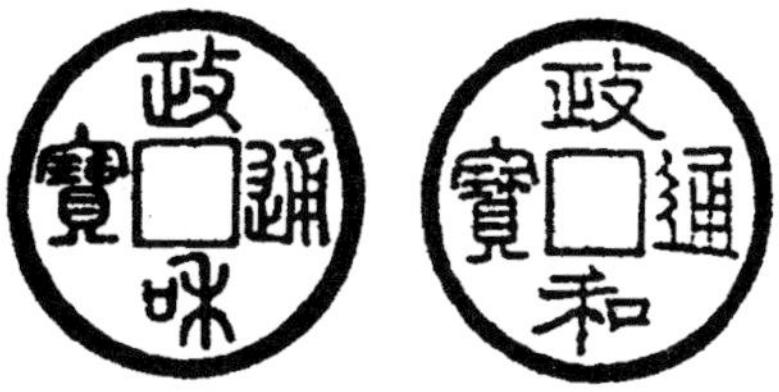

Fine Style

Some Zheng He coins come in pairs, like the two shown here, one in seal script and the other one in Li script. They may have been done by the Emperor Hui Zong himself, as he was all the time experimenting with various script styles.

G-10

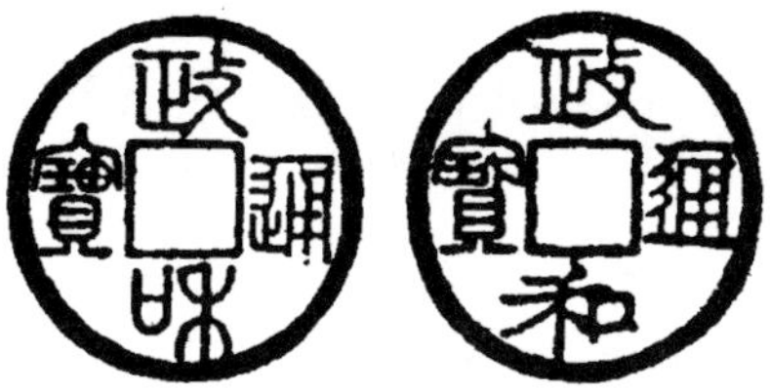

Large Characters (Zhong He Pattern)

This pair is large and beautiful. The nomenclature is rather misleading, since the reign title Zheng He came first and Zhong He (Chong He) came afterwards.

G-7

Large Characters Wen Zheng

The radical on the right side of Zheng was changed to the character Wen, hence the name. The two are accepted as a pair although the one on the left side in seal script is somewhat smaller.

G-6

Real Zheng

A variation of Wen Zheng. Written in real script (another name for regular script). The handwriting on this one comes nearest to the emperor's Slender Gold Style.

G-4

Embracing Zheng

Also a variation of Wen Zheng. The crossed right leg stretches way under the left-side radical in a hugging posture.

G-3

Pointed He

The radical on the right side of He has a pointed head. The legend is nicely written. Many Zheng He coins show up with a poorly written legend unbecoming of the master.

G-3

XUAN HE YUAN BAO & TONG BAO VARIETIES

Fine Style

Many Xuan He varieties, like the Zheng He coins, also come in pairs; one in Li script and the other in seal script. The legends on the Xuan He coins are more nicely written than the Tong Bao ones.

G-3

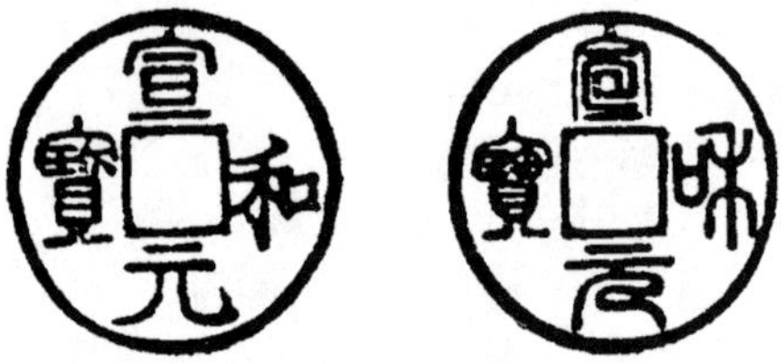

Large-foot Yuan

This is a robust pair full of vitality. The characters are superbly written and well balanced. The largeness of the coins and characters add to their attractiveness.

G-1

Broad Characters

This pair is also highly prized by collectors. All Yuan Bao coins are quite scarce. These two do not seem to be well paired, but they are still generally accepted as a pair after all.

G-2

Wide He

This one is well designed, with plenty of space in between the brush strokes. It looks like a pattern piece.

G-3

Long Xuan

The Long Xuan is a masterwork of brush art, with its square shoulders and straight strokes.

G-1

Wide Rim

Even this lowliest of Yuan Bao coins still commands a rather high grading. Yuan Bao coins were cast only in the 1st year of Xuan He, and in small amounts.

G-5

XUAN HE TONG BAO VARIETIES

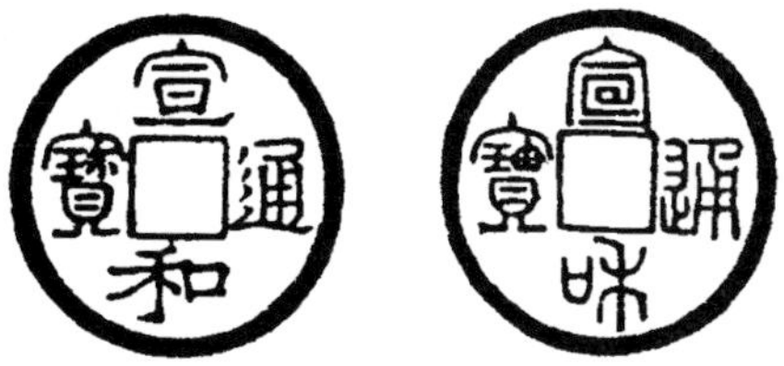

Fine Style

This is the standard version of Xuan He Tong Bao. The first is in Li script and the second one in seal script. They are available at a very moderate price.

G-8

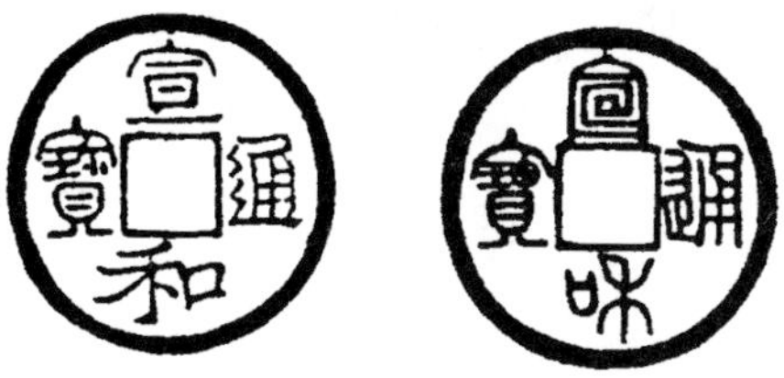

Variant Tong

There is a slight difference in writing between the Tong of this pair and the previous pair. The Tong head is long and curls upward at the left end, almost covering the left radical of Tong. These two are quite scarce.

G-3

Long Bao

The Bao is longer than the one on the first pair and the Xuan wider. Some prefer this pair over the first one. Some collectors insist the two pairs are a must for any Northern Song collection.

G-8

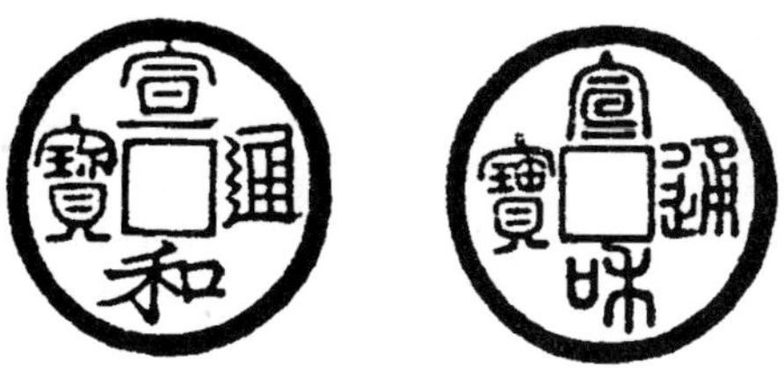

Raised Tong

The character Tong rises above the upper rim of the center hole. Cast in white bronze and finely written, they make nice collectibles. Some consider them to be pattern coins.

G-5

Robust Style

The characters are thickly built and full of vitality. They form a marked comparison with the gracefulness of other varieties.

G-8

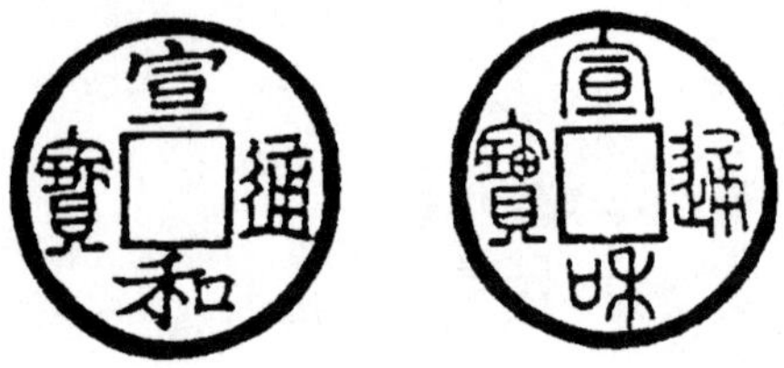

Large Characters & Wide Hole

The large center hole tends to squeeze the characters into tight postures, but they still give forth a peculiar radiance, attracting collectors despite their unattractive grading.

G-9

Tong in Regular Script

Mark the dot on the left side of the character Tong. It is a mark of the regular script. In the Li script, the left radical of Tong is written in a series of curves, while in the regular script it is composed of a dot and two curves.

G-4

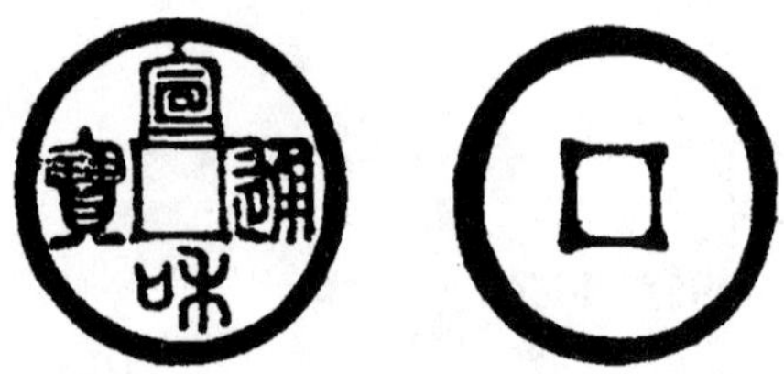

Broad Characters with Horned Rim

The legend is also robustly rendered. On both sides of the coin, the four corners of the center hole point outward like horns.

G-6

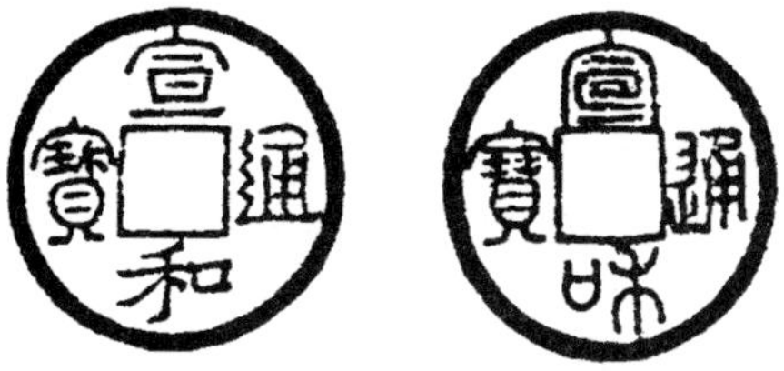

Bao With Round Radical

The lower radical of the Bao is in the shape of a circle. There are several variations of this species. The things to look for in this pair are the large Bao with the large round circle. The coins and legends are also larger than the others.

G-3

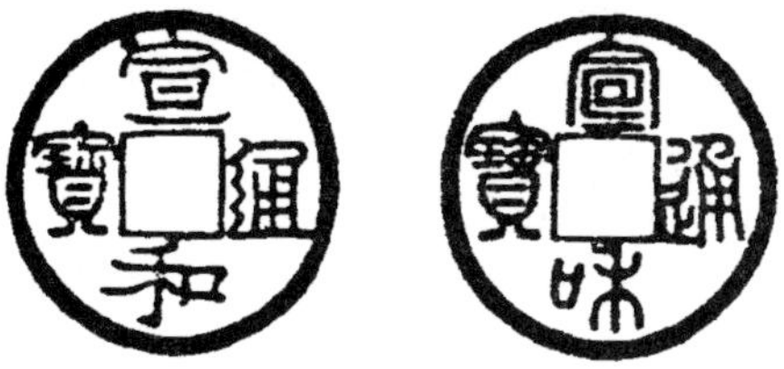

Gigantic-head Bao

This pair is the most coveted of Xuan He Tong Bao varieties, especially the one in Li script on the left. The wildness of the calligraphy make them all the more fascinating.

G-2

Concentric Legend

The characters crowd around the center hole, leaving a wide margin between the legend and the outer rim.The color of the bronze is usually white.

G-6

Eccentric Legend

The characters depart from the center hole, especially the Bao. Being thicker than normal and cast in white bronze, some numismatists take them to be trial pieces.

G-5

ASSESSING CHINESE CASH COINS

I. Methods Used in Making Fake Coins and their exposure

1. Recasting with real coins — Real coins are used to make moulds for casting fake ones. The finished products are then treated with chemicals, or covered with fake patina.

Exposure — On real coins, the surface of the characters and rims are flat; their sides go straight down and meet the coin field at right angles, and the meeting place is sharp and clear. The surface of the fake ones is somewhat rounded, and the sides curve outward where they meet the field instead of dropping straight down, so the sharply defined meeting point does not show up.

2. Mould retouching — Moulds made from real coins undergo a retouching process. Coins cast from such moulds are especially hard to detect, as the surface of the characters and rims are flat, and their sides go straight down as those of the real coins do.

Exposure — The coins are covered all over with fake patina, as any exposure of copper would give it away. The quality of the patina and the workmanship are so excellent that people fall in love with the coins at first sight.

3. Trading parts — The whole or part of a character is scraped away and a substitute is glued on.

Exposure — In this case, something is done to cover up all traces of substitution. The covered-up areas, however, do not mingle with the original coin field, so if the original coin field does not reach to the very edge of the characters, something fishy might be expected.

4. Face-lifting — The original characters are scraped away, new ones etched on the smoothed-out surface, and then the faker digs downward around the characters to raise their profile.

Exposure — The coin field around the characters sinks down, giving the characters an elevated appearance. The characters are actually on the same level as the coin field. A careful eye is sure to see through the deception.

5. Etching with acid — The legend is etched on a copper plate, covered up, and then acid is applied to the uncovered area around the characters, eating away a layer of copper; and a fake coin is made.
Exposure — The coin field is full of pock marks, like a person infected with the small pox; the sides of the characters and rim are jagged due to acid corrosion.

6. Piecing together — The obverse of one coin and the reverse of another are glued together. Another practice is to put together the outer rim of one coin and the center part of another, transforming the original into a wide rimmed coin of much higher value.

Exposure — A seam is visible on the side of the rim. Fakers try to conceal the seam by covering it up with patina. Let the buyer beware of a dirty blackish gum-like substance on the coin sides.

7. Striking with a die — This method is used to strike a mark or character onto the reverse of an ordinary coin to make it pass for an exotic variety to raise its value.

Exposure — The coin field around the struck parts shows signs of downward pressing; die marks are visible.

8. Retouching — The characters and coin field undergo recutting and scraping to make an ordinary coin pass for an engraved master coin.
Exposure — The brushstrokes are uneven in width, not matching in uniformity; and knife scratches are visible. Look at the sides of the characters and rim, which could show new knife wounds. The color of the copper is lighter than that of the master coin, which is golden yellow.

9. Faking patina — These are some of the methods used:

• Dip the coin in vinegar and then bury it for some time — The patina is thin and of a sickly green color. Wipe it and it comes off.

• Treating with chemicals like silver fluoride — The coin has a scorched, lackluster look; real coins are cool and mellow.

• Painting the coin — Paint is soft; use a knife and off it comes, but you cannot do that in the market. Real green patina comes in two colors: One appears in patches on the coin, it is rich green and shiny, hard and thick; green paint does not match the color, and it does not shine. The other is of a sand-like texture, covering the whole coin; it feels rough and prickly to the touch; paint is smooth. The red patina on coins is also prickly to the touch; paint is smooth and slippery.

• Pasting on powder ground from real patina — This type of patina is a mixture of all shades and hues, red and green specks appearing everywhere; no pattern of chemical compound distribution is evident. Smell it for the odor of glue.

• Pasting on mud — Mud mixed with glue looks different from the hard-packed dirt found on real coins; there is no sign of fine dust between the brushstrokes of the characters.

P.S. In the places where there is no mud there is paint, and where the copper does show up, that is, the surface of the characters and rims is devoid of patina, it more often than not seems a bit too shiny, like that of a newly polished shoe. The old saying holds good: Know your dealer.

SIX-WORD KEY TO ASSESSING CASH COINS

1. Legend — The rubbings or photoprints in catalogs provide a clue to dynastic coins that are known to exist. Coins not shown, or coins with legends done in styles that stray from the given samples may or may not be genuine ones. To cite an instance: only ten of the seventeen Ming Dynasty emperors issued coins with their reign titles. Coins other than these are fantasies. However, coins with the legend of the 11th emperor Zheng De were cast towards the end of the Ming Dynasty for reasons unknown. Their size, weight, alloy, design, and workmanship suggest their source to be the official mint. The brushstrokes of the legend are also taken into consideration — the strokes of the master are deft, vigorous, and spontaneous; those of the imitator are labored and lifeless.

2. Alloy — Cash coins are made from bronze, yellow copper, red copper, brass (white copper), iron or lead. Bronze was used in ancient times and in the early years of the Ming Dynasty; the color is brown. If the alloy is of any other color, they are most likely to be forgeries. However, some Wu Zhus of the Han Dynasty display a reddish hue, some Sui and early Tang coins are whitish, while the Jia Jing coins of the Ming Dynasty are of a yellowish color. Some large coins of the Qing Dynasty were made invariably with red copper, that is, the value 50 & 100 cash from the Fujian mint, and the value 500 & 1,000 cash species from the Henan and Shaanxi mints; should the alloy be yellow copper, they must be forgeries.

3. Sound — Newly made coins have a clear ringing sound, which becomes duller with the passing of years. Bouncing a coin on the table would bring the sound out. The sound of a coin is made up of two parts, the tweeter and the woofer. The high ringing tweeter sound fades with the carbonizing of the copper, until the low woofer sound remains. One should be alerted to the dull thud of the cracked coin.

4. Color — Bronze is brown in color, copper either yellow or red, and brass white. Beware of the fake coin etched out of a real bronze one. Before acquiring a coin, compare the color of the alloy and the patina with that of a real one.

5. Odor — Pasted-on patina, characters, or mud give off a smell of glue. Dealers use their noses when something about the coin arouses their suspicion. The smelling organ comes in handy in the market where scraping the patina with a knife is unacceptable.

6. Profile — A genuine coin has something about it that cannot be reproduced on a forgery. That something is called "Shen" by the Chinese. It is the essence of artistry, created through the joint efforts of the brushmaster who wrote the legend and the workers who minted the coins. An artist produces a painting through a moment of inspiration, and then goes on to make copies of it, but to the observer, there is the feeling that something is in the original that was not passed on to the copies; that something is "Shen". To cite another instance: No matter how expertly done the make-up and how similar the profile of the actor is to the real person being impersonated, one feels that something is missing — the "Shen".

   A real coin has a sharper look, the alloy more compact, the legend natural and full of vigor, and the signs of aging apparent. All these factors come together to form a profile that is inimitable. We observe a coin in its entirety, that is, we look at its profile. If the coin is genuine, the "Shen" is sure to be there; a forgery appears dull and lifeless in comparison, an empty mask devoid of "Shen".

CHRONOLOGY OF CHINESE DYNASTIES AND EMPERORS

2205 B.C.-1911 A.D.

XIA DYNASTY 夏

2205-1766 B.C.

SHANG DYNASTY 商

(Also named Yin)

1766-1122 B.C.

ZHOU DYNASTY 周

1122-256 B.C.

1. WESTERN ZHOU 西 周 1122-771 B.C.
2. EASTERN ZHOU 东 周 770-256 B.C.
   a. Spring & Autumn Period 春 秋 770-475 B.C.
   b. Warring States Period 战 国 475-221 B.C.

N.B. The rulers of the above-mentioned dynasties were named kings or princes. To the numismatist, their names are expendable. Shi Huang Di of the Qin Dynasty was the first to adopt the title of emperor. In the year 256 BC, the Eastern Zhou Dynasty split into two dukedoms — the Dong Zhou Dukedom and the Xi Zhou.

QIN DYNASTY 秦

221-206 B.C.

Emperor	Date (B.C.)
Shi Huang Di 始皇帝 (Qin Shi Huang 秦始皇)	221-209
Huang Di II 二世皇帝	209-206

HAN DYNASTY 汉

206 B.C.-220 A.D.

1. Western Han 西汉 206 B.C.-25 A.D.

Emperor		Reign Title		Date
Gao Zhu	高祖			206-194
Hui Di	惠帝			194-187
Gao Hou	高后 (Lu Shi 吕氏)			187-179
Wen Di	文帝	Hou Yuan	后元	179-156
Jing Di	景帝	Zhong Yuan	中元	156-143
		Hou Yuan	后元	143-140
Wu Di	武帝	Jian Yuan	建元	140-134
		Yuan Guang	元光	134-128
		Yuan Shuo	元朔	128-122
		Yuan Shou	元狩	122-116
		Yuan Ding	元鼎	116-110
		Yuan Feng	元封	110-104
		Tai Chu	太初	104-100
		Tian Han	天汉	100-96
		Tai Shi	太始	96-92
		Zheng He	征和	92-88
		Hou Yuan	后元	88-86

Emperor	Reign Title		Date
Zhao Di 昭帝	Shi Yuan	始元	86-80
	Yuan Feng	元凤	80-74
	Yuan Ping	元平	74-73
Xuan Di 宣帝	Ben Shi	本始	73-69
	Di Jie	地节	69-65
	Yuan Kang	元康	65-61
	Shen Jue	神爵	61-57
	Wu Feng	五凤	57-53
	Gan Lu	甘露	53-49
	Huang Long	黄龙	49-48
Yuan Di 元帝	Chu Yuan	初元	48-43
	Yong Guang	永光	43-38
	Jian Zhao	建昭	38-33
	Jing Ning	竟宁	33-32
Cheng Di 成帝	Jian Shi	建始	32-28
	He Ping	河平	28-24
	Yang Shuo	阳朔	24-20
	Hong Jia	鸿嘉	20-16
	Yong Shi	永始	16-12
	Yuan Yan	元延	12-8
	Sui He	绥和	8-6
Ai Di 哀帝	Jian Ping	建平	6-2
	Yuan Shou	元寿	2 B.C.-1 A.D.
Ping Di 平帝	Yuan Shi	元始	1-6
Ru Zi Ying 孺子婴	Ju She	居摄	6-8
	Chu Shi	初始	8-9
Wang Mang 王莽	Shi Jian Guo	始建国	9-14
(A pretender regime)	Tian Feng	天凤	14-20
	Di Huang	地皇	20-23
Liu Xuan 刘玄	Geng Shi	更始	23-25
(Prince of Huai淮阳王)			

2. Eastern Han 东汉 25-220 A.D.

Emperor	Reign Title	Date
Guang Wu Di 光武帝	Jian Wu 建武	25-56
	Zhong Yuan 中元	56-58
Ming Di 明帝	Yong Ping 永平	58-76
Zhang Di 章帝	Jian Chu 建初	76-84
	Yuan He 元和	84-87
	Zhang He 章和	87-89
He Di 和帝	Yong Yuan 永元	89-105
	Yuan Xing 元兴	105-106
Shang Di 殇帝	Yan Ping 延平	106-107
An Di 安帝	Yong Chu 永初	107-114
	Yuan Chu 元初	114-120
	Yong Ning 永宁	120-121
	Jian Guang 建光	121-122
	Yan Guang 延光	122-126
Shun Di 顺帝	Yong Jian 永建	126-132
	Yang Jia 阳嘉	132-136
	Yong He 永和	136-142
	Han An 汉安	142-144
	Jian Kang 建康	144-145
Chong Di 冲帝	Yong Jia 永嘉	145-146
Zhi Di 质帝	Ben Chu 本初	146-147
Huan Di 桓帝	Jian He 建和	147-150
	He Ping 和平	150-151
	Yuan Jia 元嘉	151-153
	Yong Xing 永兴	153-155
	Yong Shou 永寿	155-158
	Yan Xi 延熹	158-167
	Yong Kang 永康	167-168
Ling Di 灵帝	Jian Ning 建宁	168-172
	Xi Ping 熹平	172-178

Emperor		Reign Title		Date
		Guang He	光和	178-184
		Zhong Ping	中平	184-189
Shao Di	少帝	Guang Xi	光熹	189-189
Xian Di	献帝	Yong Han	永汉	189-190
		Chu Ping	初平	190-194
		Xing Ping	兴平	194-196
		Jian An	建安	196-220
		Yan Kang	延康	220-220

THREE KINGDOMS 三国

220-280 A.D.

1. Kingdom of Shu 蜀 221-265 A.D.

Zhao Lie Di	昭烈帝	Zhang Wu	章武	221-223
Hou Zhu	后主	Jian Xing	建兴	223-238
		Yan Xi	延熙	238-258
		Jing Yao	景耀	258-263
		Yan Xing	炎兴	263-265

2. Kingdom of Wei 魏 220-265 A.D.

Wen Di	文帝	Huang Chu	黄初	220-227
Ming Di	明帝	Tai He	太和	227-233
		Qing Long	青龙	233-237
		Jing Chu	景初	237-240
Fei Di	废帝	Zheng Shi	正始	240-249
		Jia Ping	嘉平	249-254
Shao Di	少帝	Zheng Yuan	正元	254-256
		Gan Lu	甘露	256-260
Yuan Di	元帝	Jing Yuan	景元	260-264
		Xian Xi	咸熙	264-265

3. Kingdom of Wu 吴 222-280 A.D.

Emperor	Reign Title		Date
Da Di 大 帝	Huang Wu	黄武	222-229
	Huang Long	黄龙	229-232
	Jia He	嘉禾	232-238
	Chi Wu	赤乌	238-251
	Tai Yuan	太元	251-252
	Shen Feng	神凤	252-252
Fei Di 废 帝	Jian Xing	建兴	252-254
	Wu Feng	五凤	254-256
	Tai Ping	太平	256-258
Jing Di 景 帝	Yong An	永安	258-264
Mo Di 末 帝	Yuan Xing	元兴	264-265
	Gan Lu	甘露	265-266
	Bao Ding	宝鼎	266-269
	Jian Heng	建衡	269-272
	Feng Huang	凤凰	272-275
	Tian Ce	天册	275-276
	Tian Bi	天玺	276-277
	Tian Ji	天纪	277-280

JIN DYNASTY 晋

265-420 A.D.

1. Western Jin 西晋 265-317 A.D.

Emperor	Reign Title		Date
Wu Di 武 帝	Tai Shi	泰始	265-275
	Xian Ning	咸宁	275-280
	Tai Kang	泰康	280-290
	Tai Xi	泰熙	290-290

Emperor		Reign Title		Date
Hui Di	惠帝	Yong Xi	永熙	290-291
		Yong Ping	永平	291-291
		Yuan Kang	元康	291-300
		Yong Kang	永康	300-301
		Yong Ning	永宁	301-302
		Da An	太安	302-304
		Yong Xing	永兴	304-306
		Jian Wu	建武	304-306
		Yong An	永安	304-306
		Guang Xi	光熙	306-307
Huai Di	怀帝	Yong Jia	永嘉	307-313
Min Di	愍帝	Jian Xing	建兴	313-317

2. Eastern Jin 东晋 317-420 A.D.

Emperor		Reign Title		Date
Yuan Di	元帝	Jian Wu	建武	317-318
		Tai Xing	太兴	318-322
		Yong Chang	永昌	322-323
Ming Di	明帝	Tai Ning	太宁	323-326
Cheng Di	成帝	Xian He	咸和	326-335
		Xian Kang	咸康	335-343
Kang Di	康帝	Jian Yuan	建元	343-345
Mu Di	穆帝	Yong He	永和	345-357
		Sheng Ping	升平	357-362
Ai Di	哀帝	Long He	隆和	362-363
		Xing Ning	兴宁	363-366
Di Yi	帝奕	Tai He	太和	366-371
Jian Wen Di	简文帝	Xian An	咸安	371-373
Xiao Wu Di	孝武帝	Ning Kang	宁康	373-376
		Tai Yuan	太元	376-397
An Di	安帝	Long An	隆安	397-402
		Yuan Xing	元兴	402-403
		Long An	隆安	402-403
		Da Heng	大亨	402-403

Emperor		Reign Title		Date
		Yuan Xing	元兴	403-405
		Yi Xi	义熙	405-419
Gong Di	恭 帝	Yuan Xi	元熙	419-420

NORTHERN & SOUTHERN DYNASTIES 南北朝

420-581 A.D.

1. Song 宋 420-479 (Liu Song 刘宋)

Wu Di	武 帝	Yong Chu	永初	420-423
Shao Di	少 帝	Jing Ping	景平	423-424
Wen Di	文 帝	Yuan Jia	元嘉	424-454
Xiao Wu Di	孝 武 帝	Xiao Jian	孝建	454-457
		Da Ming	大明	457-465
Fei Di	废 帝	Yong Guang	永光	465-465
Ming Di	明 帝	Jing He	景和	465-465
		Tai Shi	泰始	465-472
		Tai Yu	泰豫	472-473
Cang Wu Wang	苍 梧 王	Yuan Hui	元徽	473-477
(Shun Di 顺 帝)		Sheng Ming	昇明	477-479

2. Qi 齐 479-502

Gao Di	高 帝	Jian Yuan	建元	479-483
Wu Di	武 帝	Yong Ming	永明	483-494
Yu Lin Wang	郁 林 王	Long Chang	隆昌	494-494
Hai Ling Wang	海 陵 王	Yan Xing	延兴	494-494
Ming Di	明 帝	Jian Wu	建武	494-498
		Yong Tai	永泰	498-499
Dong Hun Hou	东 昏 侯	Yong Yuan	永元	499-501
He Di	和 帝	Zhong Xing	中兴	501-502

3. Liang 梁 502-557

Emperor		Reign Title		Date
Wu Di	武 帝	Tian Jian	天监	502-520
		Pu Tong	普通	520-527
		Da Tong	大通	527-529
		Zhong Da Tong	中大通	529-535
		Da Tong	大同	535-546
		Zhong Da Tong	中大同	546-547
		Tai Qing	太清	547-550
Jian Wen Di	简 文 帝	Da Bao	大宝	550-551
Yu Zhang Wang	豫 章 王	Tian Zheng	天正	551-552
Yuan Di	元 帝	Cheng Sheng	承圣	552-555
Zhen Yang Hou	贞 阳 侯	Tian Cheng	天成	555-555
Jing Di	敬 帝	Shao Tai	绍泰	555-556
		Tai Ping	太平	556-557

4. Chen 陈 557-589

Wu Di	武 帝	Yong Ding	永定	557-560
Wen Di	文 帝	Tian Jia	天嘉	560-566
		Tian Kang	天康	566-567
Lin Hai	临 海	Guang Da	光大	567-569
Xuan Di	宣 帝	Da Jian	大建	569-583
Hou Zhu	后 主	Zhi De	至德	583-587
		Zhen Ming	祯明	587-589

N.B. The aforementioned are the Southern Dynasties; the following are the Northern Dynasties.

5. Bei Wei 北魏 386-534
(Northern Wei)

Dao Wu Di	道 武 帝	Deng Guo	登国	386-396
		Huang Shi	皇始	396-398

Emperor		Reign Title		Date
		Tian Xing	天兴	398-404
		Tian Ci	天赐	404-409
Mint Yuan Di	明 元 帝	Yong Xing	永兴	409-414
		Shen Rui	神瑞	414-416
In 420 AD Bei Wei merged with the Northern and Southern dynastic group.		Tai Chang	泰常	416-424
Tai Wu Di	太 武 帝	Shi Guang	始光	424-428
		Shen Jia	神䴥	428-432
		Yan He	延和	432-435
		Tai Yan	太延	435-440
		Tai Ping	太平	440-452
		Zhen Jun	真君	440-452
		Zheng Ping	正平	452-452
Nan An Wang	南 安 王	Cheng Ping	承平	452-452
Wen Cheng Di	文 成 帝	Xing An	兴安	452-454
		Xing Guang	兴光	454-455
		Tai An	太安	455-460
		He Ping	和平	460-466
Xian Wen Di	献 文 帝	Tian An	天安	466-467
		Huang Xing	皇兴	467-471
Xiao Wen Di	孝 文 帝	Yan Xing	延兴	471-476
		Cheng Ming	承明	476-477
		Tai He	太和	477-500
Xuan Wu Di	宣 武 帝	Jing Ming	景明	500-504
		Zheng Shi	正始	504-508
		Yong Ping	永平	508-512
		Yan Chang	延昌	512-516
Xiao Ming Di	孝 明	Xi Ping	熙平	516-517
		Shen Gui	神龟	517-519
		Zheng Guang	正光	519-525

Emperor		Reign Title		Date
		Xiao Chang	孝昌	525-528
Lin Tao Wang	临 洮 王	Wu Tai	武泰	528-528
Xiao Zhuang Di	孝 庄 帝	Jian Yi	建义	528-528
		Yong An	永安	528-529
		Geng Xing	更兴	529-530
Dong Hai Wang	东 海 王	Jian Ming	建明	530-531
Jie Min Di	节 闵 帝	Jin Tai	普泰	531-531
An Ding Wang	安 定 王	Zhong Xing	中兴	531-532
Xiao Wu Di	孝 武 帝	Tai Chang	太昌	532-532
		Yong Xing	永兴	532-532
		Yong Xi	永熙	532-534

6. Xi Wei 西魏 535-556 A.D.
(Western Wei)

Emperor		Reign Title		Date
Wen Di	文 帝	Da Tong	大统	535-552
Di Qin	帝 钦			552-554
Gong Di	恭 帝			554-556

7. Dong Wei 东魏 534-560 A.D.
(Eastern Wei)

Emperor		Reign Title		Date
Xiao Jing Di	孝 静 帝	Tian Ping	天平	534-538
		Yuan Xiang	元象	538-539
		Xing He	兴和	539-543
		Wu Ding	武定	543-560

8. Bei Qi 北齐 550-577 A.D.

Emperor		Reign Title		Date
Wen Xuan Di	文 宣 帝	Tian Bao	天保	550-560
Fei Di	废 帝	Qian Ming	乾明	560-560
Xiao Zhao Di	孝 昭 帝	Huang Jian	皇建	560-561
Wu Cheng Di	武 成 帝	Tai Ning	太宁	561-562
		He Qing	河清	562-565

Emperor	Reign Title	Date
Wen Gong 温 公 (Hou Zhu 后 主)	Tian Tong 天统	565-570
	Wu Ping 武平	570-576
	Long Hua 隆化	576-576
An De Wang 安 德 王	De Chang 德昌	576-577
You Zhu 幼 主	Cheng Guang 承光	577-577

9. Bei Zhou 北周 557-581 A.D.

Emperor	Reign Title	Date
Xiao Min Di 孝 愍 帝	—	557—
Ming Di 明 帝	Wu Cheng 武成	557-561
Wu Di 武 帝	Bao Ding 保定	561-566
	Tian He 天和	566-572
	Jian De 建德	572-578
Xuan Di 宣 帝	Xuan Zheng 宣政	578-579
	Da Cheng 大成	579-580
Jing Di 静 帝	Da Xiang 大象	580-581
	Da Ding 大定	581-581

SUI DYNASTY 隋

518-681 A.D.

Emperor	Reign Title	Date
Wen Di 文 帝	Kai Huang 开皇	581-601
	Ren Shou 仁寿	601-605
Yang Di 炀 帝	Da Yie 大业	605-617
Gong Di Yu 恭帝侑	Yi Ning 义宁	617-618
Gong Di Dong 恭帝侗	Huang Tai 皇泰	618-618

TANG DYNASTY 唐

618-907 A.D.

Emperor		Reign Title		Date
Gao Zu	高祖	Wu De	武德	618-627
Tai Zong	太宗	Zheng Guan	贞观	672-650
Gao Zong	高宗	Yong Hui	永徽	650-656
		Xian Qing	显庆	656-661
		Long Shuo	龙朔	661-664
		Lin De	麟德	664-666
		Qian Feng	乾封	666-668
		Zhong Zhang	总章	668-670
		Xian Heng	咸亨	670-674
		Shang Yuan	上元	674-676
		Yi Feng	仪凤	676-679
		Tiao Lu	调露	679-680
		Yong Long	永隆	680-681
		Kai Yao	开耀	681-682
		Yong Chun	永淳	682-683
		Hong Dao	弘道	683-684
Zhong Zong	中宗	Si Sheng	嗣圣	684-684
Rui Zong	睿宗	Wen Ming	文明	684-684
Wu Hou	武后	Guang Zhai	光宅	684-685
(Wu Ze Tian 武则天)		Chui Gong	垂拱	685-689
Wu Hou assumed the		Yong Chang	永昌	689-689
title of emperor and		Zai Chu	载初	689-690
changed the dynastic		Tian Shou	天授	689-692
title fromTang to Zhou				
from the following date:		Ru Yi	如意	692-692
		Chang Shou	长寿	692-694
		Yan Zai	延载	694-695
		Zheng Sheng	证圣	695-695
		Tian Ce Wan Shui	天册万岁	695-696

Emperor	Reign Title		Date
	Wan Shui Tong Tian	万岁通天	696-697
	Shen Gong	神功	697-698
	Sheng Li	圣历	698-700
	Jiu Shi	久视	700-701
	Da Zhu	大足	701-701
	Chang An	长安	701-705
Zhong Zong 中 宗	Shen Long	神龙	705-707
(Resumed the throne)	Jing Long	景龙	707-710
Rui Zong 睿 宗	Jing Yun	景云	710-712
	Tai Ji	太极	712-712
	Yan He	延和	712-713
Xuan Zong 玄 宗	Kai Yuan	开元	713-742
	Tian Bao	天宝	742-756
Su Zong 肃 宗	Zhi De	至德	756-758
	Qian Yuan	乾元	758-760
	Shang Yuan	上元	760-762
	Bao Ying	宝应	762-763
Dai Zong 代 宗	Guang De	广德	763-765
	Yong Tai	永泰	765-766
	Da Li	大历	766-780
De Zong 德 宗	Jian Zhong	建中	780-784
	Xing Yuan	兴元	784-785
	Zhen Yuan	贞元	785-805
Shun Zong 顺 宗	Yong Zhen	永贞	805-806
Xian Zong 宪 宗	Yuan He	元和	806-821
Mu Zong 穆 宗	Chang Qing	长庆	821-825
Jing Zong 敬 宗	Bao Li	宝历	825-827
Wen Zong 文 宗	Yong He	永和	827-836
	Kai Cheng	开成	836-841
Wu Zong 武 宗	Hui Chang	会昌	841-847
Xuan Zong 宣 宗	Tai Zhong	太中	847-860

Emperor		Reign Title		Date
Yi Zong	懿　宗	Xian Tong	咸通	860-874
Xi Zong	僖　宗	Qian Fu	乾符	874-880
		Guang Ming	广明	880-881
		Zhong He	中和	881-885
		Guang Qi	光启	885-888
		Wen De	文德	888-889
Zhao Zong	昭　宗	Long Ji	龙纪	889-890
		Da Shun	大顺	890-892
		Jing Fu	景福	892-894
		Qian Ning	乾宁	894-898
		Guang Hua	光化	898-901
		Tian Fu	天复	901-904
		Tian You	天祐	904-905
Zhao Xuan Di	昭宣帝	Tian You	天祐	905-907

FIVE DYNASTIES 五代

907-960 A.D.

1. Later Liang 后梁 907-923 A.D.

Tai Zu	太　祖	Kai Ping	开平	907-911
		Qian Hua	乾化	911-916
Mo Di	末　帝	Zhen Ming	贞明	915-921
		Long De	龙德	921-923

2. Later Tang 后唐 923-936

Zhuang Zong	庄　宗	Tong Guang	同光	923-926
Ming Zong	明　宗	Tian Cheng	天成	926-930
		Chang Xing	长兴	930-934

Emperor			Reign Title		Date
Min Di	闵	帝	Ying Shun	应顺	934-934
Fei Di	废	帝	Qing Tai	清泰	934-936

3. Later Jin 后晋 936-947 A.D.

Gao Zu	高	祖	Tian Fu	天福	936-944
Qi Wang	齐	王	Kai Yun	开运	944-947

4. Later Han 后汉 948-951 A.D.

Gao Zu	高	祖	Tian Fu	天福	947-948
			Qian You	乾祐	948-948
Yin Di	隐	帝	Qian You	乾祐	948-951

5. Later Zhou 后周 951-960 A.D.

Tai Zu	太	祖	Guang Shun	广顺	951-954
Shi Zong	世	宗	Gu De	顾德	954-960
Gong Di	恭	帝	Gu De	顾德	960-960

SONG DYNASTY 宋

960-1279 A.D.

1. Northern Song 960-1127 A.D.

Tai Zu	太	祖	Jian Long	建隆	960-963
			Qian De	乾德	963-968
			Kai Bao	开宝	968-976
Tai Zong	太	宗	Tai Ping	太平	976-984
			Xing Guo	兴国	976-984
			Yong Xi	雍熙	984-988
			Duan Gong	端拱	988-990
			Chun Hua	淳化	990-995
			Zhi Dao	至道	995-998

Emperor			Reign Title		Date
Zhen Zong	真	宗	Xian Ping	咸平	998-1004
			Jing De	景德	1004-1008
			Da Zong	大中	1008-1017
			Xiang Fu	祥符	1008-1017
			Tian Xi	天禧	1017-1022
			Qian Xing	乾兴	1022-1023
Ren Zong	仁	宗	Tian Sheng	天圣	1023-1032
			Ming Dao	明道	1032-1034
			Jing You	景祐	1034-1038
			Bao Yuan	宝元	1038-1040
			Kang Ding	康定	1040-1041
			Qing Li	庆历	1041-1049
			Huang You	皇祐	1049-1054
			Zhi He	至和	1054-1056
			Jia You	嘉祐	1056-1064
Ying Zong	英	宗	Zhi Ping	治平	1064-1068
Shen Zong	神	宗	Xi Ning	熙宁	1068-1078
			Yuan Feng	元丰	1078-1086
Zhe Zong	哲	宗	Yuan You	元祐	1086-1094
			Shao Sheng	绍圣	1094-1098
			Yuan Fu	元符	1098-1101
Hui Zong	徽	宗	Jian Zhong Jing Guo	建中靖国	1101-02
			Chong Ning	崇宁	1102-1107
			Da Guan	大观	1102-1111
			Zheng He	政和	1111-1118
			Chong He	重和	1118-1119
			Xuan He	宣和	1126-1126
Qing Zong	钦	宗	Jing Kang	靖康	1126-1127

2. Southern Song (Nan Song) 南宋 1127-1279 A.D.

Gao Zong	高	宗	Jian Yan	建炎	1127-1131
			Shao Xing	绍兴	1131-1163

Emperor			Reign Title		Date
Xiao Zong	孝	宗	Long Xing	隆兴	1163-1165
			Qian Dao	乾道	1165-1174
			Chun Xi	淳熙	1174-1190
Guang Zong	光	宗	Shao Xi	绍熙	1190-1195
Ning Zong	宁	宗	Qing Yuan	庆元	1195-1201
			Jia Tai	嘉泰	1201-1205
			Kai Xi	开禧	1205-1208
			Jia Ding	嘉定	1208-1225
Li Zong	理	宗	Bao Qing	宝庆	1225-1228
			Shao Ding	绍定	1228-1234
			Duan Ping	端平	1234-1237
			Jia Xi	嘉熙	1237-1241
			Chun You	淳祐	1241-1253
			Bao You	宝祐	1253-1259
			Kai Qing	开庆	1259-1260
			Jing Ding	景定	1260-1265
Du Zong	度	宗	Xian Chun	咸淳	1265-1275
Gong Di	恭	帝	De You	德祐	1275-1276
Duan Zong	端	宗	Jing Yan	景炎	1276-1278
Di Bing	帝	昺	Xiang Xing	祥兴	1278-1279

LIAO DYNASTY 辽

916-1125 A.D.

Tai Zu	太	祖	Shen Che	神册	916-922
			Tian Zhan	天赞	922-926
			Tian Xian	天显	926-927
Tai Zong	太	宗	Tian Xian	天显	927-937
			Hui Tong	会同	937-946
			Da Tong	大同	946-947

Emperor			Reign Title		Date
Shi Zong	世	宗	Tian Lu	天禄	947-951
Mu Zong	穆	宗	Ying Li	应历	951-968
Jing Zong	景	宗	Bao Ning	保宁	968-978
			Qian Heng	乾亨	978-983
Sheng Zong	圣	宗	Tong He	统和	983-1012
			Kai Tai	开泰	1012-1020
			Tai Ping	太平	1020-1031
Xing Zong	兴	宗	Jing Fu	景福	1031-1032
			Chong Xi	重熙	1032-1055
Dao Zong	道	宗	Qing Ning	清宁	1055-1066
			Xian Yong	咸雍	1066-1074
			Da Kang	大康	1074-1083
			Da An	大安	1083-1092
			Shou Long	寿隆	1092-1101
Tian Zuo	天	祚	Qian Tong	乾统	1101-1110
			Tian Qing	天庆	1110-1119
			Bao Da	保大	1119-1125

WESTERN LIAO 西辽 1125-1213 A.D.
(Karakitai Kingdom)

De Zong	德	宗	Yan Qing	延庆	1125-1126
			Kang Guo	康国	1126-1136
Gan Tian Hou	感	天后	Xian Qing	咸清	1136-1142
Ren Zong	仁	宗	Shao Xing	绍兴	1142-1154
Cheng Tian	承	天	Chong Fu	崇福	1154 —
			Huang De	皇德	—
			Chong De	重德	—
Mo Zhu	末	主	Tian Xi	天禧	1168 —

JIN DYNASTY 金

1115-1234 A.D.

Emperor		Reign Title		Date
Tai Zu	太祖	Shou Guo	收国	1115-1118
		Tian Fu	天辅	1118-1123
Tai Zong	太宗	Tian Hui	天会	1123-1135
Xi Zong	熙宗	Tian Hui	天会	1135-1138
		Tian Juan	天眷	1138-1141
		Huang Tong	皇统	1141-1149
Hai Ling Wang	海陵王	Tian De	天德	1149-1153
		Zhen Yuan	贞元	1153-1156
		Zheng Long	正隆	1156-1161
Shi Zong	世宗	Da Ding	大定	1161-1190
Zhang Zong	章宗	Ming Chang	明昌	1190-1196
		Cheng An	承安	1196-1201
		Tai He	泰和	1201-1209
Wei Shao Wang	卫绍王	Da An	大安	1209-1212
		Chong Qing	崇庆	1212-1213
		Zhi Ning	至宁	1213-1213
Xuan Zong	宣宗	Zhen You	贞祐	1213-1217
		Xing Ding	兴定	1217-1222
		Yuan Guang	元光	1222-1224
Ai Zong	哀宗	Zheng Da	正大	1224-1232
		Tian Xing	天兴	1232-1233
		Kai Xing	开兴	1233-1234
Mo Di	末帝	Sheng Chang	盛昌	1234-1234

XI XIA DYANSTY 西夏

1002-1227 A.D.

Emperor		Date
Tai Zong (Li De Ming)	太宗 利德明	1002-1032

Emperor		Reign Title		Date
Jing Zong	景宗	Xian Dao	显道	1032-1034
(Zhao Yuan Hao)	赵元昊	Kai Yun	开运	1034-1034
		Guang Yun	广运	1034-1036
		Da Qing	大庆	1036-1038
		Tian Shou	天授	1038-1038
		Li Fa	禮法	1038-1038
		Yan Zuo	延祚	1038-1049
Yi Zong	毅宗	Yan Si	延嗣	1049-1049
(Liang Zuo)	谅祚	Ning Guo	宁国	1049-1050
		Tian You	天祐	1050-1050
		Chui Sheng	垂圣	1050-1053
		Fu Sheng	福圣	1053-1053
		Cheng Dao	承道	1053-1057
		She Du	奲都	1057-1063
		Gong Hua	拱化	1063-1069
Hui Zong	惠宗	Qian Dao	乾道	1069-1071
(Bing Chang)	秉常	Tian Ci Li	天赐禮	1071-1071
		Sheng Guo Qing	盛国庆	1071-1076
		Da An	大安	1076-1086
		Tian An	天安	1086-1087
		Li Ding	禮定	1086-1087
Chong Zong	崇宗	Tian Yi	天仪	1087-1087
(Qian Shun)	乾順	Zhi Ping	治平	1087-1091
		Tian You	天祐	1091-1091
		Min An	民安	1091-1099
		Yong An	永安	1099-1102
		Zhen Guan	贞观	1102-1115
		Yong Ning	雍宁	1115-1120
		Yuan De	元德	1120-1127
		Zheng De	正德	1127-1135
		Da De	大德	1135-1139

Emperor			Reign Title		Date
Ren Zong	仁	宗	Da Qing	大庆	1139-1144
(Ren Xiao)	仁	孝	Ren Qing	人庆	1144-1149
			Tian Sheng	天盛	1149-1171
			Qian You	乾祐	1171-1194
Huan Zong	桓	宗	Tian Qing	天庆	1194-1206
(Chun You)	純	祐			
Xiang Zong	襄	宗	Ying Tian	应天	1206-1210
(An Quan)	安	全	Huang Jian	皇建	1210-1211
Shen Zong	神	宗	Guang Ding	光定	1211-1223
(Zhun Xu)	遵	頊			
Xian Zong	献	宗	Qian Ding	乾定	1223-1227
(De Wang)	德	旺			

YUAN DYNASTY 元

1260-1368 A.D.

Tai Zu	太	祖	(Genghis Khan)	成吉思汗	1206-1227
Tai Zong	太	宗	(Ogodei)	窝阔台	1229-1241
Ding Zong	定	宗	(Guyuk)	贵由	1246-1248
Xian Zong	宪	宗	(Mongke)	蒙哥	1251-1259
Shi Zu	世	祖	Zhong Tong	中统	1260-1264
(Kublai Khan)	忽必烈		Zhi Yuan	至元	1264-1295
			Yuan Zhen	元贞	1295-1297
			Da De	大德	1297-1308
Wu Zong	武	宗	Zhi Da	至大	1308-1312
Ren Zong	仁	宗	Huang Qing	皇庆	1312-1314
			Yan You	延祐	1314-1321
Ying Zong	英	宗	Zhi Zhi	至治	1321-1324
Tai Ding Di	泰定帝		Tai Ding	泰定	1324-1328
			Zhi He	致和	1328-1329
Ming Zong	明	宗	Tian Li	天历	1329-1330
Wen Di	文	帝	Tian Li	天历	1330-1330

Emperor		Reign Title		Date
		Zhi Shun	至顺	1330-1333
Shun Di	顺帝	Yuan Tong	元统	1333-1335
		Zhi Yuan	至元	1335-1341
		Zhi Zheng	至正	1341-1368

MING DYNASTY 明

1368-1644 A.D.

Emperor		Reign Title		Date
Tai Zu	太祖	Hong Wu	洪武	1368-1399
Hui Di	惠帝	Jian Wen	建文	1399-1403
Cheng Zu	成祖	Yong Le	永乐	1403-1425
Ren Zong	仁宗	Hong Xi	洪熙	1425-1426
Xuan Zong	宣宗	Xuan De	宣德	1426-1436
Ying Zong	英宗	Zheng Tong	正统	1436-1450
Dai Zong	代宗	Jing Tai	景泰	1450-1457
(Jing Di)	景帝			
Ying Zong	英宗	Tian Shun	天顺	1457-1465
Xian Zong	宪宗	Cheng Hua	成化	1465-1488
Xiao Zong	孝宗	Hong Zhi	弘治	1488-1506
Wu Zong	武宗	Zheng De	正德	1506-1522
Shi Zong	世宗	Jia Jing	嘉靖	1522-1567
Mu Zong	穆宗	Long Qing	隆庆	1567-1573
Shen Zong	神宗	Wan Li	万历	1573-1620
Guang Zong	光宗	Tai Chang	泰昌	1620-1620
Xi Zong	熹宗	Tian Qi	天启	1621-1628
Zhuang Lie Di	庄烈帝	Chong Zhen	崇祯	1628-1644

QING DYNASTY 清

1644-1911 A.D.

Emperor		Reign Title		Date
Shi Zu	世祖	Shun Zhi	顺治	1644-1662
Sheng Zu	圣祖	Kang Xi	康熙	1662-1723
Shi Zong	世宗	Yong Zheng	雍正	1723-1736
Gao Zong	高宗	Qian Long	乾隆	1736-1796
Ren Zong	仁宗	Jia Qing	嘉庆	1796-1821
Xuan Zong	宣宗	Dao Guang	道光	1821-1851
Wen Zong	文宗	Xian Feng	咸丰	1851-1862
Mu Zong	穆宗	Tong Zhi	同治	1862-1875
De Zong	德宗	Guang Xu	光绪	1875-1908
Xuan Tong Di	宣统帝	Xuan Tong	宣统	1908-1911

Addenda

1. Sixteen Kingdoms 十 六 国 304-409 A.D.

The kingdoms, set up by the five nomadic Hun tribes and three Han generals, sprang up overnight after the upheaval of the eight princes and left the northern part of the Western Jin empire in a state of anarchy. Only four of the sixteen minted their own coinage: Former Liang, Later Zhao, Xia, and Cheng Han.

1)	Former Liang	前凉	301-376 A.D.
2)	Later Liang	后凉	386-403 A.D.
3)	Southern Liang	南凉	397-414 A.D.
4)	Northern Liang	北凉	397-439 A.D.
5)	Western Liang	西凉	400-431 A.D.
6)	Han/Former Zhao	汉/前赵	304-329 A.D.

7) Later Zhao	后赵	319-352 A.D.
8) Former Qin	前秦	351-394 A.D.
9) Later Qin	后秦	384-417 A.D.
10) Western Qin	西秦	385-431 A.D.
11) Former Yan	前燕	333-370 A.D.
12) Later Yan	后燕	383-409 A.D.
13) Southern Yan	南燕	398-410 A.D.
14) Norhtern Yan	北燕	409-436 A.D.
15) Xia	夏	407-431 A.D.
16) Cheng, Han	成汉	303-347 A.D.

2. Ten Kingdoms 902-979 A.D.

The ten kingdoms co-existed with the five dynasties, formed by the local governors who took advantage of the turbulent times and proclaimed independence, establishing reign titles and issuing their own currency.

1) Wu	吴	902-938 A.D.
2) Southern Tang	南唐	937-975 A.D.
3) Wu Yue	吴越	907-979 A.D.
4) Chu	楚	907-953 A.D.
5) Min	闽	907-948 A.D.
6) Southern Han	南汉	907-970 A.D.
7) Former Shu	前蜀	907-925 A.D.
8) Later Shu	后蜀	925-966 A.D.
9) Jing Nan	荆南	907-965 A.D.
10) Northern Han	北汉	951-979 A.D.

3. Gong Sun Shu, Emperor of Shu (Han Dynasty)	公孙述，蜀王	25-36
4. Shi Si Ming, King of Yan (Tang Dynasty)	史思明，燕王	759-62
5. Liu Shou Guang, Emperor of Greater Yan (Occupied You Zhou region, 5 Dynasties)	刘寿光，大燕帝	911-14
6. Li Shun, King of Greater Shu (Song rebel)	李顺，大蜀王	995 —
7. Liu Yu, King of Qi (Jin regime puppet)	刘豫，齐王	1130-37

8. Yuan Dynasty rebels:

a) Han Lin Er, King of Song	韩林儿, 宋王	1355-66
b) Zhang Shi Cheng, King of Zhou	张士诚, 周王	1354-63
c) Xu Shou Hui, ruler of Tian Wan	徐寿辉, 天完	1358-60
d) Chen You Liang, King of Han	陈友亮, 汉王	1360-64
e) Ming Yu Zhen, Emperor of Da Xia	明玉珍, 夏帝	1363-71

9. Southern Ming 1644-62

(Set up by members of the royal family after the collapse of the Ming regime.)

a) Prince Fu 福, title: Hong Guang	弘光	1644-45
b) Prince Lu 鲁, title: Da Ming	大明	1644-45
c) Prince Tang 唐, title: Long Wu	隆庆	1645-46
d) Prince Gui 桂, title: Yong Li	永历	1647-61

10. Ming Dynasty rebels:

a) Li Zi Cheng, Kingdom of Da Shu	李自成, 大蜀国	1644-45
b) Zhang Xian Zhong, Kingdom of Da Xi	张献忠, 大西国	1644-46
c) Sun Ke Wang, Prince Ping-dong	孫可望, 平东王	1647-55
d) Wu San Gui, Prince Ping-xi	吴三桂, 平西王	1674-78
e) Gen Jing Zhong	耿精忠,	1674-76
f) Wu Shi Fan 吳世藩 grandson of Wu San Gui		1678-81
g) Zheng Cheng Gong	郑成功	1661-83

(He recovered Taiwan for China from the Dutch in 1661 AD; his son surrendered to the Qing regime in 1683.)

11. Qing Dynasty rebels:

a) Tai-ping Heavenly Kingdom, (Led by Hong Xiu-Quan 洪秀全)	太平天国	1851-64
b) Shanghai Dagger Society (Led by Liu Li Chuan 刘丽川)	上海小刀会	1853-55
c) Chen Kai, Kingdom of Da Chang	陈 开, 大昌	1854
d) Li Wen Mao, Heaven & Earth Society	李文茂, 天地会	1855
e) Gold Coin Society, led by Zhao Qi	金钱会, 赵启	1861-92